Disasters: A Sociological Approach

Second Edition

T0369854

To Norma Anderson, who inspires us all

Disasters: A Sociological Approach

Second Edition

Kathleen Tierney

polity

First published in 2019 by Polity Press
This edition first published in 2025 by Polity Press

Polity Press
65 Bridge Street
Cambridge CB2 1UR, UK

Polity Press
111 River Street
Hoboken, NJ 07030, USA

ISBN-13: 978-1-5095-6307-4
ISBN-13: 978-1-5095-6308-1(pb)

A catalogue record for this book is available from the British Library.

Library of Congress Control Number: 2024941403

Typeset in 10.5 on 13pt Swift
by Fakenham Prepress Solutions, Fakenham, Norfolk NR21 8NL
Printed and bound in Great Britain by CPI Group (UK) Ltd, Croydon

The publisher has used its best endeavours to ensure that the URLs for external websites referred to in this book are correct and active at the time of going to press. However, the publisher has no responsibility for the websites and can make no guarantee that a site will remain live or that the content is or will remain appropriate.

Every effort has been made to trace all copyright holders, but if any have been overlooked the publisher will be pleased to include any necessary credits in any subsequent reprint or edition.

For further information on Polity, visit our website:
politybooks.com

Contents

Detailed Contents

Figures, Tables, and Boxes

Figures

Tables

Boxes

Acknowledgments

I feel so much gratitude for so many things that it is difficult to know where to start. Let me begin with thanking my outstanding team at Polity Press: Jonathan Skerrett, Karina Jákupsdóttir, Manuela Tecusan, Maddie Tyler, Evie Deavall, and Sarah Dobson. With your guidance, professionalism, attention to detail, and especially your understanding through difficult times, you have made producing this second edition a real pleasure. I am fortunate to work with such wonderful colleagues. Thanks also to the anonymous reviewers who provided suggestions on parts of the manuscript.

At the University of Colorado Boulder, my academic home, I wish to thank current and former members of the Natural Hazards Center faculty and research staff, especially Lori Peek, Jenn Tobin, Liesel Ritchie (now at Virginia Tech), and my NHC doctoral students and mentees, who have gone on to stellar careers in the field: Christine Bevc, Elizabeth Bittel, Nnenia Campbell, Simone Domingue, Brandi Gilbert, Alexandra Jordan, Erica Kuligowski, Wee-Kiat Lim, Jeannette Sutton, Jamie Vickery, and Haorui Wu. I have learned so much from all of you. I continue to cherish close ties with Jim Kendra and Tricia Wachtendorf at the University of Delaware's Disaster Research Center, with whom I shared the joys and endured the stresses of a series of challenging research projects. Thank you both for your friendship and support and for your leadership in the field.

As ever, my love and deepest thanks to my son, Justin Horner, daughter-in-law, Amy Lemley, and my granddaughters Violet and Rita Lemley. Your love and support mean the world to me.

This book is dedicated to Norma Anderson, founder of the Bill Anderson Fund (BAF). More than any other initiative, the BAF has contributed to making the field of hazards and disasters more diverse and more attuned to the needs of those who are most at risk when disasters strike.

Preface to the Second Edition

As I write this, an unknown number of bodies are being recovered from under a landslide in Papua New Guinea. Residents of Japan's Noto Peninsula are struggling to recover from a magnitude 7.5 earthquake. Canada's wildfire season has begun, forcing evacuations and threatening air quality for millions. Deadly heat waves have struck the Sahel and West Africa as well as India. In the United States new legislation is in place in the state of Florida to strike the words "climate change" from a range of policies, while major storms have struck Texas's two largest cities, causing extensive damage and large-scale power outages as temperatures soar. At the same time the future of national programs and initiatives to combat climate change and extreme events is held hostage to the 2024 presidential election.

In 2023 the earth briefly topped two degrees Celsius of warming over pre-industrial levels – warming that climate scientists predict will be the norm in the not too distant future. By the time you read this, new disastrous events will have taken place, illustrating once again how social forces continue to contribute to risk buildup and social vulnerability, and US voters will have decided whether historical efforts to reduce carbon emissions and slow the pace of climate change will continue.

This new edition is different from the earlier one in several ways. Chapters have been rearranged to bring forward theories and concepts that are at the heart of the book. Chapter 3, which presents key theoretical arguments, has been expanded to emphasize how treadmills, unequal ecological exchange, militarism, colonialism, and coloniality contribute to risk and vulnerability. A revamped Chapter 4 focuses on middle-range theories, notably on factors that contribute to organizational disasters and on new developments in warning technologies and responses.

Each chapter of this edition contains new material, for example on the Covid-19 pandemic, with an emphasis on lessons learned regarding social vulnerability and how political polarization and the "post-truth" society have intensified pandemic impacts. Chapter 5 includes new findings regarding vulnerable populations and discusses how the concept of disposability sheds light on what those populations have in common. Other discussions emphasize mid- to long-term lessons learned about the conditions that set the stage for disasters of recent years. Each chapter ends with questions and exercises designed to challenge readers to go beyond the text and further explore substantive and methodological issues.

Also discussed in this edition are recent US policies and legislation designed to both assess and improve societal resilience; newly released reports on the climate crisis and what to expect going forward; and efforts to improve the quality and coordination of disaster research, both nationally and internationally. As before, we examine together the extent to which resilience initiatives championed by disaster risk reduction experts and researchers can achieve their goals under current political–economic conditions.

Based as it is on a large body of research as well as on facts gleaned from headlines, this volume highlights the almost insurmountable challenges societies around the world must address in the face of ever-increasing risks. The argument made in the first edition is re-emphasized here with even more evidence and urgency: disaster vulnerability is a consequence of world-system, international, national, and local processes that reflect capitalist and neoliberal agendas, and these same forces stand in the way of achieving effective and equitable disaster risk reduction and climate change adaptation.

1

The Social Significance of Disasters

Introduction

Disasters are a frequent occurrence across the globe. Despite organized national and international efforts to reduce disaster losses, these losses continue to grow. In 2022 nearly 400 disasters occurred worldwide, resulting in an estimated 40,000 deaths and causing nearly $224 billion in losses; approximately 1.85 million people were adversely affected (Centre for Research on the Epidemiology of Disasters 2023). Heat waves, floods, hurricanes, and other weather-related disasters increasingly plague our warming planet. July, August, and September 2023 were the hottest months ever recorded. That year, Phoenix, Arizona saw fifty-four days, including a thirty-one-day period, when temperatures soared to over 110°F (43.3°C). In September 2023, torrential rains intensified by climate change caused vulnerable dams to fail, killing thousands in Derna, Libya. Also in 2023, Canada saw its worst ever wildfire season, as nearly 46 million acres (18.7 million hectares) – an area twice the size of Portugal – burned, releasing vast amounts of carbon dioxide and spreading smoke and particulates widely. Climate change was also implicated in hurricanes such as Harvey, which struck Texas in 2017, causing $125 billion in losses. As climate change progresses, societies around the world will be forced to grapple with more frequent extreme weather, the spread of infectious disease agents, land loss in coastal areas, and a host of other climate change-induced effects.

In addition to causing deaths, injuries, and economic losses, disasters have other profound social impacts that we will explore in this volume. Disasters are a key factor in driving people into poverty and keeping them there (World Bank Group 2017). Disasters can lead to short- and long-term health and mental health problems. Experiencing a disaster can be a major stressor for households and business owners. The extensive damage and disruption that disasters cause can result in the breakup of neighborhoods and in the loss of significant sources of social support for survivors. Many who survive disaster can find themselves living in temporary accommodations for months or even years, their daily routines disrupted and their plans for recovery stalled. After disasters, children's development may suffer as a result of interruptions in schooling, residential dislocation, and parental stress.

Key societal institutions also experience difficulties in the aftermath of disasters, as schools, churches, charitable organizations, and agencies that provide health and welfare services see their burdens increase. Communities face challenges associated with the disruption and restoration of key lifelines such as water, electrical power, transportation, and other critical infrastructure systems. Local jurisdictions may experience population decline and tax losses.

Deaths and injuries are more common in disasters in low- and middle-income countries by several orders of magnitude, while economic losses are significantly higher in wealthier nations (Centre for Research on the Epidemiology of Disasters 2016). That said, large economies such as those of the United States and other developed countries experience temporary economic setbacks in the aftermath of disasters, but there is little evidence to date that disasters cause significant economic downturns in developed nations. But this is not the case for smaller and poorer countries; there disasters can have significant economic impacts, particularly when they affect key sectors of those economies. For a nation seeking to improve its level of economic development, a disaster can be a major setback. In both large and small countries, the need to respond to and recover from disasters drains financial resources that could otherwise be employed more productively. In the United States, as billion- and multi-billion-dollar disasters continue to occur with alarming frequency, taxpayers, insurance companies, and disaster survivors themselves are forced to foot the bill. For households and businesses, disasters can generate increased debt and an inability to take advantage of opportunities for financial advancement.

Media attention typically focuses on the immediate impacts of disasters and fades away in days or weeks. As a result, the public is generally unaware of the cascading effects of disasters and of the struggles that survivors endure over time. For example, when Hurricane Maria struck the US territory of Puerto Rico in 2017, the island's already fragile electric power infrastructure was essentially destroyed and hundreds of thousands of residents were left homeless.

After the devastating 2010 earthquake in Haiti, Nepalese troops providing relief under the auspices of the United Nations brought cholera to the island. By 2016, an estimated 770,000 people, about 8 percent of the population, were infected with cholera and over 9,000 died – and those numbers are thought to be underestimates (Knox 2016). In 2011 in Japan, when the Great Tohoku earthquake triggered a deadly tsunami that caused a triple meltdown at the Fukushima nuclear power plant, the media covered that sensational story, but now there is little coverage of the ongoing effects of the large-scale population displacement and long-term nuclear decontamination efforts that this massive disaster caused.

Disasters can also challenge the competence and legitimacy of governments and institutions. The 2003 epidemic of severe acute respiratory syndrome (SARS) that originated in China created a legitimacy crisis for the ruling

Communist Party, which had attempted to cover up the outbreak even as it spread worldwide. This same pattern was repeated in 2020 and subsequent years, with the genesis and spread of the devastating COVID-19 pandemic, and with draconian containment measures in China that were widely criticized. In 2023, a massive earthquake that struck Turkey and northern Syria, which resulted in an estimated 50,000 deaths, and the flooding in Derna, Libya mentioned earlier were accompanied by widespread criticisms of the failure of institutions to protect at-risk populations from well-recognized hazards.

As we will see throughout this volume, disaster impacts and losses are not random, nor are the burdens of disasters borne equally by all members of affected populations. Rather the impacts of disasters often fall most heavily on those who are most vulnerable: the poor, racial and ethnic minorities, and other marginalized groups. Many current inquiries into the sociological study of disasters center on how various axes of inequality such as class, race, and gender, alongside other aspects of social stratification, contribute to patterns of disaster victimization and recovery.

It is not difficult to see why sociologists and other social scientists find these events and the efforts to reduce their impacts fascinating. As we have already seen, disasters have economic, political and policy, health and mental health dimensions. They frequently bring to the fore issues of inequality and social justice, shining a light on the problems experienced by marginalized and vulnerable populations. At the same time, social behavior in disasters also reveals the human capacity for altruism and creativity. We will explore together these and other themes in the chapters that follow.

Key Concepts and Definitions in the Study of Disasters

To ensure that we are working from a common set of definitions in the discussions that follow, in this section I introduce concepts that are commonly used in the sociological study of disasters and that will be employed in later chapters. Obviously one key concept is the idea of disaster itself. An important takeaway is that disasters are by their nature social events, not merely physical ones. If a major volcanic eruption were to occur in an area where human settlements did not exist or remained unaffected, that eruption would be a significant geophysical event, but not a disaster. In keeping with sociological conceptualizations, disasters involve the juxtaposition of physical forces – geological, atmospheric, technological, and other forces – and vulnerable human communities. The severity of a disaster is measured not by the magnitude of the physical forces involved, but rather by the magnitude of its societal impacts.

As subsequent discussions will show, disasters were previously seen as discrete events, concentrated in time and space, that disrupt the social order and interfere with the ability of a community or society to continue to operate, for example by interfering with governmental functions, economic activities, utility services, education, transportation, telecommunications, and housing. More recent social science formulations, such as those discussed in this volume, see disasters as arising not so much from the physical forces that trigger them at specific times as from longer-term global and societal processes, which in turn result in an increase of the potential for loss – or what I referred to in an earlier publication as "risk buildup" (Tierney 2014). Much of the discussion that follows will focus on those processes, making the point that the potential for disasters and disaster victimization can build up over long periods.

While media accounts and commonsense views of disaster tend to gloss over differences in event severity, in a search for commonalities among events, sociological formulations are attentive to such differences because of their social implications. Sociologists typically classify events into emergencies, disasters, and catastrophes (see Quarantelli 1996). As shown in Table 1.1, these different types of occurrences are associated, among other things, with differences in spatial scope, severity of the impacts, which entities respond and how, the degree of public participation in providing assistance, and recovery challenges. Examples of emergencies include multivehicle traffic accidents, large structure fires, and minor industrial accidents – incidents that may cause deaths and injuries but are localized, do not create large-scale community disruption, and are typically handled by public safety agencies such as fire and police departments. Disasters are much less common than emergencies and much more serious; in addition to producing fatalities and injuries, they have severe consequences that include large-scale social disruption. Unlike most emergencies, disasters can damage and degrade the very resources that are meant to respond to them, such as emergency communications and responding agencies. Catastrophes are larger still; they have massive repercussions, which greatly exceed the capacity of stricken communities to respond – for example long-lasting impacts that require protracted recovery efforts. Examples of twenty-first-century catastrophes include the Indian Ocean tsunami of 2004, Hurricane Katrina in 2005, the 2010 Haiti earthquake, and the triple catastrophe that struck Japan in 2011. As indicated in the table, emergencies, disasters, and catastrophes are qualitatively different. A disaster is not just a big emergency, and a catastrophe is not just a big disaster; rather the three occurrences are accompanied by differing effects, response patterns, and challenges.

The term "extreme event" is sometimes used interchangeably with "disaster." Here the reference is to events that are out of the ordinary or outside the norm – that is, rare or unlikely. The term is more appropriately applied to physical phenomena such as rainfall or wind speed than to disaster events. This is because disasters can result from events that are technically not extreme in the physical sense, but that nonetheless overwhelm a community's or society's capacity to cope.

Table 1.1 How emergencies, disasters, and catastrophes differ

Emergencies	Disasters	Catastrophes
Impacts localized	Impacts widespread, severe	Devastating physical and societal impacts
Response mainly local	Response is multi-jurisdictional, intergovernmental, but typically bottom-up	Response is initiated by central government because localities and regions are devastated
Standard operating procedures sufficient to handle event	Response requires activation of disaster plans; significant challenges emerge	Response challenges far exceed those envisioned in disaster plans
Vast majority of response resources are unaffected	Extensive damage to and disruption of key emergency services	Response system paralyzed at local and regional levels
Public generally not involved in response	Public extensively involved in response	Public only source of initial response
No significant recovery challenges	Major recovery challenges	Massive recovery challenges and very slow recovery process

Source: Compiled from data in Quarantelli 1996 and Tierney 2008.

The term "hazard" refers to an ongoing condition that has the potential for causing a disaster. Many regions around the world are exposed to earthquake hazards; many coastal areas are exposed to hurricanes and coastal flooding; flood hazards exist along rivers and streams; areas adjacent to nuclear and chemical facilities are exposed to those technological hazards; and so on. The terms "hazard" and "disaster" are not interchangeable. The former refers to the potential for a disruptive event to occur, while the latter refers to what happens when that potential is actualized. Various scientific disciplines – geology, seismology, atmospheric science, and others – seek to better understand and characterize hazards, and communities and societies worldwide seek to use that knowledge to improve their understanding of the hazards to which they are exposed and the ways in which they can respond to such threats.

The concept of vulnerability refers to the potential for experiencing adverse impacts from disasters and recovery challenges after the occurrence of disasters. This concept is applied both to (inanimate) physical systems and to individuals and social groups. For physical systems such as buildings, transportation networks, dams, and utility services, vulnerability consists in the potential for destruction, damage, or loss of function. For individuals and groups, it represents the potential for dying, being injured, losing property, being displaced, and experiencing other negative disaster impacts, as well as for having difficulty recovering after disasters. Just like the term "hazard," the term "vulnerability" relates to the potential for the occurrence of adverse experiences and outcomes – a potential that may or may not be realized in any particular disaster. Factors associated with disaster vulnerability are discussed in Chapter 5.

Disaster resilience is a concept drawn from fields as diverse as engineering, psychology, and ecology. The term refers to the ability of social units at different scales (e.g. societies, communities, households, organizations) to absorb disaster shocks, cope with disaster impacts, and successfully adapt or in some cases even improve their functioning in the aftermath of disasters. Resilience is discussed in Chapter 6.

"Risk" is a term that is also used extensively in the study of disasters. Risk is defined as "a situation or event in which something of human value (including humans themselves) has been put at stake and where the outcome is uncertain" (Jaeger, Renn, Rosa, and Webler 2001: 17). The idea that entities that have human value are "at stake" means that losses may occur. As the definition indicates, risk is always accompanied by uncertainty. The fields of risk analysis and risk management focus on clarifying those probabilities as much as possible and on undertaking risk reduction measures.

At various points in this book I will use the term "disaster agent." A disaster agent is a physical force that leads to the occurrence of a disaster, for example a tornado, a hurricane, a earthquake, a flood, or a chemical or nuclear accident. An agent and a disaster are not the same thing; a disaster occurs when an agent damages and disrupts human societies and the things that we humans value. Some disaster agents are able to produce very severe and widespread impacts and thus can be more likely than others to lead to catastrophes, particularly when vulnerability is high in an affected area. In this century, for example, a number of catastrophes and near-catastrophes have resulted in the deaths of tens to hundreds of thousands of people. Examples include the 2001 Gujarat earthquake in India (over 20,000 fatalities), the European heat wave of 2003 (an estimated 70,000 fatalities), the 2004 Indian Ocean earthquake and tsunami (over 200,000 deaths), an earthquake in Pakistan-administered Kashmir in 2005 (over 73,000 fatalities), Cyclone Nargis in Myanmar in 2008 (more than 130,000 killed), the 2008 Wenchuan earthquake in China (nearly 88,000 deaths), the 2010 Haiti earthquake (an estimated 220,000 killed), the 2011 earthquake and tsunami in Japan (approximately 20,000 deaths), and the 2023 Turkey and Syria earthquake (50,000 deaths). Note that with the exception of the 2003 heat wave and 2011 Japan disaster, these high-casualty disasters took place in less developed countries. Later we will see why the death toll is so large in those kinds of societal settings.

Climate change is a hazard that stands virtually in a category of its own. It currently affects nations, communities, and ecosystems around the world through its direct effects, for instance sea-level rise, coastal flooding, and extreme heat, and through its interaction with other disaster agents, which it makes more frequent and more severe. For example, when climate change causes sea-level rise, it makes the storm surges associated with hurricanes, cyclones, and typhoons bigger, and when it increases ocean temperatures it contributes to more intense rainfall events. In October 2023 Hurricane Otis slammed into Acapulco, Mexico as a Category 5 hurricane with wind speeds of over 160 miles per hour. Before making landfall, its rapid intensification happened in less than a day – a pattern driven by climate change. Climate change will be discussed throughout this volume, but especially in Chapter 9.

Another term, "the hazards cycle," refers to activities that can be undertaken before disasters, during and immediately after disaster impact, and during the longer-term recovery period, to reduce losses and hasten recovery. The hazards cycle consists of four elements: mitigation, preparedness, response, and recovery. Mitigation refers to measures that can be taken in advance of disasters, with a view to reducing their impacts.[1] Such measures include planning and zoning activities that direct development away from hazardous areas; building codes that require disaster-resistant construction; and strategies for retrofitting structures, so that they may resist being damaged when disasters strike. Another important aspect of mitigation involves strengthening the natural defenses that reduce the impacts of disaster agents, for example restoring wetlands so that they may absorb hurricane-force winds.

The second stage in the cycle, preparedness, consists of activities taken in advance of disasters that strengthen the ability of communities, households, and individuals to respond effectively when disaster strikes. Preparedness activities include the development of disaster plans at various governmental levels, as well as household and business disaster planning. Such measures also cover knowing what to do when a disaster threatens or strikes – for example, being aware of evacuation routes and knowing what self-protective measures to carry out in the event of a chemical or nuclear accident or some other type of disaster. Drills and exercises are another kind of common preparedness activities undertaken by emergency responders – as well as by institutions such as schools and hospitals and by private sector organizations – to ensure disaster readiness.

Response, the third stage of the hazards cycle, takes place when disasters occur; it consists of activities undertaken by individuals, households, businesses, and governmental and nongovernmental organizations and is aimed at coping with the impacts of disaster. Response activities include implementing expedient self-protective measures such as evacuating and seeking emergency shelter; activating disaster plans; searching for and rescuing persons in distress; caring for the injured and making arrangements for those who have been killed; containing immediate threats associated with cascading disaster effects such as agent-induced fires; and taking additional measures to ensure public safety, for example by issuing information about particularly hazardous areas and evolving threats.

Response activities also include improvising in various ways when plans fail to anticipate the realities on the ground. While we tend to think that disaster response consists of the activities of "first responders" – fire services, police, and emergency management personnel – actual disaster responses are diffuse and decentralized, as members of the public and entities that were not included in planning activities spur into action and new groups emerge to address pressing needs. Viewing disaster response as "what first responders do" misses the point that, as noted earlier in Table 1.1 and in the discussion around it, the public takes part in a range of response activities in the aftermath of disasters and catastrophic events. It is only in emergency incidents that public safety agencies are the main ones to handle response activities.

Finally, disaster recovery consists of efforts on the part of those affected by disasters to overcome disruption and to continue to thrive. Here again, recovery activities take place at different levels: individuals, households, businesses, communities, regions, and in some cases entire societies. Disaster recovery is often incorrectly equated with restoring and reconstructing the built environment. However, recovery also embraces recovering from trauma, reestablishing disrupted livelihoods and economic activity, and regaining a sense of community. Too often after disasters there is a rush to reconstruct and rebuild, but without attending to other, less tangible but still essential aspects of recovery. In keeping with the disaster cycle concept, recovery activities should, and often do, incorporate new mitigation measures, bringing the cycle full circle. The recovery period after a disaster can open up new opportunities to increase the safety of affected communities through the implementation of mitigation strategies. This is the period when disaster-stricken communities can make progress in areas such as hazard-aware land use policies and stricter building codes, as interest groups that may have previously opposed such measures recognize and embrace mitigation as a pressing need. Unfortunately, however, even though the recovery period presents possibilities for future risk reduction, those possibilities frequently go unrealized, leaving disaster-stricken areas vulnerable to future events.

Chapter Themes

This book provides an introduction to the sociology of disasters, and also seeks to advance the field by placing an emphasis on frameworks that help explain the causes of disasters. Many of the issues discussed here are covered in greater detail in more specialized publications that deal with topics such as disaster vulnerability and resilience, for example. In those cases, my task is to present an overview of the current scholarship and point readers to those sources for more in-depth analyses. In addition and perhaps more importantly, what I hope to do in this volume is advance new ideas about the societal origins of disasters. Much of the discussion in the chapters that follow delves more deeply into ideas that I began to develop in an earlier book, *The Social Roots of Risk* (Tierney 2014). As that title suggests, disasters and their impacts are produced through the workings of social forces to a larger extent than through the workings of natural or technological forces. Put more directly, the arguments I make here show that disasters are socially produced, not produced by natural or technological forces external to society, and that those societal forces constitute the means by which disasters take their toll on human lives and livelihoods. The root causes of disasters are to be found in the social order itself – that is, in social arrangements that contribute to the buildup of risk and vulnerability. As subsequent chapters will show, those interacting and mutually reinforcing arrangements include processes that operate within the global political economy, actions undertaken by state actors for their own purposes that ignore and increase hazards and risks, processes that contribute to social vulnerability by further marginalizing already disadvantaged social groups, and local growth-machine politics that elevates so-called economic development as a major priority, while ignoring increasing risks.

Chapter 2 offers an overview of the history of disaster research, with a focus on sociology and geography. It shows how systems thinking in sociology and the idea of "adjustments" to hazards in geography formed the basis for early research in the field. In Chapter 2 we also see how both theory and research on disasters have changed over time. Theoretical approaches such as the pressure and release (PAR) model have come to the fore that place greater emphasis on the social production of disaster vulnerability than on the physical events that cause societal disruption. While the early tradition in disaster research focused mainly on the impact and response periods of disasters, later research has begun to concentrate on other phases of the hazards cycle, for example mitigation and recovery.

Chapter 3 introduces a broad and multiscalar framework for understanding how sociological theories and concepts can be applied so as to generate a better understanding of the genesis of disasters. In this chapter the discussion focuses on insights provided by sociological research on a variety of topics: the social construction of hazard- and disaster-related phenomena; insights from environmental sociology on processes such as unequal environmental exchange; and more general approaches that focus on the political economy of the environment.

Chapter 4 moves from macro-level analyses of the global contributors to risk buildup and disasters to consider meso- and micro-level perspectives on disasters. This chapter focuses on topics of perennial interest such as the myth of disaster-induced panic. Also considered are theories that focus on public disaster warnings and warning responses. In a major departure from the earlier edition of this volume, Chapter 4 also includes extensive discussions of sociological research on organizations, risk, and disasters.

The concept of disaster vulnerability is discussed in many places in this volume, but Chapter 5 delves more deeply into it, focusing on the one hand on global and historical trends that make particular populations and groups more vulnerable than others and on the other hand on the intersectional nature of vulnerability, given that factors such as race, ethnicity, class, and gender combine to produce differential levels of vulnerability. Age and disability are among the factors explored as sources of vulnerability, as are citizenship and linguistic competence. One key point is that individuals and groups are not born vulnerable: they are rendered vulnerable through processes of social marginalization and exclusion. Another key point is that we are currently living in an era characterized by disposability, an era in which many groups worldwide lack agency and are not considered entitled to the kinds of protections available to others. This chapter also reviews efforts to measure disaster vulnerability.

Chapter 6 focuses on disaster resilience: what it is, what factors contribute to it, and why it is relevant to our understanding of why some segments of society are able to cope successfully with disasters while others are not. Discussions in this chapter focus a good deal on the concept of social capital as it relates to disaster resilience. The chapter provides an overview of efforts to measure resilience and even to improve it by reducing disaster vulnerability (among other strategies). Although the concept of resilience is ubiquitous in disaster research and practice, it is also contested, and in this chapter we will review critiques of it.

The boundaries around what constitutes the sociology of disasters are porous. Research in other social science fields – anthropology, economics, political science, and psychology – has long informed sociological understandings of disasters. In many respects, disaster sociology can be considered multi- and interdisciplinary, in that it borrows from those and other fields. The ways in which all these insights are important are discussed in Chapter 7.

Chapter 8 provides an overview of disaster research methods. This chapter is not intended to be a primer on research methods, or even on all the methods that disaster researchers employ. Rather the discussion centers on what is distinctive about conducting research in disaster settings. This includes challenges to applying conventional research approaches in disrupted social environments. The focus here is on the special operational and ethical challenges that accompany the efforts to carry out research in disaster contexts. Ethical issues always arise in research that involves human subjects. But are those issues the same or different in disasters? Do disaster survivors warrant special ethical protections? We will explore these and similar questions in Chapter 8.

Chapter 9 offers ideas about what we can expect in the future by way of disasters, as processes of global environmental change inexorably proceed.

QUESTIONS AND EXERCISES

Have you or your family ever experienced a disaster? If so, what was it like?

How do you expect to benefit from this course? By fulfilling a requirement? By learning about disasters and hazards as a way of contributing to your knowledge base? By finding out how you might have a career in the disaster space in the future?

2
Disaster Research in Historical Context

Introduction

In this chapter I offer a general overview of the field of disaster research, with an emphasis on contributions from sociology and geography. Next I discuss major critiques that were launched against classic disaster and hazards research. This discussion is followed by an overview of subsequent trends in the evolution of the field – especially the growing emphasis on vulnerability as a central topic for research, the introduction of perspectives highlighting power and inequality in the genesis of disasters and in disaster victimization, and the recognition of the importance of axes of inequality such as class, race, and gender in producing disaster impacts and outcomes. We will see how an international network of researchers has formed over time and how the field has matured, as indicated by the growing number of research centers devoted to the social dimensions of hazards and disasters as well as by that of specialist journals in the field. Chapter narratives will emphasize how particular disaster events shaped sociological research over time and will point to key ideas in the sociological study of disasters that are going to be explored in other chapters.

Disaster Research: Origins and Early Years

Notwithstanding important early research by Samuel Prince (1920) and Lowell Carr (1932), disaster research began as an organized discipline in the United States in the late 1940s. The original impetus for research on disasters came from the US military. The US use of nuclear weapons against Japan in World War II and the Soviet Union's successful nuclear test in August 1949 ushered in a period in which the two adversaries and the world at large were forced to contemplate the possibility of nuclear war. One topic of interest was how members of the public would react in the face of nuclear destruction. War planners were wondering whether panic and hysteria would result, whether collective demoralization would set in, or whether residents in bomb-stricken areas would be psychologically willing and able to cope with the terror of nuclear war and begin to rebuild their communities (Quarantelli 1987; Knowles 2011).

Initial research into the societal dimensions of disasters focused on an event that resembled what might take place in wartime. In August 1948 an air inversion in Donora, Pennsylvania resulted in a toxic smog that killed twenty residents and sickened approximately 7,000 – about half of the population in that community. The Army Chemical Center (ACC), which played a role in US chemical warfare planning, sent a team of psychiatrists to look into the deadly smog episode, in an effort to better understand the psychological effects it had on the population; the idea was that such a study could provide insights into possible public reactions to the use of chemical weapons.

The ACC asked the National Opinion Research Center (NORC) at the University of Chicago to conduct a more in-depth study of the Donora episode, but it proved difficult for the center to recruit and train enough field staff to collect all the needed time-sensitive data on public responses. The ACC went on to establish a contract with NORC whereby the latter would train University of Chicago social science graduate students and send them into the field, on a quick-response basis, after major disasters.

NORC subsequently conducted several quick-response studies on different types of community emergencies, and in 1952 it undertook its first large-scale research project after a deadly tornado that struck White County, Arkansas. The study, which involved face-to-face interviews with 342 residents, yielded a large amount of data on public responses immediately before the tornado struck; the respondents' perceptions of threat at the time of impact; their observations about the behavior of others during the impact period; psychological and behavioral responses after impact, including participation in search and rescue activities; and their emotional responses and behavior in the days and weeks after the disaster. Enrico (Henry) Quarantelli, who was among the original NORC team members, later noted that the findings from this seminal study were replicated many times in subsequent research. For example, the White County study found that

> [s]elf control is maintained in extreme threat situations. Panic or wild flight, hysterical breakdown, affective immobility are almost nonexistent. Those in danger try to help one another. Because persons are very frightened or afraid does not mean that they will fail to try and take protective actions. Passivity is not characteristic of the immediate post-impact period. The initial and by far the greatest amount of search and rescue is undertaken on the spot by survivors. Severe mental health problems are not occasioned on any scale by disasters. Convergence on a disaster site is a major problem. There may be widespread stories of looting, but actual cases of looting are very rare in post-impact situations. (Quarantelli 1988: 305)

Rather than revealing pathological or antisocial patterns of behavior, the early NORC studies characterized disaster victims as levelheaded (even though fearful) and willing to engage in a variety of prosocial behaviors.

The NORC studies were significant for their contributions to the subsequent growth of the field. Charles Fritz, who played an important role in establishing the NORC disaster teams, went on to direct studies that were conducted by the Committee on Disaster Studies and the Disaster Research Group at the National Academy of Sciences, and he became a central figure in disaster-related activities at the Academy. Under Fritz's direction, the Academy carried out approximately 160 disaster studies during the 1950s (for more detail, see Quarantelli 1987). It was also Fritz who formulated what has until recently been the best-known definition of disaster:

> [a]n event, concentrated in time and space, in which a society, or a relatively self-sufficient subdivision of a society, undergoes severe danger and incurs such losses to its members and physical appurtenances that the social structure is disrupted and the fulfillment of all or some of the essential functions of the society is prevented. (Fritz 1961: 655)

Henry Quarantelli went on to become one of the founders of the Disaster Research Center (DRC), which was the first place of its kind in the world: a center devoted to the study of the social and behavioral aspects of disasters. Established in 1963 at Ohio State University, the DRC moved in 1985 to the University of Delaware, where it continues to operate.

Initial DRC field studies focused on a variety of different disaster types, including floods, fires, a dam break in Italy, and major explosions. The 1964 Great Alaska earthquake gave the DRC its first opportunity to conduct field work in a truly major disaster. DRC field teams carried out research that began in the immediate post-earthquake period and continued until nearly two years later; they conducted over 500 tape-recorded interviews and collected numerous reports and other materials in various earthquake-stricken communities (Anderson 2014). Much of DRC's research on the earthquake focused on organizational performance, adaptation, and change after the earthquake, but there was also an emphasis on groups made up of community residents that formed spontaneously in the earthquake's aftermath. Dubbed "emergent groups," these informal responders became a continuing area of interest for the DRC and for other disaster researchers (Brouillette and Quarantelli 1971; Stallings and Quarantelli 1985).

Early theoretical approaches: Structural functionalism and symbolic interactionism

The conceptual model that guided early sociological studies of disasters was based on two related theoretical perspectives that were influential at the time: structural functionalism and systems theory. As emphasized in Fritz's original definition of disaster, communities were seen by early researchers as consisting of systems and subsystems organized around the performance of key functions such as socialization, economic activity, and education. A disaster is a damaging event that disrupts the operations of these subsystems, making such functions impossible to perform. Because communities are systems, excessive demands such as those created by disasters result in a search for ways of returning to equilibrium – in this case, they stimulate efforts to enhance community capabilities so that those demands are met. The use of the systems framework thus necessitated a focus on how organizations and service delivery systems adapt and change in the face of disaster-related demands, as well as on group emergence as a spontaneous strategy intended to cope with those demands. For example, researchers documented how responding organizations increase in size by taking on volunteers, how resources converge from outside disaster-stricken areas, how entities that previously had no disaster-related responsibilities get involved in disaster response, and how community-based groups emerge to carry out various response activities because official public safety agencies, which would normally carry out those tasks, are overwhelmed.

Originating as it did at the University of Chicago, early disaster research was also influenced by symbolic interactionism, as formulated by Chicago sociology professor Herbert Blumer. An important methodological tenet of symbolic interactionism was the notion that, to gain access to the common understandings and interpretations that members of a social setting share, it is necessary to observe that setting (Blumer 1969). This was part of the reason for entering the field as rapidly as possible after disaster impact. Early fieldworkers were not interested in retrospective interpretations of response activities – as presented, for example, in after-action reports and other official documents. Instead, they sought to get as close to the "action" as was possible in actual disaster situations and to gather information from those engaged in response activities before memories had a chance to fade. The symbolic interactionist approach also influenced field teams' data collection methods in other ways. Open-ended face-to-face interviews were favored over closed-ended surveys, because they allowed interviewees to raise issues and offer explanations in their own words.

In addition to developing the symbolic interactionist perspective in social psychology, Herbert Blumer was a founder of the sociological subfield of collective behavior – that is, the study of the social behavior that emerges in conditions of social disruption and normative uncertainty; this subfield examines behaviors such as extreme crowd enthusiasm, crowd violence, panic, and social movements (Blumer 1939). Blumer's collective behavior scholarship influenced Quarantelli, who as a graduate student set out to conduct research on panic behavior and found that panic was difficult to study because it occurred infrequently – even in dangerous, terrifying situations like disasters (Quarantelli 1954). However, early DRC studies did identify other types of collective behavior in disasters, such as the spontaneous formation of search and rescue groups, and a focus on emergence remained a part of the DRC research repertoire (for a discussion of the focus on collective behavior in early disaster research, see Wenger 1987).

From the mid-1960s to the early 1970s, the DRC branched out to conduct studies on episodes of urban unrest such as the 1965 Watts riots. Research again focused on organizations involved in responding during those disturbances, for example fire and police departments, but also emphasized innovative organizations that often developed to deal with civil unrest, for example rumor control centers and emergent groups of counter-rioters aimed at discouraging violence. DRC research also yielded important insights into the selective and symbolic nature of looting and arson during civil disturbances. These insights contradicted popular images of riots as involving irrational acts and behavioral contagion (Quarantelli and Dynes 1970).

Although pre-event preparedness and recovery were not totally ignored, the overwhelming focus of DRC studies was on the immediate post-disaster period. Most of the research centered on the performance of organizations that were officially designated as having disaster-related responsibilities – although there was also an emphasis on novel forms of collective behavior. To a large extent, the research topics that were addressed were consistent with the needs of federal policymakers and planners.

The desire to debunk both official and commonsense beliefs about human behavior in disasters was also evident in early disaster studies. Beginning with some of the first post-disaster studies such as the one conducted in White County, myths surrounding panic, "disaster shock," collective demoralization, negative mental health sequelae, and looting or other antisocial behavior were contradicted by empirical studies of disasters and replaced by images of widespread prosocial behavior and organizational problem-solving. Positive aspects of community responses were highlighted: disasters were characterized as giving rise to "therapeutic communities," as being accompanied by "status leveling" and a reduction in community conflict, and as leading to positive outcomes such as increased feelings of self-efficacy. The message emerging from pioneering studies is perhaps best summed up in the title of an article that appeared in 1977 in *Psychology Today*, which was "Good News about Disasters" (Taylor 1977). This "good news" frame masked important aspects of disaster – such as intergroup conflict and the persistence of power relations in affected communities and societies – that came to the fore in later studies (Tierney 2007).

The Natural Hazards Tradition

The second major strain of research in the United States also had its origins at the University of Chicago, in the work of geographer Gilbert White. White's 1945 Chicago dissertation focused on what he termed the "human adjustment to floods," and the concept of alternative adjustments in the face of hazards was central to his analytic approach. The dissertation is probably best known for White's assertion that "floods are acts of God, but flood losses are largely acts of man. Human encroachment upon the flood plains of rivers accounts for the high annual total of flood losses" (White 1945: 2). In other words, it is human decisions and actions that mainly determine the extent to which naturally occurring events become disasters.

An emphasis on hazard adjustments

According to White's framework, developed in collaboration with Robert Kates of Clark University, Ian Burton of the University of Toronto, and others, communities, societies, and other social actors can choose among a range of adjustments when confronting hazards. These alternative adjustments include engineered works such as levees and dams, hazard-specific adjustments such as raising properties so as to protect them from floods, land use controls, warning systems, emergency response measures, disaster relief programs, and risk-spreading through insurance. This emphasis on the spectrum of possible adjustments was in sharp contradiction to US flood management policies, which emphasized engineering solutions to the flood problem. White was suspicious of the nation's overreliance on technological solutions to flood-related problems and was convinced that such measures were solutions in name only, as indicated in a 1958 report on which he was the senior author: this report showed that federal investments in engineered flood control projects subsequent to the 1936 Flood Control Act had actually resulted in increased rather than decreased flood losses.

Countering such policies and advancing the idea that adjustments are an appropriate topic for study, White and his colleagues emphasized that there are multiple ways of reducing flood losses and that how that objective is achieved is a matter of choice. For hazard managers, bounded rather than strict rationality shapes these choices. Far from being perfectly rational human beings who weigh the costs and benefits associated with their decisions and who have complete information about alternative choices, actual human beings are "bounded" in their decision-making by their own cognitive limitations and by incomplete information. Following that logic, White made a key distinction between the theoretical range of choice – that is, all the adjustments that have been, or could feasibly be, carried out in a given setting – and the practical range of choice, which is always narrower, owing to lack of decision-maker awareness and various other social and cultural constraints (Burton, Kates, and White 1978). At the individual level, choices are influenced by such factors as hazard perception, experience, personality traits, and social roles. At low levels of hazard perception, it is likely that no adjustments will be considered, but above that threshold choices are influenced by knowledge about available adjustments and by evaluations regarding their suitability in light of criteria such as technical feasibility and the possibility of economic gain. Community-level decisions regarding hazard adjustments can shape individual choices, just as nationally adopted loss reduction policies shape choices at the community level.

White's research on natural hazard adjustments expanded further, both before and after his move to the University of Colorado in 1970. Between 1968 and 1972, under the auspices of the International Geographic Union and with funding from the US National Science Foundation, he organized and led a series of studies on the characteristics of and responses to nearly a dozen different hazards in different societal settings and communities. His main collaborators in this research were Ian Burton and Robert Kates. The results of these investigations appeared in a volume edited by White and entitled *Natural Hazards: Local, National, Global* (White 1974) and in a number of articles. In addition to its focus on specific hazards, the *Natural Hazards* volume contained sections on hazard perceptions and decision processes, general summaries of the human response to tropical cyclones, floods, and earthquakes, and reviews of hazard loss reduction policies in New Zealand, Canada, Japan, and what was then the Soviet Union. At around the same time, with funding from the National Science Foundation, White and his colleagues and students launched an assessment of hazards research in the United States. The assessment project had several goals: to document the significance of hazards in national life; to explore the social, economic, and policy consequences of the adoption of different hazard adjustments; to identify areas in which new research on hazards would yield benefits to society; and to propose a program for future research.

A key theme in the final project report for the assessment was that "[n]atural hazards research in our nation is spotty, largely uncoordinated, and concentrated in physical and technological fields" (White and Haas 1975: 5). The assessment report made a strong case for the need for more research expenditures on the social, economic, and political dimensions of hazard adjustments: they should be comparable, for example, to expenditures in the engineering disciplines. In particular, the report emphasized the need for research on five adjustments that are common to most hazards that the nation faced: relief and rehabilitation, insurance, warning systems, technological aids such as engineered works, and land use management. Among the report's other recommendations were calls for "post-audits" – that is, systematic comparative studies of disasters that would be conducted by multidisciplinary teams – as well as for longitudinal studies of disaster recovery processes.

The Natural Hazards Research and Applications Information Center

The report also called for the establishment of a clearinghouse that would facilitate communication among the people involved in studying different adjustments to hazards and the practitioners involved in developing and implementing adjustments. That recommendation became a reality with the founding of the Natural Hazards Research and Applications Information Center (NHRAIC) at the University of Colorado in 1976. With funding from the National Science Foundation and under the leadership of White and J. Eugene Haas, the NHRAIC became the second major center in the United States that was devoted to research and training in the field of hazards and disasters. In line with what had been recommended in the assessment, the NHRAIC was staffed by graduate students from different disciplines, including sociology, geography, and psychology. In line with White's original vision, much of the research conducted in the early years of the NHRAIC continued to center on specific hazard adjustments.

The "good news about disasters" theme and White's emphasis on choice and on the study of alternative adjustments to hazards reflected both broader disciplinary tendencies and personal ways of viewing the world. Sociological disaster and hazards research developed in a functionalist intellectual milieu that emphasized the smooth (if occasionally disrupted) operation of social systems and eschewed Marxian or other conflict-oriented theories about society–environment relations. Both White's Quaker faith and his intellectual projects emphasized the need for harmony with and adjustments to nature, as opposed to control over nature through technological means (Hinshaw 2006).

Ways of seeing are also ways of not seeing; by illuminating certain aspects of hazards and disasters, the activities of these pioneering centers also created blind spots. In the early decades of the field, neither center paid much attention to the role of political power or social inequality in disaster victimization. In foregrounding organizational and group responses to disasters, DRC research elided the ways in which community and supra-community factors affect disaster responses. White's vision of individuals and hazard managers exercising rational choice – albeit bounded by cognitive and other limitations – elided a point emphasized throughout this volume: that many at-risk groups have essentially no choice when it comes to shielding themselves from hazard-related risks, because those risks are imposed on them.[1]

Both centers were active in the training of subsequent generations of disaster researchers, including several that went on to found and direct other US research centers. Because the centers were so prolific, their output – both of ideas and of human resources – helped foster a kind of disaster orthodoxy.

However, over time classic perspectives began to be supplanted by new and heterodox approaches to understanding the causes and consequences of disasters.

Trends in the Study of Hazards and Disasters

Critiques of disaster orthodoxy

Disaster orthodoxy began to be seriously challenged during the 1980s. Elsewhere (Tierney 2007; 2014) I have written about the significance of the edited volume *Interpretations of Calamity*, which was published in 1983 (Hewitt 1983b). Two chapters in *Interpretations* were especially important in terms of their critique of the reigning hazards and disasters frameworks. In the first chapter of the volume, Kenneth Hewitt opened with a broadside against what he termed the "dominant consensus" in the field of disaster research. Observing that contemporary disaster research was "certainly rich in the results of scientific enquiries," he went on to argue that

> [t]he applications of scientific research are not, however, its definitive feature. It may have internal coherence or at least conviction. That does not alter my sense that it capitalizes rather arbitrarily upon scientific discovery. Indeed it accords with "the facts" only insofar as they can be made to fit the assumptions, development and social predicaments of dominant institutions and research that has grown up serving them. (Hewitt 1983a: 3)

For Hewitt, disaster orthodoxy could best be understood as reflective of, and in the service of, the societal set of power arrangements in which it had developed: the technocratic, bureaucratic, managerial state. Disasters constitute a challenge to the state's claims regarding its ability to manage and control, and the response of dominant institutions to this threat is to categorize disaster as separate from and discontinuous with "normal" social life and human–environment relations. Thus sequestered,

> [t]he geography of disaster is an archipelago of isolated misfortunes. Each is seen as a localized disorganization of space, projected upon the extensive map of human geography in a more or less random way due to independent events in the geophysical realms of atmosphere, hydrosphere, and lithosphere. More specifically, each disaster is an unplanned hole or rupture in the fabric of productive and orderly human relations with the habitat or "natural resources." (Hewitt 1983a: 12–13)

In Hewitt's telling, the discursive creation of disaster as something distinct from normal everyday life serves the interests of the state and dominant institutions by absolving them of any responsibility for creating disasters.

To be consistent with the materialist and utilitarian ideology of the state and its agents, a disaster must necessarily arise from outside the social order itself, as an accident or unanticipated event; in Hewitt's words, "to argue that government, business, science, or other institutions create disaster has been in a sense outlawed from rational discourse" (Hewitt 1983a: 17).

A second and equally fierce critique was launched in a chapter by Paul Susman, Phil O'Keefe, and Ben Wisner "Global Disasters: A Radical Interpretation" (Susman, O'Keefe, and Wisner 1983). In these authors' view, disaster does not represent a disruption to normal life, as the dominant consensus would contend; rather it is a part of normal life, the consequence of political–economic processes within the dominant capitalist world system that result in marginalization and increased vulnerability. The authors characterized poverty and "underdevelopment" not as conditions inherent in countries in the third world in need of development – what we now call the global South – but rather as consequences of domination by economically and politically powerful global actors in the global North. Because the core exercises hegemony over nations situated at the periphery, economic exchanges invariably result in negative impacts for peripheral nations, for example extreme poverty and poor governance that are recast as characteristic features of underdevelopment. Among the other effects of that hegemony are the increased marginalization of people who live in peripheral countries and their increased vulnerability to environmental stressors, including environmental extremes. At the same time, the ability of populations to adapt to change decreases, which leaves them vulnerable to both chronic stressors and the occurrence of environmental extremes such as hurricanes and other disaster agents. We will revisit these ideas in more detail in Chapter 3.

The "discovery" of vulnerability

One of the key contributions of these authors was their effort to make the concept of vulnerability central to the study of disasters. They defined disaster vulnerability as

> the degree to which different classes in society are differentially at risk, both in terms of the probability of occurrence of an extreme physical event and [in terms of] the degree to which the community absorbs the effects of extreme physical events and helps different classes to recover. (Susman et al. 1983: 264)

This emphasis on class as a factor in differential risk was in part a reflection of the authors' Marxian theoretical commitments, but was also indicative of the extent to which other contributors to vulnerability, such as gender and race, had not yet been theorized. As discussed later in this chapter, those analyses were still to come.

Just over ten years after *Interpretations*, another volume was published that was written in a similar vein. *At Risk: Natural Hazards, People's Vulnerability, and Disasters* (Blaikie, Cannon, Davis, and Wisner 1994; see also Wisner, Blaikie, Cannon, and Davis 2004) made the case that the production of vulnerability should be central to the study of disasters. Both the editors and the contributors characterize the vulnerability of individuals and groups as the result of a series of macro-, meso-, and micro-level economic and political processes, organized into what they called the "pressure and release" (PAR) model of disaster. Macro-level factors, termed "root causes," consist of broad global and national forces that affect one's access to political power and economic resources and produce social, political, and economic inequities. Another set of factors, termed "dynamic pressures," consists of the more immediate factors that represent the manifestation of root causes in particular social and historical contexts. For example, as I discuss in more detail in the next chapter, the structural adjustment programs and debt that have been forced on many countries at the global periphery are an instantiation of macro-level globalization and neoliberalization processes. Other dynamic pressures can include such factors as the imposition of export-oriented agricultural practices and rapid urbanization. Dynamic pressures lead in turn to unsafe conditions within particular contexts. Thus structural adjustments and burdensome debt lead to declining national investments in health, education, and welfare. Export-oriented agriculture leads to food insecurity and, potentially, to livelihood loss and migration. And rapid urbanization results in overcrowding, slum conditions, development of settlements in unsafe areas, and depletion of natural resources. Such factors contribute to vulnerability, which, if not offset by increases in coping capacity and access to resources that serve to release vulnerability-generating pressures, will disproportionately expose vulnerable populations to potential losses.

One key point emphasized in *At Risk* is that individuals and groups are made vulnerable through linked sets of conditions that operate at different levels of analysis. It only takes a geophysical, atmospheric, or other kind of event of magnitude for disastrous losses to occur – losses that are disproportionately borne by the most vulnerable. Another point is that it is not the physical event itself that produces those losses. The event is merely a trigger; the losses are the result of processes that are internal to the social order.

The critiques of conventional disaster research advanced in *Interpretations* and *At Risk* began to shift the field of hazards and disaster in several ways. First was the notion that disasters should be thought of not as discrete or unexpected events but rather as occurrences that are specific to the social settings in which they occur – settings characterized by inequality and vulnerability. Second was the related idea that the conditions that set the stage for disaster are the consequence of long-term political, economic, and environmental processes such as the exploitation of the natural resources of "underdeveloped" countries in the interest of capital accumulation, and subsequent resource depletion and environmental problems. Seen in this light, disasters are among the many negative consequences of the operations of the global political economy. Third was the idea that processes that are pervasive within that global system push populations in exploited regions to the margins of their societies, force them to live in increasingly unsafe conditions, and undermine their capacity to adapt, making them vulnerable when triggering events occur. As disaster scholar Steve Matthewman (2015: 136) puts it, "events are merely processes made visible." More generally, these conceptual and analytic shifts indicated an openness to using alternative paradigms such as world systems theory and Marxian critiques of global capitalism to challenge fundamental assumptions not only about the social aspects of disasters but also about the practice of disaster research itself. These ideas will be expanded on in Chapter 3.

The second assessment project

Geographers and development scholars were the main contributors to *Interpretations* and *At Risk*, and the focus of those volumes was overwhelmingly on vulnerability, hazards, and disasters in the less developed counties of the global South. However, during the decade of the 1990s, sociologists and other social scientists began to focus increasingly on issues related to disaster vulnerability within the US context. During that period and under the leadership of Dennis Mileti, the NHRAIC carried out a second assessment of the research on natural hazards. That multiyear effort was funded in part by the National Science Foundation but was mainly carried out by over one hundred researchers who volunteered to inventory knowledge on a range of hazard- and disaster-related topics. In tune with the center's historical roots, parts of the second assessment were concerned with research on hazard adjustments such as land use planning (Burby 1998), hazard insurance (Kunreuther and Roth 1998), the geographic dimensions of disasters (Cutter 2001), and disaster preparedness and response (Tierney, Lindell, and Perry 2001). However, other scholars who worked on the second assessment focused on factors associated with differential disaster vulnerability – for example gender (Fothergill 1996; 1998), race and ethnicity (Fothergill, Maestas, and Darlington 1999), and poverty (Fothergill and Peek 2004). The influence of earlier critiques of disaster orthodoxy and of work highlighting the centrality of vulnerability is clear in many of the analyses produced by the second assessment. For example, in their article on poverty and disaster vulnerability, Alice Fothergill and Lori Peek argue that

> there has been a false separation of hazards and the social system because of the lack of widespread recognition of connections between the daily risks people face and the reasons for their vulnerability to hazards and disasters.

Indeed, disasters are the products of the social, political, and economic environment, as well as the natural events that cause them. (Fothergill and Peek 2004: 89)

Space, place, and disaster

During the 1990s, researchers also began to couple a sensitivity to the role of diversity and inequality in structuring disaster vulnerability and outcomes with an awareness of the importance of understanding the forces that shape urban forms and help determine which populations are disproportionally exposed to hazards. For example, the *Hurricane Andrew: Ethnicity, Gender, and the Sociology of Disasters* compilation (Peacock, Morrow, and Gladwin 1997) contained chapters on axes of vulnerability such as gender, as well as studies that reflected insights from the fields of political ecology and critical urban studies – a synthetic approach that Peacock referred to as "socio-political ecology." In that volume, Peacock and Ragsdale argued, for example, that "[the] extraordinary influence exerted by powerful economic interests on government policy, land use patterns, and construction has important implications for disaster research" (Peacock et al. 1997: 29) and that understanding how these interests operate in different settings can tell us a lot about how and why events become disastrous and who suffers most when they do.

The *Hurricane Andrew* volume marked a return to the field's origins in the study of human ecology, but with a difference: spatial relations and patterns of settlement were highlighted, while conflicting political and economic interests and power differentials were identified as sources of disaster vulnerability and loss. When Andrew struck, the disparities between those who possessed political and economic power and those who lacked it were reflected not only in patterns of damage and destruction but also in differential trajectories and outcomes of recovery. These disparities were traceable to such factors as residential segregation by race and ethnicity, the relegation of poor residents to hazardous residential structures, discriminatory practices in homeowner insurance coverage, and inequities in the provision of post-disaster assistance.

The *Hurricane Andrew* book also brought to the fore issues of gender and disaster vulnerability. In a chapter called "A Gendered Perspective," Elaine Enarson and Betty Hearn Morrow pointed out that

> [t]he effects of gender and gender relations have been virtually ignored in most disaster research, with few sources addressing women's wide range of involvement in disaster-stricken households and communities. Women and gender still remain largely absent even as organizing categories in the disaster literature. While sex as a bipolar variable is sometimes analyzed in quantitative studies, a complex gendered analysis is rare. (Enarson and Morrow 1997: 117)

The following year, these same scholars edited *The Gendered Terrain of Disaster: Through Women's Eyes* (Enarson and Morrow 1998), which again argued for placing gender on the disaster research agenda. As will be discussed in subsequent chapters, studies have further explored the ways in which gender, other axes of inequality, and processes of marginalization have led to differential vulnerability to disasters.

Institutionalizing a discipline

The history of disaster research has also been marked by growing ties among researchers in different countries and by international collaborations. There were episodic contacts between US investigators and ones in other countries as far back as the early 1950s (Dynes 1988). However, collaborations became more common in the 1970s and 1980s. Examples include collaborative research on public responses to volcano eruptions in the United States and Japan (Perry and Hirose 1983), mass media reporting on disasters in the United States and Japan (Hiroi, Mikami, and Miyata 1985; Quarantelli, Wenger, Mikami, and Hiroi 1993), and the public response to the 1985 Mexico City earthquake (Wenger and James 1994). This period also saw exchanges between US and Italian disaster researchers regarding theory and research (Dynes, De Marchi, and Pelanda 1987). Later on, the first edition of *What Is a Disaster? Perspectives on the Question* (Quarantelli 1998) included contributions by researchers from the United States, France, Germany, Russia, Canada, and the Netherlands. Ties between US and Japanese researchers have remained strong, as can be seen in current efforts to support collaborative research funded by the US National Science Foundation and the Japan Science and Technology Agency (STA).

The international dimension of social science disaster research was strengthened with the formation of the International Sociological Association's Research Committee on Disasters (RC 39) in 1986. The membership of the research committee includes not only sociologists but representatives of other social sciences as well. The research committee meets every four years at the World Congress of Sociology and holds annual research sessions in the United States. It is the sponsor of one of the field's leading journals, the *International Journal of Mass Emergencies and Disasters* (IJMEAD).

Over time, networks have developed that are designed to encourage cross-societal and cross-discipline research, collaboration, and information sharing. For example, the Gender and Disaster Network (http://www.gdnonline.org), which was founded in 1997 and is affiliated to the University College London Institute for Risk and Disaster Reduction, serves as a hub for research, practice, and policy on gender-related issues across the hazards cycle. Recently funded by the National Science Foundation (NSF) and headquartered at the Natural Hazards Center, the Social Sciences Extreme Events Research (SSEER) network (Peek 2022) aims to identify disaster researchers and research centers around the world, offer training, and encourage research collaborations and data sharing among network participants. (See https://converge.colorado.edu/research-networks/sseer; SSEER will be discussed in more detail in Chapter 8.)

This chapter began by focusing on two pioneering hazards and disaster research centers in the United States. As the field has evolved, many other centers have been established, both in the United States and around the world. Table 2.1 lists a selected group of centers and programs whose research focuses primarily on the societal aspects of hazards, disasters, and risk. The table is meant to be only a snapshot and does not include all the social–scientific institutions and programs that currently exist.

Another indicator of the field's maturity is the proliferation of professional journals devoted to social–scientific aspects of disasters. Disaster researchers frequently publish in key journals in their own fields – anthropology, economics, geography, psychology and mental health, sociology, and so on – but they also publish extensively in specialty journals in the disaster field. Examples of such journals are the aforementioned *International Journal of Mass Emergencies and Disasters*; *Disasters*; *Disaster Studies*; the *Journal of Disaster Studies, Policy, and Management*; the *Journal of Contingencies and Crisis Management, Natural Hazards Review*; the *Journal of Homeland Security and Emergency Management*; the *Journal of Integrated Disaster Risk Management*; *Prehospital and Disaster Medicine*; *Global Environmental Change, Part B: Environmental Hazards*; *Risk Analysis*; the *International Journal of Disaster Risk Reduction*; the *Journal of Disaster Research*; *Disaster Prevention and Management*; five different *Environment and Planning* journals; and the *International Journal of Disaster Risk Science*.

Watershed Events: 9–11, Katrina, the Indian Ocean Tsunami, the Japan 2011 Triple Disaster, and Deadly Hurricanes

The first five years of the twenty-first century marked the occurrence of large-scale and even catastrophic disasters. For sociologists, the September 11 attacks on the World Trade Center called attention to various forms of emergent activity and organization at different levels of analysis. The unprecedented nature of the attacks created the demand for the performance of a variety of tasks for which there were no plans, such as evacuating tens of thousands of people from Lower Manhattan, reconstituting a big-city emergency operations center literally from the ground up, conducting search and rescue while attempting to preserve a crime scene, and simultaneously removing massive amounts of debris and searching for and identifying human remains. In the face of these and other challenges, responding agencies were forced to improvise, and researchers sought to understand how such improvisation came about. Improvisational activities had been studied before by disaster sociologists, most notably Gary Kreps (1985), but Kreps's research had relied

Table 2.1 Examples of hazard-, disaster-, and risk-related centers and programs

Center or Program	Location
Center for Public Health and Disasters University of California, Los Angeles	United States
Centre for Research on the Epidemiology of Disasters School of Public Health, Catholic University of Louvain	Belgium
Copenhagen Center for Disaster Research University of Copenhagen	Denmark
Disaster Research Center University of Delaware	United States
Hazard Reduction and Recovery Center Texas A&M University	United States
Hazards and Vulnerability Research Institute University of South Carolina	United States
Institute for Catastrophic Loss Reduction Western University	Canada
Joint Centre for Disaster Research Massey University	Australia
National Center for Disaster Preparedness Earth Institute, Columbia University	United States
Natural Hazards Center University of Colorado Boulder	United States
Population Impact, Recovery, and Resilience Program College of Global Public Health, New York University	United States
Red de Estudios Sociales en Prevencion de Desastres en America (Network for Social Studies on Disaster Prevention In Latin America)—LA RED	Panama
Research Center for Disaster Reduction Systems Disaster Prevention Research Institute, Kyoto University	Japan
Resilient Organisations	New Zealand
Risk and Resilience Program International Institute for Advanced Systems Analysis (IIASA)	Austria
School of National Safety and Emergency Management Beijing Normal University	China
UCL Institute for Risk and Disaster Reduction University College London	United Kingdom

primarily on archival material collected in past disasters. The September 11 disaster gave researchers the opportunity to observe improvisation unfolding essentially in real time, as responders grappled with the fact that, while emergency plans provided guidance for the performance of some tasks, there were literally no plans in place for others.

The largest terrorist attack in US history by many orders of magnitude, the World Trade Center disaster was followed by a massive convergence of uniformed responders, some of whom came literally from across the country – volunteers, donations of all types, and groups and organizations with no designated disaster responsibilities that simply wished to provide assistance. This large-scale response resulted in extensive emergence at the network level, as official and unofficial responders established communication, coordination, and information-sharing linkages that grew and evolved over time and space. Here again, the study of emergent response networks was not entirely new in disaster sociology; Thomas Drabek and his collaborators had studied search and rescue networks in the 1980s (Drabek, Tamminga, Kilijanek, and Adams 1981). What was new was the systematic application of network-analytic methods, including specialized computer software and analysis techniques, to an extremely large and dynamic response network. These types of methods were subsequently used in the study of other disaster events.

The 9–11 attacks ushered in a period that was marked by what many consider extreme reactions to the terrorist threat on the part of the Bush administration, Congress, and officialdom at large. Of interest in the context of sociological disaster research are such trends as the massive bureaucratization of emergency management that accompanied the creation of the US Department of Homeland Security; the framing of terrorism as a major risk to the nation, which superseded concern with hazards and disasters; and a tilt toward a stricter command-and-control approach to managing large-scale events. Before 9–11, sociological and other social science research had been somewhat successful in influencing emergency management policies and practices, as evidenced by its incorporation into widely used textbooks and training materials in the emergency management field, for example in the courses offered by the Federal Emergency Management Agency (FEMA)'s Emergency Management Institute. Sociological research had provided information on such topics as how the public responds in disaster situations – that is, in non-panicky, prosocial ways – and why more decentralized response systems that are capable of accommodating emergency are preferable to hierarchical command-and-control structures. However, many of these research lessons were lost and many disaster myths were revived after 9–11, which led to critical responses on the part of some sociologists and social scientists.

If researchers and the general public needed a reminder of the catastrophic potential of disasters, that reminder came on December 26, 2004, when a massive earthquake measuring approximately 9.0 on the Richter scale caused a tsunami that propagated throughout the Indian Ocean, killing an estimated 230,000 people in fourteen countries. Coastal areas in Indonesia, Sri Lanka, India, and Thailand were the ones hardest hit, as entire villages and their inhabitants were washed away. The tsunami catastrophe raised important questions regarding the need for effective warning systems and what should be done to assist at-risk populations in responding to disasters such as the Indian Ocean tsunami, in which warning periods may be very short. With so much devastation, the tsunami also shed light on issues related to disaster recovery, including questions about population relocation and the recovery of livelihoods for those affected.

Then came the event that marked a sea change in the sociological study of disasters: Hurricane Katrina in August 2005. While federal agencies were still in the process of devising plans for responding to terrorism, including attacks that employed all manner of exotic chemical, biological, and nuclear weapons, Katrina brought death and devastation to a wide swath of the Gulf region. Katrina's impacts shocked the nation and the world, but sociologists were not particularly surprised by what they saw during and after the catastrophe. It was well understood that hurricane-buffering natural protections such as wetlands had been depleted and that Louisiana levees would not be able to withstand the storm surge that a major hurricane would produce. It was also understood that New Orleans is essentially a "bowl" that would rapidly flood once the levees were breached. The racial and class disparities in access to self-protective measures such as evacuation were not a surprise; nor were the disparities in death rates. What perhaps did come as a shock was the sheer incompetence of responding agencies and the viciousness of the racially motivated attacks against Katrina survivors.

Many sociologists were drawn to conduct research on Katrina and its aftermath – both those who were experienced disaster researchers and those for whom disasters were a new topic of study. Studies were conducted by disaster specialists, but also by environmental and urban sociologists, demographers, gender scholars, and researchers from other sociological specialty areas. This influx of researchers from outside the disaster research community was valuable by virtue of bringing new theories, concepts, and methods into the study of disasters.

As it had after the September 11 attacks, the Social Science Research Council (SSRC) established a special website that featured scholarly commentary on Katrina from sociologists and other social scientists. The SSRC and several private foundations provided funding to a group of social scientists who worked on a project called the Katrina Bookshelf – a series of books that have been or will be published by University of Texas Press. To date, six books have been released. They focus on the experience and impacts of post-disaster displacement (Weber and Peek 2012), the role of culture and connection in the recovery of a large African American extended family (Browne 2015), Katrina as collective trauma (Eyerman 2015), children's experiences and recovery (Fothergill and Peek 2015), the recovery of African American neighborhoods (Kroll-Smith, Baxter, and Jenkins 2015), and enduring lessons from Katrina (Erikson and Peek 2022). Other funding agencies, in particular the National Science Foundation, were also active in funding research on the sociological dimensions of the Katrina catastrophe.

The body of sociological research that was developed in the aftermath of Katrina represents the culmination of several of the trends discussed earlier in this chapter. More than before, Katrina research brought home the notion that the origins of disaster are endogenous, not exogenous, to the social order and showed how these endogenous political and economic forces inscribe themselves on landscapes over time. The Katrina catastrophe provided stark examples of the ways in which processes of marginalization and vulnerability production operate at local and regional scales. And research highlighted like never before the ways in which class, race, and gender get imbricated in particular social settings and produce differential patterns of loss and recovery. Perhaps more than other recent disaster events, Katrina pointed the way forward for subsequent sociological research.

In March 2011 the Tohoku earthquake (known as the Great East Japan Earthquake) caused a massive tsunami, which killed approximately 20,000 people and triggered a triple core meltdown at the Fukushima Daichi nuclear power plant – one of only two level 7 nuclear plant disasters since the inception of that technology (the other level 7 event was the 1986 Chernobyl disaster). Taking into account the entire cascade of events, this was the costliest disaster in history, and its many dimensions have raised vital questions for sociological research. Some of the most important ones relate to the causes of catastrophic failures in risky technologies. It has been more than forty years since the publication of Charles Perrow's (1984) influential book *Normal Accidents: Living with High-Risk Technologies*, and much has been written about the ways in which organizations and institutions can discount hazards and drift into practices that cause risks to proliferate – and how they can cause disasters that in hindsight appear to have been entirely avoidable. The Fukushima disaster was a stark reminder that such pathologies continue to operate, even in advanced industrial societies that pride themselves on being safety-conscious.

Hurricanes that occurred in the United States in 2012 and 2017 highlighted the interaction between climate change and extreme events. In 2012 Hurricane (Superstorm) Sandy struck the greater New York City area at high tide, causing a storm surge that was made more intensely damaging by sea-level rise. In 2017 three major hurricanes – Harvey, Irma, and Maria – caused extensive damage respectively in Texas, Florida, and US territories in the Caribbean. In all three cases, hurricanes formed and strengthened because of warming waters in the Atlantic Ocean and Gulf of Mexico. Climate change was also a factor in the extreme rainfall that accompanied Harvey. These events added further evidence to discussions about the relationship between slow-onset phenomena associated with climate change and disaster events, as well as about the relationship between climate change adaptation and disaster mitigation.

In this chapter I focused on the origins of social science disaster research in the United States, placing an emphasis on research in the fields of sociology and geography, as embodied in the work of pioneering research centers. In addition to describing the conceptual frameworks that guided early studies, I also traced the history of critiques that were launched against those frameworks, beginning with perspectives in critical geography in the early 1980s. The field evolved as a consequence of these critiques and of new formulations such as those presented in the seminal volume *At Risk*, but also as a consequence of disaster events whose impacts on various populations raised fundamental questions regarding the inequality–vulnerability nexus. Shifts in emphasis in the sociology of disasters also mirrored trends in the larger field of sociology, albeit slowly. Originating at a time when conflict-oriented perspectives such as Marxism had reached the nadir of their influence in US academia, sociological disaster research eventually followed the broader trend of increasingly incorporating ideas influenced by those perspectives, for example ideas from political economy and political ecology. The emphasis on gender issues in disasters was also a reflection of broader trends in sociology.

In the following two chapters, I first explore general sociological theories that can help explain the incidence and severity of disasters – again, not the forces that trigger them, but rather the societal conditions that make those forces so destructive. Next, I move on to discuss middle-range theories that focus on topics such as panic, emergence, warning responses, and the social sources of organizational failures and disasters.

QUESTIONS AND EXERCISES

Go online and peruse the websites of the DRC and the Natural Hazards Center. What did you learn about these two centers and their current activities?

For each center, choose one recent publication and discuss its findings.

Take a look at Table 2.1 and choose a center to describe in depth. What kind of research is currently being done at that center (if any) and, on the basis of its publications, how relevant is that center's research to the sociological study of disasters?

Several journals that focus on hazards and disasters are mentioned in this chapter. Select one that you can access on the web and then choose and report on an article that you view as significant.

3

Theoretical Approaches and Perspectives in the Study of Hazards and Disasters

Introduction

In Chapter 2 I provided an overview of the ways in which social–scientific approaches to studying hazards and disasters have evolved over time. This chapter delves more deeply into general theories and concepts that help explain the occurrence of disasters. The focus here is on discussing three general theoretical orientations that have become increasingly important to the study of disasters: social constructionism, vulnerability science, and political economy or political ecology. Throughout this chapter I will be using the term "theory" loosely. While it is inaccurate to say that the field of disaster research is atheoretical, it would also be wrong to argue that theoretical reasoning is a hallmark of the field, especially since so much of the literature has focused on specific, individual disasters. Classifying some of the perspectives discussed here as "theory" is a bit of a stretch. Moreover, to the extent that disaster sociology is theoretical, it is mainly because there has been extensive borrowing from broader theoretical orientations within sociology. Much of what I present in this chapter, particularly in the section on political economy, represents my own efforts to add stronger theoretical reasoning to the field.

General Explanatory Frameworks

In this section I first discuss the influence of social constructionism on the study of hazards and disasters. Next I discuss vulnerability and environmental inequality research and their contributions to the sociology of disasters. To better frame the discussions that follow, saying that hazards and disasters are socially constructed is not the same as saying that they are socially produced. Scholars sometimes use these terms interchangeably, but they mean different things, as the subsequent discussion will show. A focus on social constructionism emphasizes how ideas and assumptions about hazards and disasters

– and our own understandings – are shaped by narratives, discourses, institutional practices, and other factors. By contrast, the analysis of the social production of disasters centers on how social structures and social processes operate to create the conditions that make geological, meteorological, and other physical events disastrous.

Social constructionism

Despite having its origins partly in symbolic interactionism, early sociological research took an ontological realist approach to the study of hazards and disasters. As noted in Chapter 2, disasters were conceptualized as events, concentrated in time and space, that produced damage and human harm and disrupted the existing social order. As social scientists, early researchers in the field did recognize that the meanings people attach to such events shape their responses. Notably, however, early studies predated the publication of seminal works in social constructionism such as *The Social Construction of Reality* (Berger and Luckmann 1966) and, partly owing to the practical nature of early disaster studies, researchers were not particularly interested in problematizing disaster-related phenomena. In the decades since the founding of the field, various forms of constructivism have existed alongside realism in sociological inquiry; importantly for this discussion, concepts formerly thought to be part of an obdurate reality, such as nature itself, are now theorized as social constructions. The interpretivist and postmodern turns in the social sciences have also undercut the notion that concepts such as "nature," "hazard," "disaster," and "victimization" are stable, uncontested, and non-problematic. This is not to say that forces such as wind, storm surges, and fault ruptures do not exist in the physical world. Denying the existence of these physical forces would be tantamount to denying the forces of gravity. Rather constructionist, interpretivist, and postmodern perspectives remind us that social processes are fundamental to the framings we attach to such phenomena.

Elsewhere (Tierney 2007, 2018) I have emphasized the importance of viewing disaster-related phenomena as social constructions. For example, expert models purporting to project the likelihood of disasters, claims regarding the putative causes of disasters, statistics and findings concerning the consequences of disasters (deaths, injuries, mental health problems), and programs purporting to reduce disaster losses and aid disaster victims are all outcomes of social construction practices (Tierney 2018). Framings of these and other disaster phenomena have their origins in a range of sources such as scientific knowledge, professional hierarchies that shape perceptions of expertise, bureaucratic routines, interest group mobilization, policy entrepreneurs, and hegemonic discourses and practices.

Like the larger field of science and technology studies, the field of disaster science and technology studies (DSTS) is concerned, among other things, with how so-called scientific "facts" regarding hazards and disasters are shaped by social, cultural, organizational, and institutional discourses and practices (Fortun and Frickel 2013). As other scholars have noted, except in the aftermath of particular focusing events, disasters are, typically, not constructed as social problems by the broader society, although scientific elites and a few political actors may advocate for that position (Stallings 1995; Drabek 2007). Even the capacity to acknowledge disasters, both potential and actual, is shaped by organizational cultures and practices (Clarke 1993; Cerulo 2008). As Eric Klinenberg (2002) has shown in his study on the 1995 Chicago heat wave, even a massive heat event that kills hundreds can escape official recognition as a disaster.

Constructions of disaster have shifted over time. It is often observed that in the West the dialogue between Voltaire and Rousseau concerning the 1755 Lisbon earthquake marked a shift from viewing disasters as God's punishment for sin toward seeing them as natural occurrences in which human agency plays a role. This tilt toward an Enlightenment-influenced and scientific perspective can also be seen in the post-earthquake actions of the minister in charge of recovery, the Marquis de Pombal, who directed recovery activities in ways that ensured that the rebuilt city would be more earthquake-resistant (Dynes 2000).

Secular interpretations of disaster did not supplant supernatural ones, as the Lisbon case might suggest. Religious interpretations of disaster remain very common in many societies around the world, particularly in the global South, as well as among religious and spiritually oriented groups in the global North. On the one hand, research suggests that such interpretations can lead to reduced perceptions of risk and a lack of interest on the part of adherents in adopting mitigation and preparedness measures: after all, if death and survival are determined by God's or Allah's will, why be concerned about disaster risks? On the other hand, religiosity and identification with a religious community can help adherents cope after disasters, for example by providing social and material support. Additionally, there is ample historical evidence that, even if some societies believed in the supernatural origins of disasters, that did not prevent them from engaging in mitigation and preparedness activities. (For a good review, see Sun, Deng, and Qi 2018.)

Social constructionism and Covid-19

To fully understand the power of social constructions and their influence on behavior in contemporary times, we need only consider the competing frames that were advanced – and believed and acted on by different segments of the public – during the Covid-19 epidemic. Competing claims circulated in groups and networks, often on the basis of information, misinformation, disinformation, and malinformation passed on through social media and cable news outlets such as Fox News, by the then US president Trump and other officials, and by persons claiming to be experts. To cite just a few examples of those competing claims: where did the virus start to infect humans? In a wet market or in the virology lab in Wuhan? If in the lab, was the release of the pathogen accidental or intentional? What measures are effective in reducing risk: masking, social distancing, getting vaccinated, taking drugs such as ivermectin or hydroxychloroquine, just staying healthy, exercising, or having good genes? What about vaccines: do they boost immunity? Do they cause autism? Are they a means to implant surveillance devices in recipients? How many people died from Covid? Were official statistics accurate or fabricated? What about people who "died suddenly" after taking the vaccine? Was Dr. Anthony Fauci a hero for his leadership during the pandemic, an agent of the Democratic Party, or someone seeking to profit from a newly developed vaccine?

Various explanations have been given for the rise and spread of so many competing claims that deviated from official guidance and for which there was no actual evidence. However, loss of trust in science and societal institutions, as well as the strongly polarized nature of public opinions and sentiments, were clearly factors. And while there were many dimensions of inequality and diversity that were associated with different warring constructions, political views and party affiliations stand out. As is now widely recognized, supporters of then president Donald Trump in the United States, who were generally Republicans, were particularly likely to reject official guidance on the pandemic and to gravitate toward junk science and conspiratorial claims.

That reality is socially constructed and that constructions shape social action are tenets that are widely accepted in sociology. One of the oldest dicta in sociology is the Thomas theorem (Thomas and Thomas 1928: 572), which states that "if men define situations as real, they are real in their consequences." Similarly, a central assumption of symbolic interactionism is that people act with respect to situations on the basis of the meanings they assign to them. The validity of these arguments was certainly borne out during the Covid crisis. In particular, a number of studies have found positive associations between acceptance of certain constructions such as that scientific experts are not to be trusted, belief in conspiracy theories and right-wing political orientations, and vaccine refusal (Islam et al. 2021; Kowalska-Duplaga and Duplaga 2023). Additionally, recent research conducted in Ohio and Florida has shown that party affiliation – that is, being a registered Republican voter – was associated with a higher likelihood of dying from Covid after the vaccine became available (Wallace, Goldsmith-Pinkham, and Schwartz 2023). Put another way, engagement with different socially constructed realities became a matter of life and death during Covid.

The social construction of ignorance

Social constructions are related not only to what we think we know about hazards and disasters, but also to what we are kept from knowing. While many efforts are made worldwide to educate members of the public about the hazards they face, those efforts often exist alongside other strategies, aimed at keeping the public in the dark regarding hazards. This is the social construction of ignorance.

Later in this volume we will see how psychology and behavioral economics have identified ways in which our own cognitive biases shape our views on hazards and risk. In this chapter we will draw upon insights from the field of agnotology, which is the study of the social organization of ignorance (Proctor and Schiebinger 2008), to show how information about the ways in which people are at risk can be elusive or deliberately concealed. A key insight here is that both knowledge and ignorance are the product of social and historical processes. Examples of what Frickel and Vincent term "the politics of not knowing" are abundant when it comes to hazards and disasters. Some hazards fall through organizational cracks (Beamish 2002a, 2002b), while others are intentionally concealed. In the hazards and disaster realm there are countless other examples of socially constructed ignorance, or what Linsey McGoey (2019) calls "strategic ignorance." Widely considered undesirable, ignorance becomes a strategic resource in the hands of those who hold political and economic power and do not wish to see risks and hazards reduced. There is an extensive literature documenting how "merchants of doubt" (Oreskes and Conway 2010), backed by powerful corporate actors, sow confusion concerning threats; obvious examples include the negative consequences of smoking (Oreskes and Conway 2010); toxic pollution (Cable, Shriver, and Mix 2008; Auyero and Swistun 2008); and climate change (Dunlap and McCright 2015).

Steve Rayner (2012) identified four strategies that organizations and institutions employ to keep "uncomfortable knowledge" from coming to light. Denial is "the refusal or inability of organizations at any level to acknowledge information" (2012: 114), even when it is available and there are efforts to bring that information to light. Dismissal is the rejection of available information as "unreliable, not relevant, imprecise, not timely or on the wrong spatial scale" (Rayner 2012: 116). The organized effort to deny or sow doubt about climate change and its impacts is a combination of denial and dismissal – an effort often aided by the media, which until very recently, in the name of "balance," placed as much emphasis on the claims of climate change deniers as on the broad scientific consensus on this topic (Boykoff and Boykoff 2004). A third strategy, diversion, is a "nothing to see here" approach that intentionally directs attention away from unwelcome information, such as information about hazards, and toward other issues. For example, disaster-related threats can be shuttled backstage while other concerns, such as the need to relax growth restrictions and avoid strict building codes, are foregrounded in the name of some other goal, such as housing affordability. Displacement is a strategy that seeks to direct efforts away from measures capable of addressing a real-world problem such as hazard vulnerability and toward abstract representations of the problem, such as models and scenarios. Such conceptual artifacts are of course important, but an emphasis on the need to collect more data and refine models can stand in the way of taking action on the basis of what is already known.

Various forces act to promote ignorance regarding hazards. The insurance industry is a case in point. Ideally, insurance premiums should act as signals that help current and potential property owners understand the risks associated with locating in particular areas. It is just common sense that insurance rates for homeowners and businesses should be indicative of higher levels of risk. However, such signals are often intentionally muted, particularly in high-risk areas. In the US National Flood Insurance Program (NFIP), for example, many insurance premiums are subsidized by the federal government and do not reflect risk severity, so property owners have a tendency to view flood risks as lower than they actually are. The Biggart-Waters Flood Insurance Reform Act of 2012 was intended to strengthen risk signals by allowing insurance rates to rise in ways that reflected risk assessments associated with property in flood-prone areas. This caused rates on some policies to increase by orders of magnitude, making insurance essentially unaffordable to many property owners. Outrage was so widespread that Biggart-Waters requirements were weakened in subsequent legislation – the Homeowner Flood Insurance Affordability Act of 2014. Not surprisingly, groups like the National Bankers Association and the National Association of Home Builders lobbied hard against flood insurance reform (Warmbrodt and Meyer 2017). In another example, wildfires are a major hazard in California, yet insurance premiums for property owners in high fire-hazard areas have generally not reflected the historical record or expert assessments. This is because those whose properties would be considered uninsurable on the regular market on account of very high wildfire risk can still apply to the Fair Access to Insurance Requirements (FAIR) Program, a special state-regulated risk pool. Maintaining hazard insurance subsidies has two adverse effects. Such subsidies not only shield property owners from full recognition of the perils they face but also encourage development in hazardous areas by downplaying those risks. However, as we will see later in Chapter 9, offering insurance in high-hazard parts of the United States has become increasingly untenable.

Along these same lines, the disclosure of hazards can be seen as a means of overcoming powerful actors' construction of strategic ignorance by correcting the information asymmetry between such actors and those who may be at risk. Disclosure and right-to-know policies do help lift the veil of ignorance, particularly when information falls into the hands of well-mobilized publics and social movements. Yet the record is mixed with respect to the kind of hazards considered here. Disclosure of threats is often just that – disclosure – and hoped-for risk reduction actions do not inevitably follow. For example, Seattle, Washington is located in the Cascadia earthquake subduction zone, which stretches from Vancouver Island to the north to northern California. The subduction zone is capable of producing a devastating magnitude 9.0 earthquake similar in severity to the one that struck in Japan in 2011, as well as a massive tsunami. An earthquake of that magnitude did occur in the region in 1700, and recent research shows that the threat to Seattle is even greater than previously thought, owing to the potential for a multi-fault earthquake occurrence (Black et al. 2023). The federal and state governments have launched major efforts to educate the public about the risks associated with a big subduction event and the tsunamis that would result. Hazardous buildings are another matter. Although the need for action has been acknowledged for decades, Seattle has done little to address earthquake hazards associated with its more than 1,100 unreinforced masonry buildings, which would collapse even in an earthquake less powerful than 9.0. It took until 2016 for the locations of those buildings to be made public and for residents of those buildings to be informed about their risks. Seattle has yet to take legislative action to require seismic safety upgrades.

Legislation requiring hazard disclosure can be an effective means of combatting ignorance about disaster threats, but here again having laws on the books is no guarantee that the information will reach those who need it. In the United States, the Superfund Amendment and Reauthorization Act, Title III, also passed in the aftermath of the deadly 1984 Bhopal chemical disaster. The Act required facilities that produce and handle hazardous materials to make the information regarding their inventories publicly available; it also mandated the establishment of local emergency planning committees (LEPCs) charged with reducing and responding to the risks posed by such facilities. However, after an explosion at a chemical plant in the town of West in Texas killed fifteen people, injured approximately 160, and damaged or destroyed about 150 structures in April 2013, hazardous materials inventory data were not released to the public. Those data had been kept secret on the grounds that "terrorists" might get access to them.[1] More plant accidents followed, and the dangers associated with nondisclosure became even more evident in Hurricane Harvey in 2017, when numerous hazardous materials spills occurred and when fires at chemical facilities released toxic smoke. Yet even then affected residents were left in the dark about the hazards they were facing.

Disaster vulnerability and vulnerability science

Differential vulnerability to hazards and disasters has long been a concern for the sociology of disasters, as well as for environmental sociology. The concept of vulnerability encompasses both the probability of suffering the negative effects of hazards and disasters and the likelihood that some groups will be less able than others to navigate the recovery process successfully. The emphasis on vulnerabilities associated with poverty, inequality, race, ethnicity, and gender increased as a consequence of research on disaster events such as the Loma Prieta earthquake (1989), Hurricane Andrew (1992), and the Northridge earthquake (1994); and such vulnerabilities were also highlighted in the mid-1990s, during the second assessment of research on natural hazards. On the basis of the research record, a report by the National Research Council noted that

> what happens to households during and after disasters can be conceptualized in terms of vulnerability and resilience. With respect to vulnerability, social location is associated with the severity of disaster impacts for households. Poverty often forces people to live in substandard or highly vulnerable housing ... leaving them more vulnerable to death, injury, and homelessness ... factors such as income, education, and homeownership influence the ability of households to mitigate and prepare for disasters. Social structural factors also affect the extent to which families can accumulate assets in order to achieve higher levels of safety, as well as their recovery options and access to resources after disasters strike. (National Research Council 2006: 159)

More detail will be provided in subsequent chapters on which groups are vulnerable to disasters, how, and why. The purpose here is to re-emphasize that, while they may not have been a significant concern in classical disaster research, the social and the economic dimensions of vulnerability are now a major research focus.

The idea that the study of environmental and hazard vulnerability should become a specialized field was put forth by geographer Susan Cutter, who coined the term "vulnerability science" to describe that emerging specialty area (Cutter 2003). Cutter characterized vulnerability science as a subdiscipline that

> helps us understand those circumstances that put people and places at risk and those conditions that reduce the ability of people and places to respond to environmental risk [and] integrates the constructs of risk (exposure) hazard, resilience, differential susceptibility, and recovery/mitigation. (Cutter 2003: 6)

Cutter described vulnerability science as an integrative field, which takes into account interactions among physical features of the environment that include hazards, aspects of built environments that render them susceptible to damage and destruction, and characteristics of the inhabitants of those environments that indicate a propensity for experiencing comparatively more severe disaster impacts and poorer recovery outcomes after disasters. We will take a closer look at the concept in Chapter 5.

The emphasis in disaster research on differential vulnerability and the emergence of vulnerability science mesh nicely with environmental sociology's concern with the related concepts of environmental justice (EJ), injustice, inequality, and racism, even though the two research traditions have mainly evolved on parallel tracks (Tierney 2007). With origins in two important studies conducted in the 1980s – one by the US General Accounting office (in 1983) and the other by the United Church of Christ (Commission for Racial Justice) – EJ research has focused primarily on differential racial, ethnic, and class exposures to and impacts of environmental toxins and hazardous facilities (for early work and literature reviews, see Bullard 1990; Bryant and Mohai 1992; Brown 1995; Szasz and Meuser 1997). Over time, an extensive empirical record has developed, revealing that, while both the forms of environmental inequality and the factors that are associated with it show variation across communities, general patterns hold: much more often than not, being poor and otherwise marginalized by axes of inequality translates into increased vulnerability to exposure to toxic substances and other environmental "bads" (for examples, see Bolin, Grineski, and Collins 2005; Downey 2006a, 2006b; Brulle and Pellow 2006; Downey and Hawkins 2008; Mohai, Pellow, and Roberts 2009; Grineski, Collins, Romo Aguilar, and Aldouri 2010).

Despite long-standing recognition of the differential effects of disasters, disaster vulnerability was generally not framed as a form of environmental injustice until the occurrence of Hurricane Katrina. In that disaster it was virtually impossible to ignore the social factors that influenced one's ability to undertake self-protective actions such as evacuation, the stark disparities in death rates by race and age in New Orleans, the unequal treatment of African American disaster survivors, and differences in return rates and recovery trajectories by race and class. Connections with the EJ tradition began to be made in the immediate aftermath of the catastrophe, both in terms of Katrina's immediate impacts and in terms of the hurricane's production of new toxic hazards that adversely affected people of color (Sze 2006; Allen 2007). Researchers such as the pioneering EJ scholar Robert Bullard and others later documented a range of environmental inequities throughout the impact recovery period (Bullard and Wright 2009; Bates and Swan 2010).

Scholars who study disasters are increasingly framing vulnerability and victimization in EJ terms. Flood risk has been studied through an EJ lens in different community and societal settings (Walker and Burningham 2011; Montgomery and Chakraborty 2015; Chakraborty, Collins, Montgomery, and Grineski 2014; Grineski et al. 2015). Extreme heat is the natural hazard that results in the greatest number of fatalities in the United States and many other nations. Here again, researchers are arguing that heat-related vulnerability is an EJ issue, not unlike exposure to toxic hazards. A number of US studies have documented the association between exposure to extreme heat, heat-related deaths, and low-income and minority populations (Klinenberg 2002; Harlan et al. 2006; Harlan, Declet-Barreto, Stefanov, and Petitti 2013; Wilhelmi and Hayden 2010); and scholars have now begun to frame these patterns in EJ terms (Mitchell and Chakraborty 2015).

Advances in the study of vulnerability have led to a greater understanding of the ways in which marginalized groups are disproportionately exposed to hazards and to disaster impacts. Judging from this extensive literature, it is clear that the potential for disaster-induced losses is a form of environmental injustice. While moving the field of disaster research forward in significant ways, the vulnerability literature still has two major weaknesses. First, even as evidence continues to mount, showing that patterns of inequity exist across communities and across hazards, by and large studies do not provide a full explanation as to why this is the case. Many studies of vulnerability are place-specific and tend to involve analyses that center on particular variables, such as locational information on particular toxic facilities or on natural hazards, race, and ethnicity. In consequence, a general theory of vulnerability has yet to emerge.

Second and relatedly, as can be seen in efforts to develop vulnerability indicators by using census data and other sources, the tendency in the literature is, with a few notable exceptions, to describe vulnerability as an attribute of particular segments of the population – in other words, as a state – when for theoretical purposes vulnerability is more appropriately conceptualized as a process, in which different groups are affected by changes in the broader political and economic environment that either reduce or increase their propensity for loss.

In the sections that follow I show how different sociological theories explain how social forces operating at different scales and levels of analysis – at global, international, national, and regional or community levels – set in motion the processes that contribute to disaster vulnerability.

Political economy, ecology, and critical urban studies: A framework for understanding the social production of disaster risk and vulnerability

The approach to understanding disasters put forth here applies theories and concepts from the related fields of political economy and political ecology. Simply put, the argument is that ecological change in both the natural world and human societies is shaped by political and economic forces that are part of the operation of capitalist and neoliberal regimes at different scales. This perspective makes political economy and the social relations of production, accumulation, and resource extraction at different levels of analysis central to understanding the conditions that produce hazards and disasters.

Global scale: The world system and environmental harm

We begin by considering three macro-level theories that account for the incidence and severity of environmental problems: world systems theory, the treadmill of production, and unequal ecological exchange (for an overview, see Rudel, Timmons, and Carmin 2011). Together, these complementary approaches help us understand how hazards proliferate around the world, resulting in a range of environmental harms and disasters.

World systems theory characterizes the capitalist world system as a three-tiered political and economic order consisting of core, semi-peripheral, and peripheral nations. Core nations, the wealthiest and most powerful entities in the system, which currently include the United States, Western Europe, and Japan, dominate the ones at the periphery – the so-called less developed nations that make up the global South. Semi-peripheral nations are nations that attempt either to vie for core status or to avoid sliding into peripheral status. A key dynamic of the world system is the exploitation of the labor and resources of peripheral countries by those at the core; notably, this exploitation involves compelling those countries to restructure their economies in ways that benefit the core rather than their own citizens and taking advantage of their natural resources. The notion of a multileveled world system provides a context for our understanding of the explanatory importance of the other two theories.

Treadmill of production theory argues that the continual economic expansion that is imperative under capitalism leads to resource depletion and creates other negative externalities, such as increased pollution and various forms of environmental degradation. Excessive consumption is encouraged as a means of maintaining the treadmill and is made possible, for example, when credit is made more freely available, so that consumers can spend beyond their means. Nation-states facilitate the operation of the treadmill because it is in their interest to do so – for example, because increasing expansion generates tax revenues (Schnaiberg 1980; Gould, Pellow, and Schnaiberg 2004, 2016).

Within nations, pressure to keep the treadmill operating produces conditions in which geographic areas and populations become sacrificial zones characterized by the environmental damage caused by resource extraction and concentrated production, which in turn results in pollution and waste. US examples include the coal country of Appalachia and "Cancer Alley," a stretch of land along the Mississippi River in Louisiana that has a high concentration of polluting chemical plants and is home to a mostly African American population (see Figure 3.1 for a map showing the concentration of toxic chemicals). As will be discussed later, lands on or adjacently to Native American reservations and US colonies have historically been sites for both resource extraction and environmentally damaging activities.

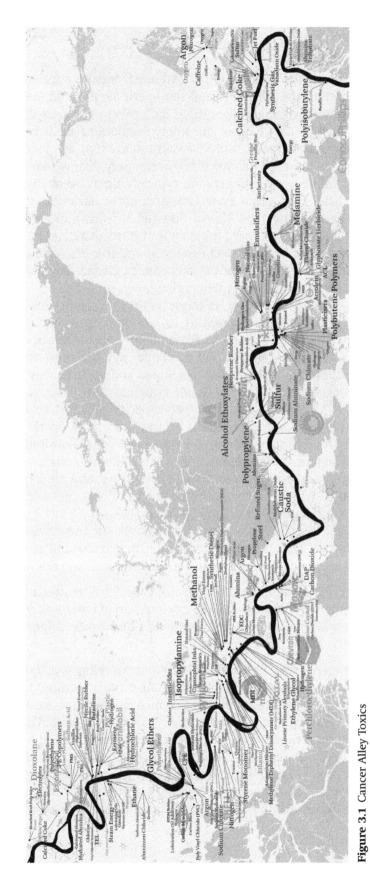

Figure 3.1 Cancer Alley Toxics

Source: Richard Misrach; Kate Orff; Aperture Foundation 2012, Norman B. Leventhal Map & Education Center. Licensed under a Creative Commons BY-ND 4.0 license.

With globalization, the treadmill has extended outside national boundaries, from the core to the periphery and semi-periphery (Gould, Pellow, and Schnaiberg 2016). Multinational corporations look to set up operations in parts of the world where labor is cheaper and safety regulations are less stringent than those in more developed countries. Many items that are produced for export to nations in the core involve extensive supply chains that originate in impoverished countries; consumers are typically unaware of the environmental damage that is part of that trade. Examples of the hazardous downsides of globalization include the 1984 Bhopal disaster, in which an accident at a Union Carbide plant in India caused thousands of immediate and longer-term deaths and injured more than 550,000 residents, and the 2013 collapse of the Rana Plaza, which housed five garment factories in Dhaka, Bangladesh. The collapse caused the deaths of over 1,100 workers.

The e-waste problem is another example of how consumption in more developed countries creates toxic hazards in less developed ones. People in affluent societies generate a continual demand for state-of-the-art electronic technologies and the industry is happy to oblige, but the resultant e-waste ends up being disposed of in "the least developed and most heavily indebted countries, such as Ghana, Nigeria, Chile, Uruguay, Viet Nam, Colombia, Peru and Ecuador" – nations that lack the capacity to effectively manage such contaminants (Abalansa et al. 2021: 2). India, with the world's largest population (over 1.4 billion), is a major generator of e-waste, but it also serves as a dumping ground for waste generated by more affluent countries. The toxic substances contained in e-waste contaminate soil, water, and air. Exposure to e-waste is associated with a range of adverse health effects, including miscarriages, stillbirths, premature births, and DNA damage.

Unequal ecological exchange theory also focuses on the environmental consequences of world-system inequalities. Rooted in Marxian and neo-Marxian political economy, the concept of unequal ecological exchange refers to

> the disproportionate and undercompensated transfer of matter and energy from the periphery to the core, and the exploitation of environmental space within the periphery for intensive production and waste disposal. (Clark and Foster 2009: 313)

Like treadmill theory, this approach argues that "developed countries with higher levels of resource consumption externalize their consumption-based environmental costs to less-developed [sic] countries which increase levels of environmental degradation within the latter" (Jorgenson 2006: 691).

Core nations extract the mineral and other natural resources of peripheral countries, in effect robbing those nations of the benefits of their own resources, while also transferring environmental harms and ravaging their environments. Nations at the core enjoy many environmental amenities, but they do so at the expense of the less developed countries they have plundered.

(For an extensive discussion of the different theoretical traditions that have influenced unequal ecological exchange theory, see Foster and Holleman 2014.)

Colonialism, coloniality, and unequal exchange

Both historically and in the present, colonialism is a key driver in unequal ecological exchange. Throughout history, imperial and colonial powers dominated subject peoples in order to extract value from their natural resources and labor, enriching themselves in the process. Beginning around the middle of the fifteenth century, European imperial and colonial powers amassed fortunes by trading in enslaved human beings and extracting gold, silver, minerals, sugar, rubber cotton, grain, spices, and other resources from their colonies. This form of unequal exchange is what made massive increases in the wealth of core nations possible.

Two points merit emphasis here for our understanding of the colonialism–disaster nexus. First, while many former colonies obtained independence during the twentieth century, coloniality, or the persistence of core–periphery inequalities, remains. In other words, colonialist relations, including relations of unequal exchange, persist even in the absence of legally sanctioned colonialism. As Hinkel et al. put it, "[u]nequal exchange enables a 'hidden transfer' of value from the global South to the global North, or from periphery to core … without the overt coercion of the colonial apparatus and therefore without provoking moral outrage" (2022: 2).

Second, while environmental sociology scholars have mainly focused on the environmental damage and pollution that result from unequal ecological exchange, disaster scholars also link unequal exchange and colonialism to disaster impacts. This was clear, for example, in both editions of *At Risk* and in the pressure and release (PAR) model, all of which highlight how extractive core–periphery relationships worsen environmental conditions to the point where they can turn into disasters when triggering events take place. As shown in Box 3.1 (see page 46), the 2010 earthquake in Haiti and that country's subsequent disasters illustrate this point.

Global institutions, organizations, and networks

Environmental sociologist Liam Downey (2015) has added another dimension to these macro-theoretical approaches by showing that there is an important layer of analysis between the world system and the national level – a layer that focuses on the role of elite, undemocratic institutions, organizations, and networks in the operations of the global political economy. Here Downey is referring to the power not of nation-states but rather of elite-controlled global financial institutions such as the World Bank and the International Monetary Fund (IMF), known as the Bretton Woods institutions, and of global

Box 3.1 Colonialism and Disasters: The Case of Haiti

Haiti was formerly a colony of France where enslaved Africans produced sugar, coffee, and other crops for export. Haiti achieved independence in 1804 as a result of a slave revolt, but in 1825 France demanded that the new nation provide compensation for the loss of its "property" or risk war – a move supported by other western nations. To pay that compensation, Haiti became deeply indebted to the French banking industry, which sapped its ability to develop its own state capacities in areas such as education and health. When the United States occupied Haiti between 1915 and 1934, debt payments continued, this time to US banks and other financial institutions. Haiti's debt was not fully paid until 1947. Over time, ordinary Haitians were forced to endure a series of dictatorial and kleptocratic regimes and became increasingly impoverished, since agricultural productivity declined as a result of poor soil conditions and exploitive international trade agreements imposed by agencies like the International Monetary Fund. Throughout its recent history, Haiti has been the poorest country in the western hemisphere, with a government so weakened by external forces and internal corruption that it proved incapable of meeting even the most basic nutritional and healthcare needs of its residents. Many outside aid organizations have operated in Haiti, in an effort to address those needs while bypassing government entities, so that Haiti came to be dubbed the "republic of NGOs" (nongovernmental organizations).

Like many poor countries worldwide, Haiti also experienced rapid urbanization, as rural residents migrated to the capital, Port au Prince, and to other cities. Informal settlements grew, often located on hillsides or in flood hazard areas. Even though Haiti was known to be vulnerable to seismic and other hazards, it lacked the ability control the growth of slums in hazardous areas or to regulate construction safety. Deforestation – a process originally initiated by France's demand for mahogany and other valuable woods, and also driven by residents' need for wood and charcoal for cooking – contributed to soil degradation, declining agricultural productivity, and increased flood risk. These were some of the conditions that set the stage for the devastation caused by the 2010 earthquake – the deadliest disaster to occur to date in the western hemisphere. As noted in Chapter 1, the earthquake was followed by a cholera epidemic that was traced back to members of a United Nations peacekeeping force. Continually buffeted by hurricanes and floods, the country struggled to recover while international aid proved insufficient, was siphoned off by corrupt elements, or went into the coffers of outside actors, including international NGOs and US corporations. Haiti's president was assassinated in 2021, and a month later another earthquake struck, killing nearly 2,000 residents. The country subsequently fell into a state of lawlessness and gang rule, further complicating recovery efforts (Oliver-Smith 2010; Gottesdiener and Graham 2021; New York Times 2022).

trade-oriented entities such as the World Trade Organization (WTO) and the General Agreement on Tariffs and Trade (GATT). These bodies and their interlocking networks, whose activities are heavily influenced by US elites, can be thought of as the regulators that make the economic hegemony of the core possible and enable the environmental exploitation of the nations from outside the core. Within the political economy of the world system, the policies and decisions of these institutions are key mechanisms through which globalized treadmills and relations of unequal ecological exchange operate.

According to Downey, elite-dominated institutions accomplish their goals through six major strategies: maintaining monopoly power over decision-making in less powerful nations; shifting both environmental and non-environmental costs onto those nations; thwarting the development of environment awareness in dependent nations; limiting the ability of non-elite actors to engage in environmentally sustainable behaviors; defining what constitutes environmentally appropriate policies and practices; and cultivating ignorance by directing people's attention away from the environmental problems created by elite dominance (Downey 2015).

Globalization, neoliberalization, and disaster risk

The macro-level and institutional approaches to the political economy of the environment discussed above highlight how the global neoliberal world order drives the production of vulnerability. Having begun to spread in the late 1970s, in tandem with globalization, neoliberalization – with its emphasis on deregulation, tax breaks for the wealthy, cuts to social welfare spending, attacks on workers' rights, privatization of formerly publicly held industries and services, pressures toward export-oriented development, and vigorous promotion of so-called free markets and free trade – has become the organizing principle for economic relations among actors in the world system.

Although neoliberalization regimes show variation across different societies, and although neoliberal practices are continually being resisted and challenged, their basic economic and political principles have gone virtually unquestioned. It is important to note, however, that the spread of neoliberal ideologies and institutional arrangements is the result of decades-long projects designed to ensure their ascendancy; and many of these projects relied on violence for their success (Klein 2007; Downey 2015; Oreskes and Conway 2023).

Globalization and neoliberalization constitute the context in which world-system treadmills and unequal exchange relationships take place, operating, as noted above, through the power of undemocratic elite-steered institutions. For example, depending on the societal setting, externally imposed neoliberal "reforms" and austerity measures can result in crippling debt that leaves societies unable to provide for their citizens' basic needs; or they can generate so-called development schemes that disrupt traditional economic activities and end up in the dislocation of populations formerly dependent on those activities; or they can trigger rapid urbanization, as those populations move to cities to seek better livelihood opportunities.

Influenced by those forces as well as by civil wars and refugee crises, migration to cities has fueled the growth of slums in the global South, increasing the vulnerability of both people and the environment (Woo and Jun 2020). In the words of urban scholar Mike Davis, we now live in a neoliberal world

> in which the claims of foreign banks always take precedence over the needs of the urban and rural poor. Everywhere the IMF and the World Bank offered poor countries the same poisoned chalice of devaluation, privatization, removal of import controls and food subsidies, enforced cost recovery in health and education, and ruthless downsizing of the public sector. (Davis 2006: 153)

Because neoliberalization and globalization also fuel increases in land and housing prices in urban centers, migrants and the poor have no choice but to live in marginal and dangerous places. Again as noted by Davis, these are "the pioneer settlers of swamps, floodplains, volcano slopes, unstable hillsides, rubbish mountains, railroad sidings, and desert fringes" (2006: 121). Other scholars observe that "urban areas are not necessarily disaster prone by nature, but 'become' disaster prone because of structural processes creating rapid urbanization, population movement and concentration" (Hamza and Zetter 1998: 292). At the same time governments, weakened by those same forces, lack the capacity to manage disaster risk – and the urban poor, who struggle daily just to meet basic needs, are in no position to do so.

National level: State action

As we move from the global to the national level, additional insights into the social production of vulnerability come from scholarship that focuses on the impact of interrelated state and corporate action on the growth of regions and metropolitan areas – and on the growth of environmental hazards. Put succinctly, "the use of geographical space is molded by the intersection of the state's strategic agenda with civilian political and economic processes" (Hooks 1994: 747). In the case of superpowers such as the United States, the needs of the military are a critical element on that agenda. As Gregory Hooks (1994) has shown, the US government's defense-related wartime investments, particularly during and after World War II, together with growth-machine politics (discussed below), help explain growth in many US regional economies. Relatedly, a variant of the treadmill of production theory known as the treadmill of destruction argues that militarism and military buildup are at the root of numerous environmental problems (Hooks and Smith 2004, 2005; Clark and Jorgenson 2012). Unlike the treadmill of production, which operates according to the logic of capitalism, the treadmill of destruction originates in geopolitical concerns and in the state's interest in projecting military power and in developing ever more lethal war-making tools. In the United States, this has turned vast lands into sacrificial zones – locations for testing chemical and nuclear weapons, for example. There is also an EJ element to the treadmill of destruction. For example, much of the land contaminated by the military is adjacent to Native American reservations (Hooks and Smith 2004, 2005). In addition to contaminating large swathes of its own territory, including communities such as Oak Ridge Tennessee and Hanford Washington, which were sites for the development of nuclear weapons, the United States also represents a global environmental threat in the form of the approximately 800 military bases it operates in countries around the world (Johnson 2004).

Returning to earlier discussions of colonialism and coloniality, Puerto Rico's islands of Vieques and Culebra, which were used as bomb-testing sites by the US Navy, remain contaminated not only with ordnance but also with hazardous substances such as perchlorate, mercury, lead, napalm, and depleted uranium (Associated Press 2021). Similarly, Guam, another US territory, is a major military outpost that is central to the projection of US military strength in the Pacific region. For decades, munitions designated for destruction were routinely burned on Guam or detonated in the open air. A recent plan to renew that program, involving tens of thousands of pounds of waste munitions annually, has been challenged in the courts (Malo 2022). The Marshall Islands, another former US colony, was for decades the site of extensive nuclear weapons testing, including for the first hydrogen bomb. The result is extensive nuclear fallout and the forced relocation of the residents of its various islands and atolls (Topol 2023). Maintaining global hegemony requires an enormous amount of resources, which is why the US military is the world's largest consumer of energy and thus among the world's largest contributors to climate change (Downey 2015). Economic growth fuels carbon emissions and climate change, but militarization amplifies that effect (Jorgenson et al. 2023).

State-sponsored development can be another source of risk when environmental impacts are ignored. For example, as globalization and neoliberalization became the organizing principles for economic activity, experimentation with the market economy became a driving force in China's regional development. But that development has resulted in greatly increased hazard exposures. For example, the city of Shenzhen, which is located on the southeastern coast of China, north of Hong Kong, was a small fishing village with a population of around 30,000 in 1979, when Deng Xiaoping declared it and other cities in the Pearl River Delta (PRD) a special economic zone, allowing for the introduction of neoliberal market-based economic activity, foreign direct investment, and export-oriented economic development. The PRD became known as the "world's factory," as all manner of goods were produced there for export. More recently it has become a financial services hub. The PRD is the largest urban agglomeration on earth in terms of both spatial scope and population size, which is estimated at over 86 million. Historically China has paid little attention to environmental hazards, and coastal economic expansion and population growth have put increasing numbers of people at risk. Development in the PRD has been accompanied by the expansion of impermeable surfaces and the destruction of natural protections such as mangrove forests, processes that further increase the region's physical vulnerability.

Because of the manner in which it has developed – in addition to the environmental damage caused by the numerous polluting industries – the region is now at greater risk of coastal and riverine flooding and typhoons, which will continue to be exacerbated by climate change and sea-level rise, and also of earthquakes. A report from Swiss Reinsurance lists the PRD as the urban region with the world's third highest vulnerability to natural hazards, after Tokyo and Manila. The PRD is the first in the world in terms of the sheer number of people exposed to hazards (Swiss Reinsurance 2014).

In recent decades, China has urbanized rapidly and to an unprecedented degree, and recent policies call for even more intense urbanization, in particular in second- and third-tier cities. Urbanization and increased density can have positive environmental effects, but density can also increase vulnerability if growth occurs in hazardous areas. Additionally, building code enforcement and construction quality are major problems in China, as seen in the 1976 Tangshan earthquake, in which an estimated 240,000 persons died, and in the 2008 Sichuan earthquake, which killed an estimated 80,000 people (Tierney 2014).

Local communities and regions

Focusing now on the local level, coalitions known as growth machines (Molotch 1976; Logan and Molotch 1976), which involve political leaders, real estate and development interests, and industry, champion economic growth to the exclusion of other values, such as the safety of those at risk from natural and technological hazards. Growth machines discursively frame continued economic expansion as an imperative. To give just one example, intensified development in coastal areas is the main driver of ever-increasing hurricane losses in the United States (Pielke et al. 2008), and climate change and sea-level rise will intensify this trend. In many cases, vulnerability results not only from exposure to hazards like hurricanes, but also from the fragility of the built environment. Under the pressure of rapid growth, it is difficult to monitor construction practices and ensure that building codes are enforced. Poor code enforcement has been identified as contributing to hurricane losses in Florida; according to one study, up to 40 percent of the insured property losses in Hurricane Andrew in 1992 were due to substandard building practices and weak code enforcement (Bragg 1999).[2]

Under current neoliberal political–economic arrangements, communities compete for private sector investment, typically by offering generous tax incentives to lure economic activity. The same is true for state-driven military and other spending, where competing communities work with their political representatives to attract government facilities such as military installations. In many cases, government investment helps growth machines achieve their objectives, while also helping to increase disaster vulnerability. For example, federal investments in activities such as levee building and beach replenishment, along with insurance subsidies, typically result in what Raymond Burby (2006) calls the "safe development paradox": while ostensibly offering protection from hazards, government investments make intensified development in hazardous areas possible. Growth-machine elites demand flood protections like levees because these enable construction in areas adjacent to the levees, but the end result is that development puts more people and property at risk. The existence of levees is one key reason for the explosive population growth that has occurred in the delta region in northern California, yet many of the delta's levees are in danger of failing and the region is at risk from storms, earthquakes, and sea-level rise (Burton and Cutter 2008).

Levees failed to protect New Orleans from catastrophic flooding in Hurricane Katrina. At the behest of growth boosters, the building of canals in New Orleans was made possible by large federal subsidies, as was the construction and continued expansion of the Mississippi River Gulf Outlet (MR-GO). Both the extensive network of canals and the MR-GO contributed to Katrina's massive impacts (Freudenburg, Gramling, Laska, and Erikson 2009).

Focusing again on Louisiana, sociologist Ian Gray calls attention to a third treadmill, which he calls the "treadmill of protection," by which state-level programs designed to reduce environmental damage and hazards from extractive activities such as oil and gas production, a category that includes land loss and coastal erosion, are locked into continually investing in such programs because states are dependent on revenues from industry. As Gray puts it, governments have little choice but to keep investing in protections, because "if public officials admit that the current built environment is untenable due to the changing profile of natural hazards, they risk both capital flight and devaluation of local property assets" (Gray 2021: 192). In Gray's telling, by promoting the treadmill of protection, officials telegraph that the environmental processes set in motion by resource extraction can be managed, thus protecting property values. At the same time they ensure that revenues from environmentally degrading industrial activities will continue to flow. And when disasters do strike, the state and the local communities can count on post-disaster assistance from the federal government. According to the logic of the treadmill of protection, "the state is forced to make increasing expenditures to secure existing areas of capitalist activities, while potentially exacerbating vulnerabilities, or 'unprotecting' less capital-intensive terri-tories" (Gray 2021: 203).

When Hurricane Harvey struck in 2017, bringing with it unprecedented rainfall, Houston and neighboring cities in Texas were inundated in what became one of the most damaging and costly disasters in US history. Disaster researchers who watched Harvey's slow march toward the Houston area feared the worst, because they understood the Houston region's vulner-abilities. A classic example of growth-machine politics run amok, Houston had become the fourth largest city in the United States by acting as a magnet for migrants who were looking for jobs and affordable places to live. In the years leading up to the hurricane, Harris County, where Houston is located, had been the second fastest growing county in the country, and at one point Houston was adding about 2,500 new residents every week. As the city grew, new roads and highways were built, adding more impermeable surfaces that increased rainfall runoff, and grasslands that could have absorbed rainfall and floodwaters were paved over. Like the state of Texas in general, Houston didn't believe in zoning, so it was not unusual for residential neighborhoods to be located directly adjacently to industrial facilities. Politically averse to anything that might stand in the way of development, the city allowed new construction in flood plains at an alarming rate in the years prior to Harvey. There had been warnings of what was to come. In 2001, Houston experienced extreme flooding and extensive damage as a result of Tropical Storm Allison, which dropped forty inches of rain on the city; but building in hazardous areas continued unabated after Allison. In May 2015 and April 2016, Houston experi-enced two "500-year" floods – that is, flood events that supposedly had a 1:500 probability of occurring in any given year.

The greater Houston area is home to the largest petrochemical complex in the world, as well as to other sources of toxics such as landfills and Superfund sites. Prior to Harvey, researchers had already documented how poor and minoritized communities were disproportionately exposed to chemical and industrial hazards. When Harvey struck, floodwaters carried and spread toxins, causing explosions and fires and exposing those in the impact area to both acute and longer-term safety and health threats, including toxic runoff from petrochemical facilities and landfills and airborne chemicals. Low-income residents, already hard-hit by the hurricane itself, faced disproportionate exposure to environmental hazards (Sherwin 2019). Additionally, as noted earlier, because of actions aimed at suppressing information about hazardous inventories, the residents, local responders, and those who came to the city to help with the response had no idea about the hazards to which they were exposed. Many environmental regulations were suspended in the aftermath of Harvey and officials downplayed the extent of the threats. One leading scientist was quoted as saying that "people are left in a state of limbo of not knowing if they were exposed or not – or, if they were, what the implications are for their health" (Bajak and Olsen 2018). EJ communities both bore the brunt of Harvey's impacts and were faced with complex recovery challenges.

Race and place: Producing environmental injustice

Growth-machine politics constitutes one set of factors that shape vulnerability at the local level. Going further to examine which groups within exposed populations are especially vulnerable to disasters and environmental toxins requires an understanding of the processes and practices that determine how these groups have come to be distributed spatially, in what types of dwellings they live, and near what types of hazards they find themselves. These are, of course, the kinds of questions that environmental inequality research seeks to address. The existence of environmental racism is well established in the literature. However, the best research on environmental racism is accompanied by a focus on the causal processes that serve as basis for an inequitable exposure to hazards. This involves exploring the concept of race itself, how racism operates, and how it is maintained.

Current sociological conceptions of race rely heavily on racial formation theory – that is, on the idea that racial categories are produced, changed, and maintained through racial projects, which are practices and processes that mark human bodies as different and unequal, as well as through hegemony, the complex of ruling practices and their cultural justifications (Omi and Winant 1994). Although notions of race and racist attitudes existed well before the development of capitalism, racism is essential to the functioning of capitalist society, in particular because it makes it possible to assign differential values to differently racialized groups (Pulido 2016, 2017). As sociologist David Pellow (2007) points out, the normal functioning of capitalist economies requires racial, class, and other forms of inequality. This is because capital accumulation, a driving force in capitalism, cannot take place unless subordinate groups such as people of color and the poor – together with what they own and the places where they live – are robbed of value. As Jodi Melamed argues, accumulation under racialized capitalism must necessarily entail loss, disposability, and the unequal differentiation of human value, and racism enshrines the inequality that capitalism provides ... it does this by displacing the uneven life chances that are inescapably part of capitalist social relations onto fictions of differing human capacities, historically race. (Melamed 2015: 77)

Historical accounts that document the ways in which racialized capitalism operates differ across places, historical periods, and oppressed groups. In the United States, in relation to African Americans, its manifestations have included slavery, violent attacks on African American communities, lynching, and race riots such as the 1921 riot in Tulsa, Oklahoma, in which whites attacked both residents and important institutions of the African American community.[3] Violent attacks against African Americans continue, but in a variety of forms, as the overt collective violence of the past has been replaced by the slow violence of segregation, discrimination, exposure to natural and environmental hazards, and the harassment and killing of African Americans such as George Floyd and Elijah McClain by agents of social control.

In the United States, violence against African Americans and other minority groups was instigated by local growth machines, but was also enabled in important ways by the state itself. Redlining for purposes of underwriting loans was initiated in 1933 by the federal government's Home Owners' Loan Corporation (HOLC), which privileged white borrowers while disadvantaging African Americans and other people of color. Further incorporating racism into loan criteria, the Federal Housing Administration (FHA) and the Veterans Administration followed HOLC practices, as did private lending institutions. Federally supported urban renewal programs, also known as "Negro removal," disrupted African American communities, and public housing projects were located in neighborhoods that were already majority–minority because white-dominated local power structures wanted it that way. The interstate highway system, originally planned for national defense, intensified the trend toward suburbanization and enabled white flight from cities around the United States (for in-depth discussions, see Massey and Denton 1998).

Actions by the state have been accompanied by other measures that have prevented people of color (and also other groups, such as Jews) from having access to a wider range of places to live. Such measures include restrictive covenants that specify who can and cannot live in particular neighborhoods, as well as various forms of exclusionary zoning. Zoning decisions are made by local governments and thus are subject to local political and economic pressure. For example, certain neighborhoods are zoned only for single-family dwellings, keeping out multifamily and apartment buildings. Others are zoned for the kinds of industries that pollute the environment. Additionally, pressure from "not in my back yard" (NIMBY) groups can also ensure that locally unwanted land uses (LULUs) are not permitted, except in low-income and minority areas.

Historically focused studies of environmental inequalities in Phoenix, Arizona (Bolin, Grineski, and Collins 2005) and in the southern California region (Pulido 2000) show how capitalist economic activity and white privilege put people of color at risk. Phoenix was established by whites, in contrast with other southwestern cities, which had originally been settled by Mexicans. Early in its history, Phoenix was segregated, Mexicans, Mexican Americans, and African Americans being relegated to the southern part of the city. The Ku Klux Klan, the vigilante groups, and hyper-discrimination in education and employment enforced this system of "sunbelt apartheid." Phoenix benefitted from the post–World War II expansion of defense spending, but these benefits accrued to whites, at the expense of people of color. At the same time zoning regulations allowed for polluting industries such as foundries, fertilizer plants, meat-packing and rendering facilities, and the city's sewage treatment facility; those facilities were located in parts of the city where people of color lived, and interstate highways were routed through Latinx neighbor-hoods, increasing air pollution. As suburbanization spread northward in the city, south Phoenix continued to decline into an area with disproportionate exposure to environmental toxins, with poor housing quality, and without environmental amenities. Later on this was revealed as the area where heat-related deaths were concentrated (Harlan et al. 2013). Bolin, Grineski, and Collins (2005) argued earlier that

> conditions in South Phoenix are not intentionally produced yet they clearly flow from a racist ideologies [sic] and practices coupled with a strong political drive to promote growth and development in the city. To promote a century of industrialization adjacent to low-income neighborhoods, without concern for the wellbeing of residents or any substantial investment in housing for its residents is environmental racism. (2005: 166)

Laura Pulido (2000) documents similar historical patterns in the Greater Los Angeles region. Like Bolin and his coauthors, Pulido shows how, over time, the exercise of white privilege was manifested in segregation, decisions about the siting of hazardous facilities, and state-enabled suburbanization that resulted in the disproportionate exposure of African Americans, Hispanics, other people of color, and low-income whites to hazards associated with polluting industrial facilities. Like Phoenix, the Los Angeles area experienced defense-related growth in the aftermath of World War II; but institutionalized racism in the form of redlining, as practiced by the Home Owners Loan Corporation and the Federal Housing Authority, ensured that segregation would persist. At the same time, the incorporation of suburban areas as new cities made it possible for those cities to use zoning regulations, restrictive covenants, and other means to maintain their "whiteness."

Pulido was primarily concerned with the ways in which white privilege was expressed spatially in Greater Los Angeles, and she emphasized how the region's evolution exposed minority residents to toxic hazards. It is thus understandable that she did not incorporate exposure to natural hazards such as earthquakes into her analysis. Yet her arguments also apply to earthquake vulnerability. For example, Los Angeles began to address the issue of collapse-hazard unreinforced masonry (URM) buildings in the mid-1980s, yet little was actually done to mitigate those hazards when the Whittier Narrows earthquake struck in 1987. A large number of multifamily URM buildings were concentrated in neighborhoods in the Pico-Union district, just west of downtown Los Angeles. This area, in which rental costs were comparatively low, was home to many Mexican Americans and recent immigrants from Central America. There was extensive damage to URM apartment buildings in Pico-Union and, after the earthquake, frightened residents began to set up improvised outdoor shelters in parks or near their apartments; such responses were common in the earthquake-prone nations of Central America. The 1994 Northridge earthquake did major damage to the housing supply of minority and low-income residents and generated the same patterns of outdoor sheltering. Understanding for the first time that the safety of damaged buildings was a major concern, city officials who conducted safety inspections after the earthquake were accompanied by translators who were able to inform non-English speakers whether they could reoccupy their buildings.

We will return to some of these themes later in discussions of disaster vulnerability. The focus in the chapter that follows is on middle-range explanations of specific topics in the disaster literature.

QUESTIONS AND EXERCISES

Blue jeans are popular apparel for everyone worldwide. Where do most of our blue jeans come from, and what is the environmental impact of their production?

What social movements have developed as a consequence of hazardous chemical exposures in Cancer Alley? How successful have these movements been to date?

On the basis of both this chapter and outside sources, identify three ways in which militarization and the military affect the environment.

4

Middle-Range Theory
Panic, Emergence, Self-Protective Actions, and Organizational Risk

A great deal of the research that is conducted in the disaster field deals not with "big picture" questions addressed by general theories such as those discussed in the previous chapter, but rather with different forms of disaster-related behavior and with concerns such as how and why organizations become accident- and disaster-prone. This chapter focuses on some key topics of concern in this mid-range space: panic, emergence and improvisation, warning responses and self-protective actions, and organizations and risk. These are all areas in which the research record is extensive but, as discussions will show, recent events and trends point to a need for further studies on some topics.

Panic

As noted in Chapter 2, the study of the social activities that relate to hazards and disasters was originally influenced by research in the sociological subfield of collective behavior. Henry Quarantelli, who is among the most influential thinkers in the field of disaster studies, began his career studying the conditions that contribute to the emergence of panic (Quarantelli 1954). Because in the early days of disaster studies there was a widespread expectation that mass panic would break out in the event of a nuclear war, Quarantelli went looking for panic in high-threat situations, but did not find it in the vast majority of the cases he studied. Although the panic myth has long been debunked by researchers, the concept of panic remains relevant to the study of disasters, because the public still clings to the idea that disasters induce panic and the media still report that it is widespread (Clarke 2002). For example, after the tragic mass shooting at a music festival in Las Vegas in 2017, which killed fifty-eight people and injured over 400, media accounts reported on the "panic" that gripped concertgoers and on the "stampedes" that ensued, even though video footage of people's attempts to move to safety showed an orderly retreat from the bullets that rained down.

Panic is so rare, Quarantelli argued, because the conditions that give rise to it are almost never present, even under circumstances that involve extreme danger, such as building fires and large explosions. According to his findings, for panic to emerge, there must be shared preexisting beliefs that particular situations, for example airline crashes or fires, are the kinds of situations that give rise to panic. Such beliefs are often based on popular culture framings of the incidents in question. Second, there must be an absence of social ties within the endangered collectivity. Third, as the threat becomes evident, members of the collectivity must develop the perception that entrapment is possible; those who come to the conclusion that they are indeed trapped in a threatening situation do not panic. Individuals must also have a sense of powerlessness and total social isolation. Finally, they must feel that, while escape from danger is possible, the chances for it are dwindling. Even under such conditions, only a small number of those facing highly dangerous situations do panic and, if panic does break out, it is short-lived (Quarantelli 1977). In his many writings on panic, Quarantelli not only challenged the myth of its frequency but also pointed to errors in the way the phenomenon has been characterized, both by scholars and in the popular media.

Panic is not irrational behavior but rather is based on realistic fears of an imminent threat, a sense of social isolation, and the belief that escape is the only option. Panic does not involve contagion; in fact, panicky reactions are typically confined to a very small segment of those who are confronting danger. The idea that panic is common is a media creation reinforced by the widespread and uncritical application of the term to a variety of emotions and behaviors. Worry about causing panic can lead to faulty decision-making, as happens for example when authorities resist issuing disaster warnings out of fear of inducing panic (Quarantelli 1977, 2001a). Quarantelli argued that, because of its potential for generating misunderstandings, the term should be withdrawn – an argument supported by decision scientist Baruch Fischhoff, who inveighed against the media's use of the word to describe the passengers forced to evacuate after a plane crash and fire in Toronto in 2005 – an evacuation that was both rapid and orderly:

> Whatever its source, the myth of panic is a threat to our welfare. Given the difficulty of using the term precisely and the rarity of actual panic situations, the cleanest solution is for the politicians and the press to avoid the term altogether. It's time to end chatter about "panic" and focus on ways to support public resilience in emergency. (Fischhoff 2005)

Despite the frequent misapplication of the term in the media and in public discourse, research continues to bear out the points originally made by Quarantelli decades ago. Those caught in frightening situations may be described as panicky in media accounts and may indeed actually believe that they have panicked, but the empirical record continues to show that social bonds do not break down even in truly frightening situations such as fires, plane crashes, crowd crushes, and the 1993 and 2001 bombings of the World Trade Center (Keating, Loftus, and Manber 1983; Johnson 1988; Johnson, Feinberg, and Johnston 1994; Aguirre, Wenger, and Vigo 1998; Clarke 2002; Kuligowski 2011). The resilience of those bonds and the dominance of prosocial behavior provide protection against the development of panic.

Emergence

A key characteristic of disaster situations is the extent to which they result in a range of emergent social phenomena. Emergence involves the development of norms, social practices, and forms of social organization that are novel in comparison with the established social order. Early ideas concerning emergence were influenced by Chicago School social psychologist Herbert Blumer, by symbolic interactionism more generally, and by Turner and Killian's emergent norm theory of collective behavior. Emergent norm theory, which evolved over a thirty-year period during the last century (Turner and Killian 1987), sought to explain three key dimensions of collective behavior phenomena:

- extra-institutionalism, that is, a departure from conventional patterns of behavior enabled, according to the theory, by the development of new norms about what is right and wrong or appropriate and inappropriate in a specific situation;
- a move from collectively shared feelings to action, depending on whether that action is collectively defined as feasible and timely; and
- the formation and maintenance of collectivities committed to carrying out the actions that the new norms require, given that these actions depend on preexisting social relationships or on an occurrence that is so unusual that it needs interpersonal interaction in order to be interpreted as to its meaning and for a collective decision on how to respond to be taken.

Paralleling this reasoning, Quarantelli's theory of emergence in disaster settings cites as conditions a shared perception that a given crisis situation requires urgent action – for example, that there are critical needs that are not being addressed by institutionalized means; a supportive social climate consisting of common norms, values, and beliefs; preexisting social relationships that are defined as relevant to the crisis situation; and the presence of crucial resources, including material resources and knowledge of how to take action. Two other factors increase the likelihood of emergence: prior planning, which sets at least some parameters around what types of actions are appropriate in crisis situations; and prior experience, which affords some opportunity to "rehearse" unconventional action (Quarantelli 1995).

Emergent groups

Research on emergence in disasters has been influenced by what is known as Disaster Research Center (DRC) typology. This is a fourfold framework that characterizes the activities organized in times of disaster according to the extent to which organizational tasks and structures after disasters differ from their pre-disaster counterparts. One organizational form, called the emergent group, involves both new tasks and new structural arrangements. Such groups have no pre-disaster existence; they form only after a disaster and its impact, in order to address crisis-related needs identified by group members. Emergent groups operating after disaster impact are often made up of people in the immediate vicinity of the disaster. For example, it has long been recognized that post-impact search and rescue activities are typically undertaken by community residents themselves (Tierney, Lindell, and Perry 2001; National Research Council 2006).

Emergent groups have been studied in a variety of pre-, trans-, and post-disaster settings (Drabek 1987; Stallings and Quarantelli 1985). As discussed in a review by Drabek and McEntire (2003), in addition to the typology, studies have identified various other forms of emergence in disaster situations: quasi- or partial emergence, task emergence, emergence based on latent knowledge not previously acted upon, and interstitial emergence in which a new group emerges that establishes linkages with existing organizations (see Quarantelli 1996 for a discussion of some of these forms). These studies argue that several factors facilitate emergence – for example shared values or what Drabek and McEntire (2003: 102) refer to as a "culture of responsibility"; the involvement of faith-based organizations in disaster-related activities; and the scope and severity of the disaster, which has a positive impact on the likelihood of emergence. Post-disaster groups can also spring from preexisting ties with groups that were formed for other purposes. For example, Occupy Sandy, a network that emerged in New York after Superstorm Sandy (2012) to provide assistance to disaster survivors, had its origins in the Occupy Wall Street protests that followed the financial meltdown of 2008.

There is also a gendered dimension to emergent group activities, but the literature on the impact of gender is equivocal. Participation in such activities is often done according to traditional gender roles, as happened for example in the 1985 Mexico City earthquake, when men organized themselves into search and rescue groups while women provided supplies and aid (Wenger and James 1994), or when groups composed of women assume "caring" roles in the aftermath of disasters (Fothergill 1996). Concern for children's welfare may partly explain why women are more likely than men to protest against technological hazards (Neal and Phillips 1990). It has also been argued that disasters result in a retreat into traditional gender roles even among those who previously espoused egalitarian values (Hoffman 1998). At the same time, there are examples of women forming their own emergent groups in order to resist being excluded from important disaster-related activities such as reconstruction (Enarson and Morrow 1998; Hoffman 1998). To complicate matters still further, some studies find no relationship between gender and involvement in emergent activities (O'Brien and Mileti 1992), while others question whether past accounts of disaster-related behavior have not been themselves biased, either by overlooking women's role in emergent groups in disasters or by inappropriately employing gender stereotypes to describe disaster-related behaviors (Scanlon 1997).

Like gender, race and ethnicity seem to be related to emergence in complex ways. Because government activities benefit those with economic and political power, in disasters we should expect to see members of racial and ethnic minorities forming emergent groups in order to provide mutual aid and carry out tasks they define as necessary. For example, Hurricane Katrina saw the creation of the Common Ground Collective, originally organized by former Black Panthers and anarchists, as well as collective mobilization on the part of the Vietnamese Americans in the neglected Village de L'Est and Versailles communities in New Orleans (Solnit 2009; Tierney 2014). However, to the extent that racial and ethnic minorities are marginalized and isolated – which includes their linguistic isolation and unfamiliarity with the operations of the disaster management system – they may lack the capacity for collective action. Isolation may be particularly acute among members of racial and ethnic groups who are undocumented and who may be afraid to organize in the aftermath of disasters.

Improvisation

Improvisation is a form of emergent activity that is enacted by both existing organizations and newly formed ones. In this case, new strategies emerge for carrying out disaster-related tasks – typically with new tools, including informational ones – which are collectively defined as appropriate in a given disaster setting. Disasters invariably contain elements of surprise; even the best disaster plans can fall short, because by their nature disasters have unanticipated effects. As described by Tricia Wachtendorf (2004) in her study of the 2001 World Trade Center attacks in New York City, improvisation in disasters ranges from activities that differ from what was originally planned but attempt to reproduce it to entirely new sets of activities, never envisioned in the original plan. For example, as a result of the Trade Center attacks, New York City lost its emergency operations center at the height of the attacks, yet was able through improvisation to reproduce organizational configurations and communication capabilities at a new site, in a matter of days. In other cases, however, such as the search for human remains and crime-scene evidence at the Fresh Kills landfill, procedures and practices had to be improvised on the fly, because there was no preexisting "roadmap" for how such tasks would be performed (Wachtendorf 2004). Similarly, the water-borne evacuation of approximately 500,000 persons from Lower Manhattan on the day of the attacks, which was carried out spontaneously by hundreds of watercraft of different types, was almost entirely improvised (Kendra and Wachtendorf 2016).

Improvisation is a relatively new line of sociological inquiry, and much existing scholarship relies on insights developed from the study of jazz and acting. One key lesson from that body of work is that improvisation is not the completely spontaneous creation of new lines of action on the spur of the moment; it is best carried out by professionals who are highly knowl-edgeable about different musical forms and performance repertoires. While it may appear spontaneous, jazz improvisation reflects the ability to draw upon knowledge that is both broad and deep (Berliner 1994; Weick 1998). Improvisation does not consist of making music on the fly. The great jazz stylist Charles Mingus was once quoted as saying: "you can't improvise on nothing, man. You gotta improvise on something" (Tierney 2014).

Researchers find that the same goes for improvised emergency response activities. As Wachtendorf and James Kendra put it, "an emergency responder – whether a formal or informal responder – must be able to draw upon a reper-toire of training or education, experience, knowledge of the community, and a shared vision with other organizations":

> Improvisation also involves the ability to use resources that are on hand (whether or not they have been pre-designated as emergency response resources) as well as the ability to decide how much deviation from previous plans is appropriate. Rigid hierarchical forms of command and the compart-mentalization of organizational roles discourage improvisation. In contrast, improvisation thrives when local actors have autonomy when confronting surprise. (Wachtendorf and Kendra 2006)

This same notion is emphasized in Diane Vaughan's (2021) study of air traffic controllers faced with dangerous and potentially disastrous situations involving aircraft that may be on a collision course. Extensively and rigorously trained to deal with routine situations, they use that training as a starting point, to improvise in situations for which they may not have been trained.

Emergent multiorganizational networks

Emergence in disasters also occurs at the network level. Emergent multi-organizational networks (EMONs) are novel, complex, heterogeneous forms of organization that consist of a mix of preexisting organizations with designated disaster responsibilities and new entrants, including preexisting entities without prior involvement in disaster-related activities and emergent

groups. These different types of organizations may themselves undergo structural changes, such as increases in size as volunteers converge to provide
additional assistance. EMONs are an outgrowth of efforts at improvisation,
formed out of a common recognition among network participants that urgent
action is needed, namely action that reaches outside pre-disaster institutional
arrangements. Subnetworks typically organize themselves around key tasks
(Bevc 2010). As noted earlier, one example is that of civilian mariners who
coordinated their activities to evacuate Lower Manhattan by water after the
9–11 World Trade Center attacks. In that instance, operators of commercial
watercraft of all types self-organized to evacuate hundreds of thousands of
people from Lower Manhattan – a waterborne evacuation comparable in size
to, or perhaps even larger than, the evacuation of Dunkirk during World War
II. Without any central coordinating body, the EMON was able to function
effectively owing to a variety of factors. Important among them were mariner
culture, which calls for action on behalf of those in distress; a shared vision of
what needed to be done; and the mariners' extensive local knowledge (Kendra
and Wachtendorf 2016).

The most sophisticated studies on disaster EMONs draw extensively on
interorganizational theory and on network theory and analytic methods, but
with a major difference: while those fields tend to concentrate on network
relationships that develop and operate in relatively stable environments,
research on disaster EMONs focuses on network phenomena in turbulent,
unstable environments, typically characterized by the rapid emergence of new
network relationships and by dynamic change. Still, EMON researchers remain
committed to studying central network-analytic topics such as network
structure (e.g. centrality, connectedness), brokerage, communication, coordination, influence, and factors that help explain network relationships (e.g.
homophily, geographic proximity). The difference is that the emphasis is on
the ways in which network attributes and associated behaviors depart from
pre-event institutional arrangements such as disaster plans. One challenge in
EMON studies is that this research tends to focus on post-impact networks,
without the benefit of having baseline data. (For representative studies and
discussions of methodological issues, see Petrescu-Prahova and Butts 2005;
Butts, Petrescu-Prahova, and Cross 2007; Bevc 2010; Spiro, Acton, and Butts
2013; Schweinberger, Petrescu-Prahova, and Vu 2014; Kapucu and Garayev
2016).

Online emergence and crisis informatics

The study of online emergence and emergent networks is a new area in disaster
research known as crisis informatics, a field that developed in the early 2000s
through collaborations among computer and information scientists, disaster
sociologists, and other social scientists. The field had its origins in the study

of manifestations of disaster-related collective behavior such as convergence and group emergence; scholars found similarities between these kinds of behaviors in real-world crises and virtual-world activities that employed information and communication technology in the context of disasters and other emergencies (Palen et al. 2007; Palen and Liu 2007; Palen and Hughes 2018). Tracking the rapid evolution of information and communication technologies (ICT) and Web 2.0, crisis informatics is a rapidly evolving field.

Research on crisis informatics spans a wide range of topics (for an overview and bibliography see Palen et al. 2020). In this section I will selectively discuss research that involves online emergent activity in disasters. I will also discuss newer crisis informatics research that focuses on disinformation and misinformation, using the Covid-19 pandemic as an example.

The next section, on warnings and warning responses, discusses the implications of crisis informatics research for the study of warnings and will deal with warnings and warning responses. There I will briefly look at research on how and to what effect ICT is changing the way warnings are issued and disseminated. I will leave out the use of social media by established (as opposed to emergent) disaster responders, or ICT-enabled one-way and two-way communications between officials and members of the public, which are also addressed in crisis informatics research (see e.g. Hughes, St. Denis, Palen, and Anderson 2014; Sutton, League et al. 2015; Chauhan and Hughes 2017).

Collective sense-making is a critical element in disaster-related collective action. Prior research on sense-making has described how the process develops in real-world situations – or fails to do so (Weick 1993). Crisis informatics research looks at how online convergence, emergence, and collaboration can contribute to sense-making and to situational awareness for participants within and outside disaster-stricken areas. For example, in one early study Leysia Palen and her collaborators described how Facebook was used during and after the 2007 Virginia Tech mass shootings, both as a means to disseminate "I'm OK" messages and in order to arrive at an account of those who had perished in the attacks. Noteworthy in this study were Facebook participants' ability to identify victims more quickly than university authorities and participants' ongoing editing of posts for accuracy (Vieweg et al. 2008). In other work on sense-making and the use of spatial and visual information, Palen and colleagues studied the role of the photo-sharing platform Flickr in documenting the impacts of six different disaster and crisis events (Liu et al. 2008). Among publications by the Palen group are also studies on the use of OpenStreetMap after the 2010 Haiti earthquake (Soden and Palen 2014) and on emergent neo-geographic practice, or the use of social media platforms and mash-ups to convey crisis-related information both spatially and temporally (Liu and Palen 2010).

In addition to sense-making, crisis informatics researchers study a variety of other online phenomena. Project HEROIC (the acronym stands for "hazards, emergency response, and online information communication") has developed models of EMONs based on Twitter (now known as X) messaging, for example in the 2013 Boston Marathon bombing (Sutton et al. 2013). In related work that is also based on Twitter messaging, project HEROIC investigators studied the EMON that developed after the 2010 Deepwater Horizon oil spill and used network-analytic techniques to explore network attributes such as reciprocity, hierarchy, power, and influence (Sutton et al. 2013). Focusing on the Boston Marathon bombing, Andrea Tapia and her colleagues explored what happened when two online groups (Reddit and Anonymous), interacting with authorities and with "virtual bystanders," attempted to aid law enforcement by finding the perpetrators of the bombing (Tapia, LaLone, and Kim 2014).

Online rumoring is another phenomenon these researchers explore. According to collective behavior theory, rumor behavior is a form of collective sense-making that typically emerges in uncertain situations, including disasters. Crisis informatics research has explored various aspects of online rumoring; there are for instance studies on rates of rumor propagation, expressions of confidence in information that is passed on through ICT affordances such as X (Twitter), the ways in which rumors are corrected and affirmed online, and methodological strategies for increasing the accuracy of research on crisis-related rumoring (see, for example, Starbird et al. 2016; Zeng, Starbird, and Spiro 2016; Arif et al. 2017; Fitzhugh, Gibson, Spiro, and Butts 2016).

The Covid-19 pandemic saw an explosion of an especially pernicious form of online rumoring: the spread of misinformation, disinformation, and malinformation about the pandemic (Donovan, Dreyfuss, and Friedberg 2022). Crisis informatics researchers have begun to launch inquiries into the development and dynamics of such campaigns and have established research centers such as the Center for an Informed Public at the University of Washington, which is led by crisis informatics researcher Kate Starbird (Calo et al. 2021).

The spread of Covid misinformation, alongside online disinformation and malinformation campaigns, has taken place within a context that saw the rise of the post-truth social order; extreme political polarization; efforts on the part of political figures, social movements, and right-wing entrepreneurs to capitalize on the public's fears; and declining trust in institutions, which led to excess illness and death among consumers of online lies (Tanne 2021; Wallace et al. 2023). In yet another indication of the politization of Covid, Kate Starbird from the University of Washington has been sued by right-wing groups on "free-speech" grounds (Blitzer 2023). Joan Donovan, an internet researcher whose work at Harvard's Kennedy School focused on disinformation campaigns, was dismissed despite having substantial funding for her research.

Warning Responses

Public responses to disaster warnings are among the best studied topics in the field of social science disaster research. This body of research, which has spanned nearly six decades, has resulted in the formulation of conceptual models and in a large number of hypothesis-testing studies (for an excellent review of the topics covered, see National Academies 2018). Classic research on disaster warnings characterized the process in more or less linear terms, using Lasswell's (1948) source–message–channel–receiver–effect–feedback model. Investigators sought to identify the factors that determine successful transmission at each stage in the chain. For example, for message sources, attributes such as legitimacy, credibility, and believability were identified as important. Similarly, researchers identified attributes of messages, channels, and receivers that were deemed important for message effectiveness. Models of warning response drew heavily on more general principles of risk communication, while recognizing that risk communication challenges are different for imminent threats from what they are during non-disaster times. As discussed later in this section, in the many decades since the first research was conducted, the warning landscape has changed enormously, in ways that make linear models of warnings invalid.

Sociological theorizing regarding warning responses relies either implicitly or explicitly on the emergent norm theory of collective behavior. As noted earlier, emergent norm theory focuses on how members of collectivities develop new norms or courses of action that depart from conventional everyday activity, typically in conditions of uncertainty and urgency. In a general sense, the process of arriving at decisions on protective actions such as evacuation can be characterized as a form of "milling" (Blumer 1939; Turner and Killian 1987; see also Wood et al. 2018) or intensified collective information seeking, in which participants attempt to develop new definitions of the situation or emergent social constructions when they perceive that something out of the ordinary and potentially threatening is happening. Milling begins when members of the public become aware of a possible threat by receiving information about it through interpersonal networks, conventional media, or social media. Once the information is received, milling continues as the public attempts to go through other stages of the response process: understanding the information, believing that it is true, feeling personally at risk, confirming the information, and responding accordingly (Mileti and Sorensen 1987). Research on warning makes three key points: an active response will not take place without the satisfactory resolution of those stages; action is never automatic and always depends on social interaction; and message recipients must verify warning messages with the help of other information sources before taking further action.

Sociologist Dennis Mileti and geographer John Sorensen have produced some of the most important research on the attributes of effective warnings, arguing for the importance of the following: (1) a description of the impending threat or event that indicates what is taking place; (2) guidance on what form of protective action is required, for instance evacuating or sheltering in place; (3) the location of the threat and of populations at risk; (4) the moment when the population at risk needs to take action; (5) the identity of the message source; (6) the time when the threat is no longer present and the warning message expires; and (7) what consequences can be expected as a result of the threat (e.g. structural damage to buildings, flooding, flying objects). Other characteristics of effective warning messages include clear, unambiguous language; specificity; completeness; and, importantly, consistency across platforms and across the various organizations issuing warnings (Mileti and Sorensen 1990; Mileti and Peek 2000; Kuligowski et al. 2023).

An overarching concern, and one that is increasingly problematic in the current communications landscape, is trust in warning communications. This means trust not only in information sources themselves but also in key elements of the warning content and guidance. This point is perhaps best illustrated in the case of the Covid-19 pandemic, when large segments of the US population lacked trust in communications issued by institutions such as the Centers for Disease Control and Prevention and experts such as Dr. Anthony Fauci (Bruine de Bruin, Saw, and Goldman 2020; Pollard and Davis 2022). In essence, whether the elements of effective warnings are present or not is moot if members of the public do not trust the information that is being disseminated.

New technologies, new questions

A substantial amount of the research on warning responses and self-protective action was carried out during a period when information sources were significantly fewer than they are today and when information channels were more limited and employed conventional broadcast technologies such as radio and television. The communication landscape is now very different and much more complex. The public in the United States and in many other developed societies is continually awash with media that may contain information on numerous threats, imminent or distant, on which sources, messages, and channels abound, but without being vetted for their legitimacy and trustworthiness. What is more, new technologies are continually coming online to communicate public warnings and advisories, and an increasingly diverse public is accessing information in increasingly diverse ways.

Now that large segments of the public have access to cell phones, many recent efforts at improving warnings and risk communications involve the use of cell phone technologies. The wireless emergency alert (WEA) system in the United States is a key example. Issued through the Integrated Public Alert and Warning System (IPAWS), which aggregates warning information from different official sources, WEA involves the issuing of short warnings to phone users. Previously limited to 90 and 140 characters, WEA warnings can now be issued in 360 characters. WEA messages are designed to geotarget at-risk populations as well as to follow social science research by incorporating the kinds of attributes of effective warnings discussed above.

WEA has been the focus of a number of studies exploring issues regarding its efficacy (for an excellent review see Kuligowski et al. 2023). For example, in one study, communication researcher Hamilton Bean and colleagues developed simulated 90- and 140-character WEA messages involving a nuclear hazard and used interviews and focus groups to determine the responses of study participants. They found the main initial responses to the messages were fear and confusion; participants displayed low levels of understanding of the messages and expressed frustration about what they saw as incomplete information; there were varying assessments of the believability of the messages; and participants had difficulty personalizing the risk (Bean et al. 2016). More recently, Bean conducted a nationwide survey after a 2021 test of the WEA system and found that survey participants lacked an understanding of the uses of the system, which indicated that system improvements and more public education are needed (Bean and Grevstad 2023). Studies of other hazards have yielded comparable findings. For example, analyses of a large corpus of WEA messages involving wildfires showed that the messages issued were deficient in many of the key message content areas described above. Not a single one of the thousands of messages analyzed, which covered a large number of wildfires, contained all the recommended content and message characteristics discussed here (Kuligowski et al. 2023).

A National Academies study on emergency alert and warning systems identified a number of challenges that warning systems need to address. Among such challenges is a need for these systems to take into account the needs of members of the public whose first language is not English. For example, while 208 different languages are spoken by residents of New York City, warnings are issued in only eighteen languages. Warnings should also be tailored to the needs of persons with different physical and mental abilities and constraints. Geotargeting needs to be improved too, so as to avoid problems with under- and overwarning potentially at-risk populations. And there are challenges associated with whether warning systems involve opting in or opting out (for these and other recommendations, see National Academies 2018). On top of such challenges, the kinds of information-seeking activities that are required in order for recipients to confirm the warnings and decide on the actions to take are complicated by the plethora of applications through which the public can currently access information: not only official warning systems such as WEA but also Facebook, Google, X, Instagram, TikTok, and many others.

Warning technologies such as WEA show enormous promise in terms of their ability to deliver warning messages that are timely and accurate and that provide the kinds of guidance their intended audiences require in order to take self-protective actions. That said, as Bean notes, today's mobile warning systems will be effective "only if improvements in technological capabilities accompany changes in professional training, public policy and education, and community preparedness. Like sirens, radio, television, and the Internet before it, mobile technology is no panacea for the problems of warning people at risk" (Bean 2019, xv).

Organizations and Risk: Origins of Accidents and Disasters

Another group of middle-range theories and empirical observations centers on why and how organizations fail at managing risks, thereby causing emergencies and large-scale disaster events such as the Fukushima nuclear plant meltdowns and other nuclear plant disasters, the Bhopal Union Carbide disaster, the Deepwater Horizon oil platform blowout and oil spill, and the more common and prosaic but no less deadly and destructive accidents that occur regularly in organizational settings worldwide. We begin this section by focusing on two frameworks for understanding organizational susceptibility to accidents and system failures – normal accidents and high-reliability organizational theory – and then move on to discussing research findings concerning factors that generate risk buildup within organizational systems.

It is important at the outset of this discussion to stress once again that many organizational failures at managing risks take place within the context of globalized capitalism, which too often prioritizes profits over safety. When organizations are more concerned with shareholder returns on investments than, say, protecting their workers and the environment, we should not be surprised that major accidents occur. And as we shall see, public entities are not immune from some of the same forces that produce risks among private sector actors.

Normal accidents and high reliability: Competing or complementary?

The best-known sociological theory explaining organizational accidents and disasters was put forth by Charles Perrow in his seminal study *Normal Accidents: Living with High-Risk Technologies* (1984). Perrow argued that the roots of organizational failures – for example industrial accidents and disasters – lie in two structural features of the systems involved: interactive complexity and tight coupling. In interactively complex systems, components and operations are interdependent in such a way that failure in one part of a system automatically triggers other failures and can produce unanticipated outcomes. Interactively complex systems contrast with linear ones; with the latter, failures in one part of a system can be isolated and cascading failures can be avoided. When complex interactive systems are also tightly coupled, problems that develop in one component or process automatically trigger runaway problems in others, and this can lead to disaster. In contrast, loosely coupled systems are characterized by redundancies and multiple means of containing problems in system operations. They are also characterized by slack vis-à-vis resources such as supplies and equipment, as they allow for work-arounds and multiple means of avoiding failure.

Thinking in terms of a fourfold typology, the systems that are least disaster-prone are those that are linear and loosely coupled. Perrow argues that most manufacturing activities fall into this category. In contrast, chemical and nuclear power plants are complex and tightly coupled systems and thus are susceptible to dangerous cascading failures. These are the kinds of systems that societies and organizations should be most concerned about. Exemplars of intermediate categories include mining operations (complex but loosely coupled), electrical power grids, and marine shipping (both linear but tightly coupled).

In a later work, *The Next Catastrophe* (2006), Perrow added another dimension to our understanding of risk buildup: size and concentration. Here he was concerned with three aspects of those conditions. First, the sheer physical size of hazardous facilities and activities and their geographic concentration mean that failures will have more serious consequences than they would otherwise. As an illustration, the Fukushima Daichi nuclear complex contained not just one nuclear reactor, but six; all were at risk from the tsunami caused by the 2011 9.0 earthquake, and three of them experienced core meltdowns. The massive petrochemical complex in Houston is another example of how size and concentration contribute to heightened risks. In 2017, Hurricane Harvey caused numerous hazardous materials releases, explosions, and fires. A second source of vulnerability is the size of populations that live in high-hazard areas. Earlier discussions have noted that China's Pearl River Delta, Manila, and Tokyo are massive agglomerations in which tens of millions of residents are at risk from earthquakes, floods, and other hazards, and that intensified population growth in areas around the globe constitutes a key source of vulnerability. Here Perrow argues for efforts designed to shrink the size of the "targets" exposed to hazards.

Finally, Perrow warns against threats generated by concentrations of political and economic power. Power translates into the ability to lobby for eased regulations over potentially disastrous activities, silence opponents and critics, and erode guardrails intended to reduce risk buildup. Power operates in multifarious ways, for example as an ability to water down and block the implementation of risk reduction measures and support industry-friendly politicians. Without countervailing political and economic forces, concentrated power may be the most pernicious influence of all on the buildup of organizational risk.

High-reliability organization theory also addresses the organizational aspects of risk, but from a different point of view. Here the emphasis is on organizational practices that allow systems to operate safely despite the fact that they may be complex and tightly coupled and thus disaster-prone. Early studies used to focus on aircraft carriers, in which all systems must operate safely and in sync in order to avoid accidents. Air traffic control is considered another example of a system that operates with a very high degree of reliability. (For examples of this scholarship, see Roberts 1990; 1993; Weick, Sutcliffe, and Obstfeld 1999; Roberts and Bea 2001; Weick and Sutcliffe 2007.)

High-reliability scholarship identifies a number of factors as key to avoiding disaster in otherwise risky systems. Sensitivity to operations involves deep knowledge of system characteristics and processes. Reluctance to simplify consists of an appreciation for and understanding of system complexity – how elements in a system are interconnected and how they influence one another. Preoccupation with failure refers to organizational vigilance about potential accident precursors and near misses. While many organizations may ignore or actively conceal small accidents, high-reliability organizations highlight them as opportunities to learn more about how to operate safely. Another characteristic, deference to expertise, involves listening to and heeding the advice of knowledgeable organizational personnel, even if – indeed especially if – those individuals rank low in the organization's hierarchy. For example, lower-level employees, who are most familiar with actual day-to-day operations, must be able to express concerns and have the organization act on those concerns without fear of being ignored or retaliated against. High-reliability organizations also practice resilience through active learning and training.

Researchers have identified several other characteristics of highly reliable organizations. Their leaders are emphatic about prioritizing safe operations; a strong, widely accepted culture of safety is practiced extensively; and the organization's ability to learn from mistakes is emphasized. As discussed earlier, slack, too, is important: operational and safety systems have built-in redundancy, and organizational resources aren't stretched too thin.

Normal accidents and high-reliability theories are sometimes framed as opposites; for example, Charles Perrow once noted that normal accidents theory is pessimistic about the ability of organizations that exhibit interactive complexity and tight coupling to operate safely, while high-reliability theory is optimistic. In his research on nuclear weapons arsenals in the United States and elsewhere (interactive complexity, tight coupling), Scott Sagan (1993) sought to compare the applicability of the two perspectives to that case and found in favor of normal accidents theory. In his telling, despite extensive efforts to keep nuclear weapons technologies as safe as possible, hazardous incidents and near misses abound, although largely out of sight of the public.

That said, the general consensus is that it is incorrect to view the two perspectives as competing or to argue that one is accurate and the other is not. Rather they should be seen as complementary, addressing different aspects of the safety problem. For example, Perrow's work is particularly strong in its emphasis on the inherent structural sources of system failure and on the importance of taking into account the role of external forces such as power in shaping organizational vulnerability and safety. High-reliability scholars place more emphasis on organizational culture, sense-making, and learning as safeguards against organizational disasters; and, as will be discussed in the next section, how organizations deal culturally with the threats they face is important in explaining why some organizations have better safety records than others. There are also areas of agreement. For example, both perspectives stress that organizations require substantial resources and investments in redundancy to counteract threats to safety.

Factors that contribute to organizational disasters

In various studies researchers have also identified organizational attributes and processes that contribute to the occurrence of disasters. Here I briefly discuss six contributors: regulatory capture, production pressures, the drift into deviance, ignoring near misses and close calls, eschewing "possibilistic" thinking about risks, and outright criminality. These factors are not mutually exclusive; they often combine to produce disasters.

As its name suggests, regulatory capture occurs when agencies charged with regulating entities that could pose threats abandon their objectivity and authority, aligning instead with the objectives of those entities rather than their own regulatory missions. Capture and the efforts to bring it about are ubiquitous features of capitalist political economy, so much so that it is difficult to imagine industry–government relationships that are entirely free of them. Capture is facilitated, for example, when industrial sectors and organizations succeed in lobbying on a regular basis for weakened controls and when negotiations with regulators result in arrangements that favor the regulated entities. Indeed, it is quite common for the laws and regulations that are meant to keep industries in line to be written by representatives of those industries. According to an International Monetary Fund paper on lobbying in the banking sector, typical strategies include "providing policy research, sponsoring think tanks, mobilizing grassroots constituencies, building and maintaining relationships with key decision makers and influencers, drafting and amending bills, and assisting agencies in writing complex rules" (Igan and Lambert 2019: 4).

Such activities tend to succeed because the areas covered by regulations are on the whole complex, government regulatory agencies are stretched thin, and industries can afford to hire highly skilled lobbyists and experts to promote their agendas.

Regulators can face conflicting expectations, which cause them to downplay safety while promoting the aims of regulated entities. For example, focusing on the BP Deepwater Horizon blowout and oil spill, the Minerals Management Service, the agency responsible for monitoring the safety of offshore drilling, was also charged with collecting the royalties generated from oil production. This created contradictory incentives – promoting safety while promoting profits. The same is true of Japan's Science and Technology Agency in the lead-up up to the 2011 Fukushima disaster: it had the dual mission of both promoting nuclear power in Japan and other international markets and overseeing plant safety. To make matters worse, the government's nuclear industry in Japan was organized in ways that likely worked against risk-reduction efforts. Japan is well known for its revolving-door personnel shifts, in which individuals move among industry, government regulatory agencies like the STA, and research universities, fostering a common mindset across sectors (Aldrich and Crook 2008). Of course, the Japanese "nuclear village" is not that unusual in reality; we have only to look at the cozy relationships that existed between the US banking and financial services industry, its regulators, and the legislative bodies that failed in their oversight roles in the run-up to the 2008 crash.

Production pressures have been extensively documented as factors that contribute to disasters within organizations. Such pressures take a variety of forms: employers speed up industrial processes, reduce investments in safety and worker well-being, reduce personnel so workers have to work faster and harder, continually require workers to work overtime, give them little control over their schedules, and cut back on their breaks and sick days. Such measures contribute to organizational profits while placing extreme burdens on workers and allowing threats to safety to proliferate.

The US rail industry is a poster child for the ways in which production pressures have contributed to risk buildup, accidents, and disaster. One example is the case of a train derailment that took place on February 3, 2023 in East Palestine, a small town in northeastern Ohio directly adjacent to the Pennsylvania border. In that case, 49 cars in a Norfolk Southern train derailed (out of 141 loaded and 9 empty cars), 20 of them being loaded with hazardous materials. Fires burned in a number of rail cars for about 48 hours, triggering the evacuation of residents who lived within a one-mile radius of the derailment. Fearing a hazardous materials explosion, local fire officials and the railroad decided to conduct a "controlled burn," which released hydrogen chloride and phosgene into the air and nearby waterways – a measure later assessed to have been unnecessary. Residents subsequently complained of a variety of symptoms such as headaches, nausea, respiratory, skin, and eye irritation, and nosebleeds. In 2024, a settlement topping $310 million was reached with the US Department of Justice and the Environmental Protection agency; it covered cleanup costs, a fund to monitor the health of community residents and provide mental health services for them, and a civil penalty for violations of the Clean Water Act. This was in addition to $600 million designed to settle a class action lawsuit brought by East Palestine residents and businesses.

Like the hundreds of derailments that occur annually in the United States, the East Palestine event took place in the context of intense production pressures, which had a direct effect on safety. Under a regime known as Precision Scheduled Railroading (PSR), Norfolk Southern, like other rail carriers, reduced its workforce and ran longer and heavier trains. The train involved in the East Palestine incident was 1.76 miles (2.8 km) long and had only one engineer, one conductor, and one conductor trainee on board. The railroad had also reduced the number of car inspectors in 2019 and sidestepped a federal inspection requirement, cutting the required 90 to 105 point checks down to 19.

Production pressure is an industry-wide problem. Overall, since 2016, the number of personnel working on Class 1 railroads in the United States has been cut by 25 percent. At the same time, the exceedingly long trains operating under PSR have proved hazardous to local communities, even to the point of causing deaths. Trains stopped at rail crossings impede the flow of traffic, including emergency vehicles. People traveling on foot, children among them, now crawl under stopped trains to get where they are going, rather than making long treks around. All this so that railroad shareholders may enjoy stock buybacks and the industry may be made more attractive for investors. (For more details on the East Palestine derailment and rail safety, see Salcedo, Lazo, and Powell 2023.)

An organization may have a stated commitment to safety and yet still drift into deviance. The notion of deviance drift as a contributor to organizational disasters was first put forth by sociologist Diane Vaughan in her classic study of the 1986 space shuttle Challenger disaster, in which the shuttle disintegrated just over a minute after launch, killing all seven crew members (Vaughan 1996). While many postmortem analyses focused on the proximal cause of the disaster, namely a failure of O-ring seals in a joint in the rocket booster, Vaughan's decade-long investigation delved deeply into the institutional, structural, and cultural context in which O-ring problems were not taken as seriously as they should have been. Vaughan focused on how the launch was approved despite concerns expressed by some expert advisors.

Vaughan's analyses showed that NASA's regulators were in a weak position when it came to requiring more stringent risk management, including during the period that led up to the disastrous launch. On top of that, production pressures were also at play: the launch was scheduled to take place on the same day as then president Ronald Reagan's annual state-of-the union address, and plans had been made for him to discuss the launch during that speech. Educator Christa McAuliff, a Challenger crew member promoted as the first "teacher in space," was also going to be featured in the administration's public relations efforts around the launch.

Vaughan had another opportunity to provide insights into NASA's problematic practices when the space shuttle Columbia caught fire on re-entry on February 1, 2002, killing everyone on board. Serving as a member of the Columbia Accident Investigation Board, she and others emphasized how, just as in the Challenger disaster, NASA chose to discount problems related to the foam insulation system on the spacecraft. Some of that insulation broke off when the shuttle was launched and caused the spacecraft to go up in flames as it re-entered the atmosphere.

The NASA examples also highlight the ways in which organizations whose operations have the potential for catastrophic failures can ignore or downplay the significance of accident precursors and near misses. For example, in the two NASA disasters that Vaughan studied, there were many examples of operations that involved anomalies (e.g. O-ring problems) that did not result in disaster. This prompted organizational decision makers to gradually discount such anomalies rather than seeing them as accidents waiting to happen. The notion of "pushing the envelope" is relevant here: if a small problem develops, say, in a system component and no major failure occurs, why not continue with operations as planned? Such reasoning can predispose organizations to accommodate ever-increasing levels of risk, particularly when their focus is on the bottom line. (For more in-depth discussions of this tendency within organizations, see Cerulo 2008.)

Experts on organizational risk have emphasized the importance of focusing on near misses and identifying and ameliorating their root causes. But, as the NASA examples show, organizations can also experience pressure to downplay anomalies. Additionally, recalling discussions of social constructionism in the previous chapter, near misses need to be recognized by organizations and their leaders as accident precursors – something that does not occur automatically. Instead, the tendency is often to ignore or "normalize" occurrences that do not develop into full-blown crises. Indeed, even when such crises do occur, organizations may fail to construct them as indicators of future problems. For example, British Petroleum (BP) had experienced a number of plant accidents in the years leading up to the catastrophic Deepwater Horizon blowout and oil spill. These include an explosion at one of its refineries that occurred just five years earlier and killed fifteen people and injured nearly two hundred; and there were other accidents too, which preceded that explosion. Subsequent investigations tied BP's lack of vigilance in addressing plant hazards to production pressures, extensive cost-cutting measures, and a pervasive sense among personnel that, given its concern with the bottom line, the company was not willing to invest in measures that would reduce risk (Tierney 2014).

Other analyses of both organizational and other types of disasters point to the kinds of issues that were brought up in the aftermath of the 9–11 terrorist attacks on the United States, and more recently after the terrorist attacks that precipitated the Israeli–Hamas war in 2023: that such debacles represent a "failure of the imagination." Sociologist Lee Clarke has called attention to errors that result from the inability or refusal to think in "possibilistic" as opposed to "probabilistic" ways when it comes to risks (Clarke 2006; 2008). The current emphasis on probabilistic risk analysis as a method of gauging risks of all types and as a guide for risk management strategies can lead us into ignoring that the potential still exists for truly catastrophic outliers that probabilistic analyses discount. Worst cases can and do happen. There was another event, similar to the March 2011 earthquake and tsunami in Japan, in roughly the same location: the 869 Jogan earthquake, estimated at magnitude 8.4 but possibly larger, which generated a massive tsunami; yet a worst-case repeat was never contemplated by government and nuclear power planners. Nations around the world have engaged in all manner of pandemic preparedness programs, but came up shamefully short when confronted with Covid-19. And nations continue to be at risk from climate change while clinging to the idea that its catastrophic potential can be avoided.

Finally, we can identify situations in which it is difficult to conclude that organizational disasters are anything but the consequences of ongoing patterns of deviant behavior displayed by the organizations involved. Here I am not referring to situations in which organizations drift into deviance or fail to attend to near misses, although those issues can also be present. Rather in these cases disasters result from established patterns of ignoring and circumventing regulations and covering up extensive rule breaking. The world is now familiar with convicted fraudsters such as Elizabeth Holmes and Sam Bankman-Fried, whose companies, Theranos and FTX respectively, were built on elaborate schemes meant to deceive investors, but there are many other examples of intentional deviance and deception throughout the corporate world that resulted in disaster. The 2008 financial meltdown has often been interpreted as a normal accident, but both Charles Perrow himself and other analysts have highlighted the role of the financial industry's greed and deception in the lead-up to the collapse (Perrow 2011; Bryant and Sigurjonsson 2022). In their telling, that crisis, the largest since the crash that ushered the Great Depression of the 1930s in, was not due primarily to the interactively complex and tightly coupled nature of the global financial system – although the system did have those attributes – but rather to decisions that were intentionally made by leaders in the financial services sector to rack up profits in what was essentially an industry-wide house of cards built on providing predatory home loans to applicants who had little chance of being able to pay them back. Triggered by events such as the collapse and bailout of Bear Stearns in March 2008 and those of Lehman Brothers and Merrill Lynch in September of that year, the house of cards fell in short order. Other factors such as regulatory capture and production pressures within the financial sector can of course not be discounted, but sheer greed and the intent to deceive undoubtedly played a major role.

Box 4.1 The Upper Big Branch Mine Disaster: Ongoing Rule Breaking and the Social Production of Disaster

On April 5, 2010, a coal dust explosion initiated by methane emissions at a mining operation owned by Massey Energy in the company's Montcoal mine in Raleigh County, West Virginia killed twenty-nine of thirty-one mine workers at the site, in the deadliest US mine disaster in forty years. Subsequent investigations uncovered a pattern of violations that stood out even in an industry known for its disregard for worker safety. The litany of proven accusations against Massey is shocking by any standard. In the year before the disaster, the Mine Safety and Health Administration issued 515 citations against the company regarding safety violations, but levied no fines. Worker testimonies revealed a systemic pattern of intimidation, in which they were told not to report safety violations or else they would lose their jobs. Workers also felt forced to maintain production goals in order to avoid being fired, and retaliation against those who pointed to safety issues was common in what investigations later termed a "pervasive culture that valued production over safety" (US Department of Labor 2010: 157). Worker safety programs were deemed inadequate.

To further sidestep accountability, the company was typically informed in advance when federal health and safety inspections were going to take place, and it secretly kept two sets of books – one that recorded safety violations and one that did not, which was the version shown to safety inspectors. Just before the disaster, the company failed to address problems of inadequate ventilation and air monitoring in the mine – problems that led directly to the deadly explosion. The company had also been found to be in violation of mandatory safety inspection requirements (US Department of Labor 2010).

After the disaster, the US Mine Safety and Health administration issued 369 violations against the company and levied $10.8 million in penalties – the largest fines in the agency's history. The company settled with the US Department of Justice for an additional $200 million, which included awards of $1.5 million to each of the families of those killed, plus those of the two survivors.

Mine superintendent Gary May was sentenced to twenty-one months in prison for conspiring to violate Mine Safety and Health Administration laws. Massey CEO Donald Blankenship, scion of a politically well-connected West Virginia family with a long history of profiting from mining operations, was sentenced to one year in prison on a single misdemeanor charge of conspiring to violate mine safety standards. He ran for US Senate in 2018 and for the US presidency in 2020, as a Constitution Party candidate.

Other examples abound in which organizational actors go beyond trying to circumvent safety rules to flouting them outright, as a way of doing business – and with disastrous results. Box 4.1 on page 77 discusses one such disaster: the 2010 Upper Big Branch mine disaster.

As noted earlier, the factors discussed above do not operate in isolation but more often occur together to contribute to organizational disasters. The Boeing 737-MAX airliner is a case in point. The plane was involved in two fatal crashes: one on October 9, 2018, which resulted in the deaths of 189 persons on board, and another on March 10, 2019, which killed 157. Without going into detail about the causes of the two crashes, or why the planes were not grounded after the first crash, subsequent analyses pointed to two key reasons for the increased likelihood of those accidents: regulatory capture and production pressures. The airline's regulator, the US Federal Aviation Administration, had essentially ceded critical safety design and inspection issues to the airline itself (US House of Representatives 2020; Bourke 2021). The airline was also in keen competition with its main rival, Airbus, which was in the process of bringing a new plane, the Airbus 320 neo, onto the worldwide market. Both circumstances, combined with a relentless corporate focus on the bottom line, undermined safety at Boeing. The airplane manufacturer's problems were further magnified in January 2024, when a part of the fuselage where there could have been an emergency exit in a different seating configuration ripped off a 737-9 on an Alaska Airlines flight while it was airborne, causing extensive damage and sucking parts of the plane and passengers' belongings out into the air. Early analyses once again pointed to capture and profit seeking as factors that compromised Boeing's safety culture (Isadore 2024).

We turn in the next two chapters to two concepts that are fundamental to understanding disasters and their societal impacts: vulnerability and resilience.

QUESTIONS AND EXERCISES

Do some additional reading on the Boeing corporation and its safety record. What new information has come to light since this book was published? Do you see additional evidence of the safety-related factors discussed in this chapter, such as regulatory capture and the drift into deviance?

Collect additional information from published sources on the spread of Covid-19 misinformation and disinformation online. How should we think about such patterns sociologically? What entities benefitted from misinformation and disinformation?

What warning systems exist for tornadoes? For hurricanes? What about earthquake early warning systems in Japan, Mexico, and the United States? How are they supposed to work, and how effective are they?

5

Disaster Vulnerability

Introduction

Throughout the history of sociological disaster research, scholars have focused on disasters not as physical phenomena but as social ones. No matter how large, a physical event such as a massive earthquake or a tropical cyclone is not considered a disaster unless it results in losses to human communities and the things they value and in the disruption of the social fabric. Disasters are marked by death and injury, damage to homes and businesses, displacement of populations, short- and longer-term economic losses, and threats to the functioning of social institutions such as educational and healthcare systems. However, the burdens of a disaster are not borne equally; some groups suffer disproportionately. Understanding how and why these disparities exist is a fundamental question for the sociology of disasters. Using an intersectional lens, this chapter provides a partial answer to that question by taking a closer look at the concept of disaster vulnerability and at vulnerable groups.

The Concept of Vulnerability

In a 1990s article, geographer Susan Cutter noted that scholars had advanced a number of definitions of the concept of vulnerability and that those definitions were not necessarily consistent among themselves (Cutter 1996). Since then, there have been additional clarifications but no clear definitional consensus. The United Nations International Strategy for Disaster Reduction (UNISDR) (2017) defines vulnerability as "[t]he conditions determined by physical, social, economic and environmental factors or processes, which increase the susceptibility of a community to the impact of hazards." Bolin and Kurtz (2018: 183) assert that the vulnerability perspective "works to identify an ensemble of sociospatial and political economic conditions and historical as well as current processes which can explain how specific hazard events become disasters." Other definitions take into account both pre-event susceptibility and coping capacity. For Wisner, Blaikie, Cannon, and Davis (2004: 11), vulnerability consists of "the characteristics of a person or group and their situation that influence their capacity to anticipate, cope with, resist, and recover from the impact of a natural hazard." Similarly, Joern Birkmann (2006: 14) argues that vulnerability "has to be seen as the estimation of the wider environment and social circumstances, thus enabling people and communities to cope with the impact of hazardous events or, conversely, limiting their ability to resist the negative impact of the hazardous event ... vulnerability can also take into account the coping capacity and resilience of the potentially affected society." For our purposes, following Cutter, Boruff, and Shirley (2003), we can begin this exploration by thinking of disaster vulnerability as a set of conditions indicative of the potential for loss: loss of life, of physical and mental well-being, of the ability to function, of the functionality of physical systems such as buildings and infrastructure, of livelihoods and personal assets such as wealth and savings, and of environmental diversity and sustainability. The concept of vulnerability has already been introduced in earlier chapters; we learned, for example, that the pioneering volume *At Risk* made the study of vulnerability central to disaster research and provided a model – the pressure and release model – for understanding how vulnerability is produced through macro-, meso-, and micro-level social forces. Earlier discussions in Chapter 3 also highlighted the idea that vulnerability production is a process; vulnerability is not a state but rather an evolving set of conditions driven by a variety of forces that include the dynamics of the world system, processes that marginalize groups on the basis of ideologies such as racism, actions taken by states and communities that adversely affect particular segments of the population, and other forces that create, maintain, and reproduce inequality. Researchers typically take into account three different dimensions of vulnerability: the hazardousness of different geographic places; built-environment and infrastructure vulnerability; and social vulnerability, which is our main focus here.

Drivers of Vulnerability

Hazardousness of place

What is often referred to as "the hazardousness of a place" (Hewitt and Burton 1971) takes into account the fact that particular geographic areas are simply more prone than others to events that arise from hazards. This facet of vulnerability is often referred to as exposure. Coastal areas and their residents are exposed to hazards such as hurricanes, while places adjacent to rivers and streams are exposed to the potential for riverine and flash floods. Along what is known as the Ring of Fire, parts of Japan, China, Chile, and New Zealand have experienced a number of devastating earthquakes in the twentieth and twenty-first centuries, a fact that testifies to the high levels of exposure to earthquake hazards in these regions. Mexico and countries in Central America such as Nicaragua and El Salvador have a long history of violent earthquakes and deadly hurricanes. Turkey has experienced devastating earthquakes in recent years, again owing partly to its high seismic hazards. In the United States, exposure to earthquake hazards is high to moderate not only in California but also in Washington, Oregon, the New Madrid Seismic Zone in the Midwest, and even South Carolina and Massachusetts. One of the most hazard-prone places on earth, the Philippines, faces multiple hazards such as tropical cyclones, floods, volcanic eruptions, and earthquakes. Similarly, as seen in the case of Hurricane Maria and Hurricane Irma in 2017, islands in the Caribbean are at risk of being struck by hurricanes that originate in the eastern Atlantic Ocean and are vulnerable to the high winds and flooding that those storms produce. Bangladesh regularly experiences major flooding, and many countries in Africa are prone to both drought and large-scale flooding.

With respect to technological hazards, as discussed earlier in connection with Hurricane Harvey, Houston is not only prone to hurricanes and floods but also home to the largest chemical complex in the United States, which means that Houston's population is exposed to the risk of impacts from hurricane winds, storm surges, and industrial accidents. Many other communities host numerous facilities that manufacture, process, or store hazardous chemicals. Others are sites of nuclear plants, which makes those communities more vulnerable than others to accidents comparable with the 1979 Three Mile Island disaster, the 1986 Chernobyl disaster, and the 2011 Fukushima triple meltdown. Understanding the different hazards to which communities and societies are exposed is thus an important element in understanding societal vulnerabilities.

Our goal in this chapter is to show how and why not all populations and groups exposed to hazards are equally vulnerable. Taking earthquake exposure as an example, exposed populations show variation in their capacity for mitigating and preparing for earthquakes, knowledge of what to do in the event of an earthquake, and ability to undertake those self-protective actions. Some groups may be living in dangerous structures, while others live in safer buildings. Evacuation is the most effective self-protective measure when a hurricane threatens, but members of some groups may be unable or unwilling to evacuate for a variety of reasons: lack of transportation, inability to afford gas and stay in a hotel, or concern about potential lost wages. Because of climate change, there will be more heat waves in the future, in the United States and around the world; but, as we will see later, population groups are differentially vulnerable to extreme heat.

Built-environment vulnerability

The concept of vulnerability also encompasses the built environment, which includes not only buildings and infrastructure – highways, bridges, electrical systems, ports, and so on – but other constructed systems such as levees, seawalls, and other works that are intended to offer protection against extreme events. Here again, built-environment vulnerability is related to the likelihood of loss through destruction, damage, and functional degradation. Assessments of built-environment vulnerability center on such issues as the overall condition of built-environment elements and questions about when they were built and under what codes and standards, how well the hazards to which the structures are exposed were understood at the time when those structures were designed and built, whether they have been adequately maintained, whether, if needed, they have been retrofitted, and whether they are approaching or exceeding the period of time for which they were designed – as is the case, for example, with many US nuclear plants whose permits have nonetheless been extended.

One element of the built environment, the US electrical power grid, is a case in point. Although the power grid normally operates with very high levels of reliability, under certain conditions the grid is prone to cascading, and even to catastrophic loss of function. This is what happened, for example, in August 2003, when what would have been a minor accident in part of the power grid resulted in a massive blackout that affected major cities in the United States and Canada.

More recently, winter storms that struck in mid-February 2021 caused a failure in Texas's electric power grid, precipitating the worst energy infrastructure disaster in the state's history. Winter Storm Uri originated in the Pacific Northwest and spread to the southern United States, and even to parts of northern Mexico. As a result of the storm, temperatures in some parts of Texas dipped to an astonishing −2°F (−19°C). Demand for electrical power soared, but Texas does not require utilities to maintain reserves; in other words, there was an absence of resource "slack" in the power system. On top of that, the electrical power infrastructure in Texas is not hardened to resist low temperatures. The extreme cold also led to large-scale water shortages, burst water pipes, and indoor flooding.

The grid failure resulted in a loss of power to an estimated 4.5 million homes and businesses – about one third of electrical power customers and nearly $300 billion in economic losses. The official death toll from the massive outage stands at 246, but actual numbers may be higher, perhaps topping 700 or even 800 (Buchele 2022). Approximately 300 cases of carbon monoxide poisoning were reported, as residents attempted to stay warm by running their cars or using improperly vented generators. Occurring as it did during the Covid pandemic, the power grid failure also disrupted the response to it, for example by slowing vaccine deliveries. It also produced heightened psychosocial stress for those affected, especially in households with children under the age of eighteen and with disabled and elderly family members and among younger and lower-income households (Ritchie, Gill, and Hamilton 2022).

Chapter 4 discussed conditions that contribute to organizational disasters, and such conditions were certainly present in the Texas power grid disaster. To avoid federal government regulation, Texas maintains its own power grid, the Electric Reliability Council of Texas (ERCOT), which is separate from the nation's other two grids, the Eastern and the Western Interconnections, meaning that, unlike the rest of the US grid, ERCOT was virtually unable to import power during the disaster. Along with the cost-cutting measures mentioned above – lack of winterization of the grid and of excess capacity – this isolation was a major cause of the disaster. The grid failure led to a shake-up on the ERCOT board and to efforts to harden the power system against extreme weather. Efforts are also underway to allow Texas to gain access to power from outside the state under emergency conditions. (For more details, see Monroe 2022; Golding 2023.)

As this example shows, advanced societies are highly vulnerable to power grid disruptions. This element of the built environment literally provides the backbone on which societies depend, making it possible to use the internet and banking services, pump gasoline, heat and cool structures, operate transportation and other infrastructure systems, supply water, use grocery store checkout systems, and more. Perrow (2006: 213) calls the power grid "the single most vulnerable system in our critical infrastructure," noting that it is vulnerable to attacks by terrorists as well as to extreme weather events such as excessive heat and cold, hurricanes, and floods.

Social vulnerability

Place-based and built-environment vulnerabilities must be taken into account in developing a full picture of why and in what ways societies and communities are at risk of experiencing disaster losses because, as we have seen in earlier discussions, community residents become vulnerable to disasters in part because they often live in high-hazard areas. In the absence of effective affordable housing policies, many community residents have no choice but to live in unsafe and overcrowded housing units that are physically vulnerable to disaster impacts, for example in manufactured housing and old, poorly maintained apartment buildings. Worldwide, poor people have few options other than to live in slum conditions and in areas that are hazard-prone, such as steep hillsides and flood plains.

Sociologists who study hazards and disasters are fundamentally concerned with social vulnerability – that is, with the social origins and aspects of the differential potential of individuals and communities to experience short- and longer-term losses as a consequence of disasters. For the purposes of the discussions in this volume, we can conceptualize social vulnerability to disasters as a condition that is the consequence of historical and ongoing societal forces that create a disproportionate potential for loss, and also for experiencing poorer outcomes as a result of loss. Put another way, vulnerable groups are those groups that are more likely to experience a range of negative impacts when disasters strike and less likely to experience positive outcomes in the aftermath of disasters. A number of publications focus on social vulnerability (see Pelling 2003; Bankoff, Frerks, and Hilhorst 2004; Enarson and Chakrabarti 2009; Thomas, Phillips, Lovekamp, and Fothergill 2013; Enarson and Pease 2016; Enarson, Fothergill, and Peek 2018; Bankoff and Hilhorst 2022). Here I distill some of the many insights from these and other studies while offering a slightly different way of thinking about disaster vulnerability – one that places primary emphasis on the effects of class, race, and gender, as well as on state actions that produce or exacerbate vulnerability.

Some parts of the definition provided in the preceding paragraphs need to be clarified. The first is that social vulnerability has temporal, spatial, and situational dimensions. It exists at particular points in time and in particular locations; disaster vulnerability is shaped by historical trends, and conditions can evolve and vary in ways that make individuals and groups more or less vulnerable in terms of both impacts and outcomes. Regarding impacts, for example, discussions in Chapter 3 showed how racial and ethnic segregation resulted in disproportionate exposure to toxic hazards in cities like Phoenix and Los Angeles. Regarding outcomes, vulnerability to experiencing negative outcomes during the post-disaster recovery period results in part from preexisting conditions of vulnerability, but also, importantly, from the resources that are available to survivors in the aftermath of disasters – for example, recovery policies and the extent to which people are able to take advantage of post-disaster relief programs and to take other steps to put their lives back in order. Outcomes for those who lose their homes are shaped in part by policy decisions that can shift over time; but, as we will see later in this chapter, such policies can reinforce preexisting inequities.

Often the conditions that affect post-disaster recovery outcomes are unrelated to the disaster itself, or even to disaster relief policies. For example, high rental vacancy rates in one community that experiences a disaster can make it easier for displaced low- to moderate-income renters to find adequate post-disaster housing, and this situation renders them less vulnerable to long-term dislocation, while low vacancy rates in another disaster-stricken community may cause serious difficulties for displaced renters in those same income groups. For a business, disaster recovery can be affected by the overall economic climate; other things being equal, businesses probably have better prospects during periods of economic growth than when the economy is stagnant. Consequently, vulnerability can best be thought of as a combination of long-term disadvantages such as those typically associated with race and social class and situational conditions that vary over time and across communities.

Another key point is that, while impact and outcome vulnerabilities are often highly correlated, sometimes losses experienced as a result of disaster impacts can be offset by policies that seek to improve outcomes for those affected. To take one example, communities and businesses that depended on the fishing industry suffered significant losses as a result of the 2010 British Petroleum (BP) Deepwater Horizon oil rig blowout and oil spill. In the aftermath of the spill, the company quickly devised a compensation scheme and began payouts to victims. In contrast, the long and drawn-out process of compensating fishing-oriented communities and businesses after the 1989 Exxon Valdez oil spill, which was caused by Exxon's intransigence in fighting legal settlement efforts, led to long-term stress for those who were awaiting payouts, as well as to loss of community cohesion and trust in institutions such as the government and the courts (Ritchie 2012; Ritchie, Gill, and Farnham 2013). The Oil Pollution Act of 1990, which was passed after the Exxon spill, clarified the role of so-called responsible parties in compensating those who are negatively affected by oil spills. While the compensation arrangements made after the BP disaster were still a source of community conflict and psychological stress for those affected (Gill, Picou, and Ritchie 2012; Ritchie, Gill, and Long 2018), the 1990 statute at least clarified who should pay for spill-induced losses; and, because compensation came more quickly than in the Exxon disaster, longer-term negative psychological consequences of stress were likely avoided.

We will see later how Covid-19 affected vulnerable groups, but here it is important to note that policies enacted during the pandemic did help to ameliorate some of its negative effects. Legislation like the American Rescue Plan, programs such as the Paycheck Protection Program, and monetary aid offered directly to individuals and households represented a $5 trillion effort to shield households, businesses, and industries from the massive negative economic impacts of Covid. Not everyone was helped to the same degree by such assistance, but it is difficult to imagine how the country would have fared during and after the pandemic without them. The point here is that policies and programs can make a big difference when it comes to addressing – or ignoring – social vulnerability.

Ideally, in the aftermath of disasters efforts should be made to level the playing field so that those who have lost the most by comparison with their pre-disaster circumstances should receive the most assistance during the recovery process; but, as we will see in the discussions that follow, this is often not the case. Rather, what happens to those who have experienced losses in disasters is yet another manifestation of what sociologist Robert Merton (1968) referred to as the Matthew effect: those in society who already have advantages tend to accumulate more, while those who lack advantages fall farther behind.[1]

Vulnerable groups? The significance of intersectionality

In both scholarship and public policy, there has been a tendency to characterize a wide range of groups as vulnerable to hazards. A partial list of these groups includes women, poor people, members of racial and ethnic minorities, elderly persons, persons with ongoing health problems and disabilities, and children. Categorizing entire segments of the population in this way can be useful. For example, special disaster-related programs may be developed to target those who live in poverty, or children. Such categorizations also point to characteristics of group members that can make them particularly vulnerable in disaster situations: only women can get pregnant and need prenatal care, and women, as opposed to men, are typically victims of domestic violence that occurs in the wake of disasters. While this chapter will shine a light on the ways in which members of different groups are made vulnerable in the context of hazards and disasters, it will also make two related points. First, it is important to move away from the kind of essentialism that sees vulnerability as an inherent or intrinsic characteristic of members of particular groups – for example by arguing that all women or all children are vulnerable. To look at vulnerability this way would be to ignore the often immense differences that exist within such groups, and also the point that, as noted earlier, people are not born vulnerable, they are made vulnerable. Moreover, as we will see in the next chapter, while individuals and groups are vulnerable differentially, they are also resilient differentially – and high levels of resilience can overcome social deficits that are typically associated with vulnerability.

Second, sociologists have long used the concept of intersectionality to refer to the ways in which multiple dimensions of stratification and inequality come together to shape people's life circumstance and life chances. Originally formulated by legal scholar Kimberlé Crenshaw (1991) and developed further by sociologists who study race, class, gender, and other forms of inequality (see e.g. Andersen and Collins 2016; Collins and Bilge 2016), the concept highlights the fact that different axes of inequality combine and interact to form systems of oppression – systems that relate directly to differential levels of social vulnerability, both in normal times and in the context of disaster. Intersectionality calls attention to the need to avoid statements like "women are vulnerable" in favor of a more nuanced view that asks, for example: "Which women are more vulnerable and which are less so, under what conditions, and why?" There is a vast difference in levels of social vulnerability between a woman who is a recent immigrant of color, non-English-speaking, and working as a night janitor for hourly wages and a white woman with a PhD who is a high-ranking and hugely compensated executive in a major social media company. Intersecting statuses place people who might otherwise be considered similar – toddlers and teenagers, for example – in very different positions when it comes to their social vulnerability. Thus, even though I will refer to particular groups as vulnerable in these discussions, we must also keep in mind gradations in vulnerability that result from intersecting dimensions of inequality. As Maureen Fordham and her colleagues put it,

> It is not that children, people with disabilities, women, and other social groups are vulnerable as such; it is a particular amalgamation of factors in place and time that dictates that some groups will be harder hit and less able to recover successfully. (Fordham et al. 2013: 12)

Key Dimensions of Social Vulnerability: Class, Race, and Gender

Social class

The most straightforward way of thinking about social class is to see it as having three main dimensions: income and wealth, education, and occupation. Income consists of what is earned by individuals and households, which can encompass wages and salaries, dividends on investments, and cash benefits such as social security payments. In contrast, wealth is what is owned: the assets individuals and households possess. Wealth can encompass equity in a home, savings, stocks, bonds, other financial instruments, and other possessions. The net worth of a household consists of its assets minus what it owes, for example in the form of household mortgages and other debt. In the United States, both income and wealth are highly unequal, most of the advantages accruing to those who are extremely well-off, while the income and wealth of other groups remain stagnant or are in decline. For example, at the end of 2022 the top 20 percent income quintile held about 71 percent of US wealth, or just under $98 trillion, and 60 percent of income earners between the highest and lowest quintiles experienced a steady decrease in their share of the country's wealth. In the third quarter of 2023, two thirds of the nation's total wealth were owned by the top 10 percent of earners, while the lowest 50 percent owned a tiny 2.6 percent of the total wealth (USA Facts 2023).

Education is a second marker of social class membership. This marker spans both educational attainment and more subtle distinctions such as where individuals received their educations. High educational attainment is characteristic of the upper-middle and upper classes. Adding to their advantages, members of the wealthiest groups are typically educated at elite primary and secondary schools and colleges – often the schools their parents and grandparents attended – which serves to separate them from members of the lower classes even further.

Occupational status has several dimensions, including the prestige that members of the public assign to an occupation, the amount of independence associated with different occupations, whether individuals earn salaries or hourly wages, and median income levels within occupations. Such differences point to the importance of not only how much individuals earn, but also how they earn that income and the value that others place on particular occupations. For example, physicians and scientists have high occupational prestige, while real estate agents and automobile salespersons are much less admired by members of the public, even if they may earn high incomes through commissions.

Scholars differ in how they distinguish among the various social classes. In the United States, for example, classic research by W. Lloyd Warner (1949) recognized three social classes – upper, middle, and lower – each with upper and lower gradations. Currently, the sociologist Dennis Gilbert (2018) divides US society into six classes: capitalist, upper-middle, middle, and working, along with the working poor and the underclass. Members of the capitalist class are individuals with "old money" that has existed for generations, corporate chief executive officers, and others who have amassed very high net worth. This is the group that is often referred to as "the 1 percent." Members of the capitalist class have very high income and wealth levels, often do not earn their money through actual work, and are likely to have achieved their wealth by inheriting it. This is also the class that possesses the highest amount of political power and influence. Members of the upper-middle class are doing well financially, but not as well as those in the upper class. They have generally attained their class position in their own lifetimes, by receiving advanced degrees. They work for a living but, unlike those who are lower in the class hierarchy, their occupations involve little supervision, and they are generally salaried professionals. Doctors, lawyers, and other highly paid professionals fit into this category. Those in the middle class have at least a high school education and can be involved in minor management or supervisory positions. The working class consists of manual workers and many low-paid clerical and retail sales workers. The working poor are the lowest-paid manual, clerical, and other workers. These individuals may be working full time and still fall below the 2023 poverty line of $30,000 a year (for a family of four) as a result of their low wages. The underclass, the lowest group in the class hierarchy, is made up of people who are unemployed, who work part time for low wages, or who obtain their income through public assistance.

What has come to be called the precariat is a distinctive group that does not fit easily into traditional class categories, which assume that individuals have at least somewhat consistent earnings, even if those earnings are low. As the portmanteau suggests, this group has a precarious economic position, which is highly dependent on the vicissitudes of the market. Members of the precariat are characterized by a lack of predictability in terms of income and employment, along with a lack of the kinds of employment protections and benefits that were traditionally enjoyed by many members of the middle and working classes. This group includes involuntary part-time workers who have little say over the hours they work, participants in the gig economy, and so-called private contractors such as Uber drivers, who may make well below the minimum wage for the hours worked. The precariat also includes people who have experienced downward mobility, for example in response to economic downturns, have lost their homes, are unable to live on their meager pension or social security benefits, and may even have been forced into a nomadic existence based on taking advantage of seasonal work in places such as Amazon warehouses. This aspect of precarity was recently captured in the book and film *Nomadland*, which focused on individuals and groups that are not exactly homeless, but are not housed either, and travel the country in recreational vehicles in search of often backbreaking work.

Social class exerts a profound influence on virtually every aspect of people's lives. Lower-class individuals have lower life expectancies and poorer health outcomes than better-off people, in part because they are likely to smoke, to exercise less, and to have poorer diets. Mental health problems are also more common among the lower classes, but, despite the higher incidence of these kinds of physical and psychological problems, those in the lower classes are less likely to have adequate medical insurance (Barr 2014). Divorce, too, is more common among the lower social classes, which in part accounts for the higher incidence of female-headed households in these groups (Bureau of Labor Statistics 2013). Members of less privileged groups, especially African American men, are also more likely to be arrested and to find themselves in jail or prison and on parole and probation – circumstances that typically result in poor life chances (Western 2006; Western and Pettit 2010). Home ownership is increasingly less common moving downward in the class hierarchy. Because rents have increased faster than wages in many US cities, working- and lower-class families find it increasingly difficult to get affordable housing and often must resort to living in overcrowded conditions (Semple 2016; Kotkin and Cox 2017); they are also forced to cut back on spending for basic necessities such as food, transportation, and medical care. Overcrowding is known to have significant negative effects on children, for example higher stress, problems with sleep, and difficulties with school performance and academic achievement (Solari and Mare 2012). The effects of overcrowding on children can persist throughout their lives. The Covid-19 pandemic only worsened these already dire conditions, because it caused rents and living expenses to soar.

Within the subdiscipline of medical sociology, researchers have found significant support for fundamental cause theory, which holds that socioeconomic status is a key determinant of many adverse health conditions and outcomes (see Phelan, Link, and Tehranifar 2015 and Clouston and Link 2021 for discussions). Members of higher-status groups enjoy better health owing to their ability to draw upon "flexible resources," which include knowledge, money, power, prestige, and beneficial social connections. In contrast, members of lower-class groups possess fewer flexible resources and are also burdened by structural forces such as racism, stigma, and other forms of social isolation and exclusion – forces that have a direct bearing on their ability to access the health resources they need. As later discussions will show, fundamental cause theory can be expanded beyond the medical and health realm, to broader concerns regarding social vulnerability and vulnerability to disasters.

Disasters can add to the everyday injuries associated with being lower in the class hierarchy. According to fundamental cause theory, those who rank lower in the class system typically have few resources available for coping with any sort of emergency, including a disaster. For example, out of necessity, poor people depend a great deal on their place-based networks of social support, which help them overcome poverty by providing free support in the form of childcare, transportation, food, and moments of respite from stressful situations at home. But because disasters damage or destroy residences and neighborhoods and can result in temporary or permanent residential dislocation, they can disrupt those social support networks. Disasters frequently do the most damage to substandard and rental housing (which is typically made of inferior materials, generally not used for owner-occupied housing), putting poor people at greater risk of residential dislocation.

In addition to damaging support networks and causing displacement, disasters can bring about, in the affected communities, changes that make life even more difficult for those at the lower end of the social hierarchy. Regarding financial resources, to the extent that disasters are responsible for a decline in the availability of rental housing, they cause rents to rise. Increased rents affect displaced people at all income levels, but are most burdensome for those who were struggling before disaster struck. For example, in 2017, Hurricane Harvey displaced hundreds of thousands of homeowners and renters while also destroying or rendering uninhabitable thousands of rental units. Those forced out of their owner-occupied dwellings, as well as renters, needed to find places to rent in order to achieve some sort of stability in their lives, and so, as a result of this increased demand, rental costs increased (Sarnoff 2017). Temporary federal rental assistance is designed to help displaced residents, but the living conditions that are typical of many lower-class and underclass people (and others) can threaten their eligibility even for this form of aid. An article that appeared in *Texas Monthly* after Hurricane Harvey in 2017 noted how living arrangements can disqualify disaster survivors for aid:

> People are denied FEMA [Federal Emergency Management Agency] aid for a wide number of reasons, and in some cases, it might seem, for no reason at all. Aid eligibility rests on being able to prove US citizenship and residence at an address rendered unlivable. This might seem easy, but pitfalls abound: people who lived with roommates or family and might not be listed on a lease or a utility bill; people who lived with too many other applicants; people whose homes could be owned by incarcerated spouses or exes; exchange students, foreigners, and undocumented people who cannot offer

proof of citizenship; people who lost their identification in the storm, or their landlord's phone number. The list goes on. (Young 2017)

A look at the US social class system reveals a society that is sharply divided between the haves and the have-nots, between those who are able to live stable lives, have access to a range of amenities, and feel secure in their social class positions and those whose lives are marked by instability, stressful experiences, and other forms of insecurity. Disaster-related burdens fall most heavily on the have-nots. Superimposed on these class disparities are other inequities associated with race and ethnicity; and we turn next to these.

Race and ethnicity

Recalling our earlier discussion of racial formation, race is a social construct that is used to mark racialized persons and groups for unequal treatment within society. Racialized categories serve as the basis for practices such as racial segregation, job discrimination, and other forms of social exclusion. Race and ethnicity tend to co-vary with social class, African Americans, Native Americans, and people of Hispanic descent being more likely to have lower-class status than whites and consequently to have fewer flexible resources with which to protect themselves against disasters and to cope when they occur. At the same time, racial designations bring with them additional disadvantages that cannot be explained solely by reference to social class markers. For example, in comparison with whites, African Americans and people of Hispanic descent earn less at the same educational levels, amass less wealth at similar income levels, and tend to pay more for equivalent goods and services, largely owing to higher prices in the areas where they live (Williams, Mohammed, Leavell, and Collins 2010).

Regardless of their socioeconomic status, racial and ethnic minority group members face unique burdens, which are attributable to race alone. These burdens include not only day-to-day expressions of racism but also ongoing disadvantages, such as living in hyper-segregated areas, living in close proximity to hazardous facilities, living in food deserts that offer limited access to healthy foods, and having reduced access to quality schools and community amenities such as parks and open spaces. Even when we control for socioeconomic status, being a member of a racial or ethnic minority has profound negative effects; for example it contributes to disparities in mortality and other health outcomes (Williams, Priest, and Anderson 2016).

Income and wealth data reveal the extent of racial disparities in the United States. Data on average incomes tend to mask the extent to which earnings vary as a function of race and ethnicity – and they do so significantly. For example, in 2022 the median income for all US households was $74,580 but the median income for whites was $81,060, while the figures for Hispanics and African

Americans were $62,800 and $52,860 respectively. In other words, Hispanic income comes up no higher that to 77 percent of white income, while African American income comes up only to 65 percent. Those of Asian descent earned significantly more than any of these groups: their median income was $108,700.

Since the publication of Melvin Oliver and Thomas Shapiro's (1995) ground-breaking study *Black Wealth, White Wealth*, sociologists have been increasingly focusing on racial and ethnic disparities in wealth, in addition to income disparities. Here the picture is even starker: Hispanics and African Americans possess substantially less wealth than whites. For example, in 2022, Black households had a median net worth of $49,900 and the net worth of Hispanic households was $61,600, while the figures for white and Asian households were $285,000 and $536,000, respectively (Luhby 2023). Adding to these inequities, Hispanics and African Americans have accumulated significantly less than whites in retirement savings, in part because they are less likely to be participating in retirement plans. Whites are five times more likely than Hispanics or Blacks to have received large gifts and inheritances that add to their assets (Urban Institute 2017).

What these income and wealth disparities mean in the disaster context is that racial and ethnic minority group members lack the financial cushions that whites typically take for granted and that contribute to their disaster resilience. Like members of the lower classes, minority group members have fewer financial resources on which to draw when emergencies occur; and, like poor people, they may see their social support networks weakened in the event of disaster, which lowers their access to informal sources of aid.

As just one example, in research that was conducted after Hurricane Katrina, Bevc, Nicholls, and Picou found that African Americans suffered a range of negative effects of that disaster. Summing up their findings, they observed:

> African Americans throughout the primary impact region have suffered disproportionately more problems than other racial or ethnic groups. African Americans were more than twice as likely to have received major damage or have their homes totally destroyed. Large proportions of African Americans had to move out of their residences and proportionately more were separated from family members. Post-Katrina financial problems were most acute for African Americans. A similar pattern persisted for African Americans in terms of insurance and state grant program claims. [They] had fewer claims fully settled and had more claims partially settled. (Bevc, Nicholls, and Picou 2010: 155)

Gender and vulnerability

As used here and in keeping with sociological treatments of the concept, gender refers not to biological sex but rather to the differential assignment of rights, privileges, and cultural and behavioral expectations that are associated with the designation of persons as male or female, along with the identities that are shaped by those social forces. Gender is the basis not only for signaling differences in expectations regarding "appropriate" behavior, but also and more importantly for producing disparities in such areas as social privilege, socioeconomic status, economic opportunity, and political power.

Like social class and racial–ethnic disparities, gender inequality is pervasive. For women, particularly those in less developed countries, gender inequality can translate into limited personal autonomy, limited access to educational and livelihood-related resources, restrictions on property ownership and the ability to inherit, ongoing threats to physical safety, and lack of access to political power. Worldwide, women bear burdens that are similar to those borne by racialized groups; these come in the form of actions designed to "keep them in their place." Such actions range from micro-aggressions to physical and sexual violence and the denial of basic human rights – for instance rights regarding reproduction or control over one's own body. In the United States, the #Me Too revelations that began in 2017 regarding the extent of the sexual harassment, assault, and humiliation suffered by women from all walks of life attest to the fact that unequal and exploitive gender relations are strongly embedded in the social fabric even of highly developed societies. As we will see later in this chapter, individuals who deviate from the traditional gender binary, as do lesbian, gay, bisexual, and transgender persons, are at risk of similar and even harsher treatment. Indignities rooted in gender-based oppression, like those rooted in race and ethnicity, exert their influence at all levels of the social class hierarchy.

Since 2006 the World Economic Forum (WEF) has been gathering and disseminating information on the male–female gender gap with the help of a Global Gender Gap Index it developed, which focuses on a collection of variables associated with economic participation and opportunities, educational attainment, survival and health, and political empowerment. Its report for 2023, which contains data on 146 countries, provided both overall rankings and rankings on the four key dimensions of gender achievement. The survey showed that, while no nation has succeeded in eliminating the gender gap, some countries are doing a much better job of addressing it than others. Overall, the WEF estimates that women have achieved 68 percent parity with men, but countries' success in closing the gender gap ranges from a high of 90 percent (Iceland) to a low of 4 percent (Afghanistan). The five countries with the lowest gender gaps were Iceland, Norway, Finland, New Zealand, and Sweden. The United States ranks forty-third on the index, at 75 percent parity, behind a number of lower- and middle-income countries. Gender inequities are considered such a serious problem worldwide that the United Nations has included gender equality and the empowerment of women and girls among its major sustainable development goals (World Economic Forum 2023).

Gender inequality is inextricably linked to economic and racialized inequalities. In the United States, women currently earn 80 cents for every dollar earned by men, but African American and Hispanic women earn respectively 63 and 54 cents on the dollar. Adding further to their burdens, women in the United States lag far behind their counterparts in other affluent countries when it comes to paid family leave and childcare opportunities. Recent years have also seen their reproductive rights severely curtailed, for example as a result of the Supreme Court's decision to strike down *Roe v. Wade*, let alone draconian legislation passed in many states.

The US Census set the 2023 poverty line at $30,000 for a family of four. Poverty rates vary considerably across states, from a low of 7 percent of the population in New Hampshire to a high of 18.7 percent in Mississippi. The US territory of Puerto Rico, which experienced catastrophic losses in Hurricane Maria in 2017, had a poverty rate of 43 percent in 2023.

Poverty in the United States is both gendered and race-based. A report by the National Women's Law Center (Sun 2023) notes that, since 2021, just over one in nine women in the United States have been living in poverty; but, again, poverty rates vary considerably across racial and ethnic groups. For example, while 10 percent of Asian women and 8.9 percent of white women were living below the poverty line in 2021, the rates for Black, Latinx, and Native American women were respectively 18.8, 17, and 21 percent. Additionally, the poverty rate for women of all races who were born outside the United States was 14.7 percent.

That same year, approximately 11 million children were living in poverty, and just under half of that group in what is considered extreme poverty. Notably, in 2021 government pandemic aid programs resulted in an historical decline in children's poverty – an illustration of how state policy can ameliorate some aspects of social vulnerability. Unfortunately, those poverty-fighting policies have since been rescinded.

Jennifer Tobin-Gurley and Elaine Enarson (2013) enumerate the many ways in which gender matters in both non-disaster and disaster times. To provide just a few examples, pregnancy creates special needs for women. For men, expectations regarding masculinity may limit the ability to ask for psychological help when they are experiencing stress, which can lead to self-medication through substance abuse. Women are more risk-averse than men, which means that they may take disaster warnings and evacuation orders more seriously than their male counterparts. In Hurricane Katrina, for example, men were twice as likely as women to resist evacuating (Haney, Elliott, and Fussell 2010). Because of their lack of power and authority, women may be overruled by men when it comes to disaster-related decision-making.

Poverty is gendered, and that gendered dimension is reflected in women's struggles in the aftermath of disasters. As just one example, Jessica Pardee studied fifty-one African American women who had been living in public housing before Hurricane Katrina and who were displaced. Relocating was bound to be difficult for this group of women, who "were among the least likely to have savings for rental deposits, funds to purchase basic furniture, or access to job transfers that would ensure a steady stream of income" (Pardee 2012: 68). To make matters worse, of the twenty-one who had been employed before Katrina struck, only four were able to obtain employment afterwards. Almost all the women received federal government or Red Cross assistance after the hurricane, but they still struggled to find stable housing arrangements, many moving multiple times in the months after the storm. Landlords took advantage of the hurricane to raise the rent and to place restrictions on those to whom they would rent, further disadvantaging these women. Pardee observed:

> In an ideal scenario, the rehousing process would have been simple – find a place, sign a lease, get an inspection, submit the voucher, and ... Welcome home! In reality, the women in this study faced multiple barriers imposed by private rental actors and assisting institutions – the people charged with "helping" them after the storm. These women were almost always left after Katrina with less money than they had before to pay the rent or for other needs. (Pardee 2012: 76–77)

The demolition of four public housing projects in New Orleans narrowed these women's options of returning to the city, as did rising rents, cumbersome application requirements and fees for rental housing. Many women suspected that landlords and city decision makers were deliberately trying to make it as difficult as possible for people like them to return to New Orleans – suspicions that have been largely borne out.

Gender is associated with disaster-related mortality, but in complex ways. Some studies find that men are at greater risk of losing their lives in disasters, while others point to the vulnerability of women and girls. Women's lack of access to needed health services both before and after disasters can put them at risk for adverse health outcomes. Gender role expectations can mean that men experience greater risk of injury during disaster response and recovery periods, while women are exposed to high levels of stress associated with their caring and supportive roles.

According to the Enarson et al. (2018) review, while after disasters men may die from suicide at higher rates than women, women tend to experience more mental health problems than men. The authors also note that research on recent disasters, in less developed and developed nations alike, continues to show that women experience higher risk of violence after disasters, both in the home and in other settings, for instance temporary shelters.

These researchers attribute gender differences in disaster mortality and morbidity to factors such as gender norms, the gendered division of labor in households and workplaces, and other societal practices that result in differential exposure to hazards and their impacts. As a recent example, women of color are overrepresented in lower-paying jobs in the service sector. These are the kinds of "essential service" positions that made them more vulnerable during the Covid pandemic.

The Importance of an Intersectional Approach to Vulnerability

As the preceding discussion shows, the intersecting forces of class, race, and gender translate into divergent levels of opportunity and success for individuals and groups. While social class achieves prominence in this respect, race, ethnicity, and gender co-determine class effects, magnifying the benefits that accrue to men and whites to the detriment of non-white racial and ethnic groups and women. At all levels of the class hierarchy, women and the less privileged racial groups fall behind; they do not reap the benefits afforded to members of the dominant group because they have fewer flexible resources available to cope with day-to-day emergencies as well as with disasters.

The social forces that are active and evident in everyday life manifest themselves perhaps even more starkly when it comes to hazard exposure and disaster impacts and outcomes. Those at the lower end of the social class hierarchy are more likely to live in physically vulnerable places and in vulnerable housing types (McCoy and Dash 2013). Lower-income individuals and households must settle for whatever housing they can afford, even if it is unsafe and in poor repair. Renters have little or no leverage over landlords in terms of housing safety. As noted earlier, those with greater financial resources are better able to evacuate – and to do so early – than the less well-off, putting themselves out of harm's way (Elliott and Pais 2006).

After disasters, recovery opportunities are structured by the same pre-disaster class, racial, and gender disparities. Again, if we consider fundamental cause theory, flexible resources matter: as the statistics above indicate, social classes, racial and ethnic groups, women and men differ significantly in the degree to which they possess resources that help them prepare for, respond to, and recover from disasters. Those living in poverty, including many members of racial and ethnic groups and women, typically have little or no discretionary income after paying for housing, food, transportation, and other basic expenses, which means that they are highly unlikely to be able to take measures to reduce their disaster risks such as stockpiling supplies or acquiring the wherewithal to evacuate. Incomes vary significantly across class, race, and gender divides, but the glaring disparities in wealth discussed earlier are perhaps even more indicative of inequities in the ability to cope with disaster-induced problems and to make progress toward recovery.

As we saw in Chapter 3, many of the disadvantages African Americans and other minority group members currently experience, such as racial segregation and barriers to accumulating wealth, are part of the legacy of discriminatory governmental policies. As Bolin and Kurtz observe,

> [t]he state is a major agent in the production, transformation, and enactment of constructions of race. Through law, policy, and a complex suite of institutional arrangements, racial discrimination in myriad forms is shaped by state-sanctioned practices in civil society. (Bolin and Kurtz 2018: 182)

These inequities can also be found in governmental disaster assistance programs. Individual and household resources are directly related to the ability to gain access to adequate amounts of disaster assistance. In the United States, apart from those who have experienced disasters directly, most people are unaware that the major source of federal government recovery assistance for households and businesses comes in the form of loans. Direct assistance of other kinds is quite limited – for example funds for temporary repairs designed to make dwellings livable, or rental vouchers for those who have been displaced. For larger recovery expenditures such as housing reconstruction and major repairs, the main source of assistance is loans from the Small Business Administration – loans that are made on essentially the same basis as private bank loans, that is, by taking into account such factors as a good credit history and an income that permits paying back the loan. On the positive side, in 2024 the Federal Emergency Management Agency (FEMA) began a new policy of providing $750 directly to disaster survivors on an expedited basis – an indication that the agency understands how much survivors need immediate assistance with living expenses.

In a society in which access to financial services and credit is important on a day-to-day basis, this kind of access can become even more crucial in disasters. However, here again, certain groups have more access than others. Overall about 6 percent of US adults are "unbanked," meaning that they and their households have no checking, savings, or money-market accounts, but that percentage rises to 17 percent for households with incomes under $25,000. For whites and Asians, the proportions of unbanked households are respectively 3 and 5 percent, but the proportions for Latinx and Blacks are 10 and 13 percent. Those who are without access to conventional banks typically turn to the use of money orders and check-cashing services (Board of Governors of the Federal Reserve System 2023). Being unbanked also rules out having access to the debit and credit cards that banks offer. During Covid, stimulus funds were deposited directly into the bank accounts of those who had them, while the unbanked had to wait longer to receive assistance. The same will presumably be the case in FEMA's new direct financial assistance programs.

Access to credit and having good credit, which is indicated by an individual's credit score, can be all-important in the aftermath of disasters, particularly for those who seek recovery-related loans. However, credit availability is, again, structured along race and class lines. An estimated 26 million Americans are "credit-invisible," meaning that they have no credit score at all – a population in which Black and Latinx persons and residents of low-income neighborhoods are overrepresented. These are the same groups that tend to have lower credit scores and to be denied credit or offered unfavorable predatory credit terms regardless of income level; among credit applicants, 46 percent of those with incomes under $50,000 are turned down, with significantly higher rates of denial for Blacks and Hispanics, again holding income constant (Campisi 2021; Board of Governors of the Federal Reserve System 2023). The burdens of seeking and obtaining credit are unequally distributed; lower-income credit applicants, particularly minoritized persons, face "higher initiation fees and interest rates, harsher penalties, and steeper overdraft fees" (Wherry and Chakrabarti 2022: 134).

A key rationale for establishing the credit scoring system in the first place was that it was supposed to make "color-blind" lending more feasible. But in reality racial and class biases are baked into the system itself. According to one commentator (Ludwig 2015: n.p.), credit ratings "embed existing racial inequities in our credit system and economy – to the point that a person's credit information serves as a proxy for race." Those inequities can be traced in turn to a history of redlining in minority communities and to the targeting of minority groups for predatory lending practices. In other words, by its very nature, the information that serves as the basis for credit lending, including post-disaster loans, is discriminatory.

After Superstorm Sandy, the Fair Share Housing Center, a civil rights group, found evidence of discrimination toward disaster assistance applicants in New Jersey that adversely affected African American and Hispanic disaster survivors. Around 38 percent of Blacks and 20 percent of Hispanics who applied for resettlement grants were rejected, by comparison with 14.5 percent of whites. The same pattern was found among applicants for repair and reconstruction assistance: 35 percent of African Americans and 18 percent of Hispanics were rejected, while the figure was 13.6 percent for whites (*New York Times* Editorial Board 2013).

The Role of the State in Vulnerability Production

In a volume titled *The Wrong Complexion for Protection*, Robert Bullard and Beverly Wright argue that the US government has a poor track record when it comes to the risks faced by African Americans and members of other minority groups with respect to natural and technological hazards. With regard to the latter, "[n]umerous bad [government] decisions have turned communities of far too many low-income people and people of color into 'sacrifice zones' and toxic dumping grounds, lowering nearby residents' property values (thereby stealing their wealth) and exposing them to unnecessary environmental health risks" (Bullard and Wright 2012: 102). Bolstering their argument, they cite cases in which federal agencies such as the Environmental Protection Agency acted, or failed to act, to the detriment of minority communities exposed to a range of toxic hazards. In many of those cases, appropriate governmental responses to those hazards had to be forced through class action lawsuits.

Native Americans living on reservations are often exposed to toxic hazards – vulnerability that can also be traced to discriminatory governmental practices. As Durham and Miller (2010) observe, Native American tribes are recognized as sovereign nations, but at the same time they are subject to US government and corporate activities that can put them at risk. Durham and Miller's research indicates that, of the five hundred Native American nations, more than 300 are exposed to toxic hazards. Because of their poverty and powerlessness, Native Americans have been unable to resist corporate and government actions that increase their vulnerability. Tribal lands such as those inhabited by the Western Shoshone nation have served as sites for nuclear weapons testing and have been targeted as locations for nuclear waste facilities such as the controversial Yucca Mountain nuclear waste storage site, which has never been implemented and will probably never be. Traditional Mohawk lands in New York State are exposed to pollutants released by nearby industries.

There are more than 500 abandoned uranium-mining sites on the Navajo Reservation in Arizona. Those living on the reservation were not aware of uranium-related hazards until 1979, when a dam break released 94 million gallons of mining byproducts and 1,100 tons of radioactive sludge onto reservation land. Tribal members subsequently learned that decades of uranium mining were polluting their soil and drinking water, exposing them to elevated risks for lung cancer and putting them at risk for kidney damage and various inflammation-related diseases (Arnold 2014). As Bolin and Kurtz observe,

> The casual disregard of Indian miners and their families' health by corporations, the decades of delay in federal compensation for radiation exposure victims and in EPA [Environmental Protection Agency] clean-up and hazard mitigation all speak to the marginality of American Indians. (Bolin and Kurtz 2018: 198)

The Road Home Program, a federally funded Hurricane Katrina recovery program that was the largest of its kind in US history, presents yet another example of how governmental policies and practices reproduce and reinforce racial and class hierarchies. As the name suggests, this program's ostensible purpose was to provide assistance to Louisiana renters and homeowners so that they could avoid long-term displacement and return to their homes. Aid came in the form of forgivable loans to owners of rental properties (so that tenants could return) and to homeowners. Payouts were calculated on the basis of the lower of two numbers: a property's pre-storm market value; or the cost of storm-related damages. However, as Kevin Gotham (2014: 783) shows,

"African–American applicants for Road Home grants received smaller compensation awards and therefore a fraction of the funds needed to rebuild their homes because they were residents in historically segregated neighborhoods with depressed property values." Gotham explains that about 93 percent of the homes owned by African Americans in New Orleans were valued at less than $150,000, by comparison with 55 percent of white-owned homes. African Americans, particularly those whose homes were extensively damaged, were thus significantly more likely than whites to receive compensation that was far lower than what they required to rebuild or make major repairs. Inequities in Road Home Program assistance led to protests and a federal class action lawsuit.

Focusing again on New Orleans, Elizabeth Fussell (2015) summarized what is known about the characteristics of Hurricane Katrina evacuees, returnees, and people who experienced long-term displacement. Those with higher incomes and higher educational levels and access to transportation were able to evacuate before Katrina struck, while those with fewer resources either stayed in their homes to ride out the storm or sought emergency shelter at the last minute. African Americans, lower-income, and younger residents were displaced farther away from the city, which complicated the recovery process for those groups. One year after the storm, flexible resources again determined who was able to return home; early returnees were older, better educated, and better off financially. Renters had difficulty returning to New Orleans for several reasons: rental properties had been vulnerable to damage, owners of rental properties may have been unable to make the needed repairs, and, because the supply of rental housing dwindled, rents increased.

Again illustrating the impact of governmental decisions on disaster outcomes, as noted earlier, the Housing Authority of New Orleans demolished several low-income housing complexes and then opted for replacing them with mixed-income developments, seriously curtailing rental options for the very poor. In 2010, five years after Katrina, the New Orleans neighborhoods that lost the most – if we compare their population levels at the time with pre-storm levels – tended to have larger numbers of minority and low-income residents, renters, individuals who lived in subsidized housing, and individuals who received lower levels of FEMA disaster assistance.

Other Aspects of Vulnerability: Children, Older Adults, and Others

The disaster literature indicates that children, elderly persons, people with disabilities, sexual minorities, and various other groups – for example people whose language ability is limited, immigrants, both legal and undocumented, and incarcerated persons – are in greater danger of suffering a range of negative outcomes when disasters occur. It is important to remember, however, that vulnerability is conceptually defined as a potential for loss. Whether that potential is realized in any given disaster depends on a variety of factors, for example the type of hazard, whether a disaster affects less developed or developed societies, the severity of disaster impacts, the proximity of at-risk populations to high-impact areas, the extent to which societies and communities have implemented disaster risk reduction strategies, and even situational factors such as the time of day when a disaster may strike. As shown throughout this chapter, especially in earlier discussions about intersectionality, variables such as age and physical ability are never the sole determinants of negative disaster impacts and outcomes; they exert their influence in combination with other factors.

Additionally, our knowledge of various forms of social vulnerability is not necessarily cumulative. Studies of the differential effects of disasters have used a range of methodologies – some more sophisticated than others – and have defined impacts in different ways, making it difficult to compare them across disaster events (Bourque, Siegel, Kano, and Wood 2007). Even concepts as seemingly straightforward as "disaster-related deaths" and "affected populations" are measured in a variety of ways (Guha-Sapir and Hoyois 2015), and the same is the case for other types of impacts, such as those that involve mental health. Further complicating matters, even though disaster impacts are greater in less developed societies, most studies focus on disasters in more developed ones. Ideally, there should be large-scale comparative studies that employ identical definitions of the variables of interest and identical state-of-the-art methods across different societies and hazard types, but such studies do not exist at present. Despite such limitations, over time, researchers have been able to develop a better understanding of why different groups are vulnerable, and they have identified patterns and trends in disaster victimization that indicate differential vulnerability. The discussions that follow do not consider all the sources of vulnerability, and even those that are highlighted are not discussed exhaustively. Rather the intention is to provide illustrative examples from different types of disasters and to focus on the reasons why groups such as children and the elderly can be more vulnerable in disasters.

Children and disaster vulnerability

The hazard- and disaster-related experiences of children have not been studied extensively until fairly recently. Early in this century this dearth of understanding led sociologist William Anderson (2005) to call for an increase in the research focus on children. Subsequently sociologist Lori Peek (2008), making the same point, argued that children (defined as young individuals up to the age of eighteen) constitute a significant proportion of those worldwide who are at risk in disasters, and for three main reasons. First, young children are physically vulnerable and dependent on their caregivers for their physical safety. Second, unless they are specifically targeted for help, children are likely to be overlooked by service providers in the aftermath of disasters. But the fact that the needs of the adults in a household are met does not simply guarantee that children's needs will be addressed. Third, disasters have the potential for adversely affecting children's health and psychological and psychosocial development. When disasters strike, children may lose loved ones and friends, experience residential dislocation, or have their schooling and academic progress interrupted. These types of traumas can have lasting effects. At the same time, on the positive side, Peek also pointed out that children can play a constructive role by engaging in disaster risk reduction strategies, both in their households and in their communities.

In another review of research, Weissbecker, Sephton, Martin, and Simpson (2008) echoed these themes, highlighting a number of findings from studies worldwide on the ways in which disasters can affect the psychological and physical well-being of children and adolescents. Disasters can expose children to a variety of stressful life events, such as loss of loved ones, of home, and of educational opportunities, relocation, and changes in family dynamics that result from parental stress. Stress can in turn lead to physiological and neurological changes accompanied by the disruption of sleep patterns, cognitive and memory impairments, and a reduction in immune functioning. Children are at risk of mental health conditions such as post-traumatic stress disorder (PTSD), anxiety, and depression. Because disasters disrupt the social fabric, children's daily routines are altered, but at the same time children need structure; its absence can lead to behavioral and developmental problems and increased feelings of vulnerability. Children and adolescents are also more susceptible than adults to health problems such as flu-like symptoms that are stress-related and can persist over time. Weissbecker and colleagues also pointed to research on factors that can reduce or exacerbate the effects of disasters on children. Problems may be more severe for children who were already experiencing stress and having difficulty coping and for children whose parents exhibit the effects of pre- and post-disaster stress. Moderating factors include children's coping capacities, social support, and a positive overall family environment. Children's post-disaster difficulties tend to be more severe in less developed countries and in countries that do a poor job of mitigating and preparing for disasters.

A more recent review took into account eight decades of research (Peek et al. 2018), noting that almost half of all studies on children and disasters have been published since 2010 and that the focus of such work tends to be on psychological and mental health impacts, just as it used to be in earlier research. Structural–ecological emphases are still lacking in research on children, as are approaches that take intersectionality into account. Additionally, more attention needs to be paid to children's resilience, to their own voices regarding their disaster-related experiences and needs, and to the ways in which children participate in disaster risk reduction activities.

What the literature is able to tell us so far is that children can be vulnerable to disasters in a variety of ways. A survey of deaths caused by disasters among youths found that very young children – those in their first year of life – present a high risk of mortality in extreme events. While statistics indicate that girls in less developed countries are more at risk of dying as a result of disasters, the picture is different in the United States, where male children and adolescents may be more at risk (Peek 2013). Different hazards appear to have differential effects on children; infants are disproportionally affected by extreme heat, while older children are more affected by floods, storms, and extreme cold (Zahran, Peek, and Brody 2008).

By comparison with adults, children can be especially vulnerable to the secondary effects of natural disasters, such as the toxic mold and other environmental pollution that typically accompanies flooding, as well as to technological disasters. For example, in the aftermath of the 2010 BP/ Deepwater Horizon oil spill, researchers from the National Center for Disaster Preparedness (2013) documented a range of health problems in children in heavily affected communities, including bleeding from noses and ears, skin rashes, gastrointestinal problems, and blurred vision. Depending on such factors as disaster severity, pre-disaster mental health state, and the availability of supportive services, children can be at risk of developing various psychological conditions, for example PTSD, in the aftermath of disasters (Norris, Friedman, Watson et al. 2002; Peek 2008).

The Sandy Child and Family Health (S-CAFH) study was conducted between August 2014 and April 2015, with a randomly selected cohort of respondents in nine New Jersey counties that were most seriously affected by Superstorm Sandy in 2012 – those living in areas that experienced storm surge, flooding, and widespread property damage. In that study, 18 percent of parents reported that their children were struggling with anxiety and depression, were having problems sleeping, or were having difficulty getting along with their friends. Difficulties were more pronounced for households that experienced damage, particularly minor damage, and for children from homes whose income fell below $20,000 per year. For the latter, the incidence of reported children's problems rose to 35 percent, which is indicative of the effects of social class on children's capacity to cope. Negative effects were also more pronounced when the parents themselves were fighting mental health problems (National Center for Disaster Preparedness 2015).

Being displaced can be particularly hard for children. Five years after Hurricane Katrina, one study found that "[a] startling 60 percent of children displaced by Katrina either have serious emotional disorders, behavioral issues ... or are experiencing significant housing instability." The same study found that 52 percent of parents believed that their children needed professional help in order to cope with those kinds of problems but were not receiving it for reasons to do with insurance coverage and the shortage of qualified professionals (Children's Health Fund and National Center for Disaster Preparedness 2010: 5). An earlier study had also showed that southern Mississippi and southern Louisiana children from areas affected by Katrina were less likely than unaffected children nationwide to get access to personal healthcare providers. Children who experienced Katrina were also more likely to be Black, to be living in poverty, in single-parent families, and in unsafe neighborhoods, and also to be in fair to poor physical health (Stehling-Ariza, Park, Sury, and Abramson 2012). Here again, it appears that the children who are in the greatest need of health and mental health care after disasters are the ones least likely to receive these services. Box 5.1, on page 106, provides more information on what the children went through in the aftermath of Katrina.

Two of the most devastating disasters in US history occurred in 2017: the hurricanes Harvey and Maria. A study called the Health of Houston Survey was already under way prior to Hurricane Harvey. The hurricane disrupted data collection, but the survey was able to continue six months later, making pre- and post-disaster comparisons possible. The study indicated that children experienced poor health outcomes, which were related to disruption to household life and to home damage, and that immigrants, Hispanics, Asian, and "other race" children and those in the five- to nine-year-old age group experienced the most severe declines (Raker 2022).

After Hurricane Maria in Puerto Rico, a large-scale survey was conducted with public school students in third grade and above. The study revealed severe effects on children and youths across geographic areas and status groups, for example "witnessing one's home and other homes being damaged; having belongings damaged; being forced to evacuate; having a family, friend, or neighbor experience injury or die; or fearing death or injury of self" (Orengo-Aguayo, Stewart, and de Arrelano 2019: 6). Other impacts included experiencing shortages of food and water, having friends and family members leave Puerto Rico, and experiencing neighborhood violence. About 7 percent of respondents exhibited symptoms of PTSD, girls being more likely to experience such symptoms (Orengo-Aguaryo et al. 2019).

Two cautions merit emphasis here. The literature on children and disasters remains unbalanced in several ways. Psychological and psychosocial impacts are emphasized over other considerations, such as educational outcomes, overall adjustment, and post-disaster resilience and growth. As most of the studies discussed above indicate, research has focused on disaster impacts on children in the relatively short term, as opposed to following children and their families over time (Peek et al. 2018).

Second, as intersectional considerations and studies like the one conducted by Fothergill and Peek indicate, simply being young does not predict children's vulnerability to disaster impacts and poor recovery outcomes. Other factors need to be taken into account, if we are to understand which children and youths are most vulnerable. These researchers frame children's disaster vulnerability as involving multiple disadvantages:

> Age alone does not make a child vulnerable to disaster. Instead, age interacts with many other factors that may render children particularly at risk. Moreover, vulnerability factors tend to build over time and cluster together, resulting in what we refer to as cumulative vulnerability ... a racial minority child with a physical disability who lives in an impoverished household in a hazard-prone area will experience multiple, intersecting forms of social, environmental, physical, and economic vulnerability that will shape that child's experiences – and likelihood of survival – in a disaster ... it is not solely age or race or ability status or poverty or hazards exposure, but how these risk factors accumulate in a child's life. (Fothergill and Peek 2015: 23)

Elderly persons and disaster vulnerability

Around the world, nations differ considerably in the demographic makeup of their populations. As a general rule, less developed countries "tilt young," with majorities of their populations often under the age of eighteen. In contrast, developed countries "tilt old." Japan, the world's oldest country, is an extreme example: in 2022, the proportion of those aged sixty-five or older was 29.9 percent, and one in ten were eighty years old or older. In 2015, one in six people in the world was living in more developed countries, but one third of the world population that was sixty-five and older and one half of the world population that was eighty-five and older were living in those countries. These ratios are expected to change over time, as fertility rates continue to decline and life expectancies increase in developed societies (He, Goodkind, and Cowal 2016). What this means is that in the future more and more older adults, including very old ones, will be exposed to natural and technological hazards.

Keeping in mind the role of intersectionality in shaping vulnerability, research does suggest that elderly persons are especially vulnerable to disasters (Tatsuki 2013; Feather 2014; Campbell 2019), but other factors also come into play. For example, a large proportion of older adults have chronic conditions such as high blood pressure, diabetes, and heart disease, which require continual management. If a disaster causes them to stop taking their medication – for example, if their prescriptions go missing as a result of a disaster and they cannot get them refilled – their physical conditions could worsen and become life-threatening. When disasters threaten, older adults may be limited in their ability to undertake self-protective actions. Just over 40 percent of those over sixty-five have functional limitations that may interfere

Box 5.1 The Children of Katrina

Alice Fothergill and Lori Peek (2013, 2015) conducted extensive long-term research on New Orleans children and youths who had been displaced by Katrina in order to understand more clearly how that experience affected their lives. They found that those children spent a great deal of time in a sort of limbo, a "permanent temporariness." Many children moved more than once after the hurricane – for example from home to emergency shelters, then to FEMA-provided trailers, and later back to New Orleans or to new communities. While displaced, many continued to miss their former homes. Those who lived with their mothers in single-parent families had typically had the chance to interact with their fathers on a somewhat regular basis before the hurricane, but those opportunities no longer existed in their new homes. Similarly, they lost contact with grandparents, aunts, uncles, and other members of the extended family, who were either left behind or relocated to other communities. Children who were permanently displaced had to adjust to living in new communities and attending new schools, which was stressful for them, while those who returned to New Orleans were under stress because the city had changed so dramatically as a result of Katrina. They were likely to return to different schools, and in many cases the friendship networks they had before the storm no longer existed. Back in New Orleans, they also feared that another hurricane would strike. However, not all children were equally likely to confront such stressors. On the basis of their research, Fothergill and Peek concluded:

> While all the children in our study experienced some degree of permanent temporariness, children who were marginalized, whose families had fewer resources, who were poor, and who were Black, were likely to experience this state more profoundly. Indeed, children's pre- and post-disaster experiences were clearly shaped by their racial background and class status. (Fothergill and Peek 2013: 138)

with their ability to seek safety. Older persons may be reluctant to evacuate when orders are issued, preferring the security and familiarity of their own homes. They may have a stronger tendency to base their evacuation decisions on previous experiences of disaster events that did not harm them.

To the extent that elders are socially isolated, they may be overlooked during an emergency and not receive the help they need. The vast majority of elderly persons live at home, but they are increasingly living alone, which may cut them off from sources of social support (Klinenberg 2002; Peek 2012). Social networks can become frayed as people get older; support networks may be especially weak for those who have lost a spouse, are childless, are living in poverty, and are disabled.

Being elderly is typically accompanied by sensory impairments such as decline in visual and hearing capacities and a lessening of cognitive abilities. Mayhorn (2005) notes that these kinds of impairments can interfere with the ability of older adults to pay attention to and comprehend warning messages in disaster situations, as well as to respond appropriately to warnings. After disasters, physical and cognitive limitations may make older individuals less likely to access sources of aid, even if such assistance is badly needed. Weaker social networks may mean that seniors never have the opportunity to learn about recovery programs; and, even for those who are aware, bureaucratic barriers may be difficult to overcome (Peek 2013).

Applying fundamental cause theory again, social class and other factors are important in understanding the disaster vulnerability of elderly persons. In the United States, those who are sixty-five and older are better off financially than the youngest members of the population, which potentially offsets some vulnerability factors. For example, in 2015 the poverty rate for the elderly stood at 8.8 percent, which contrasts with a rate of 19.7 percent for children under eighteen. Those aged sixty-five and older constituted 14.9 percent of the population and 6.9 percent of the very poor (i.e. households earning less than 50 percent of the poverty level), while children represented 23.1 percent of the population and 33.6 percent of the very poor. However, poverty rates for elderly persons differed by gender, older women being more likely than older men to be living in poverty (He et al. 2016). As we saw earlier, race and ethnicity matter: in 2014, among those sixty-five and above, 18 percent of Latinx and 19 percent of African Americans were living in poverty, by comparison with 8 percent of non-Hispanic whites (Population Reference Bureau 2015).

Major disasters in the United States and around the world have highlighted the vulnerability of elderly persons. To cite just a few examples, in the 1995 heat wave in Chicago, just under three quarters of those who died were older adults, and social isolation was a significant contributor to their mortality (Klinenberg 2002). In Aceh Province, Indonesia, the hardest hit area in the 2004 Indian Ocean tsunami and the place where the majority of the deaths occurred, women were significantly more likely to be killed, but being elderly and being very young were also significant risk factors (Doocy et al. 2007). Of those who died in Hurricane Katrina in New Orleans, those over sixty made up 75 percent of the total, those over seventy accounting for 40 percent of that total – even though those over sixty made up only about 15 percent of the population (Adams, Kaufman, Van Hattum, and Moody 2011). The 2011 earthquake and tsunami in Japan killed an estimated 20,000 people. In that disaster, the death rate increased with age, people aged sixty-five and older totaling around 58 percent of those killed. Unlike in the Indian Ocean tsunami, mortality was low for children and no significant gender differences were found (see Nakahara and Ichikawa 2013). In the wildfires that struck northern California in October 2017, forty-two people were killed, most of whom were over seventy. The oldest victim was 100 years of age (NBC News 2017). Elderly victims died in their homes, which indicates that they were either unwilling or unable to evacuate, as fires spread rapidly.

Elders who are dependent on assistive devices that rely on electricity can become endangered if a disaster causes a power outage. Some persons who live in high-rise apartments are unable to go to and from their homes without elevators, but elevators become inoperative when power is disrupted. When Superstorm Sandy struck in 2012, many elderly New York residents were stranded in their apartments when the power went out. With so many medical records now in electronic form, access to medical information can be compromised, which could affect disproportionately older persons in need of medical treatment (National Institute of Standards and Technology 2016).

For reasons discussed earlier, vulnerabilities associated with age are perhaps most evident in extreme heat events. The heat wave that struck Europe in the summer of 2003, which began in June and peaked in August of that year, resulted in approximately 77,000 excess deaths – that is, deaths over and above "normal" and expected levels.[2] A study on mortality in the sixteen most affected countries in the Eurozone found that age as well as gender were major risk factors for dying and that, as age increased, so did death rates. For example, in France, which was especially hard-hit, death rates in the over ninety-five age group increased by 46 percent, as compared with the number that would have been expected had the heat wave not occurred (Robine et al. 2007). In a study of heat-related deaths that occurred between 1987 and 2005 in 105 cities, Bobb, Peng, Bell, and Dominici (2014) note that, while the risk of dying from extreme heat declined during that period for all age groups, those over seventy-five were most at risk at the beginning of the study. The authors attribute the decline in overall mortality over the eighteen-year period to improvements in responding to heat-related hazards, such as heat–health warning systems and public health programs targeting elderly persons.

While many research findings point to older age as a risk factor for dying in disasters, it should be emphasized that, as in the case of youths, focusing on being elderly alone is insufficient for understanding disaster-related mortality. Indeed, it has been argued that, on its own, age is not necessarily associated with the overall risk of dying from disasters (Bourque et al. 2006). For example, although in the Great Hanshin-Awaji (Kobe) earthquake of 1995 in Japan older persons were significantly more likely to die, that was because they tended to live on the lower floors of traditional Japanese residential structures, which collapsed and crushed them when the earthquake struck (Bourque et al. 2006; Wood and Bourque 2018).

A key message here is that, like other axes of vulnerability, age exerts its influence when combined with other risk factors. As Wood and Bourque (2018:

373) note, "[a]n important concern for the study of morbidity and mortality associated with disasters is the generally weak methodology of most studies." Research to date has done a poor job of separating individual risk factors such as age from other potentially confounding factors. For example, focusing again on the 2003 European heat wave, Richard Keller studied nearly one hundred deaths that occurred in Paris and found that, while age was a key factor in predicting death, it can also be a proxy for other influences, such as exposure to more extreme heat conditions and social isolation. Elderly persons in Paris with limited means tended to reside in very tiny apartments on the top floors of classic Parisian buildings. Those apartments, known as *chambres de bonne* because in earlier times they housed domestic servants, typically lacked air conditioning and cross-ventilation. Heat rose and built up in those apartments, exposing their occupants to temperatures greatly in excess of those that prevailed in other types of dwellings. Keller also made the point that, while elderly persons were at high risk from dying in the heat wave, so were younger marginalized individuals such as addicts and persons without sources of social support (Keller 2015).

Like Keller, others argue that to gain a full picture of how and why elderly persons are at risk in heat waves, a number of other factors have to be taken into account. The actual amount of heat exposure is one such factor. Extreme heat is not uniform within communities; environmental conditions such as building density, paved-over surfaces, and lack of vegetation can create urban heat islands, exposing some segments of the population to even higher temperatures during heat waves. Sharon Harlan's research on heat-related deaths in Maricopa County, Arizona over a nine-year period identified age as a risk factor, while also singling out other influences on increased mortality such as the combined effects of being elderly and living alone, living in areas exposed to urban heat island effects, for example inner-city neighborhoods and places that lack vegetation, and being vulnerable according to socioeconomic indicators. At the same time, "higher neighborhood income and education, younger white populations, greener landscapes, AC [air conditioning], and cooler microclimates were associated with reduced heat vulnerability" (Harlan, Declet-Barreto, Stefanov, and Petitti 2013: 203). Similarly, a study conducted on heat-related deaths in cities in Michigan found that deaths from cardiovascular disease were associated with living in zip codes where there were larger numbers of people over sixty-five and living alone – but also with being unmarried and living in zip codes with less green space and more homes built before 1960 (Gronlund et al. 2014). However, that same study noted that the literature on heat-related deaths is inconsistent in its findings on these kinds of factors. Here again, as we saw with children and youths, elderly persons who are most at risk are those who experience cumulative vulnerability.

Elderly persons living in congregate care facilities such as nursing homes and rehabilitation centers are highly dependent on those institutions during disasters. While all US nursing homes are required by federal law to have emergency plans, the quality of those planning efforts is uneven (US Department of Health and Human Services n.d.). Nursing home emergency planning tends to focus more on facility-specific emergencies such as fires, as opposed to large-scale community disasters. Disasters create a range of problems for nursing homes, for example damage to or complete destruction of facilities, utility service outages, and the need to evacuate patients at short notice, when many of them may be frail and dependent on life supports. In Hurricane Katrina, seventy nursing home residents died in thirteen different facilities. In Hurricane Rita, which occurred shortly after Katrina, twenty-four nursing home residents died when the bus that was being used to evacuate them caught fire (Belli and Falkenberg 2005).

When Hurricane Irma struck Florida in 2017, the storm resulted in approximately ninety deaths, including deaths caused by falls, drowning, and carbon monoxide poisoning in households where generators were being used. However, fourteen deaths took place in a single nursing home facility in the community of Hollywood, Florida. The storm resulted in a loss of power to the facility's air conditioning system, causing temperatures inside the facility to skyrocket. Residents began showing symptoms of hyperthermia, but despite their own pleas and those of their family members, their problems were not adequately addressed, even though the nursing home was across the street from a hospital that could have provided emergency care (Darrah 2017).

Disabilities and disaster vulnerability

Any discussion of disabled persons in the context of disasters has to begin with an understanding of different models or conceptualizations of disability. In their discussion of disability and disaster, Davis et al. (2013) identify three main conceptual formulations that have been applied to the construct of disability: the medical model, the sociopolitical model, and the functional model. The medical model, which was ascendant until well into the late twentieth century, framed disability as an individual-level characteristic associated with medical conditions, diseases, or traumas that cause individuals to deviate from "normal" expectations regarding their physical and mental capabilities. The medical model conceptualizes disability as "real," in the sense that being disabled is thought to be tied to particular diagnosable diseases and conditions that place limitations on individual functioning.

By contrast, the sociopolitical model, which arose out of the disability rights and independent living movements in the latter part of the twentieth century, emphasizes how societies place limitations on differently abled individuals through socially constructed images of disabilities and through policies that create disabling environments. In this view, disability is both socially constructed and socially produced: constructed, because societies develop stereotyped beliefs about those who are defined as disabled; and produced, because policies related to issues such as physical accessibility, educational and occupational opportunities, and the availability of assistive technologies limit what those marked as disabled can accomplish.

Finally, the functional model of disability, which is also consistent with sociological conceptualizations of disability, focuses on the diversity of populations defined as disabled and on abilities as well as on limitations within those populations. Like the sociopolitical model, the functional model focuses on societal barriers to the inclusion of those labeled as disabled and on overcoming those barriers through appropriate policies and assistive technologies. By focusing on functional limitations as opposed to medical diagnoses, this model also brings to the fore the idea that so-called "normal" people can find themselves more or less disabled at various times in their lives: after having an accident that results in mobility, cognitive, or other challenges, after experiencing a severe illness, in some cases while pregnant, after giving birth or having surgery, when suffering the ravages of famine, or when finding oneself in an unfamiliar environment that presents outsized physical challenges. The acronym TAB – temporarily able-bodied – is commonly used in disability rights communities to express the idea that everyone is at risk for becoming disabled at some point in their lives. Recognizing that any one of us can be disabled at one time or another blurs the distinction between being able-bodied and being disabled.

In discussing the vulnerability of disabled persons to disasters worldwide, Stough and Kelman (2018) argue that such persons can be thought of as constituting a minority population in its own right. They have experienced discrimination, been stigmatized, and even been targets of violence. Members of disabled groups are sometimes considered second-class citizens in their own societies; for example, they may face barriers to employment and education and denial of their human and civil rights. They are frequently stereotyped as incompetent, stupid, and dependent, and their life circumstances are socially constructed as tragic (McDonald, Keys, and Balcazar 2007; Swain and French 2008) – stereotypes that fail to recognize the agency and capabilities of those labeled as disabled. As will be discussed later in this chapter, many of the reasons why people are "disabled" stem from societal policies and practices that place limitations on differently abled groups.

Institutional definitions of disability – that is, the manner in which governments and other institutions quantify and classify disabled persons – can be useful as a way of developing an understanding of the prevalence of disabilities, both in general and in specific population groups. Focusing on the United States, on the basis of 2015 and 2016 census data, Lewis Kraus (2017) provides a picture of the disabled population that includes both general and more specific statistics. The data indicate that an estimated 12.6 percent of the US population are disabled people, but that percentages differ significantly by state, running from a low of 9.9 percent in Utah to a high of 19.4 percent in West Virginia. In ten states, which are mostly located in the southern United States but include Alaska, rates of elderly persons with disabilities reach 40 percent or more. Rates of hearing, vision, and cognitive disabilities, challenges with being ambulatory and with being capable of living independently are positively correlated with age, ranging from less than 1 percent for those under five years of age to 35.4 percent for those who are sixty-five and older.

Disability rates in the United States vary as a function of social class, race, ethnicity, and gender – which shows the importance of taking an intersectional approach to social vulnerability. Those with higher household incomes and higher levels of education are less likely to be disabled. In contrast, almost half of all adults with household incomes under $15,000 are disabled. African American non-Hispanic adults have higher rates of disability than other groups. Women have higher rates of disability than men. Nearly one in four women have one or more disabilities, by comparison with about one in five men (Courtney-Long et al. 2015). Here again, vulnerability is the result of cumulative circumstances, such as being impaired in one or more ways, living in poverty, having lower earnings and less education, and being a member of a racial minority group.

Newer statistics focusing on working-age persons with disabilities indicate that disabled persons have higher rates of unemployment than those who are not disabled; in 2023 their unemployment rate was twice that of their non-disabled counterparts. Those who did have jobs were also more likely to be working part time. Disabled persons have lower educational attainment than those considered able-bodied – an indication of the barriers they encounter in the educational system (US Department of Labor 2023).

It is easy to understand why having a disability can be a risk factor for experiencing more severe disaster impacts and poorer recovery outcomes. Mobility impairments constitute the most common disability in the United States (Courtney-Long et al. 2015), and such impairments can make it more difficult to undertake recommended self-protective actions when disaster strikes. For example, earthquakes occur without warning and, when they strike, the recommended self-protective action is to duck (under a table, for example), cover, and hold on. An individual has only a few seconds in which to take cover once the shaking begins; this puts mobility-impaired persons at a disadvantage. One study that focused on three US hurricanes (Bonnie, Dennis, and Floyd) found that people with mobility, sensory, and other physical impairments were less likely to evacuate and that some disabled persons were not even aware that evacuation orders had been issued (Van Willigen, Edwards, Edwards, and Hessee 2002). As noted earlier, Mayhorn (2005) found that sensory and cognitive limitations associated with aging can make it difficult for people with those disabilities to perceive and interpret warning messages.

As summarized by Stough and Kelman (2018), research suggests that persons with disabilities have been at greater risk of being killed or injured in disasters. However, even though this may well be the case, there is a great deal we do not know when it comes to assessing their vulnerability. Disabilities are many and varied, and within any particular category of disability (e.g. mobility, cognition) impairments can be more or less severe. Some individuals with mild impairments may be able to cope with disasters quite well on their own, while others with the same impairments may be almost totally dependent on others in those situations. Then, just as they can be differentially vulnerable, people can also be differentially resilient, depending on their financial resources and their levels of pre-disaster preparedness, for example. Further, there is almost no research that focuses on disability alone, as a risk factor taken in separation from other factors it is associated with, such as race, class, and gender. This is a shortcoming in disaster research, but it is also a shortcoming in disability studies more generally, where axes of diversity and inequality within disabled populations have been given little attention (McDonald et al. 2007). There simply has not been enough well-designed systematic research for us to state definitively that being disabled, in and of itself, is a contributor to disaster victimization and poor recovery outcomes.

It is also important to keep in mind that, according to the sociopolitical and functional approaches to disability, the extent to which being disabled leads to disproportionate disaster victimization may have less to do with disabilities themselves than with societal responses to the needs of disabled persons, both in normal times and in disasters. In the United States, for example, as a result of the disability rights movement and of laws such as the Americans with Disabilities Act, the everyday needs of those who are disabled have been recognized and, while much remains to be done, accommodations for those needs have been implemented. At the same time, even with such advances, there is also considerable evidence to show that the US disaster response system has been unprepared to address the needs of disabled persons, particularly those with the greatest needs, in disasters.

After Hurricane Katrina and Hurricane Rita, the National Council on Disability (2006) issued a scathing report that documents the difficulties experienced by, and the unjust treatment of, disabled residents in the affected areas. In the immediate emergency period, people with sensory disabilities lacked access to emergency warnings. For example, those with hearing impairments could not comprehend evacuation instructions or information about emergency shelters because no closed captioned or sign language messages accompanied that guidance. The Federal Communications Commission reminded local broadcasters that they would have to comply with laws that required communications accessibility, but compliance was spotty. Similarly, informational websites provided by government agencies did not comply with laws regarding access to information for the visually impaired. People with disabilities experienced difficulties regarding evacuation from their homes and from nursing homes and hospitals because of the lack of transportation and assistance personnel. Those who did manage to get to transportation hubs found that many buses lacked ramps and lifts.

The report stated, further, that the authorities did not seem to be fully aware of the needs of disabled persons in disasters. Mass shelters operated by the Red Cross were not equipped to serve persons with disabilities. Instead, "special needs" shelters were set up; but this often resulted in splitting up families. After the two disasters, information regarding services was not provided in ways that addressed the distinctive needs of people with different disabilities.

Deaths in hospitals and nursing homes tell a similar story of institutional failure. Sheri Fink's (2013) detailed reporting on deaths that occurred among seriously disabled and medically dependent patients in Memorial Hospital in New Orleans reveals that, after Katrina, patients' physical conditions deteriorated rapidly and that, unable to evacuate some patients in the aftermath of the hurricane, medical personnel resorted to "mercy killings," using large doses of major painkillers and tranquillizers. One physician and two nurses were initially accused of second-degree murder, but the grand jury that was subsequently impaneled to investigate the matter declined to indict them. Thirty-five patients died in St. Rita's nursing home in St. Bernard Parish outside New Orleans during Hurricane Katrina. The owners of the nursing home were charged with negligent homicide and cruelty, but were found not guilty of those offenses at trial (Cobb 2013). As we learned earlier from the discussion on Hurricane Irma in 2017, nursing homes continue to be places where patients are largely at the mercy of facility operators and staff, often with tragic consequences when disasters strike. Reports like these reveal the extent to which laws and regulations designed to assist and protect persons with disabilities are often ineffective in disasters. They also point to other ways in which, even in the most prosperous societies, institutions can fail disabled and dependent persons during and after disasters.

Other vulnerable groups

The literature also identifies other groups that can be vulnerable in the context of disasters. The homeless population is one of those groups. Ben Wisner was among the first to note that homeless people in high-risk megacities such as Tokyo and Los Angeles are socially invisible; when people encounter them, "the common reaction is to avert the eyes" (Wisner 1998: 32). Consequently, their needs were not being addressed in disaster preparedness planning. Around that same time, Brenda Phillips (1998) argued that almost nothing was known about how those who are homeless fare in disasters. She went on to describe the experiences of homeless people in Santa Cruz, California after the 1989 Loma Prieta earthquake. As a consequence of research conducted in the past three decades, we now have a better understanding of the disaster vulnerabilities of homeless populations. Some progress is also being made in the development of policies and plans that target the needs of the homeless population in disasters.

Homeless individuals and families are vulnerable to disasters in a number of ways. They live on the margins of society, a situation that can cut them off from information on disaster forecasts, warnings, and disaster assistance. Because homelessness is increasingly being criminalized in cities around the United States, for example through ordinances that forbid sleeping in public or living in a vehicle, homeless persons are further stigmatized and often forced into living in marginal places and spaces, such as areas along riverbeds and in forests, which are exposed to flooding and wildfires (Vickery 2017). Many adults and children who are homeless have experienced traumatic events in the past, which makes them especially vulnerable when disasters strike (Bush 2014). Homeless women have often been victims of domestic and sexual violence, and homeless children are likely to have been present during domestic violence episodes (National Center on Family Homelessness 2014). Homeless veterans may also have experienced or been exposed to traumatic events while in the service. Adults and youths may suffer from alcoholism and substance abuse problems (National Coalition for the Homeless 2017). For reasons like these, homeless individuals and families may lack the capacity or the will to seek out assistance during and after disasters. They may also be discriminated against when seeking assistance during disasters, even emergency shelter (Edgington 2009; Vickery 2017). Like community-based organizations more generally, organizations that provide services to homeless individuals and families, for example shelters and transitional living facilities, often lack the capacity to prepare effectively for disasters; they also tend not to have connections to emergency services agencies in their communities (Gin, Kranke, Saia, and Dobalian 2016; Gin et al. 2017; for other discussions of the disaster vulnerability of community-based organizations, see Ritchie, Tierney, and Gilbert 2010).

US government agencies have made some progress in developing guidance toward assisting homeless individuals and families in disasters. For example, in its guidance for service providers, the US Department of Health and Human Services (n.d.) emphasizes the need for a "trauma-informed approach" in planning and response activities that target members of the homeless population. What is not known is the extent to which resources like these are actually being used in local communities and, if they are, to what effect.

Homelessness results from a number of factors, but principally from a lack of affordable housing. As the affordability crisis becomes more acute, more people are living on the streets, in vehicles, on public transportation, and in remote areas far from services, or are moving around from facility to facility.

In a later section we examine the implications of climate change for this population.

Those who deviate from societal heteronormal expectations can also be at risk in disasters. LGBTQIA+ persons can become targets of discrimination after disasters – and in a variety of ways. One obvious way is that same-sex unions are not recognized in many countries around the world. Until the landmark 2015 Supreme Court decision in *Obergefell v. Hodges*, same-sex unions were not universally recognized in the United States. Worldwide, disaster aid generally targets "households," but what is considered a household can vary. A family consisting of husband, wife, and children is most likely to meet that definition; but what about an unmarried lesbian or gay couple, with or without children, in a country where being gay is criminalized?

Phillips and Jenkins (2013: 324) note that in disasters "lesbians, gay men, and bisexual or transgender individuals are among those whose survival, safety, and well-being may be contingent upon finding safe space and sensitized emergency services." Despite these distinctive needs, researchers note that sexual and gender minorities are consistently overlooked in disaster-related laws and policies (Dominey-Howes, Gorman-Murray, and McKinnon 2014; Gaillard, Gorman-Murray, and Fordham 2017). Like those who are homeless, individuals and groups that depart from the established gender binary are typically stigmatized. LGBTQIA+ persons are routinely discriminated against and can become targets of hate crimes, even of deadly attacks. LGBTQIA+ youths may become homeless as a result of their sexual orientations, which compounds their vulnerability. In the United States, right-wing and conservative religious figures have even blamed gay men and lesbians for *causing* disasters (Blumenfeld 2016).

Although the topic of sexual minorities in disasters is relatively new, there are already examples of the unequal treatment these minorities receive. For example, in Indian society, the Aravani are males who reject male identity and choose to live as women, while seeing themselves as neither male nor female. The marginalization of the Aravani, who are sometimes referred to as the "third sex," was evident in the aftermath of the 2004 Indian Ocean tsunami. A report on gender issues in that disaster noted:

> Pre-tsunami socio-cultural as well as policy-induced discrimination rendered the Aravani population invisible in the relief, rehabilitation, and reconstruction agenda. There were no official records of deaths and losses incurred by this group or the subsequent trauma and neglect they experienced. Their vulnerabilities were further exacerbated by their systemic exclusion from the mainstream gender discourse and thereby from post-disaster planning exercises. (Pincha 2008: 25)

This pattern repeats itself in other societies. Gay men and lesbians are stigmatized in Haiti, and reports concerning their treatment in the aftermath of the catastrophic 2010 Haiti earthquake reveal that in many cases they were denied disaster assistance services and were subjected to rape and other forms of violence. They were also blamed for causing the earthquake and were sometimes attacked on that basis. Organizations serving LGBTQIA+ persons were also destroyed or damaged in the earthquake (International Gay and Lesbian Human Rights Commission n.d.).

Gaillard et al. (2017) document the disaster experiences of gender minorities in the Philippines, Indonesia, and Samoa. The Bakla in the Philippines are biological males who identify as females and assume both male and female roles in the gendered division of labor. In Indonesia, Waria are men who take on a feminine identity and often work in the beauty industry. In Samoa, the Fa'afafine are biological males who dress as women and who, like the Bakla, perform both male and female tasks. Members of these three groups experience marginalization and stigma every single day; they are "discriminated against, mocked, and deprived of access to resources and the means of protection available to men and women" (Gaillard et al. 2017: 440). Many have experienced various forms of exclusion in disaster situations, such as being denied access to emergency shelters and short-term housing and not being able to obtain sufficient food in the aftermath of disasters.

As often happens in US disasters, fundamentalist Christian clergy blamed the gay community for the Hurricane Katrina catastrophe. After the hurricane, members of the LGBTQIA+ community faced various kinds of harassment and discrimination. Some faith-based organizations, including churches, were not interested in providing aid to gay hurricane victims. Obtaining support was especially hard for gay African Americans and persons with HIV/AIDS. Louisiana did not recognize same-sex unions at the time of the hurricane, which rendered gay couples ineligible for some forms of aid (Monroe 2016).

This situation becomes more dire when we consider how the political backlash against advances in LGBTQIA+ rights in the United States might affect the provision of disaster services to members of those groups. FEMA has acknowledged the risks faced by the LGBTQIA+ population owing to factors such as discrimination, stigmatization, and marginalization (Frank 2020). The Center for Disaster Philanthropy (n.d.) also enumerates the ways in which sexual minorities are at a disadvantage in disasters, from agencies' failing to recognize differing family structures to aid-seekers being met with disrespect, harassment, and even violence. Similarly, the US Department of Health and Human Services (2023) points to a number of adverse effects experienced by members of the LGBTQIA+ population in disasters. Discrimination and stigmatization against the LGBTQIA+ community is even harsher outside the United States: countries like Uganda have passed laws that mandate life imprisonment and even the death penalty for relationships involving same-sex couples.

In their review of issues related to language ability and literacy, Santos-Hernández and Morrow (2013) discuss several widely recognized dimensions of literacy. To touch on just a few of them, literacy means being able to read and understand the meaning of texts (prose literacy); understand signs and images (visual literacy); comprehend documents and have the ability to fill out forms (document literacy); and have access to and be able to use digital devices (digital literacy). Just as in everyday life, the ability to prepare for, respond to, and recover from disasters requires these kinds of skills. Difficulties with achieving competence in these different areas can be a source of social vulnerability when people are exposed to hazards and confront disasters.

The Organisation for Economic Co-Operation and Development (OECD) consists of the twenty-two most developed countries. The Survey of Adult Skills, which focuses on different forms of literacy, is conducted every ten years in the nations that are part of the OECD, plus two other nations. The most recent available data are from 2013. Recognizing that what counts as literacy skills has changed in the twenty-first century, the OECD focuses on three types of literacy among adults aged between sixteen and sixty-five: being able to understand, use, and evaluate written texts in the nation's main language – or what we commonly think of as literacy; numeracy, or the ability to access, use, and interpret mathematical and statistical information; and the ability to access and use digital technology in order to acquire information. Comparing OECD countries, the US population scores well below average in all three areas; it is also distinctive in that younger persons in this country (persons aged between sixteen and twenty-four) did not score better than older persons in literacy and numeracy when last surveyed. (Most countries have seen improvements, as younger generations acquire more skills.) The United States has significant numbers of people – perhaps as many as one third of the adult population – who, by OECD criteria, cannot perform problem-solving tasks even at a minimal level (Organisation for Economic Co-Operation and Development 2013). This raises questions about the extent to which ordinary Americans can access and understand a range of disaster-related information, including information on climate change and its impacts, hazards and risks, disaster forecasts and warnings, self-protection guidance, and, when disasters strike, information on available relief and recovery services. For example, many of the forms that are required in order to access government assistance after disasters are web-based, favoring those who can navigate the internet well. After disasters, aid applications can be submitted at physical disaster assistance centers with the help of trained staff, but not everyone can travel to those centers to apply for aid in person.

About 14 percent of the US population is foreign-born, and the literacy rates in this population segment differ from those of native-born Americans. Foreign-born residents make up a high proportion of the population in disaster-prone metropolitan areas such as Miami (37 percent) in Florida and San Jose (36 percent), Los Angeles (34 percent), and San Francisco–Oakland

(29 percent) in California. Overall, immigrants have lower prose, document, and quantitative literacy than their native-born counterparts, as measured by the National Assessment of Adult Literacy. Hispanic adults have the lowest literacy scores, followed by Blacks and Asians; but there are also large intra-racial differences in literacy. Santos-Hernández and Morrow (2013) note that women immigrants have lower levels of literacy than their male counterparts, which raises concerns about the extent to which they are able to access and comprehend information on disaster risks and recommended preparedness measures.

In New York City, an estimated 192 languages other than English are spoken in residents' homes. The totals for Los Angeles and Houston are 185 and 145 respectively. The US government currently provides various forms of disaster-related online guidance in just over one dozen languages, which is not reflective of the country's linguistic diversity. It is unclear how many people are actually accessing this foreign language information and to what effect. What is clear is that those with high levels of English-language literacy are most advantaged with respect to being able to obtain, under-stand, and use disaster-related information of all types. This is yet another example of the "flexible resources" that persons of higher socioeconomic status possess.

Closely related to immigration, citizenship is another factor to consider in understanding social vulnerability. According to the Institute on Statelessness and Inclusion (2014), which notes that data are difficult to obtain in many parts of the world, there were at that time an estimated 10 million people worldwide who were not citizens of any state. This approximate number included refugees, asylum seekers, internally displaced persons, and residents of countries in which, for one reason or another, they lacked the privileges of citizenship. One such group is the Rohingya of Myanmar. The estimated 1 million Rohingya have not been recognized as citizens of Myanmar and have been consistently discriminated against by Burmese institutions. Their communities have been subject to violent attacks, which intensified in 2017, causing nearly one million to flee to neighboring Bangladesh, where they live in squalid conditions in refugee camps, lack access to livelihoods, and are exposed to major disasters like Cyclone Mocha, which struck Bangladesh in 2023 (USA for UNHCR 2023).

Throughout the world, stateless persons are robbed of their human, political, and economic rights, sometimes to the point where they do not even exist for official purposes. Depending on the country, stateless persons may be forced to contend with lack of access to the ballot, education, health care, social services, and employment opportunities; with severe restrictions on travel, both in their country of residence and abroad; and with not having any form of official identification (Institute on Statelessness and Inclusion 2014). Essentially, if citizenship consists of the "right to have rights" (Somers 2008), then those – such as stateless persons – who do not enjoy full citizenship privileges are especially vulnerable, both on an everyday basis and in disasters.

In the United States, non-citizens – both permanent residents (green-card holders) and other immigrants – theoretically have almost the same rights as citizens. Non-citizens face restrictions in areas such as voting and running for office, but otherwise they enjoy roughly the same constitutional protections as citizens. However, with regard to disaster assistance, the situation is different. While the government is required to provide emergency assistance services such as emergency transportation for evacuation and emergency shelter, food, and medical services to non-citizens, the key word here is "emergency." When it comes to other forms of assistance, restrictions do apply. Undocumented immigrants are not eligible for federal programs such as FEMA's Individuals and Households Program, which provides short-term recovery assistance, for example home repairs and rental vouchers for those who are displaced, nor can they apply for Small Business Administration housing or business loans. However, if some member of a household headed by an undocumented immigrant is a US citizen (e.g. a US-born child), then applications for these forms of assistance can be made on that person's behalf (American Red Cross, National Immigration Law Center, and National Council of La Raza 2007). Nongovernmental organizations (NGOs) can also provide assistance regardless of an applicant's immigration status, or can refrain from asking about citizenship entirely.

Even though undocumented immigrants in the United States do have access to some forms of disaster assistance, there is reason to believe that they will avoid seeking such services, especially in the current political climate. As long ago as the Loma Prieta earthquake, which occurred in 1989, Brenda Phillips (1993) noted that immigrants from Mexico and Central America tended to avoid official disaster shelters as a result of the presence of military personnel, because its members were widely feared in their native countries and they were scared of being picked up by immigration authorities. Those same kinds of fears caused immigrants along the Gulf Coast to stay behind when evacuation orders were issued for Hurricane Gustav in 2008 (NBC News 2008). In 2017, when Hurricane Harvey was bearing down on Texas, the state indicated that it would be providing services to all residents regardless of immigration status, but at the federal level the US Customs and Border Control (CBP) was still operating checkpoints that were designed to round up undocumented persons. At the time Harvey struck, Texas had already passed a law permitting police officials to work with CBP and Immigration and Customs Enforcement in apprehending undocumented persons. Although that law had not yet gone into effect at the time of Harvey, its passage had already resulted in increased fear and declining trust in authorities among immigrants.

Writing about immigrants' lack of trust in government and their vulnerability, journalist Dara Lind noted:

Unauthorized immigrants are often wary of seeking government assistance even in the best of circumstances, and their isolation can keep them from finding out important information: Many immigrant residents of Flint, Michigan, for example, found out about the prohibition on drinking the city's lead-contaminated water months after the rest of the city did. High-profile immigration enforcement makes that even harder. (Lind 2017)

In the current political climate, when refugees and asylum seekers around the world are being demonized and when their needs are greater than ever, serious questions remain about the extent to which their disaster-related needs are being met.

Climate change, Covid, and vulnerability

Climate change and its tendency to intensify disaster events such as hurricanes, wildfires, and extreme heat is increasing negative impacts on many vulnerable groups. Providing a comprehensive review of the impacts of climate change on social vulnerability is beyond my scope, but a few examples should suggest future directions for study. Children, particularly those in low-income countries, are vulnerable to conditions that are being exacerbated by climate change: more severe droughts, floods, and heat waves, vector-borne diseases, and food insecurity. Children with preexisting respiratory conditions are vulnerable to climate-driven atmospheric conditions such as increase in the levels of ozone and other pollutants (Bartlett 2008). A recent review outlined a framework for conceptualizing how climate change is affecting children's health and will do so going forward. First, direct effects will be felt as a result of the increasing effects of climate-related events such as heat waves, floods, and wildfires. Next, climate change will result in secondary effects such as ecosystem disruption, air pollution, food insecurity, and forced migration. Taking direct and indirect effects into account, a multiplicity of negative effects will result, ranging from disaster-related deaths to vulnerability to infectious diseases and poor nutrition. The authors conclude:

Through its far reaching impacts on all parts of society, climate change will challenge the very essence of children's rights to survival, good health, wellbeing, education, and nutrition. (Hellden et al. 2021: e164)

Hotter temperatures have a disproportionate impact on elderly persons; extreme temperatures – defined as starting at 95 degrees Fahrenheit (35 degrees Celsius) – make it impossible for bodies to cool themselves through perspiration alone, and the body's temperature regulation system becomes less effective as people age. Older individuals are also increasingly likely to have chronic conditions that are exacerbated by high heat, such as cardiovascular,

respiratory, and renal illnesses and diabetes. Additionally, some of the medica-
tions elders take for their health problems can interfere with the body's
temperature regulation system (US Global Change Research Program 2016).
Because elders rely on assistive and life-support technologies and because
disaster impacts intensify, disruptions of power and water systems will have
greater negative effects on them than on younger members of the population
(National Institute of Standards and Technology 2016).

Adverse effects from increasing heat and heat waves also hit disproportionately those who experience homelessness. For example, as Chapter 1 notes, at
the time of this writing 2023 was the hottest year on record, and the city of
Phoenix Arizona underwent a record heat wave that summer. A report issued
by Maricopa County, where Phoenix is located, indicated that 645 county
residents died in that historic heat wave – a 52 percent increase in deaths
over the previous year. Being over fifty years of age, having a substance abuse
problem, and having preexisting physical and mental health conditions were
factors that contributed to heat-related deaths. However, a glaring statistic
is that 45 percent of those who died were experiencing homelessness at the
time (Maricopa County 2024). Taking into account that the population of the
county was nearly 4.6 million at the time, the proportional toll taken on
members of the homeless population is astounding. At the same time, we
can envision how the other key risk factors identified in the report can be
associated with homelessness – which, again reflects the cumulative nature
of vulnerability.

Incarcerated persons are an understudied population, but what is known is
that carceral institutions place little emphasis on planning for disasters and
that the widespread use of prison labor in disaster response – for example,
in firefighting – exposes prisoners to environmental hazards (Purdum 2019;
Purdum and Meyer 2020). Large numbers of those who are imprisoned are
members of vulnerable populations, with high rates of physical and mental
health problems. Prisoners regularly experience social isolation, physical
vulnerability, and exposure to overcrowding and unsafe conditions such as
poor sanitation and ventilation. At the same time, they lack protection from
disasters owing to facilities' lack of preparedness (Glade et al. 2022). On top
of that, recent research indicates that in the face of climate change many of
the 2 million members of the imprisoned population in the United States lack
access to cooling options during high-temperature periods and that many
states do not require their prison facilities to provide such relief (Toholske
et al. 2024). Thirteen states do not require facility-wide air conditioning; for
example, the state of Texas has no such requirement, even though temperatures in its prisons can soar to 110°F (43.3°C) (Purdum, Dominick, and Dixon
2022).

Despite the carceral state's decades-long punitive turn, a fundamental
principle remains that depriving convicted persons of their liberty should

be the sole punishment for their crimes. That other forms of punishment are inflicted on those who are caught up in the criminal justice system and imprisoned is a major injustice. The fact that those in jails and prisons, where minoritized populations are overrepresented, are disproportionately put in positions of vulnerability to climate change and disasters via the conditions that exist in carceral institutions only compounds that injustice.

In light of what is known from studies of disasters and fields such as medical sociology, it came as no surprise that the negative impacts of the Covid-19 pandemic fell disproportionately on already vulnerable populations. Elderly persons, Blacks, Native Americans, and the Latinx population experienced more adverse impacts from Covid than their younger, white, and better-off counterparts (Magesh et al. 2022). Preexisting conditions were also predictors of poor Covid outcomes; but, as we have seen, such comorbidities are also associated with lower-class and minority status. In the polarized political landscape in the United States, vaccine skepticism and refusal were associated with political views, and there is evidence to suggest that party affiliation was a factor in excess Covid deaths (Wallace, Goldsmith-Pinkham, and Schwartz 2023). However, it also appears that difficulty in obtaining access to the vaccine when it became available was also an issue for some members of the population, such as those who were nonwhite, unmarried, disabled, less educated, and of lower class status (Monte 2021).

A detailed and comprehensive review of Covid health outcomes, both globally and in the United States, indicates that US fatalities were associated with age (being elderly), gender (male), race and ethnicity (being Black or Latinx), and living in a rural place. The authors of the review point to long-standing structural forces and comorbidities as key determinants of Covid outcomes, arguing that "health inequity exists and will even increase unless the political and social determinants of health and healthcare access are addressed" (Cutter and Huang 2022: 14).

Perhaps more than any other catastrophe, Covid revealed the glaring disparities that exist between society's haves and have-nots. While the population of "essential workers" – made up largely of minoritized, lower-wage, hourly, and contingent workers – had no choice but to work through the pandemic in order to put food on the table for themselves and their families, higher-status members of the population were given the opportunity to shelter in place, work from home, and otherwise avoid exposure to the virus. Some "digital nomads," with their secure salaries and financial resources, could even decamp for sunnier climes and other destinations that offered reliable internet connections and other amenities, while their hourly laboring "essential" compatriots and their families had little choice but to expose themselves to the virus.

Around the world, Covid survivors are currently facing the specter of long Covid, a little understood set of pandemic sequalae. To the extent that vulnerable populations were more susceptible to Covid in the first place, we can expect the burdens of long Covid to fall disproportionately on those populations. The contributions of long Covid to short- and longer-term disabilities and who bears their burdens is a topic for future research.

Vulnerability as disposability

Scholarship surrounding the concept of disposability sheds light on the relationship between reigning political–economic structures and processes, vulnerability, and disasters. Scholars of different stripes are increasingly pointing to the ways in which neoliberal capitalism and associated processes such as globalization and growing inequality have produced winners and losers, and also to the ways in which losers are increasingly treated as disposable – that is, as having little or no value, voice, or power. In the current political–economic regime, the needs and rights of disposable individuals and groups need not even be recognized, much less prioritized. These people are instead marginalized, silenced, made invisible, or in some cases eliminated.

In this vein, Zygmunt Bauman (2017) observes that modernity and globalization have created not only human waste but "wasted humans": refugees, asylum seekers, poor members of minoritized and marginalized groups, and others deemed useless and unproductive. Similarly, reflecting on the impacts of Hurricane Katrina on poor people of color, Henry Giroux observes that "the category 'waste' includes no longer material goods but also human beings, particularly those rendered redundant in the global economy" (2007: 308). Saskia Sassen (2014; 2015) argues that "expulsions" are characteristic of the "savage sorting" that occurs in the current global economy, where the expelled include people thrown into precarity as a result of housing and financial crises, workers whose jobs have been lost as a consequence of globalization, international migrants, people confined to refugee camps, and incarcerated persons.

As Dipali Mathur (2022) puts it bluntly in her research on toxic hazards in India, this means that entire populations are "available to be poisoned," as exposure becomes a normal, accepted, unquestioned form of life:

> The exposure to toxic harm and its debilitating consequences is disproportionately borne by the bodies and the environments of those least equipped to defend themselves against such harms, for instance among the most dispossessed in developing countries … Toxicity under the conditions of ruthlessly extractive capitalism, has been weaponized to "make killable" already disadvantaged populations living on the margins of society. (Mathur 2022: 8–9)

Viewing those vulnerable to hazards through the lens of disposability reveals what Native Americans exposed to the hazards of uranium mining, residents of Cancer Alley, people who live near other kinds of toxic sites, stateless persons, poor Blacks, homeless persons, prisoners, and others discussed here have in common: their lives simply have less value than the lives of those who enjoy the benefits of current political–economic arrangements. Connecting vulnerability with disposability and expulsion reflects realities that have been discussed in this chapter and elsewhere, especially in Chapter 3. Both are consequences of broader processes such as colonialism, coloniality, unequal ecological exchange, widespread social and economic inequality, systemic racism, climate change, and the disaster events it is continually intensifying.

Measuring Vulnerability

Systematic efforts to measure vulnerability began early in the twenty-first century. Just as there is no agreed-upon definition of vulnerability, there is no general consensus as to which set of indicators captures best its various dimensions – social vulnerability included. Vulnerability and its measurement are central to conceptual frameworks that focus on society–environment relations, for example sustainable development, sustainable livelihoods, global environmental change, and hazards and risk (Birkmann 2006; Kok, Narain, Wonink, and Jager 2006; Patt, Schroter et al. 2010). These frameworks have a good deal in common, but they also differ, for example in the processes on which they focus and in the indicators they employ to measure vulnerability. It will not be possible here to review all these different approaches. The focus in this section will be instead on those measurement frameworks that deal most directly with hazards and disasters and, even then, only on the most widely used ones. Readers will notice that the frameworks briefly reviewed below differ in scale as well as in the aspects of vulnerability they address.

The Disaster Deficit Index (DDI) is one in a suite of indicator frameworks that were developed under the auspices of the Inter-American Development Bank to assess vulnerability at the country level for Latin American and Caribbean countries. Its main focus is on economic and financial vulnerability as well as on countries' capacity to obtain resources that may offset disaster losses. The DDI models the degree to which major natural disasters would adversely affect countries' national treasuries and cause the countries to go into debt, or even to experience economic collapse. A related set of measures, the Local Disaster Index (LDI), focuses on less serious but recurrent disasters that could affect those same countries. Data on potential deaths, numbers of people affected, and economic losses are measured at the municipal level and then aggregated at the country level. The logic behind the LDI is that, in addition to major disasters, frequent low-level events can negatively affect countries' development trajectories. The Prevalent Vulnerability Index (PVI), a national-level index, comprises three sets of indicators and indices, which center on populations and economic activities exposed to hazards, on social and economic vulnerability, and on coping capacity. As an example, Nicaragua, the Dominican Republic, El Salvador, and Honduras have high levels of vulnerability, judging from these three indices (see Cardona 2011; also Cardona 2010 for more in-depth discussions of the indices themselves).

The Global Natural Disaster Risk Hotspots project, which was led by Columbia University and the World Bank, focuses on two types of vulnerability at the country level: the risk of disaster-related deaths and the risk of economic losses, each one calculated as a function of the population exposed and gross domestic product (GDP). Six natural hazards are considered: earthquakes, volcanoes, landslides, floods, droughts, and cyclones. The goal of the project was to identify "hotspots," that is, countries and regions with the highest vulnerability to those six hazards. Levels of vulnerability were calculated on the basis of historical data on deaths and economic losses. For the purposes of this project, countries were divided into seven geographic regions and four classes of national wealth: high, upper-middle, lower-middle, and low wealth. According to the measures used in this project, mortality risks are significantly higher in countries with lower levels of wealth, many of which are exposed to multiple natural hazards. Examples of these high-risk countries are Bangladesh, Nepal, El Salvador, the Philippines, Costa Rica, Burundi, and Haiti (Dilley et al. 2005).

The Social Vulnerability Index (SoVI), which was developed initially for US counties at the Hazards and Vulnerability Research Institute (now the Hazards and Resilience Research Institute) at the University of South Carolina (Cutter, Boruff, and Shirley 2003), provides more fine-grained information on vulnerability than the country- and regional-level measures that were just discussed.[3] Based largely on data collected as part of the US Census, the SoVI provides measures of vulnerability at the county level; SoVI data can be further disaggregated to focus on smaller geographic areas within counties. When SoVI was originally developed at the start of this century, researchers identified variables that were considered important in influencing social vulnerability on the basis of findings in the disaster research literature. The index was developed to include forty-two variables; most of these are indicators of population diversity, but they also take into account measures of economic viability and characteristics of the built environment. Using factor analysis, these forty-two variables were reduced to eleven factors that explain differences in vulnerability nationwide. Those factors are personal wealth, proportions of children and elderly persons in the population, race, ethnicity, density of built-environment elements such as housing units and manufacturing and commercial establishments, dependence on one versus multiple economic sectors, quality of the housing stock and percentage of home ownership, occupational makeup of the population, and a measure that takes into account a county's debt level and the percentage of the population employed in infrastructure services such as transportation and public utilities.

The 2010–2014 version of SoVI used twenty-nine indicators that make up eight different components of social vulnerability: wealth, race and social status, elderly residents, Hispanic ethnicity and residents without health insurance, special needs individuals, service industry employment, Native American populations, and gender. Additionally, in 2019 SoVI underwent an update in which seven multivariable factors were singled out as explaining nearly three fourths of the variance in vulnerability: lacking wealth, being Black, Latinx, or Native American, being elderly, having a disability, and being employed in the service sector.

As an assessment tool, SoVI has several advantages. The data on which the index is based are available for the entire United States, making it possible to compare counties and communities. Because SoVI uses census data, expenses for costly data collection are largely avoided. Because it takes into account multiple variables, the index enables researchers and decision makers to understand which variables are most important in influencing social vulnerability in different community contexts, which can in turn help with identifying groups that can be targeted in vulnerability reduction efforts. Because SoVI is based on geographic information systems (GISs), maps can be developed to educate the public and decision makers about the risks their communities face. The index has also proved to be adaptable for use in other societies and communities, for instance in regions and states in Brazil (de Loyola Hummell, Cutter, and Emrich 2016) and in the Lisbon metropolitan area in Portugal (Guillard-Gonçalves, Cutter, Emrich, and Zêzere 2015). (For a review of SoVI's history and applications, see Cutter 2024).

In addition to SoVI, the HVRI developed and regularly updates the Spatial Hazard Event and Loss Database for the United States (SHELDUS). SHELDUS compiles data on fatalities, injuries, and economic losses caused by a wide range of disaster types over the period 1960–2022. With the help of SHELDUS 22, disaster losses can be aggregated and mapped at the county, state, or regional level, as well as by year.

The SoVI analytic approach now forms the basis for important US decision support and public education tools. A logic similar to the SoVI approach underpins the Social Vulnerability Index, which was developed by the US Centers for Disease Control and Prevention, as well as the FEMA's National Risk Index for Natural Hazards. The National Risk Index, which was developed on the basis of HVRI vulnerability research and inputs from subject matter experts from government agencies, private firms, and universities, includes an online tool that makes it possible to assess vulnerability and resilience at US county and even census tract levels (see Figure 5.1). The Risk Index, which includes data on eighteen hazards the nation faces, is made up of three multivariable elements: expected annual losses, social vulnerability, and community resilience (see US Department of Homeland Security, FEMA: https://hazards.fema.gov/nri/determining-risk).

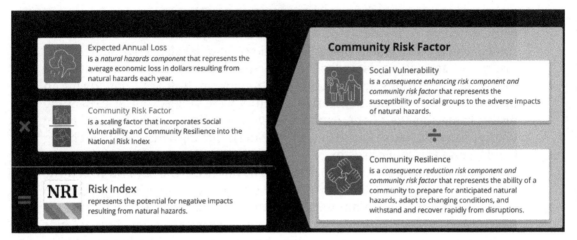

Figure 5.1 Elements of the US National Risk Index
Source: US Department of Homeland Security, Federal Emergency Management Agency.

Concluding Comments

This chapter has focused on three dimensions of vulnerability: hazardousness of place, built-environment vulnerability, and social vulnerability, which has received the strongest emphasis. We learned that social class is perhaps the most important determinant of social vulnerability to disasters, but also that, even within the social class hierarchy, race, ethnicity, and gender are significant predictors of vulnerability. In the United States, being well-off from the standpoint of income and wealth and also being white and male confer advantages; in contrast, a lower position in the social class hierarchy, coupled with being a member of a racial or ethnic minority group and being female, translates into disadvantage, both in normal times and in disasters. Other dimensions of social vulnerability that were explored in this chapter are being young, being elderly, having a disability, being homeless, belonging to a gender minority, being of limited language ability and literacy, having less than full citizenship status, and being incarcerated. A thread running throughout the chapter is that states themselves can set into motion processes that privilege particular groups at the expense of others – for example by institutionalizing exclusionary and vulnerability-producing practices, or by withholding full citizenship rights and access to services. I have also looked (although in a limited way) at efforts to measure vulnerability at different scales.

Throughout the discussion of the factors that produce social vulnerability, four points have been emphasized. One is that an intersectional approach is essential for understanding vulnerability – that is, a perspective that takes into account the influence of multiple axes of inequality, which combine to make individuals and groups more or less vulnerable. A second and related point is that vulnerability should be thought of as cumulative – the result of a range of social forces that, taken together, shape the fates of individuals and groups on an everyday basis, but also when they confront disasters.

A third point is that, while research is strong with respect to some predictors of vulnerability such as race, class, and gender, it can be difficult to reach conclusions regarding other factors because the empirical record is less definitive at this time. What is needed is more multivariate comparative studies on disaster vulnerability that are well designed, systematically conducted, and capable of teasing out the relative contributions of the various factors that can influence social vulnerability.

Fourth, as indicated at several points in this chapter, focusing on factors that contribute to disaster vulnerability only tells a part of the story. Just as individuals and groups can be differentially vulnerable, they can also be differentially resilient. Social deficits produced by forces such as class, race, and ethnicity can be offset by other factors, such as social support, disaster preparedness, and post-disaster learning. Those whose social positions and capabilities could render them vulnerable also have the capacity to overcome those disadvantages in a variety of ways. Structural forces act on individuals and groups, but agency can modify those forces. It is the combination of structural advantage–disadvantage and resilience that shapes disaster impacts and outcomes. To complete this picture, I turn in the next chapter to the topic of disaster resilience.

QUESTIONS AND EXERCISES

Turkey is mentioned in this chapter as an example of the "hazardousness of place," but other factors account for its massive earthquake losses. Focusing on two earthquakes, the 1999 Izmut earthquake and the 2023 Turkey–Syria earthquake, discuss, on the basis of what you have learned so far, why they were so damaging and deadly.

Go online and gather information on how the National Risk Index characterizes disaster vulnerability in your home town or where you live now.

The US experienced the highest Covid-19 death tolls among the G-7 nations – that is, among the most developed and wealthy countries. Why?

6

Disaster Resilience
Concepts, Measures, and Critiques

Introduction

In disaster research and risk reduction policy and practice, it is difficult to find a concept that has achieved as much influence as the notion of disaster resilience. The concept has an interesting history. Decades ago, the idea of resilience began to be employed in the study of complex adaptive systems such as ecological ones, as well as in psychology, where it was advanced to explain why some children and youths who were exposed to stressful situations were able to cope despite those stressors, while others were not (Rutter 1987). With the contributions of scholars such as Holling (1973), Adger (2000), Folke et al. (2002), and others, frameworks used in the study of ecological systems began to be applied to social systems – although, as we will see later, there are problems with that parallelism. Economists have also focused on resilience as a way of understanding how individual firms and regional and national economies recover from external shocks such as hikes in the price of energy (Dhawan and Jeske 2006) and production losses (Park, Cho, and Rose 2011). The concept is also prominent in work on environmental and development economics (Perrings 1998; 2006). Like vulnerability, resilience increasingly emerged as a theme in development studies and in research on global environmental change, including climate change (Gallopín 2006; Janssen and Ostrom 2006; Pelling 2011; Denton et al. 2014).

With respect to disaster studies, resilience was discussed in the summary volume of the Second Assessment of Research on Natural Hazards (Mileti 1999) and began to rise to prominence a few years later. An article on earthquake resilience (Bruneau et al. 2003) is an early example of this trend, as are other works published around that time (see Pelling 2003). There has been an avalanche of books since then (e.g. Comfort, Boin, and Demchak 2010; Shaw and Sharma 2011; Miller and Rivera 2011; Kapucu, Hawkins, and Rivera 2013; Ross 2014; Masterson et al. 2014; McEntire 2022), and also hundreds of articles on various aspects of societal resilience in the face of hazards and disasters.

Resilience has become increasingly dominant in disaster risk reduction discourse and policies. Somewhat arbitrarily, we can associate the beginning of this shift toward resilience in the policy arena with two events: the publication of a US federal government document entitled Grand Challenges for Disaster Reduction (Subcommittee on Disaster Reduction 2005), which emphasized the need for measuring and improving disaster resilience; and the United Nations International Strategy for Disaster Reduction's (2007) Hyogo Framework for Action, which was released after a major disaster-related conference in Kobe, Japan in 2005 that marked the tenth anniversary of the Great Hanshin-Awaji (Kobe) earthquake. Within the nongovernmental sector, the US National Academies of Sciences, Engineering, and Medicine also engaged in a number of activities that focused on community and societal resilience, as evidenced, for example, in a report on public–private partnerships as vehicles for enhancing community resilience (National Research Council 2011). The Academies report entitled *Disaster Resilience: A National Imperative* (National Research Council 2012) pressed for action on resilience conceptualization, measurement, and initiatives.

A variety of other efforts signaled a growing concern with disaster resilience. The World Bank made resilience in the face of disasters and climate change a key priority in its programs targeting developing countries (World Bank Group 2013). The Asia-Pacific Economic Cooperation forum (APEC) also emphasized disaster resilience as a major concern (Asia-Pacific Economic Cooperation 2015). In the United Kingdom, the influential Department for International Development (DFID) made enhancing disaster resilience a core approach in its strategy for providing aid to less developed countries (Department for International Development 2011). In 2013 the Rockefeller Foundation launched its 100 Resilient Cities program, which aimed at making communities worldwide more resilient in the face of both acute shocks such as disasters and chronic stressors. Later it teamed up with the US Department of Housing and Urban Development (HUD) on a national competition for enhancing community resilience in the United States.

Australia has adopted resilience as a guiding principle in its own humanitarian efforts. New Zealand, which suffered a series of damaging earthquakes in 2010 and 2011, developed a national resilience strategy, and many nongovernmental organizations (NGOs) have also been formed in that nation under the resilience rubric. The European Commission prioritized resilience in its provision of development and humanitarian assistance, and the United Nations International Strategy for Disaster Reduction (UNISDR) Hyogo Framework, which ended in 2015, was superseded by the Sendai Framework for Disaster Risk Reduction 2015–2030, which made risk reduction and resilience (taken together) one of its four major priorities.

More recently the US government has made a historic commitment to promoting both climate and disaster resilience. This began in 2021, with Executive Order 14008, which focused on addressing the crisis of climate change. With substantial funding from the Bipartisan Infrastructure Law, the

Inflation Reduction Act (2022), and other sources, the federal government embarked on the largest ever set of programs to respond to climate change and associated extreme events. Priorities are laid out in the National Climate Resilience Framework (White House 2023), which focuses on mobilizing federal and other resources to ameliorate the impacts of climate change and disasters. The Framework articulates the following high-level goals for the national resilience effort:

- Embed climate resilience into planning and management.
- Increase resilience of the built environment to both acute climate shocks and chronic stressors.
- Mobilize capital, investment, and innovation to advance climate resilience at scale.
- Equip communities with the information and resources needed to assess their climate risks and develop the climate resilience solutions most appropriate for them.
- Protect and sustainably manage lands and waters to enhance resilience while providing numerous other benefits.
- Help communities become not only more resilient but also more safe, healthy, equitable, and economically strong.

Other federal vulnerability and resilience executive actions include Executive Order 14096, which focuses on environmental justice, and Justice 40, which requires the channeling of select hazard-related federal investments to communities defined as disadvantaged. These efforts were accompanied by the development of the Climate and Environmental Justice Screening Tool, which can be viewed as a measure of both community vulnerability and community resilience.

In this chapter we will explore the meaning of the concept of resilience, look at approaches to measuring resilience, and investigate the applicability of the concept to the study of disaster response and recovery. We will also consider criticisms of the concept and conditions that place limits on resilience capacities. As we did with vulnerability in the previous chapter, we will focus on issues that are relevant to a social–scientific understanding of disaster resilience.

What Is Disaster Resilience?

Conceptualizations and definitions

As is so often the case in academic and policy circles, there is no universally agreed-upon definition of resilience. In a broad overview of the use of the term in various fields, Plodinec (2009) identified no fewer than forty-six different definitions of the concept. Community psychologist Fran Norris and her colleagues (Norris et al. 2008), who focused more on the societal aspects of resilience, listed twenty-one different framings of the concept. Here I offer a few commonly used definitions that provide a sense of how resilience is used in the social science disaster literature. Bruneau et al. (2003: 735) defined earthquake resilience as "the ability of social units (e.g. organizations, communities), to mitigate hazards, contain the effects of disasters when they occur, and carry out recovery activities in ways that minimize social disruption and mitigate the effects of future earthquakes." Similarly, Cutter et al. (2008: 600) define disaster resilience as "the ability to survive and cope with a disaster with minimal impact and damage ... [along with] the capacity to reduce or avoid losses, contain the effects of disasters, and recover with minimal social disruption."

In a thoughtful review of the social and psychological literature, Norris et al. (2008) refer to the concept of resilience as a metaphor borrowed from fields outside the social sciences and as a theory focused on adaptation after shock and trauma, as a set of capacities, and as a strategy for reducing disaster losses. According to their definition, resilience is "a process linking a set of adaptive capacities to a positive trajectory of functioning and adaptation after a disturbance" (2008: 130–131).

The 2012 National Academies report defined disaster resilience as "the ability to prepare and plan for, absorb, recover from and more successfully adapt to adverse events" (National Research Council 2012: 2). A comparable World Bank publication defined resilience as "the ability of a system, community, or society exposed to hazards to resist, absorb, accommodate, and recover from the effects of a hazard promptly and efficiently by preserving and restoring essential functions" (Jha, Miner, and Stanton-Geddes 2013: 10).

The current definition of disaster resilience adopted by the UNISDR frames resilience in an almost identical way:

> In the context of disaster risk, the ability of a system, community, or society exposed to hazards to resist, absorb, accommodate, adapt to, transform and recover from the effects of a hazard in a timely and efficient manner, including the preservation and restoration of its essential basic structures and functions through risk management. (United Nations International Strategy for Disaster Reduction 2017)

These definitions convey two ideas that most researchers and practitioners would agree are central to discussions of resilience. The first is that resilience involves resistance or absorptive capacity; a resilient person, household, organization, community, or built-environment system is one that can experience a major stressor or shock and still function reasonably well, even if part of its functioning has been reduced. Second, resilience involves the ability to cope and adapt when disasters strike and to move on to recover. Put another way, depending on the size and severity of a disaster, some or even many resistance measures may fail in a disaster, but adaptive strategies can help overcome those failures.

The resistive and absorptive aspects of resilience, sometimes referred to as inherent resilience, encompass several types of activities that were previously identified in the literature as "disaster mitigation," or measures that can be taken to reduce the likelihood that a hazard would produce impacts such as death, injury, damage, disruption, and economic loss. As we've seen earlier, the best way of minimizing disaster impacts is to avoid dangerous locations in the first place by ensuring that people and structures are not situated in places where they are exposed to hazards – for example in hazardous coastal zones, floodplains, sites adjacent to active earthquake faults, and places at the wildland–urban interface that present a high risk of wildfires. This is the purpose of hazard-related land use and zoning regulations; but, as we have seen from earlier discussions, in many parts of the world such regulations are lacking or are not enforced: where they do exist political and economic actors frequently work to circumvent them. There is also the problem that certain hazards may not have been well understood when human settlements were first established, and this left a legacy of hazard exposure. At the same time, as noted at various points in this volume, the ongoing tendency to develop land even when hazards are recognized is a key contributor to burgeoning disaster losses.

If hazards cannot be avoided entirely, a second line of defense is to ensure that the built environment can resist the forces unleashed by disasters. As more is learned about how elements in the built environment can fail in disasters, this knowledge serves as guidance for improving disaster resistance – for example, through measures such as building codes that encourage or require hazard-resistant design and building practices and through programs that retrofit older structures to make them safer. Around the United States, many communities have steadily improved their requirements for building and infrastructure safety – but many others, typically facing opposition from political and economic interests, have resisted making such changes.

Two earthquakes illustrate the significance of the resistance element in resilience. On January 12, 2010, a magnitude 7.0 earthquake struck Haiti, causing widespread devastation in the capital of Port-au-Prince and surrounding areas and killing upwards of 200,000 people. Just a few weeks later, on February 27, a massive 8.8 earthquake struck off the coast of Chile, causing intense ground shaking and a tsunami. Although the effects were very severe everywhere, including in Chile's capital, Santiago (which had a population of just over 6 million), estimates suggested that just over 500 people died as a result of the earthquake. A key factor that contributed to mortality in Haiti was the lack of earthquake resistance in the built environment; large numbers of people died because they were crushed by collapsing buildings. In Chile, a nation that has a long history of violent earthquakes, the story was different. Many structures survived because they were designed and constructed to resist earthquake forces. Keeping in mind earlier discussions about vulnerability, the quality of the built environment in the two countries was in large measure a reflection of their relative prosperity: Haiti, an island nation and the poorest in the western hemisphere; Chile, still a poor country, but well-off enough to be able to invest in higher levels of earthquake safety.

When strategies to resist disaster impacts fail, those affected by disasters must cope and recover. The activities associated with this aspect of resilience, which were formerly termed "preparedness," "response," and "recovery," enable individuals, households, organizations, and communities to enact coping strategies. Disasters can disrupt a range of critical community activities such as economic functioning, livelihoods, schooling, public health and welfare, transportation and other critical infrastructure systems, and housing. The adaptive dimension of resilience seeks to provide temporary and longer-term fixes that address these disruptions. As Paton and Johnston (2006) note, this set of adaptive processes involves not merely a return to the *status quo ante*. Rather adaptation always brings about change of some kind, and successful adaptation should lead to improved resistance and adaptive strategies. In this sense, adaptation after disasters can be seen as "bouncing forward" instead of merely "bouncing back."

Keeping these two aspects of resilience in mind, many discussions of the concept represent resilience graphically, in terms of degree of degradation of key community and societal functions and length of the time required to restore those functions. Following Bruneau et al. (2003) and taking the community and its various systems (e.g. transportation, lifelines, educational institutions, economic activities, healthcare systems) as units of analysis, the graph in Figure 6.1 represents a fictitious community in which effective resistance measures are in place and coping and adaptive strategies are working well enough for the community to overcome disaster-induced disruption and

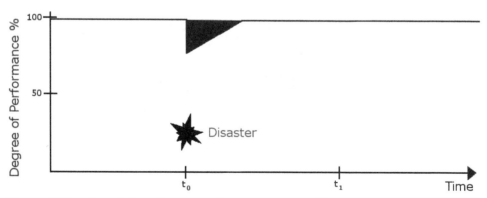

Figure 6.1 Less degradation of system performance, more resilience
Source: Bruneau et al. 2003.

losses. The triangular dark area represents the extent to which systems are not resilient, but in this case the "resilience triangle" is small. In the graph in Figure 6.2, resistance strategies are weaker. This situation leads to a significant loss of system performance, while coping measures are not enacted in a timely way or are insufficient to address disaster impacts and losses. In this case, as indicated by the size of the dark resilience triangle, there is less resilience. The goal of resilience-enhancing measures is to make that loss of performance – that triangle – as small as possible.

It is easy to assume that resilience is the opposite of vulnerability – in other words, that the most socially vulnerable individuals and groups are the ones that have the greatest difficulty being resilient in the face of disasters. While the two concepts are clearly related, resilience is not the obverse of vulnerability. Vulnerability is indicative of the potential for experiencing disaster losses; but, as we will see later, members of vulnerable groups can be resilient as a consequence of factors such as social support and social capital.

Resilience domains

The resilience literature and the guidance on becoming resilient point to various aspects of community life that can become the focus of resilience-building strategies. Bruneau et al. (2003) emphasize four resilience domains: technical, organizational, social, and economic. Paton and Johnston (2006) identify six elements of community resilience: knowledge of hazards, shared community values, established social infrastructure, positive social and economic trends, partnerships, and resources and skills. Renschler et al. (2010) identified seven dimensions of community resilience: population and demographics, environmental and ecosystem, organized governmental services, physical infrastructure, lifestyle and community competence, economic development, and social and cultural capital. Susan Cutter and her collaborators view

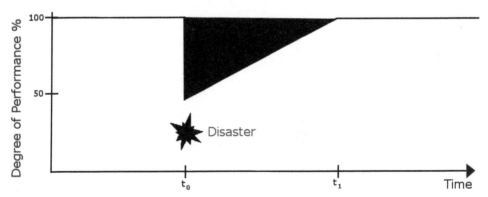

Figure 6.2 Greater degradation of system performance, less resilience.
Source: Bruneau et al. 2003.

resilience as having six dimensions: ecological, social, economic, institutional, infrastructural, and community competence-related (Cutter et al. 2008). A recent review of resilience measurement frameworks identified six domains: economic, social, health (this one includes healthcare facilities), physical (built environment and infrastructure), governance, and the environment (Hisham, Patherage, and Fernando 2021).

As we saw in Chapter 5 regarding vulnerability, built-environment characteristics need to be taken into account in assessing vulnerability. The same is the case with resilience, as indicated by how frequently elements in the built environment are mentioned when efforts are made to identify key dimensions of resilience such as those just discussed. However, for our purposes we will home in on more societally relevant aspects of resilience. In particular, our focus will be on social capital, because it is closely related to other forms of capital such as economic, political, and cultural and because it is the concept that has received the greatest emphasis in the social science disaster literature.

Approaches that are most relevant to the sociological analysis of resilience tend to emphasize the role of different forms of social and community capital in shaping this capacity. Following Bourdieu's (1986) original formulation, capital of this kind is the accumulation, transmission, and reproduction of wealth and monetary value (economic capital) – which is the basis for the other forms of capital, for credentials such as academic qualifications and other symbols of status (cultural capital), and for network-based resources gained through connections with others (social capital).

Social capital is fundamentally about social networks and connections. Bourdieu defined social capital as "the aggregate of the actual or potential resources which are linked to possession of a durable network of more or less institutionalized relationships of mutual acquaintance or recognition" (Bourdieu 1986: 248). Robert Putnam, an influential pioneer in social capital research, defines it as "features of social organization such as networks, norms, and social trust that facilitate coordination and cooperation for mutual benefit" (Putnam 1995: 67). Other definitions of the term are similar: "the ability of actors to secure benefits by virtue of membership in social networks or other social structures" (Portes 1998: 6); "friends, colleagues, and more general contacts through whom you receive opportunities to use your financial and human capital" (Burt 1992: 9); and "resources embedded in a social structure which are accessed and/or mobilized in purposive actions" (Lin 1999: 35).

Social capital gives rise to norms, obligations, and a sense of trust among the members of a network and provides channels through which information can flow (Coleman 1988). Belonging to a network entails the expectation of reciprocity: someone does a favor for another individual in her friendship network that the other person will repay at a later point, on account of feelings of obligation. Social embeddedness and a sense of belonging are characteristics of social capital, as are civic mindedness and civic engagement. As Putnam's definition indicates, being connected enables network members to engage in collective action to realize their goals – for example, to achieve political or economic objectives.

Scholars generally recognize three forms of social capital that confer different types of benefits. Bonding social capital refers to the relationships that exist within a particular group, such as a local group working on issues of homelessness. Bridging capital consists of linkages that exist between two or more groups of different types, for instance groups composed of people with different ethnic backgrounds, or entities that were formed for different purposes. In effect, bridging capital widens the network of participants who work toward a common objective, making more resources available. Using the same example, bridging capital exists if a number of community groups that work on different aspects of the homeless issue (housing, mental and physical health, legal rights) agreed to join forces and to form a coalition to press for more services for those who are unhoused. Linking capital involves relationships between groups and centers of power and influence, such as governmental entities. For example, to bring about that linkage, the coalition concerned with addressing the needs of the homeless population might get one of its members elected to the city council, establish connections with state or national policymakers, or obtain a large grant from a major foundation.

Without bonding social capital, individuals are isolated and lack access to the kinds of resources – for example financial, informational, and emotional support – that members of cohesive groups enjoy. Without bridging capital, a group's resources may be too limited to address members' needs, or some group members may feel overburdened when asked to provide support. Without linking capital, groups lack connections to more powerful entities that would be in a position to increase their resources in relation to other groups. Where all three forms of capital are present, network members have the best chance of getting access to resources and achieving their goals (for extended discussions of these forms of social capital in disaster contexts see Aldrich 2019).

Different approaches to conceptualizing social capital have yielded a variety of empirical indicators of the concept. Typical ways of identifying social capital take into account measures of political participation (voting), volunteering, density of and individual or household involvement in community NGOs, embeddedness in social networks, social support, community attachment (e.g. length of residence in a community, home ownership), frequency of participation in social activities, and feelings of trust and belonging. By contrast, low political and community participation, social isolation and marginality, transience, lack of community engagement, and sparse or weak NGOs are associated with low levels of social capital.

The influence of scholarship on social capital can be seen in efforts to identify the elements of disaster resilience and link them to disaster-related processes and outcomes. Yuko Nakagawa and Rajib Shaw (2004) were among the first to argue that social capital is a key element in resilience. In their research, which involved recovery from the 1995 Great Hanshin-Awaji (Kobe) earthquake and the 2001 Gujarat earthquake in India, they demonstrated a relationship between bonding, bridging, and linking social capital at one end and participation in, and satisfaction with, response and recovery efforts at the other.

Russell Dynes (2006) also linked social capital with disaster resilience, arguing that effective disaster responses both build upon and contribute to the development of social capital. He noted that emergent groups and emergent multiorganizational networks (EMONs) can be thought of as new forms of social capital that come about in order to address disaster-related challenges (see later discussions on resilient disaster responses). Social capital is also associated with the development of norms – in this case, the altruistic norms that have added force in disaster situations, leading to extensive helping behavior. These points are echoed by Rebecca Solnit, whose book *A Paradise Built in Hell: The Extraordinary Communities That Arise in Disaster* (Solnit 2009) details how disasters are accompanied by strong feelings of community solidarity and a variety of forms of prosocial collective action.

For Norris et al. (2008), the key components of disaster resilience are information and communication, community competence, social capital, and economic development (which can be viewed as economic capital). Sociologists Liesel Ritchie and Duane Gill (2011) base their understanding of the dimensions of community disaster resilience on Flora and Flora's (2008) community capitals framework, which identifies seven types of capital: natural (e.g. natural resources and ecosystems), financial, built, political, social, human, and cultural. Kendra, Clay, and Gill (2018) identify nine components of disaster resilience:

- capacity for improvisation in disasters,
- number and quality of physical and infrastructural resources,
- community capital,
- natural resources,
- institutional capital,
- political capital,
- human capital,
- economic capital,
- social capital.

In a comprehensive review of the literature on social capital and disasters, Michelle Meyer (2018) identified a number of studies that show that social capital, measured at either the individual or the community level, has a positive impact at various stages of the hazards cycle. For example, social capital is associated with mitigation and adaptation activities, adoption of disaster preparedness measures, evacuation behaviors, disaster responses, and positive recovery outcomes.

Studies abound on the role of social capital in disasters. In one frequently cited study, Eric Klinenberg (2002) conducted research on the factors that contributed to mortality in the 1995 Chicago heat wave, which caused approximately 750 deaths. Selecting two apparently similar Chicago neighborhoods in which heat-related mortality differed significantly, he found that social ties and other variables associated with social capital were key factors contributing to low death rates. In the neighborhood where death rates were higher, fear of crime kept people isolated in their homes, many residents were transients, and levels of social interaction and participation in community organizations were low. The neighborhood where mortality was low was a bustling commercial center where people interacted on a daily basis in stores and in the streets. Ties with extended family members were strong in that largely immigrant community and the Catholic Church served as a major community hub. Klinenberg concluded that high levels of social capital had a protective function for otherwise vulnerable community residents.

Other research reveals the connection between social capital and positive health and mental health outcomes after disasters. Following Hurricane Katrina, Adeola and Picou (2012) employed survey research methods to assess the link between social capital measures (e.g. home ownership, feelings of self-efficacy, involvement with community organizations) and physical health outcomes such as respiratory problems, headaches, nausea, and high blood pressure among Katrina survivors in hard-hit parts of Louisiana and Mississippi. They found that those with high levels of social capital had fewer health problems than those with low social capital. These same researchers looked at long-term patterns of psychological distress following Katrina and found that low levels of social capital were predictive of depression and psychosocial stress, and also that these negative mental health impacts were more common among blacks, older adults, unmarried adults, women, people with less education, and people with weak social networks (Adeola and Picou 2014).

Heid, Pruchno, Cartwright, and Wilson-Genderson (2017) studied the mental health of New Jersey residents between the ages of fifty-four and eighty who experienced Hurricane Sandy in 2012. Controlling for other factors that could have influenced outcomes, they found that the severity of storm exposure was associated with more symptoms of post-traumatic stress disorder (PTSD), while respondents' perceptions of neighborhood social cohesion (a measure of social capital) were associated with fewer symptoms. Additionally, even for those with greater exposure to the storm, perceived social cohesion was associated with lower levels of PTSD. (For a review of other studies on social capital and post-disaster health outcomes, see Aida, Kawachi, Subramanian, and Kondo 2013.)

Technological disasters and social capital

Research by Liesel Ritchie and her collaborators (Ritchie 2004, 2012; Ritchie, Gill, and Farnham 2013; Ritchie, Gill, and Long 2018) focuses on the relationship between disasters and social capital. These researchers see social capital as an asset at all phases of the disaster cycle. However, much of their work documents the ways in which disasters can damage social capital and community cohesiveness, particularly when the disaster agent is technological and the recovery period is protracted and accompanied by litigation-related community conflict. The idea here is that, rather than giving rise to thera-peutic communities, as emphasized in many studies, technological disasters tend to give rise to "corrosive communities." Ritchie's research on the long-term impacts of the 1989 Exxon Valdez oil spill in one fishing community in Alaska is a case in point. That 11-million gallon spill, the largest in history before the 2010 BP Deepwater Horizon blowout and oil spill in the Gulf of Mexico, was a catastrophe that had far-reaching consequences not only for the environment, marine life, and fisheries but also for the affected communities. Lawsuits seeking damages from Exxon dragged on for more than twenty-five years, during which the residents of those communities were under significant psychological and financial stress and the social fabric became frayed. Attitudes and behaviors associated with social capital – such as trust and goodwill, or the willingness to socialize – and feelings of efficacy declined.

Other researchers who have studied technological disasters also contend that those kinds of events, which trigger blame for their occurrence, disputes over the magnitude and severity of impacts, lingering and uncertain effects, and lawsuits, can have a corrosive effect on individual and community social capital (Erikson 1995; Freudenburg 1997; Gill and Picou 1998; Picou, Marshall, and Gill 2004). For example, Mayer, Running, and Bergstrand (2015) studied the residents of four communities affected by the BP Deepwater Horizon oil spill and found that, even though the victims of the spill began to be compensated relatively soon after that disaster, many residents were critical of the compen-sation process, which they saw as random and arbitrary. As a consequence, individual claimants and businesses that had experienced losses felt as if they were in competition with one another for resources, and many avoided interactions where money-related conflicts might surface. The perception that some residents had filed fraudulent claims or profited in a major way from the spill and cleanup created feelings of distrust that also had corrosive effects. The researchers concluded that "residents felt themselves pulled apart rather than together by the claims process during what were already difficult times" (Mayer et al. 2015: 384).

A note of caution regarding toxic threats

Findings like these are consistent across a range of studies but, as I have argued elsewhere (see Tierney, Lindell, and Perry 2001; Tierney 2014, 2018), framing technological disasters as uniquely corrosive glosses over some important points. While some researchers focus on toxic emergencies that result in diminished social capital and corrosiveness, others point to situations in which communities have responded to such threats with apathy and denial. For example, Auyero and Swistun (2008) studied an Argentine shantytown ironically called Flammable that is literally located on top of a toxic industrial site. They found that, even though residents suffered a number of health problems, they were doubtful and confused about whether the toxic exposure was harmful, denied the hazard, or blamed their illnesses on sources other than industrial pollution. Gunter, Aronoff, and Joel (1999) studied communities where toxic contamination was present and found in them complacency and an absence of conflict. Kari Norgaard (2011) conducted research in a community in Norway where residents could see evidence of climate change all around them but still engaged in collective climate change denial. Findings like these indicate that, although the literature is replete with studies showing that anthropogenic hazards can lead to community conflict and social capital losses, there are exceptions.

In considering how disasters can give rise to community conflict and erode social capital, it is also important to recall a key point made earlier in Chapter 3, namely that hazards, disasters, and their impacts are socially constructed. Discourses centering on blame and responsibility for hazards and disasters reflect epistemic and socially situated perspectives in which consensus is elusive. Was Hurricane Katrina a natural disaster caused by a Category 3 hurricane, or was Katrina's devastation the consequence of a major technological hazard – weakened and failing levees – and therefore caused by the Army Corps of Engineers, which was largely responsible for the construction of the levee system? Or was the oil and gas industry responsible, because its activities caused land loss and a reduction in natural protections? To what extent can we attribute the impacts of other devastating hurricanes such as Harvey, Irma, and Maria to the meteorological characteristics of those events, as opposed to human agency in the form of human-induced climate change and the political-economic precursors that shaped the devastation? Here again, a constructivist perspective cautions against making sharp distinctions between "technological" and "natural" disasters.

The downside of social capital

So far we have focused on the ways in which social capital contributes to disaster resilience; but the effects of social capital are not always positive.

Daniel Aldrich (2012) refers to social capital as "Janus-faced" – that is, as a set of resources and capacities that can be used for good or ill. Pioneering researcher Alejandro Portes (1998) provided various examples of what he termed "negative social capital," for example ethnically based business monopolies that keep competitors out, or groups that control unions and succeed in denying membership to those considered undesirable (typically, people of color). Strong ties can pressure group members to remain in deviant lifestyles associated for instance with drug dealing and gang involvement, even though they would rather quit. We need to keep in mind that Bourdieu's original interest in social capital centered on how it functions as a means of distinguishing higher-class "haves" from lower-class "have-nots." For him, social capital was just as much about being able to exclude others as it was about creating in-group solidarity.

Along these same lines, with respect to hazards and disasters, there are examples of how the strong social capital of some groups works to the detriment of others. The environmental justice literature is full of examples of how well-off and well-connected – and typically white – communities succeed in avoiding "environmental bads" such as chemical factories and hazardous landfills, pushing them onto minority communities. When groups with high social capital organize behind the banner of "not in my backyard" (NIMBY), they ensure that environmental harms are thrown into someone else's backyard; and this "someone else" is, typically, a vulnerable group deprived of the capacity and political power to resist.

Daniel Aldrich provides examples of how the strong social capital of some groups can result in the exclusion of others. In a study of the recovery of villages and hamlets in Tamil Nadu, India after the 2004 tsunami, Aldrich (2011) found that local councils, which had strong bonding social capital, were able to link to external sources of aid such as humanitarian NGOs and higher levels of government. However, he also found that, once those councils obtained recovery resources from the outside, they distributed them in ways that excluded certain groups within the community, such as women (especially female heads of households), elderly residents, and Dalits – members of the lowest caste, formerly known as "untouchables." Communities that did not have local councils received less aid and had difficulty recovering, but at least they had bonding social capital, often in the form of kinship networks, and the aid that was obtained there was distributed more equitably.

The devastation wrought by Hurricane Katrina in New Orleans created a desperate need for temporary housing, and the solution that the Federal Emergency Management Agency (FEMA) devised was to provide trailers and trailer parks for displaced residents who remained in the city. A preliminary list of approved sites was developed, and final siting decisions were made by the New Orleans city government. Working with a database of 114 zip codes in and around New Orleans, Aldrich and Crook (2008) documented the number of trailers and trailer parks that actually ended up being located in each zip code. They then looked into the extent to which social capital played a role in where trailers were placed. Using voting rates in the 2004 presidential election as a measure of social capital (because voting rates were closely associated with other forms of civic participation) and controlling for a number of other variables (among them race, income, education, and flood damage), they found that the higher the voting rates in a zip code, the fewer trailers and trailer parks were located in that zip code. Trailers and trailer parks, along with those who live in them, generally come with a certain stigma and are often targeted for NIMBY actions. The authors interpreted their findings as an indication that city leaders were consciously trying to avoid neighborhoods where civically engaged residents were likely to organize in order to resist the siting of trailers.

In September 2013, communities in Colorado's Front Range region experienced massive flooding in what was at that time the costliest disaster in the state's history. Located at the confluence of two rivers, the community of Lyons experienced extensive damage, especially to its infrastructure systems, and the entire town had to be evacuated for a time. Two mobile home parks that had housed mainly low-income and elderly residents were essentially destroyed. Housing costs were already high in the town, a significant proportion of the housing stock was destroyed in the flood, and rents subsequently went up, making it difficult for displaced mobile home residents to return to Lyons. Local advocates of affordable housing and their allies banded together, conducted studies, and developed a proposal for building a sixty-six-unit affordable housing development on six acres of a twenty-five-acre public park. The plan had strong community support, but an opposition faction emerged. That faction, which had backing from major business leaders in the town, claimed to be motivated by the need to preserve parks and open space, but there was also a strong undertone of NIMBYism. An election was held to determine whether the affordable housing development could go forward, and the measure failed. This led to the long-term displacement of mobile home residents who had been flooded out. Nnenia Campbell (2016), who studied the aftermath of the flood in Lyons and other communities, noted that, while social capital was high among groups on both sides of the issue, housing advocates were no match when it came to their opponents' economic and political power. Observing that the controversy resulted in bitterness and recriminations on both sides, she also cites the case as an example of the corrosive effects of disasters.

Daly and Silver (2008) point to other problematic aspects of the concept of social capital. They note that the World Bank has embraced the concept and has argued for its importance in economic development and good governance; but they also point out that, in the Bank's framing, women and the poor are expected to generate social capital as a way of solving their own problems, while the state is assigned a lesser role. These authors express concern that "social capital can provide a rationale for the state to exit poor communities and leave the problem-solving to civil society or individual action" (2008: 553). I will return to this idea later in this chapter, when I discuss critiques of the resilience concept.

Measuring Disaster Resilience

A focus on resilience and its dimensions leads logically to questions about resilience measurement. If improving resilience is a goal, how do we know whether communities and societies are reaching that goal? Which aspects of resilience are functioning well, and which ones need improvement? Do specific elements of resilience need to be prioritized? What baseline data are available that would enable researchers to measure changes in resilience in the aftermath of disasters? Measurement strategies are needed to answer questions like these. The literature on individual, organizational, community, and national resilience is vast. In this section we will consider measurement approaches that explicitly address disaster resilience, as opposed to resilience in general, although the two concepts are obviously related.

When so much attention is being paid to disaster resilience in both research and practice communities, it is not surprising that measurement approaches have also proliferated rapidly. Schipper and Langston (2015) analyzed eighteen sets of indicators that measure resilience at different levels, some of which focus on disaster resilience. Stevenson et al. (2015) discuss thirteen different resilience assessment frameworks. Cutter (2016) reviewed twenty-seven different measurement schemes that address different resilience domains and units of analysis. Sharifi (2016) identified thirty-six different assessment tools at different analytic levels. The Resilience Measurement Evidence and Learning Community of Practice (2016) has compiled an inventory of thirty-nine resilience measurement approaches and frameworks. Hisham, Patherage, and Fernando (2021) identify, review, and classify thirty-six resilience measurement approaches. These comparative analyses are a good source of information on the details, strengths, and weaknesses of different resilience metrics. Important to note is that, while there is some degree of convergence on key concepts associated with resilience across measurement schemes, concepts are operationalized differently. Frameworks also vary in terms of the hazards they take into account. Some frameworks are not specific with respect to the hazards considered, or take an all-hazards approach. Others focus on resilience in the face of particular hazards, such as droughts and floods, or on specific dimensions of social life, such as livelihoods and food security.

Measurement approaches can be distinguished in a number of ways. Disaster resilience is a multilevel concept; the resilience of nations, regions, economic sectors, communities, organizations, households, and individuals can all be assessed, which means that measurement schemes should focus on various levels of analysis. A nation as a whole may score one way on resilience criteria, while lower-level social units may score differently. Frameworks can be primarily quantitative or predominantly qualitative. Another aspect on which resilience measurement schemes differ is whether they rely on "objective" data – that is, data that employ social indicators or other objective measures – or on self-reported data or self-assessments. Examples of the latter could include data collected through focus groups and community discussions organized around the concept of resilience, where the perceptions of community members are emphasized. Cutter (2016) makes several further distinctions. Measurements can take various forms: indices made up of quantifiable indicators or variables; scorecards involving assessments of progress toward resilience goals and using numerical scores or letter grades; mathematical models of resilience such as those used by economists; or toolkits that provide step-by-step guidance on developing resilience scores. Further, frameworks can either be tailored to focus on individual communities by using locally available data or be designed to allow for comparisons across multiple units such as countries or cities. In what follows I focus on a few examples of sociologically relevant resilience measurement approaches of different types, with the goal of providing a general sense of the logic that undergirds different frameworks and the types of indicators that are employed. The discussion next provides examples of resilience measurement tools applied at different levels of analysis.

Community-Level Measurement Frameworks

Baseline resilience indicators for communities (BRIC)

Like the Social Vulnerability Index (SoVI), which was discussed in the previous chapter, BRIC was developed by Susan Cutter and her colleagues (Cutter, Burton, and Emrich 2010; see also Cutter, Ash, and Emrich 2014) at the Hazards Vulnerability and Resilience Institute. BRIC is a composite measure of disaster resilience made up of variables drawn from secondary sources such as the US Census and other less costly and widely available data sources. The conceptual framework on which BRIC is based is called the "disaster resilience of place" (DROP) model (Cutter et al. 2008). The unit of analysis is the community or, more specifically, the county. BRIC focuses on six resilience domains, also referred to as capitals: social, economic, housing and infrastructure, institutional, community, and environmental. On the basis of findings in the disaster research literature, multiple variables were selected for inclusion within each of those domains – forty-nine variables in all. For example, the concept of social resilience is measured by variables associated with equality in educational attainment, English language competence within the population, food security, fewer elderly and disabled residents, and the extent to which transportation, phone service, health insurance, and mental health services are available. The community capital dimension of resilience is made up of variables indicative of place attachment, political engagement, and residents' disaster preparedness and response training. Institutional resilience is measured by variables related to investments in disaster mitigation, flood insurance coverage, the ability of jurisdictions to coordinate with one another, and disaster experience. Because data are available for all counties in the United States, BRIC allows researchers and decision makers to make cross-county comparisons and to judge how their communities stack up against others. Details of the BRIC framework, including lists of indicators, can be found in Cutter, Burton, and Emrich (2010). BRIC indicators form the basis for the resilience portion of the US National Risk Index, which was discussed in Chapter 5.

Communities advancing resilience toolkit (CART)

CART is a comprehensive set of resilience assessment and improvement tools that was developed by a group of researchers based primarily in the Terrorism and Disaster Center at the University of Oklahoma, the Geisel School of Medicine at Dartmouth University and the National Center for Post-Traumatic Stress Disorder, and the US Centers for Disease Control and Prevention (Pfefferbaum et al. 2013). The conceptual framework that underpins CART derives from theory and research findings on community capacity and competence from the fields of social psychology, community psychology, and public health. One of the initial publications that laid out this resilience framework was Norris et al. (2008), which was discussed earlier in connection with resilience domains. CART is meant to be applied at the community level, where "community" can also be defined as a neighborhood or some other unit of analysis; participants in the CART process are the ones who decide what the community boundaries are. A core element of the CART assessment, in contrast with that of BRIC, is based on data provided by community stakeholders who take part in a resilience assessment process. Like BRIC, CART uses widely available secondary data sources such as the census (for population, housing, and other community characteristics), the Department of Health and Human Services' Community Health Status Indicators, and other community-level indicators that give a snapshot of community resilience capacities. In this measurement process, the community itself also collects what it considers to be relevant data through strategies such as key informant interviews and what the CART developers call "community conversations." In addition to instructions on how to conduct interviews and community conversations, other components of the toolkit are guidance on stakeholder analysis, capacity and vulnerability assessment, and participatory strategic planning aimed at enhancing resilience.

Although its core concepts and assumptions remain the same, CART has evolved over time in terms of what the research group considers to be the key elements of resilience and how they can be measured. An earlier formulation (Pfefferbaum et al. 2007) specified seven elements that the literature identifies as important for resilience: connectedness, commitment, and shared values; participation; support and nurturance; structure, roles, and responsibilities; resources; critical reflection and skill building; and communication. Further refinement prompted the CART group to reduce these concepts to five: general community resilience; connection and caring; resources; transformative potential; and disaster management. The assessment process involves collecting extensive data in these five areas. Listed below are examples of the interview questions that are associated with each area:

- *General resilience* Does the community help people in need? What resources are available for disaster and terrorism readiness, response, and recovery?
- *Connection and caring* Do community members share similar values? Are members committed to the well-being of the community?
- *Resources* Are disaster response and recovery services available in the community? Are they available to all community members?
- *Transformative potential* Does the community have or collect information in order to improve its ability to adapt and learn from crises? Are members able to take part in problem-solving regarding community issues?
- *Disaster management* What does the community do to prevent disasters and terrorism? Is the community currently doing anything to improve its disaster and terrorism response?

CART is used extensively in community participatory resilience assessments. Full details of the CART toolkit are available online at https://medicine.ouhsc.edu/academic-departments/psychiatry-and-behavioral-sciences/terrorism-and-disaster-center/cart-community-resilience-toolkit.

Disaster resilience scorecard for cities

This assessment tool was developed by the UNISDR to enable communities to assess their progress toward the "ten essentials for making cities resilient" identified in the Sendai Framework for Action. Different versions of the tool, developed through short stakeholder workshops, can be used for preliminary assessments as well as for more detailed ones, which would necessitate longer stakeholder engagement. The detailed tool contains 117 indicators, each measured on a scale of 0 to 5, covering ten major sets of activities that map onto the "ten essentials." The scorecard enables cities to assess their overall resilience and also to identify areas in which they are performing well and areas that need improvement. Table 6.1 lists the activities scored in the detailed assessment and provides examples of positive indicators for each.

Table 6.1 Scorecard activities and selected indicators

Resilience Essential	Examples of Indicators
Organize for resilience	City plan incorporates risk considerations; stakeholders are included and kept up to date on plans
Identify, understand, and use current and future risk scenarios	Comprehensive risk analyses, updated in last three years and approved by a third party; risk assessments include socioeconomic, spatial, physical, and environmental assets at risk, estimated from most probable and most severe scenarios
Strengthen financial capacity for resilience	Dedicated responsibility within city to access national and international resilience financing; budget for resilience measures exists, is adequate, and is protected
Pursue resilient urban development	No loss of employment from "most severe" disaster scenario; systematic use of design solutions to improve city's resilience, enforced by codes
Safeguard natural buffers to enhance the protective functions offered by natural ecosystems	Critical ecosystem services are identified and monitored annually using key performance indicators; city undertakes transboundary assessments of ecosystem assets and works with neighboring jurisdictions to manage assets
Strengthen the institutional capacity for resilience	Disaster risk reduction stakeholders have memoranda of understanding with relevant NGOs; there are systematic hazard-related public information campaigns using multiple media platforms
Understand and strengthen societal capacity for resilience	In every neighborhood, organizations exist that address the full spectrum of resilience issues; all vulnerable groups confirm that they are regularly engaged in disaster resilience issues
Increase infrastructure resilience	Protective infrastructure is in place to deal with "most severe" disaster scenario with minimal social and economic impacts; no loss of electrical power, even in "most severe" scenarios
Ensure effective disaster response	Comprehensive plans exist in relation to scenarios, and they have been tested in actual emergencies; equipment and relief supplies are defined in relation to scenarios and take into account the use of volunteers
Expedite recovery and "build back better"	Comprehensive plans exist for economic, infrastructure, and community recovery under "most probable" and "most severe" disaster scenarios; stakeholders are involved in "build back better" planning

Source: Compiled from data in United Nations International Strategy for Disaster Reduction 2017.

Organizational-Level Measurement of Resilience

The literature on organizational resilience mainly focuses on business enterprises, as opposed to other types of organizations. Many lessons regarding organizational resilience are based on case studies of businesses that have coped and adapted in the face of extreme events (see for example Sheffi 2005, 2017). In contrast with the case study approach, other researchers have developed metrics for organizations that are similar to the metrics for communities just discussed, and these make it possible to assess the resilience of organizations. Other insights on what makes organizations resilient come from post-disaster surveys of large numbers of businesses. Additional insights on organizational resilience come from research carried out by economists and from bodies that produce standards and engage in resilience assessment.

Resilience measurement for organizations

Resilient Organisations, a research and consulting enterprise based in Christchurch, New Zealand, has developed and implemented a web-based survey questionnaire that enables organizations of all types to measure their resilience (Stephenson, Vargo, and Seville 2010; Lee, Vargo, and Seville 2013). In developing survey items, the Resilient Organisations team drew on several lines of research: studies on organizations that employ risky technologies but nevertheless exhibit nearly error-free performance, research on organizational failures, and inductive research on New Zealand organizations that experienced crises. The survey tool focuses on four main areas: the organization's resilience ethos; situation awareness; management of what is termed "keystone vulnerabilities" – that is, those parts of an organization's system that could cripple the whole organization if they failed; and adaptive capacity. The team developed multiple indicators in each of these areas. These indicators take the form of statements with which participants agree or disagree on a Likert scale. The sum of these items produces an overall resilience score. Table 6.2 lists some of these statements, as outlined in one of the group's research papers (Lee et al. 2013).

On the basis of an extensive review of the literature on organizational performance in crises, Somers (2009) developed a tool called the Organizational Resilience Potential Scale (ORPS), which was designed to measure what he terms "latent resilience"; and he tested the tool using a survey with a sample of municipal public works managers. These managers were asked to rate their departments on the following factors: goal-directed solution seeking; risk avoidance; critical situational understanding; team members' ability to fill multiple roles; reliance on information sources; and access to resources. Information was gathered on six additional measures: managers' risk perceptions; decentralization of decision-making, which is believed to be related to

Table 6.2 Resilience measures developed by Resilient Organisations

Resilience Component	Examples of Survey Items
Resilience ethos	Our organization has a culture where it is important to make sure that we learn from our mistakes and problems.
	Our organization is able to collaborate with others in our industry to manage unexpected challenges.
Situation awareness	Our organization has clearly defined priorities for what is important during and after a crisis.
	Our organization is able to shift rapidly from business as usual mode to respond to crises.
Management of keystone vulnerabilities	I believe our organization invests sufficient resources in being ready to respond to an emergency of any kind.
	Our organization understands that having a plan for emergencies is not enough and that the plan must be practiced and tested in order to be effective.
Adaptive capacity	People in our organization are known for their ability to use their knowledge in novel ways.
	There is an excellent sense of teamwork and camaraderie in our organization.

Source: Compiled from data in Lee, Vargo, and Seville 2013.

an organization's capacity to respond in crises; extent of continuity of operations planning; managerial information seeking; whether the department had outside accreditation; and the department's involvement in community planning.

Extrapolating from post-disaster business studies

Although not carried out under the rubric of resilience or specifically for measurement purposes, much of my past work has focused on challenges that businesses experience in disasters and on factors that are predictive of positive short-term and long-term business recovery outcomes (see Dahlhamer and Tierney 1998; Webb, Tierney, and Dahlhamer 2000, 2002; Tierney 2007). Those studies had the advantage of employing stratified random sampling, large sample sizes, and multivariate analytic methods. That body of research led to insights into the pre-disaster characteristics and post-disaster experiences of the businesses that tended to fare better than others in the aftermath of disasters – which is one way of thinking about business resilience.

One weakness of my research on businesses and disasters was that the samples were limited to businesses that had survived disasters. Other research that also used stratified random sampling methods focused on both surviving businesses and businesses that collapsed after a disaster – in this case,

Hurricane Katrina (Marshall, Niehm, Sydnor, and Schrank 2015; Sydnor et al. 2017). Researchers have also employed qualitative methods to delve more deeply into factors that are associated with positive post-disaster outcomes (Alesch, Holly, Mittler, and Nagy 2001); or they have used a combination of quantitative and qualitative approaches (Hall, Malinen, Vosslamber, and Wordsworth 2016).

Findings across studies are not entirely consistent, but do help us both identify what makes businesses vulnerable to poor recovery outcomes after disasters and suggest business resilience factors. Generalizing from these and other, similar studies, we can hypothesize that business disaster resilience is linked to four sets of factors: business characteristics, owner characteristics, disaster impacts, and exogenous economic conditions. Regarding business characteristics, in line with sociological research on organizations, being a large business in terms of number of employees and revenues appears to make those businesses more resilient than small ones. Business type is also important; businesses in economic sectors that are highly regulated, such as financial institutions, are generally more resilient because they are required to be, while businesses in highly competitive sectors where there are higher rates of failure during non-disaster times, for instance in the retail and service sectors, are likely to be more at risk for failure or poor recovery outcomes. Businesses that are involved in post-disaster repair and reconstruction, such as construction companies and hardware stores, may fare better after disasters, with the caveat that those gains are, typically, temporary. Being located in a structure that is owned rather than rented appears to add to resilience. Older businesses, unlike recently established ones, appear to be better able to weather stressors brought on by disasters. There is also some evidence that partnerships and other ownership forms are more resilient than sole proprietorships. Businesses that were faring well financially before disaster struck also appear to register more positive outcomes. Finally, it appears that businesses that serve a wide market outside the disaster impact area – for example, by having an internet sales component or by placing their goods in stores in multiple locations – may have fewer difficulties than businesses with a local focus only, because disasters can create problems with customer, supplier, or shipper access or can alter customer behavior.

With respect to business owner characteristics, being male and not being a member of a minority group appear to be associated with greater resilience. Women- and minority-owned businesses tend to have fewer economic resources, which makes them more vulnerable to experiencing difficulties in the aftermath of disasters. The educational attainment level of the business owner is another resilience factor; this indicates that an owner's social capital plays a role in business resilience. Resilience is higher when owners have more industry experience and more disaster experience, and there is also an indication that an owner's flexibility, capacity for innovation, and entrepreneurial spirit matter for business recovery.

Disaster impacts are also important for understanding business resilience. Other things being equal, businesses are less likely to be able to cope when disaster damage to structures, inventories, and equipment is very severe and when disruptions of infrastructure services such as electrical power and communications are prolonged; both of these can lead to business closure for longer periods. When a business is located in an area that has been highly damaged, even if the business itself has not, it could face significant recovery challenges. Additionally, where there has been residential damage and dislocation, a business may be in danger of losing its customer base, and this could be especially problematic for businesses that earn their income locally.

Finally, like all businesses, those that have experienced disasters are affected by the overall economic climate and trends within their specific sectors. Generally speaking, resilience levels should be higher in good economic times than in poor ones. Positive economic conditions should favor business recovery, while recessions and periods of high unemployment (and hence less discretionary income for households) should have adverse effects. Disasters typically bring additional funds into affected regions via disaster assistance and insurance payouts, but such funds do not benefit all businesses equally.

Insights from economics

Although economists who do research on disasters tend to focus on disaster effects at the national and regional level, some economists also collect and analyze data on individual businesses. Adam Rose is an economist who has done research on economic impacts and resilience at all three levels. Rose defines and measures business resilience in ways that differ to some degree from previous discussions. He defines static economic resilience as the ability of a system – in this case, a business – to maintain functionality when it experiences an external shock such as a disaster. By contrast, dynamic economic resilience consists of actions taken to recover from a disaster or some other shock (Rose 2007). Rose also makes a distinction between inherent and adaptive resilience. Inherent resilience already exists in pre-disaster times; examples include large business inventories and other resources, or arrangements that have been made to ensure that a business can receive the supplies and components it needs even when a disaster occurs. Adaptive resilience consists of strategies that ensure continuity of business operations and recovery after disasters, for instance the ability to continue to operate on generators if the electrical power supply fails, or to relocate the business if needed. Also included in this category is the ability of a business to understand how the disaster has affected the demand for its goods and services, either positively or negatively, and to respond accordingly. Framed in this way, resilience results from a combination of pre-disaster organizational strengths and post-disaster ingenuity (Rose and Krausmann 2013).

Rose's approach to quantitatively assessing business resilience is relatively straightforward and intuitive: as a first step, think of the maximum disruption a business or some other economic unit could experience as the result of a disaster in the form of economic losses, then calculate what percentage of those losses was avoided. That percentage is a measure of resilience. Put another way, resilience is the ratio of losses avoided to potential maximum losses. Rose and his colleagues (Rose, Oladosu, Lee, Asay 2009) demonstrated this resilience metric using the example of businesses affected by the 2001 World Trade Center terrorist attack. Their focal concern was the firms' resilience in the face of business interruption. They obtained a dataset on the 1,134 firms that were forced to relocate after the attack because they had been doing business in the two collapsed Trade Center towers or the immediate vicinity. Between them, these firms employed over 100,000 people. An estimate of the losses that would result if all those businesses ceased to operate (i.e. on an indicator of zero resilience) provided the upper bound of how serious the economic impacts could be. Conversely, estimating losses if all businesses relocated immediately, never experiencing any interruption, provided the lower bound (i.e. an indicator of full resilience). Using data on actual business interruption losses, the researchers determined that 72 percent of potential losses (the upper bound) had in fact been avoided. In their terms, then, the resilience factor for businesses was 72 percent.

Subsequent work focused on a range of resilience strategies both private firms and public-sector entities can employ to avoid losses from disaster-induced disruptions. For example, organizations can relocate if their premises are damaged or destroyed, find new suppliers to overcome supply-chain problems, or give employees the opportunity to work longer hours to make up for missed production (Dormady, Roa-Henriquez, and Rose 2019).

Normative approaches to organizational resilience measurement

In contrast with the empirically based approaches to resilience described here, normatively based strategies for assessing organizational resilience take into account how an organization measures up to consensus-based standards for organizational preparedness and crisis response or to other types of standards. Standards developed by the International Organization for Standardization, known as ISO, are widely accepted and used worldwide. One standard, ISO 22316: 2017, focuses specifically on organizational resilience. That standard sets out activities that indicate compliance within nine areas of organizational performance:

- shared vision and clarity of purpose
- an understanding of the context in which the organization operates

- effective and empowered leadership
- a supportive organizational culture
- shared information and knowledge
- adequate resources
- development and coordination of management disciplines
- support for continual improvement
- the ability to anticipate and manage change.

ISO has also produced a suite of detailed standards associated with risk assessment, risk management, and ensuring the continuity of business operations in the event of disruption that may arise from various sources, such as disasters and terrorist attacks. Compliance with such standards could be taken as indicative of organizational resilience.

The Insurance Institute for Business and Home Safety (IBHS), which receives funding from the insurance industry and other sources, has developed a toolkit called Open for Business EZ (OFB-EZ), which consists of guidance aimed at ensuring business continuity after disasters and places special emphasis on small businesses. IBHS makes this toolkit available online at no cost, and also provides an app that businesses can use to guide their own business continuity planning processes. OFB-EZ recommends best practices in many different areas, including risk assessment and prioritization, operations, finances, human resources, and information technology. Although not framed as a resilience assessment method, OFB-EZ could in principle be converted to one.

Measuring Household Resilience

By comparison with what is available for community-level measures, there are relatively few checklists or toolkits for measuring household resilience to disasters. I begin this section by discussing findings from the disaster research literature that indicate the types of factors likely to be associated with household resilience. I then move on to provide a brief overview of the extensive literature on family psychosocial resilience as it relates to disaster resilience. Finally, I consider some measures that are commonly used to assess household resilience in less developed countries.

Long before the concept of disaster resilience came to the fore, researchers conducted extensive studies on household hazard mitigation and preparedness for a wide range of disasters, as well as for terrorism (for summaries of earlier research, see Drabek 1986 and Tierney et al. 2001; see also Lindell and Perry 2000; Bourque, Mileti, Kano, and Wood 2012). Although it is difficult to generalize because study results are not entirely consistent, we can tentatively identify household characteristics that may be associated with resilience potential, just as we did for businesses. Some studies suggest that minority households are less likely than white households to adopt mitigation and preparedness measures and that home ownership and higher levels of income and education are associated with carrying out such measures. Households that actively seek out information about hazards are more likely to prepare, as are households that have previously experienced disasters. Perceived risk tends to be associated with the adoption of protective and preparedness measures, but generally exerts its influence in combination with other factors. Findings such as these need to be put into context: levels of household preparation for disasters are low, even in high-risk areas. Taking into account the many forms of disaster vulnerability that were discussed in the previous chapter, it is not difficult to see why many households would have difficulty coping with a disaster.

The topic of family resilience has been prominent in the psychological sciences for decades, and there are literally hundreds of models that seek to identify family resilience factors, both during normal periods and in the face of stressors (for examples, see Black and Lobo 2008; Becvar 2013; Masten and Monn 2015; Walsh 2016).[1] The vast majority of this work has focused on the psychological well-being of family members, factors associated with psychological vulnerability, and protective factors that help family members avoid negative psychological and social outcomes such as anxiety, depression, and substance abuse. This literature focuses on stressful circumstances of all types, examples of which include illness and bereavement, crime and community violence, wars and civil wars, terrorism, and in some cases disasters. On the basis of the finds presented in this literature, Vogel and the Family Systems Collaborative Group (2017; see also Vogel and Pfefferbaum 2016) identify four sets of factors that they consider to be associated with family resilience. First, family members should possess a set of beliefs and attitudes that include seeing crises as shared challenges for the family, accepting that distress is to be expected under stressful conditions, having hope, but of the realistic sort, avoiding feelings of blame or guilt, being in touch with religious and other prosocial belief systems, and viewing adversity as a meaningful and even positive experience. Second, under stress, households that are resilient stick to their daily routines and rituals as much as possible and adapt in situations where that is too difficult. This covers maintaining family roles, for example by ensuring that parents retain their authority. A third set of resilience factors involves communication. In resilient households, family members communicate, but in appropriate ways. For example, adults avoid giving young children more information about a disaster or a stressful situation than they can handle at their developmental level. Household members allow for the expression of a range of emotions, including negative ones, but are also able to find joy under difficult circumstances. Finally, resilient families employ a range of coping and problem-solving skills.

There are a number of other measurement frameworks that are used in assessing household resilience in the developing world. The Secure Livelihoods Research Consortium (SLRC) is an alliance composed of researchers from eight institutions in North America, Europe, Asia, and Africa and from the United Nations Food and Agricultural Organization, whose work focuses on household livelihoods and well-being, with an emphasis on household resilience in the face of conflict. The SLRC conducted longitudinal research with households in the Democratic Republic of Congo, Nepal, Pakistan, Sri Lanka, and Uganda. Its measurement tool focuses on three main areas: livelihoods, which consists of food security, income sources, and assets; access to and experience with services, including health and education services and water access; and relationships with governance processes, including civic participation. Through its project Building Resilience and Adaptation to Climate Extremes and Disasters (BRACED), the Overseas Development Institute in the United Kingdom has also developed a suite of instruments for assessing household resilience.

Programs for Enhancing Resilience

Recent years have seen the development of a number of programs aimed at improving resilience. In this section I focus on three such efforts: a program sponsored by the Rockefeller Foundation; resilience planning sponsored by the National Institute of Standards and Technology; and resilience measurement and enhancement efforts at the National Academies of Sciences, Engineering, and Medicine.

As its name indicates, the Rockefeller Foundation's program 100 Resilient Cities (100RC) focused on urban resilience. This initiative began in 2014 and at its peak provided funding to large and small cities on every continent (except Antarctica). The program framed resilience as the capacity to respond to two types of problems or stressors that cities face. Chronic stressors, which are ongoing for cities, include problems such as high unemployment, food and water shortages, and climatic change. Acute stressors include natural disasters, disease outbreaks, and terrorist attacks. Each participating city was required to develop a resilience strategy aimed at reducing the impacts of both types of stressors. One of the key elements of 100RC was the funding of chief resilience officers (CROs) in participating cities. The CRO, who ideally was expected to report directly to the city's mayor, was responsible for developing a resilience vision and for bringing together city departments and authorities so that they could coordinate their resilience-related activities. Rather than working in isolation, CROs participated in a global CRO network that enabled them to share information on resilience plans and activities.

In collaboration with Arup, a London-based consulting firm, Rockefeller developed the Community Resilience Framework, an assessment tool centered on four key elements of urban resilience: leadership and strategy; infrastructure and environment; economy and society, or social and financial systems that contribute to resilience; and health and well-being. The initiative ended somewhat abruptly in 2019, when the leadership of the Rockefeller Foundation changed hands. Some funding and activities were spun off to a new set of programs, headquartered at the Adrienne Arsht-Rockefeller Foundation Resilience Center at the Atlantic Council.

The National Institute of Standards and Technology (NIST) developed the Community Resilience Planning Guide to assist communities in assessing and improving their resilience in the face of hazards. The Guide, which was released in 2015, provides direction on a six-step planning process that contains the following elements (National Institute of Standards and Technology 2015a, 2015b):

- forming a collaborative planning team,
- understanding the community's social and built environment and their linkages,
- determining community goals and objectives,
- developing a resilience plan and implementation strategy,
- preparing and reviewing the plan and obtaining approval from authorities,
- implementing, evaluating, and updating the plan.

Accompanying the planning guide is a series of planning briefs that instruct communities on how to address various elements in the planning process, for instance how they can characterize their populations and social institutions, set resilience goals, and identify and prioritize resilience shortfalls. NIST also provides funding for the Center for Risk-Based Community Resilience Planning, which is a multidisciplinary consortium of researchers from twelve universities led by Colorado State University.

Following the passage of the Community Disaster Resilience Zones Act in 2022 and employing the National Risk Index and the Climate and Economic Justice Screening Tool, FEMA has identified nearly five hundred at-risk US communities that are most in need of programs and resources to increase their resilience. An online platform has also been developed to show which communities are included in the program. The program is being expanded to include tribal lands and US territories. It will be important for researchers to follow designated communities to chart the initiative's progress.

The National Academies of Sciences, Engineering, and Medicine (the Academies), nonprofit institutions that offer analysis and advice on issues of societal significance in the United States, are also extensively involved in efforts to conceptualize, measure, and improve resilience. Within the Academies, there are a number of groups whose activities focus on building resilience for disasters, disease outbreaks, security threats such as terrorism, and critical infrastructure risks. The Resilient America Roundtable, which is part of the Academies Science and Technology for Resilience Program, meets regularly and focuses on a variety of resilience-related activities and topics, such as reviewing governmental resilience policies and programs and considering emerging threats such as complex, compounded disasters. The Academies' Gulf Research Program (GRP) was established with $500 million in criminal settlement funds paid by the organizations that were found responsible for the 2010 BP oil spill. The GRP provides funding for a range of research and capacity-building projects, a significant proportion of which deal with disaster and climate change resilience.

Resilient Disaster Responses

There are many books and reports that provide guidance for emergency managers and others who are interested in understanding current policy approaches and programs for effective ways of responding to disasters. My objective here is different: it is to offer an introduction to what sociological research has found regarding how resilience is manifested and achieved in the context of disasters.

A key insight from past research is that resilient disaster responses are nonhierarchical. Ideally, decisions are made at the appropriate level – usually that of the local incident – and by those who are closest to emerging problems. While responses require coordination, they do not require centralized command; in fact, centralization can slow down responses and can lack on-the-ground situational awareness. The response to the 1995 Kobe earthquake was slower than it needed to be because local authorities were waiting for the prefectural governor to give orders, while the governor, who was initially unreachable, was waiting for orders from the central government in Tokyo, and those were slow in coming. The US Coast Guard is frequently lauded for its performance in disasters, and this is largely because that organization emphasizes a principle of on-scene initiative. Those in charge of vessels do not wait to be told what to do; they take action on the basis of identified needs (Tierney 2014). As disasters unfold, there are always people who complain about "chaos" and lament that it looks as if no one was in charge. Wanting a centralized structure or a command-and-control model of response flies in the face of what decades of disaster research tell us, namely that disasters are complex and multifaceted, that they requirie diverse sets of expertise, and that hierarchy is the enemy of rapidity and adaptability.

Along these same lines, resilient responses are able to accommodate emergence. As discussed in Chapter 4, emergent groups are always a part of the response landscape. Organizations may expand in size and may take on tasks they normally do not perform, and volunteers may converge. To focus again on lessons from the Kobe earthquake, hundreds of thousands of people offered volunteer services of all kinds to those in the affected region, but local authorities had difficulty working with volunteer groups. Reasons for their exclusion included Japan's state-centered view of how disasters should be managed and its general suspicion of voluntary organizations. In the aftermath of the earthquake, 1995 was referred to as "the first year of the volunteer," voluntary organizations active in disaster (VOADs) were formed, and laws were changed to make it easier for voluntary groups to function (Tierney 2012).

EMONs are also an invariant feature of disaster responses. Organizations typically cluster around problem-solving tasks, many of which are unique to specific disasters. For example, Christine Bevc (2010) studied the EMON that developed during the emergency period that followed the terrorist attacks on the World Trade Center in 2001. That EMON consisted of more than 700 different public, private sector, and nonprofit organizations as well as newly emergent entities, all of which were organized around forty-two different tasks. Some of those tasks, such as caring for those who were injured, were typical tasks performed in disasters, while others, for example investigating the rubble from the towers as a crime scene, were not typical. Bevc's network analyses showed that some organizational entities rose to prominence unexpectedly by taking on roles that were not specified in disaster plans, because particular activities were necessary. The Trade Center response was typical of what happens in large-scale disasters.

Butts, Acton, and Marcum (2012) studied EMONs that developed during warning and emergency periods in the multistate area that was struck by Hurricane Katrina. They identified 187 distinct networks that clustered around different tasks and changed over time. Regarding how organizations coordinated their activities, they noted that

> coordination roles in the inner core of the Katrina EMON appear to be filled by a combination of organizations with a standing mandate to bridge diverse groups and organizations whose centrality emerges from tasks and resource considerations that are peculiar to the specific event. (Butts, Acton, and Marcum 2012: 25)

Disaster planning seeks to identify and address problems that could emerge during disasters, but disasters always contain an element of the unexpected. This is one of the reasons why emergence is so common. A resilient disaster response is flexible enough to incorporate groups that were not identified in prior planning.

As discussed earlier in Chapter 4, scholars have pointed to the role of improvisation in disaster response (Weick 1998; Kendra and Wachtendorf 2003, 2006; Wachtendorf 2004; Mendonça and Wallace 2007). Because disaster impacts cannot be planned for in totality, disasters almost always create problems that were not envisioned in the original plan. Like jazz pianists and improvisational actors, responders must depart from scores and scripts in order to put together an effective performance. Let us return to the World Trade Center attacks. The Mayor's Office of Emergency Management (OEM) in New York was located in one of the buildings of the World Trade Center complex – a building that caught fire and collapsed on the afternoon of September 11. Surprisingly, the OEM did not have a backup site from which to coordinate emergency operations, which forced the organization to improvise an emergency operations center (EOC) in the middle of a major crisis response. After moving to different locations and not having enough room for all the organizations and personnel that were taking part in the response, the OEM reestablished the EOC in one of the massive piers that line the Hudson River on the west side of Manhattan. The pier accommodated both the entities that had been involved in pre-disaster planning and other organizations, which joined the response team for specific purposes, such as producing maps to show damaged areas and assistance sites, since the OEM had lost its map-making capabilities (Wachtendorf 2004).

Approximately 1 million people were in Lower Manhattan at the time of the attacks, and the subways and trains were not operational. Many people walked uptown and over the Brooklyn Bridge to get home, but an estimated 300,000 people were evacuated by water, by means of a spontaneous, improvised system that brought together ferries, tugboats, fishing boats, dinner boats, sightseeing vessels, government watercraft, and other types of vessels. Mariners saw the need that day; they understood the waterways around Manhattan like no one else, so they immediately began a process of self-organizing (Kendra and Wachtendorf 2016). Similarly, in the aftermath of Hurricane Katrina, private boat owners spontaneously organized what they called the Cajun Navy and headed to New Orleans to rescue people who had been trapped by the flood waters. Some of these same boat operators left Louisiana to perform rescues after Hurricane Harvey in 2017.

Improvising response activities does not mean making up those activities out of whole cloth. Just as students of jazz view improvisation as the outcome of mastering many musical forms, students of disaster responses see improvisation as arising from previously acquired knowledge. In New York, members of the OEM staff had a mental picture of how the EOC needed to be organized and what groups needed to participate. At the same time, they needed to make room for new players who had resources and skills to offer. Boat operators had a thorough understanding of the waters surrounding Manhattan, but they also found creative ways of identifying who needed to go where and of labeling origins and destinations in ways that evacuees could understand. As these examples show, improvisation involves retaining pre-disaster knowledge when it makes sense to do so while also using ingenuity to tackle unexpected challenges.

Continuing with this theme, those who are involved in responding to disasters must know that they can and should improvise and adapt when the situation calls for it. Organizational practices that confine actors to narrow roles and responsibilities and want things done "by the book" discourage improvisation. Organizational scholars point to conditions that increase the likelihood that disasters are averted and, when they happen, are managed well. Such conditions include extensive experience on the part of organizational actors; diversity in terms of competencies, experiences, and perspectives; and effective communication among actors. Researchers point to the importance of nonhierarchical relationships within organizations, such that lower-level staffers know that they have permission to speak up when they see anomalies or signs of impending disaster (Weick and Roberts 1993; Weick, Sutcliffe, and Obstfeld 1999). Resources are also important. Schulman (1993) refers to the importance of "resource slack," that is, personnel, funds, and material resources that exist over and above what an organization needs for its daily operations and can be rapidly accessed should the need arise. If organizations do not possess those resources themselves, they should have easy ways of obtaining them, which is one reason why various types of mutual aid pacts – for example, among police departments, utility companies, and states – are common in emergency management. Similarly, health and public health organizations have devised ways of increasing their surge capacity in disasters and other emergencies, for instance disease outbreaks.

Resilient disaster response involves anticipating disaster impacts on the built environment and exposed populations while also expecting the unexpected. Pre-disaster hazard assessments, impact and loss estimates, scenarios, and policies designed to identify specific vulnerabilities and vulnerable groups help communities understand the likely consequences of different types of disasters. A knowledge-based planning process increases the chances that the community will be able to respond effectively. At the same time, community leaders and those charged with carrying out response activities should take a critical stance and question their assumptions, both about impacts and about their own response capabilities. What if hazard assessments are based on outdated science? What if community vulnerability analyses overlook important population changes? How current (or outdated) are the resource lists kept by emergency management organizations?

Along with the need to base response plans on sound information, outside-the-box thinking is also required. What if some impacts that have been envisioned do not materialize, but other unanticipated impacts occur? Will the response system be flexible enough to deal with those impacts? Do entities that are planning to respond have significant blind spots, and could they benefit from seeking out external and dissenting perspectives? We saw earlier that, before the earthquake–tsunami–nuclear-plant meltdowns in Japan in 2011, there was evidence that a major earthquake that occurred hundreds of years ago in the same region had generated a gigantic tsunami. Tokyo Power Company (TEPCO), which owned and operated the Fukushima nuclear plants, had been informed that the facilities could be disabled by a very large tsunami. However, echoing discussions in Chapter 4, there was a failure to engage in possibilistic thinking, and TEPCO did not take steps to enact countermeasures.

Relatedly, disaster response organizations should be learning organizations. They should learn from the disasters they experience, from the experiences of other communities, and from drills and exercises. One reason why after-action reports are developed after disasters and exercises is to identify lessons learned. Equally if not more importantly, however, in order to be resilient, response organizations must incorporate those lessons into their procedures and practices. Sadly, organizations and communities have a tendency to content themselves with pointing out lessons learned and areas in need of improvement, without adapting or changing.

Resilient Disaster Recovery

Although progress has been made in the past few years, recovery remains the least studied of the stages of the hazards cycle – a carryover from the days when disaster response was receiving the lion's share of research. Still, researchers can point to factors that predict positive recovery outcomes, which is one way of conceptualizing resilience. Earlier discussions of resilience have focused to some extent on recovery, for example by homing in on conditions that appear to be associated with either positive or negative outcomes for households and businesses. Here we focus on factors that influence recovery at the community scale.

Disaster recovery is "the differential process of restoring, rebuilding, and reshaping the physical, social, economic, and natural environment through pre-event planning and post-event actions" (Smith and Wenger 2007: 237). Several aspects of this definition are important to note. First, recovery is differential in the sense that different aspects of disaster-stricken communities recover at different rates, as do different social groups. Second, recovery should be thought of as a process or series of processes, not an end point; and, particularly in cases where disaster impacts are severe, such processes can go on for years, or even for decades. Third, recovery is complex, encompassing multiple aspects of community life. Box 6.1 on page 164 lists just a few dimensions and domains in which recovery processes operate. As the definition given here and the items on the list indicate, disaster recovery involves much more than physical reconstruction. It takes social, psychological, cultural, and institutional dimensions.

If we focus on this short list of recovery domains, it is evident that many dimensions of recovery are interdependent and that some of its aspects

---

Box 6.1 What Needs to Recover after Disasters? Examples of Disaster Recovery Domains

Temporary and permanent housing   Household quality of life
Infrastructure: utilities, roads, etc.   Physical well-being
Public buildings   Psychological well-being
Commercial and industrial buildings   "Community spirit" and attachment
Businesses and jobs   Distinctive aspects of community
Disrupted economies   culture
Key community institutions: schools,   Environment, ecosystems, and
neighborhoods hospitals, etc.   natural resources

---

assume priority. For example, it will be difficult to restore housing if major utilities such as power and water are unavailable; and it will be difficult to restore neighborhoods without homes, schools, and businesses. Similarly, lost jobs and economic activity will not be able to recover unless businesses can reopen; businesses also depend on the availability of utilities and buildings from which to operate, and they need transportation systems to be restored, so that they are able to receive shipments and customers are able to reach them. Additionally, transportation systems must be functional and ensure that the supplies needed to repair and rebuild public, commercial, and industrial buildings are available. Household quality of life, psychological well-being, community spirit, and cultural recovery all depend, at least to some degree, on the restoration of the built environment and on the recovery of key community institutions. Researchers have explored these interdependencies through modeling and simulation, with an eye on identifying which pre-disaster measures (e.g. utility-system mitigation measures) and post-disaster actions (e.g. rapid debris removal, utility-system restoration) contribute to better, more resilient recovery outcomes (Miles and Chang 2003, 2006, 2011). To ensure resilient recovery, those in charge of the process must understand interdependencies across domains and scales and guide recovery activities accordingly.

Studies of disasters in the United States and around the world have uncovered a variety of factors that encourage resilient disaster recovery. Laurie Johnson and Robert Olshansky (2016) studied recovery processes after major disasters in six different countries: the 1995 Kobe earthquake and the 2011 earthquake and tsunami in Japan; the 2001 World Trade Center attacks; the 2001 Gujurat earthquake in India; the 2004 Indian Ocean earthquake and tsunami in Indonesia; hurricanes Katrina and Rita in the United States in 2005; the 2008 Wenchuan earthquake in China; the 2010–2011 Canterbury earthquake sequence in New Zealand; and Hurricane Sandy in the United States (2012). In some of these cases, such as the 2008 earthquake in China and the 2010–2011 earthquakes in New Zealand, recovery plans and policies were directed by the central government. In others, such as the Japan earthquakes, there was strong central government involvement but also ties with other levels of government. In Indonesia and India the recovery planning and management were more decentralized and balanced; there were multiple entities at different levels that coordinated their activities.

Although these disasters took place in different societies that had different forms of governance and systems for providing recovery aid, Johnson and Olshansky saw commonalities across the cases they studied, and these commonalities led to recommendations about how to achieve positive disaster recovery outcomes – what I call resilient recovery. One key recommendation concerns the locus of recovery decision-making and direction. As we saw with disaster response, in contrast with decentralized and community-based approaches, centrally controlled recovery activities have a downside. In the Wenchuan earthquake, for example, recovery was directed by China's central State Council and aligned with central governmental priorities such as urbanizing the countryside and promoting tourism, as opposed to local concerns and preferences. Rebuilding took place rapidly and entire communities were moved and rebuilt, but in most cases recovery activities were carried out without public involvement and relatively little attention was paid to restoring livelihoods and social networks and addressing community needs. Although the political and economic conditions were different, this same pattern was seen in China after the devastating 1976 Tangshan earthquake, which destroyed 95 percent of the buildings in that city of 500,000 and killed approximately 242,000.[2] As in the Wenchuan case, the central government developed a recovery process for Tangshan that was consistent with its own goals, the emphasis was on physical reconstruction, and public participation was lacking (Zhang, Zhang, Drake, and Olshansky 2014).

Less centralized processes may be more difficult to manage and recovery may take longer, as more actors are involved and there is broader community participation, but the outcomes are likely to be more satisfactory. In addition to recommending that it is important to decentralize recovery decision-making and management as much as possible, build capacity, and empower the residents of disaster-stricken communities, Johnson and Olshansky (2016) offer the following recommendations:

- obtain and distribute recovery funding efficiently, effectively, and equitably;
- collect and disseminate information to all parties in the recovery process, for example by employing newsletters, websites, paid liaisons, and entities that bring together key personnel from lead agencies and the public;

- support collaboration, both horizontally (across similar types of organizations and at the same level of governance) and vertically (across scales and levels of governance);
- meet immediate, urgent needs in disaster-affected areas while thinking ahead to plan for longer-term community improvements;
- plan and act simultaneously; take actions that are feasible right away while still paying attention to situations that need longer-term deliberation;
- budget for the costs of communication and planning, revise budgets over time, and plan for contingencies in case things go wrong with some aspects of recovery;
- avoid the permanent relocation of residents and affected communities, except when it is clearly necessary, and then take steps to ensure full participation on the part of residents;
- reconstruct quickly, but do not rush; do not sacrifice to speed other important elements of recovery, such as community participation.

Sociologist Brenda Phillips has studied post-disaster recovery extensively. She argues that six principles characterize positive and sustainable disaster recovery: (1) an inclusive, participatory recovery planning and implementation process; (2) a focus on community quality of life; (3) a commitment to economic vitality and diversity; (4) a concern with social and intergenerational equity; (5) a focus on preserving and improving the natural environment and ecosystems; and (6) activities aimed at reducing the impacts of future disasters (Phillips 2009). Other scholars, too, offer guidance on how to accomplish holistic and sustainable community recovery. Mileti (1999) and Smith and Wenger (2007) point to five conditions that make for better recovery outcomes. Community involvement is essential. Recovery policies should be based on as much relevant information as communities can gather, including details on the population and the built environment, the local economy, and the available sources of recovery funds. Recovery requires an organizational structure that comprises not only government agencies but also other community organizations, including emergent ones. Attention should be paid to modifying policies in light of the community's disaster experience, for example by changing land use patterns or by upgrading building codes to reduce future losses. There should also be an emphasis on identifying diverse ways of financing recovery.

Coordination among actors around providing assistance is essential for a resilient disaster recovery, but is often difficult to achieve. This is particularly true in less developed societies, which must rely on outside entities and international NGOs (INGOs) for recovery assistance. Disasters in less developed countries often spur into action various freelancers and organizations that want to demonstrate the efficacy of their particular disaster recovery solutions, with little interorganizational coordination. The 2010 Haiti earthquake is a case in point. As we saw in Chapter 3, Haiti was known as a "republic of NGOs" on account of the extensive involvement of nonprofits in virtually all aspects of community life and the weakness of state institutions. After the earthquake, many of those NGOs sprang into action and were joined by newcomers to Haiti who wanted to assist in any way they could, as well as by for-profit entities that provided assistance. At the same time, many government ministries had been destroyed in the earthquake and many officials were killed, which further eroded government capacity. That scarcely mattered, because NGOs were accustomed to bypassing the state, which they continued to do after the earthquake. The United Nations, which had a large presence in Haiti, was attempting to coordinate INGOs by clustering them together around key recovery tasks such as housing, but those efforts were largely ineffective in Haiti. NGO leaders rotated out of Haiti and were replaced so often that there was little continuity of effort. Decisions were made without input from the residents of the affected areas and, rather than coordinating, officials from different hard-hit jurisdictions competed for aid. The result was a disorganized relief and recovery effort fraught with duplication, service gaps, and ill-informed decision-making – for example, temporary housing was located in areas prone to flooding (Ritchie and Tierney 2011; Katz 2013). United Nations troops that were sent to Haiti from Nepal after the earthquake caused a cholera epidemic that killed thousands. Five years after the earthquake, National Public Radio and the investigative journalism group ProPublica documented massive waste and lack of transparency by the Red Cross in Haiti (Elliott and Sullivan 2015). It was subsequently revealed that aid workers from Oxfam International, an INGO, held sex parties with earthquake victims and paid to have sex with residents, who were forced into prostitution to make a living.

Social capital and disaster recovery

Political scientist Daniel Aldrich has explored the relationship between social capital and recovery in a range of disaster situations. In *Building Resilience: Social Capital in Post-Disaster Recovery* (Aldrich 2012a), he analyzed the role of social capital in facilitating community recovery in three major disasters: the 1923 Great Kanto (Tokyo) earthquake, the 1995 Great Hanshin-Awaji (Kobe) earthquake, and the 2004 Indian Ocean tsunami. In all three cases he found that social capital – variously measured as voter turnout, political activism, civic and social movement participation, and "linking" connections to higher governmental levels – was a predictor of recovery outcomes such as a more rapid repopulation of damaged areas. With respect to the Kobe earthquake, Aldrich (2010) also noted that weak or absent social capital ties proved harmful. After that disaster, elderly survivors were randomly assigned to apartments in large complexes, but no consideration was given to keeping their pre-disaster social networks intact. With little opportunity to socialize, receive social support, or have someone to look after them on a regular basis, many of these elders died alone, and suicide was suspected in some of those cases. After the earthquake, the Japanese word *kodokushi*, "lonely death," was used to describe such situations (see also Otani 2010).

Aldrich later turned his attention to studying recovery after the 2011 Japan triple disaster. Among other topics, he focused on the role of community elders and of the concept of *ibasho* in the recovery process. The term *ibasho* designates a place where people come together to interact informally and where they feel at home. In one of the worst affected communities, an NGO called Ibasho established the Ibasho Café as an informal community space, with the intention of building social capital and empowering elderly residents. In its first year, the café served more than 5,000 people and hosted more than fifty community-oriented events. In their research, Aldrich and his collaborators found that, for those who took part in its activities, the café encouraged the formation of social networks and restored a sense of belonging. Elders developed a sense of solidarity, as well as confidence in the progress they were making toward recovery. Moreover, through their participation in café events and activities, elderly disaster survivors found a renewed sense of purpose:

> By demonstrating the knowledge, skills and experience they have to offer [elders] have proven that they are not just a vulnerable population who needs to be looked after and protected. Rethinking their roles in the community made many elders realize that they still want to be active participants in the community life. (Kiyota, Tanaka, Arnold, and Aldrich 2015: 32)

In *Black Wave*, Aldrich (2019) presents data from a number of communities in the three prefectures most hard-hit by the triple disaster (Iwate, Miyagi, and Fukushima), in order to show how social networks were important throughout the hazards cycle and at different units of analysis. For example, family and neighborhood relationships influenced the evacuation process for individuals and households, and social ties affected how survivors fared in emergency shelters and temporary housing. Residents of close-knit neighborhoods and local organizations self-organized during the period immediately after disaster impact, when some local governments were not functioning. Prefectures and local communities relied on their ties with the central government as well as on international sources of aid (i.e. social capital of the linking type) to seek out needed response and recovery resources, although with varying levels of success.

Researchers affiliated with the Mercatus Center at George Mason University conducted a series of studies and have published extensively on post-Katrina recovery (Chamlee-Wright 2010; Chamlee-Wright and Storr 2009, 2010, 2011). Their research provides a number of examples of how social, cultural, and religious ties influenced rates of return and recovery in the aftermath of Katrina. On the basis of their studies, they argue that financial assistance alone, even if substantial, does little good without the participation of civil society institutions in the recovery process. They also argue that local, bottom-up, non-bureaucratized recovery activities are more likely to be successful than top-down programs, because they are more closely aligned with the needs and values of those affected by disasters. Like other researchers, the Mercatus Center group argues that, when governmental entities become involved in disaster recovery, they should do so in ways that restore and support social capital ties.

More rapid or better, more sustainable recovery?

For many years, recovery processes were seen in a positive light if they resulted in a smooth and timely return to the *status quo ante*. Early discussions of the concept of resilience (e.g. Bruneau et al. 2003) emphasized rapidity as a key dimension of resilience. It is now recognized that, while speed is important in some respects – for example, in getting victims the medical treatment they need and in restoring or replacing critical services such as the provision of water and other lifeline services – it is not necessarily associated with more resilient recovery outcomes. Acting in haste, communities may close off desirable future options: for example, after a flood they may permit reconstruction in known flood-prone areas when they really should be taking other steps, such as buying out flood-prone properties or revising their land use plans. Community residents and business owners understandably want recovery to take place as swiftly as possible so they can get back to their lives, but there are many aspects of community recovery that require study and deliberation.

The recovery period is a time when communities have an opportunity to take steps that make them more resilient to future disasters and more sustainable overall. The tiny rural town of Greensburg, Kansas is one example. Greensburg experienced a devastating tornado in May, 2007 that almost wiped the town off the map. Facing such ruin, the community developed a long-term recovery plan aimed at making Greensburg a "green community." Recovery policies specified that all public buildings over 4,000 square feet would have to be rebuilt to meet the highest standards established by the US Green Building Council, known as LEED-Platinum, and that they had to use renewable energy sources. Greensburg was successful in carrying out that vision. The idea spread to the private sector, with the result that Greensburg now has what may be the world's only LEED-Platinum tractor dealership. In keeping with the town's vision, the owners of that business went on to set up a wind-energy company. Greensburg attracted attention from around the world for its sustainable recovery practices and became the subject of documentaries, including one narrated by Leonardo di Caprio, as well as of books such as *The Greening of Oz: Sustainable Recovery in the Wake of a Tornado* (Fraga 2012). The town is unlikely to experience a direct hit from a tornado in the future (although that cannot be ruled out), but it did seize recovery-period opportunities to build a more sustainable future. Tulsa, Oklahoma is another example of a community that steadily improved its disaster resilience over time as a result of a series of deadly and damaging floods. (See Box 6.2 for details of Tulsa's story.)

Critiques of the resilience concept

The concept of resilience is not without its critics. One problem with the term is that it is so widely used, and by so many different constituencies, that its meaning has become increasingly vague. Diverse actors infuse the concept with diverse meanings, and there is little clarity or consensus on what actually constitutes resilience. In many quarters resilience has supplanted old disaster terminology, which refers to mitigation, preparedness, response, and recovery; so those concepts, which have more concrete meanings, are subsumed under the "resilience" rubric.

Critics also focus on what they see as the ideological aspects of the concept, noting how it consistently meshes with neoliberal constructions of the state and of social life (for discussions of neoliberalism, see Peck and Tickell 2002; Peck 2010). Neoliberalization, the reigning ideological and practical framing of state–society relations, envisions a diminished role for the state while privileging private sector and civil society solutions for societal challenges. Among other things, the process of neoliberalization presupposes devolution to the private sector of activities formerly performed by the public sector, for instance the delivery of services by private contractors and public–private partnerships, as a means of addressing societal problems.

Neoliberalization typically brings about a rollback of state services and the requirement that recipients of assistance meet conditions set out by service providers – for example, by making work a requirement for government aid, even if recipients are unable to work. It pressures individuals to be entrepreneurial by seizing opportunities for themselves; they should be flexible and adaptable – in other words, they should be resilient. If they are not, then they are not worthy of receiving support. By putting the onus of qualifying for assistance on the individual, neoliberalism treats receiving assistance as a privilege rather than as a right. To be resilient, individuals are to adapt in the face of forces such as rapid urbanization and climate change – forces that are framed as inevitable (see, for example, Rodin 2014). As Julian Reid observes, the pressure to cope in the face of those sorts of chronic and acute stressors aims at producing a resilient subject, "which must permanently struggle to accommodate itself to the world[,] a subject that accepts the disastrousness of the world it lives in as a condition of partaking in that world" (Reid 2013: 355). Resilient subjects are not political subjects with rights, but rather individuals who have "accepted the imperative not to resist or secure themselves from

Box 6.2 Building Resilience into Recovery and Beyond: The Case of Tulsa, Oklahoma

Located on the Arkansas River and within the Mingo Creek watershed, Tulsa, Oklahoma has a long history of flood disasters: there were major floods in 1923, 1970, 1974, and 1976, as well as an especially deadly and damaging flood in 1984. Over all that period the city's flood losses increased steadily, in part because the city had relied on levees and dams for flood protection and had allowed intensive development in the floodplain.

In response to repeated floods and other disasters (at one point, Tulsa led the nation in the number of federal disaster declarations), Tulsa devised a range of strategies meant to reduce flood losses. After the flooding in 1974, the city designed and initiated the Mingo Creek Improvement project, which protected approximately 700 homes from future flooding. After another damaging flood in 1976, the city received federal funds to begin acquiring land in the floodplain. The city also passed a moratorium on building in the floodplain, developed comprehensive floodplain and storm water management programs, and established a flood early alert and warning system. After the 1984 flood, which left fourteen people dead, the city relocated 300 homes and a mobile home park, began a detainment basin project with the Army Corps of Engineers, established a city department of stormwater management, and initiated a stormwater utility fee. Over time, the city acquired 1,000 flood-prone properties, made decisions designed to preserve one quarter of the floodplain as open space, and adopted strict flood-resistant building codes.

Owing to its flood management initiatives and efforts, Tulsa received special recognition from the FEMA in 2000 and from the Department of Homeland Security in 2003. The city currently receives a rating of 2 (the second-highest rating) on the Community Rating Scale for flood risk reduction and, as a result, the flood insurance rates for Tulsa residents are significantly lower than those in other flood-prone communities around the country.

Tulsa is also a national leader in preparedness programs for floods, tornadoes, and other disasters. The city received funding during the 1990s under FEMA's short-lived Project Impact program, which provided support for loss reduction-planning projects, community education, and the development of public–private disaster preparedness partnerships. When that program ended, Tulsa developed a spin-off organization called Tulsa Partners, which continued that work and was especially successful in public–private partnership building. One notable public education project involved a 2003 partnership designed to distribute disaster preparedness materials in thirty-two McDonald's restaurants in Tulsa. The city also became active in Citizens Corps, a Department of Homeland Security program that was meant to engage community volunteers in disaster preparedness and response activities. In 2006, Tulsa Partners joined with the insurance industry–supported Institute of Business and Home Safety in order to establish a Disaster Resistant Business Council. Another collaboration, with the nonprofit organization Save the Children, focused on disaster preparedness for day-care centers.

Recent activities and efforts in Tulsa have extended beyond preparedness for extreme events. For example, in collaboration with the Tulsa Zoo, Tulsa Partners launched the Millenium Center for Green and Safe Living. The center, located at the zoo, provides environmental education programs for the public as well as information on both disaster-resistant and sustainable building materials and construction practices. The city also participates in the Mayors' Climate Protection Agreement, a project of the US Conference of Mayors.

Decisions regarding floodplain management and other disaster loss reduction programs came about in a variety of ways. Repeated flooding made flood hazards difficult to ignore and led to the formation of citizen groups that pressured the local government to act. Although community pressure was initially ignored, flooding in 1976 and the subsequent involvement of a member of Congress helped with gaining additional support. The Army Corps of Engineers was a source of needed technical information, and the passage of the Water Resources Development Act, which was championed by the same Congress member, also provided a stimulus for further action. The 1984 floods occurred only nineteen days after the election of a new mayor, who subsequently organized a flood hazard mitigation team for the city. The mayor was assisted in these efforts by other committed local officials, including a city attorney, and by engineering consultants. Later on, FEMA Project Impact funds provided support for coordinated local disaster loss reduction activities, and local businesses stepped in to continue those efforts when federal support ended.

Tulsa Partners changed its name to the Disaster Resilience Network in 2016. The city continues to garner recognition for its resilience-enhancing efforts. Tulsa also joined the Rockefeller Foundation's 100 Resilient Cities initiative, which provides support for a chief resilience officer position as well as various types of technical assistance. (For additional discussions, see Patton 1994; Meo, Ziebro, and Patton 2004; Bullock, Haddow, and Haddow 2008.)

the dangers they face but instead adapt to their enabling conditions" (2013: 355). This view is echoed by other critics – such as Jonathan Joseph, who has argued that "the recent enthusiasm for the concept of resilience across a range of policy literature is the consequence of its fit with neoliberal discourse" (Joseph, quoted in Reid 2013: 38), which shifts the responsibility for public welfare and well-being from the state to the individual. The resilient subject has no choice but to adapt in the face of societal and global changes that are framed as inevitable.

Some disaster scholars observe that the diminished role envisioned for the state and the privileging of the private sector in activities like disaster recovery – both of which are embedded in the neoliberal political economy and resilience discourse – inevitably create problems. In the United States, where neoliberal principles hold sway and shape disaster recovery practices, recovery activities have been increasingly privatized. Services delivered by the private sector are very expensive because private providers have to make a profit, which leads to bloated budgets. Giving private sector actors large amounts of money to perform services that are necessary in disaster recovery leads to a decline in transparency and accountability. Without adequate oversight – which is difficult to achieve in large-scale disasters – private contractors engage in wasteful practices and are often free to decide for themselves who is worthy of receiving services. Benefits typically accrue to disaster survivors who have the means, connections, and cultural competence to navigate in the disaster assistance landscape – in other words, to survivors who are resilient by virtue of their high levels of social capital. Those who are unable to become "empowered consumers" in the post-disaster environment – the poor, the vulnerable, those who lack bureaucratic savvy – often receive far less than they deserve (Gotham 2012; Adams 2012).

Disaster management and resilience discourses tout the idea of a "whole-of-community" approach to addressing hazard- and disaster-related problems, typically without recognizing that burdening civil society with tasks formerly carried out by government is part of the neoliberal playbook. Focusing on the Covid pandemic, for example, Marybeth Stalp and her collaborators describe how literally thousands of quilters, sewers, and 3D print experts were called into service to produce masks and other personal protective equipment (PPE) for hospital personnel and the general public when government entities were unable to meet the demand. Like a good deal of crisis volunteering, this work was done primarily by women. While many PPE-makers were happy that they were able to contribute to reducing pandemic risks, others reacted with a combination of astonishment and anger at being asked to perform tasks and contribute materials gratis because of government's inability to meet Covid PPE needs (Leap, Stalp, and Kelly 2022). While the activities of these groups are an excellent example of emergence, as discussed in Chapter 4, they are also indicative of neoliberalism's rollback of state responsibilities for public health and safety.

Some resilience theorists emphasize that true resilience involves not only adaptation in the face of shocks and stressors, but also transformative activities that overcome those stressors by drastically reducing them. Such activities would require, for example, shifting from fossil fuels to 100 percent renewable energy as a way of reducing the impacts of climate change (Pelling 2011), or greatly reducing income inequality as a way of reducing disaster vulnerability. These kinds of transformative changes can be brought about only by overcoming systems of power and privilege. But resilience discourse is largely silent on issues of power that come to the fore when the focus is on social systems. In ecological systems where the concept of resilience originated, species adapt, but human communities can resist, and in some cases bring about large-scale change.

Relatedly, along with eliding issues of power, resilience discourse seldom acknowledges the political–economic drivers of the problems that resilience-enhancing activities are supposed to overcome – arrangements that have been emphasized at various points in this volume. As one critic of the concept puts it:

> Homelessness, global warming-induced environmental disaster, and poverty are consequences of capitalism[, which] depends upon exploitation and the expropriation of human and other natural resources. Resilience framing obscures collective comprehension of how capitalism produces these disasters, and it redirects human energy away from pursuing collective projects, politics, and ways of living that would pose the best chance of collective survival rather than adaptation to ever-worsening catastrophe. (Saltman 2024: 9)

Concluding Comments

In this chapter we have explored the concept of disaster resilience from a variety of angles: how it is defined, how it is measured at different levels of analysis, what factors contribute to resilience, and what constitutes resilient disaster response and recovery. We have also looked at programs that seek to enhance resilience in the face of hazards and disasters. Additionally, we have considered critical perspectives on resilience, particularly on the way it is framed and practiced in the context of neoliberalism. These critiques are important, but it is also important to recognize that resilience does exist. As we have seen, some communities, societies, and groups are better than others at mitigating, preparing for, responding to, and recovering from extreme events. This chapter has attempted to show why that is the case by emphasizing the importance of avoiding hierarchical notions of command and control, of insisting on flexibility and adaptability in response and recovery activities, and of understanding the needs of communities that have experienced disasters.

QUESTIONS AND EXERCISES

Based on your reading, describe the characteristics of a disaster-resilient community.

Using FEMA's Hazard Vulnerability and Resilience Tool and its Resilience Zone designations, focus on a "resilient" community/zone. Does the designation make sense to you?

Take a deeper dive into the neoliberalism–resilience nexus. How do some critics view the resilience concept?

7

Key Contributions from Other Disciplines

Introduction

The ingredients necessary for the sociological study of disasters do not reside solely within the discipline itself. Sociology and its various subfields are broad and often merge into adjacent or complementary fields. Cross-fertilization is also evident in the area of methods; for example, while originally developed by geographers, various mapping and spatioanalytic methodologies are now widely employed by sociologists and other social scientists. As fields have become increasingly multi- and interdisciplinary, disciplinary boundaries have become more porous. This is particularly true in problem-focused fields such as disaster research (and environmental studies more generally), which can involve teams of researchers from different fields and a good deal of borrowing and synthesis across disciplines.

We should therefore take a broad view of what constitutes the sociology of disasters, regarding it as a sociological subfield that draws upon research conducted in other social and policy sciences and is catholic in its methods. Under this big umbrella, the field has evolved both by employing perspectives that are sui generis and by borrowing creatively from ones developed in other disciplines. What matters is not so much whether specific disaster studies are carried out by bona fide sociologists, but rather whether their findings are sociologically relevant and rest upon assumptions that are consistent with sociological reasoning.

With those caveats in mind, I focus here on perspectives and methods from six other disciplines that contribute to our sociological understanding of disasters: anthropology, economics, geography, political science and public administration, psychology, and urban planning. This is not meant to be an exhaustive review of each and every contribution from outside sociology; rather the intent is to provide examples of contributions from a select group of disciplines that have had a significant influence on sociological thought on the subject of disasters.

Contributions from Selected Disciplines

Anthropology

Anthropology scholars who study hazards and disasters are relatively few in number, but they have had a significant impact on the sociological study of disasters (for overviews of past and current research in the field, see Oliver-Smith 1996; 2015a; 2015b; Oliver-Smith and Hoffman 1999; Hoffman and Oliver-Smith 2002; Faas and Barrios 2015; Barrios 2017). Like sociology, anthropology stresses that the meanings associated with disasters are not given, but are rather socially and culturally constructed.

Key strengths of anthropological approaches are their focus on culture in its various manifestations, their commitment to long-term engagement in disaster-stricken communities, their emphasis on societies other than the western ones in which many other social scientists conduct research, and their related concern with problems of global poverty and marginalization (see e.g. Barrios 2017; Garcia-Acosta 2020; Faas 2023). Anthropologists remind us that nature, space, and the built environment are imbued with symbolic significance and that it is important in a disaster context to understand the meanings people attach to them. Further, in line with ideas advanced here, anthropological scholars document historical processes that contribute to disaster and vulnerability production, point to the significance of power imbalances in shaping both vulnerability and resilience, and critically interrogate the reigning concepts and practices of neoliberal "development."

The use of in-depth ethnographic methods is a hallmark of anthropological research that has enabled anthropologists to develop a nuanced understanding of such topics as variations in the cultural interpretations of hazards and disasters across societies and over time, how cultural beliefs and practices influence adaptation strategies in the face of extreme events, and the role of culture in individual and community disaster experiences and disaster recovery. In an example of the anthropological approach to studying recovery, shortly after the Katrina catastrophe, anthropologist Katherine Browne began following a large extended African American family that was displaced by the hurricane. Subsequently she spent more than eight years documenting their experiences. Her book *Standing in the Need: Culture, Comfort, and Coming Home after Katrina* (Browne 2015) and the accompanying documentary *Still Waiting* tell the story of how family members were able to sustain their distinctive "cultural cycle" through reliance on family traditions such as cooking and eating special meals together and on institutions such as the Black church.

The edited volume *Contextualizing Disasters* (Button and Schuller 2016) is another example of an anthropological approach to disaster studies. Two overarching themes are evident in that compilation. The first emphasizes the diversity of narratives that frame understandings of disaster phenomena, for instance mass media views, survivors' perspectives as expressed in their own narratives, and officially produced narratives. That such accounts quite often diverge is a reflection of different institutional priorities, efforts at a hegemonic control of information, and often the silencing of survivors' voices.

A second theme highlights the importance of the connection between the operation of the global political economy – processes such as globalization, neoliberalization, and the imposition of economic restructuring and austerity measures – and ethnographical accounts of the local, on-the-ground impacts of such processes in different societal contexts – along with the importance of merging our knowledge of these two sides.

Cognitive psychology, behavioral economics, and economics

These three areas of inquiry are discussed together here, although they are in many ways dissimilar. With respect to hazards and disasters, cognitive psychology and behavioral economics, which also form the foundation of the interdisciplinary field of decision science, focus primarily on individual perceptions and decision-making, while the more general field of economics tends to be meso- and macro-oriented, emphasizing for example the impact of extreme events on losses and recovery at business, community, regional, and national levels and on the costs and benefits associated with different strategies for managing hazards.

Decision-making and heuristics

Psychologists Amos Tversky and 2002 Nobel laureate in economics Daniel Kahneman influenced disaster studies primarily through their contributions in the areas of risk perception and decision-making. They are best known for developing prospect theory, a descriptive theory of decision-making that stands in contrast to expected utility theory – the normative "rational actor" paradigm that is favored by classical economists (Kahneman and Tversky 1979). While expected utility theory argued that people mentally tally the costs and benefits of their decisions and choose the option that secures the greatest amount of value, prospect theory showed that the options that yield identical values can be selected differently depending on how they are framed – for example, whether they are presented to individuals as gains or losses, probabilities or certainties. One insight from this influential theory is that people are more sensitive to the potential for losses than to the potential for gains, a pattern that is referred to as the endowment effect.

In important related work, Kahneman and Tversky demonstrated that, in order to avoid psychic overload, individuals typically take cognitive shortcuts, called heuristics, when forming judgments in uncertain situations (see Kahneman and Tversky 1972; Tversky and Kahneman 1973, 1974). Thus availability, one of the original heuristics they identified, refers to the ease with which information can be drawn from memory. Information can be more readily available if it is recent or vivid and dramatic, but for this reason the availability heuristic can also create perceptual distortions regarding risk. After learning, say, about a horrible airline crash, a person may be unwilling to fly and may drive to her destination instead, even if airline accidents are exceedingly rare and driving is statistically more dangerous.

Tversky and Kahneman identified other heuristics too, such as anchoring and representativeness, and subsequent research has uncovered additional patterns that often characterize how we think about risks. For example, status quo bias (Samuelson and Zeckhauser 1988) refers to people's tendency to want things in their lives to remain the same – as opposed to making choices that involve change. Particularly when faced with many choices, they tend to decide not to decide. Optimistic bias (Weinstein 1980; 1989) leads individuals to think that the risks they face in areas such as health and safety are lower than those others face. Another heuristic, myopia, relates to bias toward short-term thinking – and specifically to the inability to take the long view when thinking about risk. The affect heuristic (Slovic, Finucane, Peters, and MacGregor 2007; Slovic 2010) refers to the influence emotions have on decision-making; in the words of Paul Slovic and his collaborators, "images, marked by positive and negative affective feelings, guide judgment and decision making" (Slovic et al. 2007: 1335; see also Kahneman 2011). Rooted in experience, judgments involving what is good or bad are accompanied by feelings. This happens automatically, often at the unconscious level, and it can influence judgments regarding risk.

A veritable industry has developed around the identification of heuristics, which are too numerous to be discussed here. However, the few heuristics I briefly highlighted have clear implications for how people perceive hazards and act toward them. Status quo bias suggests that, to the extent that people have to make changes in their lives – purchase an insurance, adopt mitigation measures, or perhaps even relocate if they live in a hazardous area – to protect themselves against the potential for disaster, they will tend not to do so. Optimistic bias could lead them to downplay the risks they face. Myopia may limit their ability to think in the present about losses they could well experience over the longer term. The affect heuristic may lead individuals to overestimate the likelihood of risks that trigger especially negative feelings (nuclear power and similar "dread" risks are examples; see Slovic, Fischhoff, and Lichtenstein 1979, 1981), while underestimating prosaic but more probable threats.

Familiarity with heuristics and behavioral economics is important for understanding perceptions and behaviors related to hazards, and also for shaping them. For example, Zaval and Cornwell (2016) argue that, while certain cognitive heuristics lead to inaction about climate change, people may begin to make different judgments on the basis of direct, unpleasant experiences with phenomena such as heat waves, which will become more common as climate change progresses. This is an example of the operation of availability. Noting that many types of decisions – such as not saving for retirement – are not in the best interest of those who make them, Richard Thaler and Cass Sunstein (2008) have advocated policies that "nudge" decision makers in more prudent directions by changing their "choice architecture." In the hazards area, other behavioral economists have suggested ways of nudging homeowners into protecting themselves against disasters, for example through the purchase of insurance (Kunreuther, Pauly, and McMorrow 2013). Because homeowners have a tendency to purchase flood insurance in the aftermath of a flood (availability) and then drop the insurance after periods without flooding (myopia), one way to nudge them into protecting their property would be to make multiyear insurance policies available rather than the annual ones that are currently being offered (Kleindorfer, Kunreuther, and Ou-Yang 2012).

Economic impacts of disasters

Another contribution to the sociological understanding of hazards and disasters comes from economists' research on the global, national, and regional economic impacts of disasters. At the global level, economic losses are highest in developed societies, while death tolls are highest in less developed societies. At the national level, most studies concur that the macroeconomic impacts of disasters are generally small and short-lived (Albala-Bertrand 1993; 2006). Even catastrophic events such as Hurricane Katrina and the 2011 Great Tohoku earthquake, tsunami, and triple nuclear power plant meltdown caused relatively little macro-level economic disruption, except in the short term. It should be noted, however, that these two mega-disasters affected developed societies with very large economies. Some studies suggest that disasters can result in economic downturns in certain societal contexts – for example in small island nations with less diversified economies (Hochrainer 2009). But in many such cases the negative effects on GDP and economic growth may be relatively small and may be offset by external aid, remittances, and investments in reconstruction.

As currently employed, the economic modeling of disaster impacts has four main objectives. First, economic loss estimates are conducted in the immediate aftermath of a disaster, to help determine an event's scope and severity – for example as a way of establishing assistance needs or giving the insurance industry information on potential insured losses. Many rapid economic analyses are carried out by catastrophic modeling firms whose main clients are insurers and reinsurers. The US Geological Survey also employs its Prompt Assessment of Global Earthquakes for Response (PAGER) system to develop rough economic impact estimates for earthquakes around the world. The second and most common type of modeling studies in the academic literature focuses on the economic impacts of disaster events, either in the (relatively) short term or over longer periods. The objectives of such studies include understanding economic recovery processes and analyzing how disasters affect economic trends (see e.g. Chang 2000; Miles and Chang 2006; Chang 2010; Chang and Rose 2012).

Third, economic modeling is also used to estimate losses from disaster events that have not yet occurred. This is done either through probabilistic loss estimation modeling, which takes into account a range or suite of disaster events, or through the analysis of the impacts of scenario events. An example of the latter approach is the US Geological Survey's use of modeling to estimate economic losses in its well-known ShakeOut (earthquake) and ArkStorm (atmospheric river/floods) scenarios.

Finally, economic modeling can be used to estimate the costs and benefits of disaster risk reduction programs – for example, by developing loss estimates with and without particular mitigation measures. An example of this type of analysis is the Natural Hazard Mitigation Saves project (Multihazard Mitigation Council 2019), which used economic modeling to demonstrate that disaster mitigation measures save between four and eleven dollars in avoided losses for every dollar spent, depending on the mitigation measure and disaster agent under consideration.

Geography and spatial social science

As discussed in Chapter 2, geographic research formed part of the foundation for contemporary disaster studies. This involved contributions from US-based researchers like Gilbert White and his collaborators, who emphasized alternative adjustments to natural hazards, as well as from scholars in other countries whose primary focus was on the hazards–disasters development nexus.

Geographers are uniquely positioned to shed light on the conditions that make particular places either more or less hazardous. Geographic information science (GIS) and spatial social science introduced important tools for the study of disasters through their ability to integrate various mapping layers in order to better understand and compare levels of disaster exposure and vulnerability – for example, by combining databases with hazard maps and databases that show built-environment characteristics and census-based population and community characteristics. GIS analyses form the basis of hazard-mapping and loss estimation methodologies. Advances in remote sensing, such as the capacity to use satellite and radar imagery to map hazards and assess disaster impacts on the natural and built environment, have further contributed to geographic understandings of the "hazardousness of place" (for examples, see Poursanidis and Chrysoulakis 2017).

The most influential center for the geographic analysis of hazards and disasters is the Hazards Vulnerability and Resilience Institute (HVRI) at the University of South Carolina. Researchers affiliated with HVRI have conducted research on a wide variety of topics: spatial patterns of hazard risks and disaster losses (Cutter 2001; Ash, Cutter, and Emrich 2013), the analysis and measurement of social vulnerability (Cutter, Boruff, and Shirley 2003; Emrich and Cutter 2011; Cutter 2017), disaster resilience conceptualization and measurement (Cutter, Burton, and Emrich 2010; Cutter, Ash, and Emrich 2016; Cutter 2016), and disaster recovery (Finch, Emrich, and Cutter 2010; Burton, Mitchell, and Cutter 2011; Cutter, Emrich et al. 2016).

Critical geographic perspectives include Marxist theoretical orientations that prioritize the analysis of capitalism and class as drivers of vulnerability. Critical geography reminds us that the patterns we observe vis-à-vis the spatial distribution of populations and social activities are the result of the exercise of political power, both in the present and over time. For example, according to the geographer Edward Soja (2009), gerrymandering, redlining in real estate sales and mortgage lending, exclusionary zoning, and apartheid are examples of the "political organization of space." Other examples abound, for instance ones associated with "not in my backyard" mobilizations, the siting of locally unwanted land uses (LULUs) in low-income neighborhoods, and inequities in the provision of environmental and other amenities.

Political science and public administration

Important foci for political science and public administration research include policy development, agenda setting, policy learning after disasters, and the analysis of the effectiveness of policies and programs aimed at reducing disaster impacts that span pre-, trans-, and post-disaster activities.

One area of inquiry focuses on the extent to which disasters spur policy change. Disasters do not rank high on policy agendas during normal times. The need to reduce disaster risks is most likely to attract attention in the immediate aftermath of disasters, as policy windows that were formerly closed are forced open by those events – and particularly by the way they are framed in the media. As emergency management researcher Claire Rubin has noted in her analyses of emergency management and homeland security legislation and programs over past decades, "certain focusing events drive changes in laws, regulations, systems, and practices. In fact, virtually all major federal laws, executive directives programs, policies, organizational changes, and response systems have resulted from major and catastrophic disasters" (Rubin 2012: 6–7).

There are many examples of such connections. The discovery of major toxic pollution in Love Canal, a neighborhood in Niagara Falls, New York, in 1978 led to the passage of the Comprehensive Environmental Response, Compensation, and Liability Act (CERCLA), known as Superfund, in 1980. The 1984 Bhopal catastrophe in India, in which, as seen earlier, a toxic release from a Union Carbide plant killed thousands and injured half a million people, was followed in 1986 by the passage of the Emergency Planning and Community Right to Know Act, an amendment to the Superfund law that required handlers of hazardous materials to make any information on their inventories available to the public. After the massive Exxon Valdez oil spill, which occurred in 1989, Congress passed the Oil Pollution Act of 1990. The terrorist attacks of September 11, 2001 resulted in the passage of the USA PATRIOT Act and the formation of the Department of Homeland Security (DHS); and, after Hurricane Katrina, Congress passed the Post-Katrina Emergency Management Reform Act and the Pets Evacuation and Transportation Standards Act, known as the PETS Act.

However, not all disasters become focusing events – in fact the majority of them do not. Political scientist Thomas Birkland has identified the conditions under which disasters come to be seen as requiring policy changes. The disaster must be severe and must be framed as representing a failure of policy, and both the lessons learned and candidate policy remedies must be identified. Most disasters and threats never reach this threshold, and even when they do, the policies promoted most strongly by advocates and the media have the greatest chance of being adopted – even if those policies are merely symbolic (Birkland 1997, 2007). Indeed, the crisis-induced tendency to pass legislation and create programs can result in ever-shifting policy frameworks and recommendations and can fail to address root causes of governmental dysfunction (Roberts, Ward, and Wamsley 2012).

Even when threats and disasters become focal points for policy advocacy and adoption, policy implementation introduces new complications. In some cases policies are misguided and resources are squandered. After the terrorist attacks of September 11, for example, policy advocates of many different stripes exaggerated the magnitude of the terrorist threat, which led to controversial legislation such as the PATRIOT Act, along with massive expenditures on homeland security. Approximately ten years after 9–11, John Mueller and Mark Stewart estimated that about $1 trillion had been spent on the terrorism threat, not counting the cost of the wars in Afghanistan and Iraq, even though the likelihood of anyone dying in a terrorist attack remained vanishingly small, as indeed it had been prior to 9–11. As a consequence of hastily adopted laws and policies fueled by the climate of fear generated after 9–11 and by interest groups that wanted to capitalize on that fear, the homeland security funds that were allocated were grossly out of proportion with the threat of terror attacks (Mueller and Stewart 2011a, 2011b, 2012). Moreover, in the decades after 9–11, DHS and other federal anti-terrorism and law enforcement agencies grossly underestimated threats posed by domestic right-wing terrorism.

Psychology and related fields

An earlier section in this chapter discussed key contributions of cognitive psychology to our understanding of risks and threats. The present section outlines other contributions made by psychological fields, for example social and community psychology and the study of psychological trauma. Among the many topics studied by psychologists, the three that are of greatest interest to sociologists – and to which they have contributed alongside psychologists – are risk perception, risk communication and warning responses, and the psychosocial effects of disasters.

Risk perception and communication

The topic of risk perception has been approached from a variety of disciplinary perspectives, but what is now known as the psychometric approach has generally been dominant. As I have discussed elsewhere in greater detail (Tierney 2014), psychologists' initial interest in the perception of risk was driven by concerns about how the public perceived certain technological hazards, particularly those associated with nuclear power, and why public perceptions differed so markedly from those of experts, who were thought to be in a better position to understand such risks. The insights into cognitive heuristics provided by the work of Kahneman and Tversky (discussed earlier) offered some guidance; people use heuristics or cognitive shortcuts in assessing risks.

Further research within the psychometric paradigm explored how even the perceived characteristics of risks influenced perception. Among the most important findings from this strain of risk perception research was the conclusion that the perceived severity of risks was influenced by whether those risks were seen as voluntarily accepted or imposed, as commonplace or exotic, as familiar or unfamiliar, as dreaded or not. Other perceived characteristics of risks were their being especially deadly, their affecting large numbers of people, and their having intergenerational negative effects. These attributes could explain, for example, why people had such an elevated sense of the risks associated with nuclear power (Slovic et al. 1979, 1981).

Another development within the psychometric framework involved taking into account the sociodemographic characteristics of individuals as they related to risk perception. Here both race and gender emerged as important influences on how risks were perceived: women in general and members of minority groups in particular turned out to perceive risks differently from Caucasian males (Slovic 1999; Finucane et al. 2000). Other research in this vein has explored how individual characteristics such as gender, education, and income, combined with other factors such as information-seeking, influence the perception of various types of risks (Cummings, Berube, and Lavelle 2013).

A different line of research focuses on the influence of emotions on risk perceptions. While in the past there had been a tendency to contrast "emotional" judgments and decisions with "rational" ones and to view emotions as biasing factors in the perception of risk, current approaches emphasize that perceptions are shaped by a combination of emotions and "slower," more analytic forms of thinking, and also that emotions function in positive, adaptive ways. The large body of research on emotions and risk perception includes work on the affect heuristic, which was discussed earlier (Finucane et al. 2000; Slovic 2010), along with studies of the ways in which specific emotions shape the perception of risk. Negative emotions are generally associated with pessimism and greater concern about risks, while positive ones are associated with optimism and a tendency to downplay risks.

Another approach within the psychometric paradigm focuses on the role of people's mental models in shaping perceptions of hazards and other risks. This method seeks to elicit from individuals, through open-ended interviews, their understandings of various aspects of hazards, such as how people get exposed to the hazard, how it affects them, and what can be done to reduce or control it. These mental models, which are typically expressed as hierarchically organized influence diagrams, are then compared with models developed on the basis of information obtained from experts on those same risks (for examples of how this is done, see Bostrom, Fischhoff, and Morgan 1992 and Morgan, Fischhoff, Bostrom, and Atman 2002). The analysis of mental models helps identify areas in which there are misunderstandings about the causal processes that characterize hazards, and this can be important for crafting effective risk communication messages.

Risk communication – which aims to assist recipients of risk information in making sound choices, the kind that lead to health and safety – can be thought of as a blend of insights from the study of risk perception, persuasive communication, social marketing, attitude and behavior change, and organizational crisis communication. Although the focus here is on communication in relation to hazards and disasters, findings from research that involves other types of risks – for example communicable diseases and other health conditions, or risks associated with medical procedures – are also relevant. Within the area of hazards and disasters, a distinction can be made between communicating about risks during non-disaster times and communicating in the context of imminent threats – for example, by issuing warnings and providing guidance on necessary protective actions.

Janoske, Liu, and Sheppard (2012) identify several general theories and models of risk communication that are relevant within the disaster context. These include the Centers for Disease Control and Prevention's crisis and emergency risk communication (CERC) model, which focuses on the types of communication that are appropriate during the different stages of a disaster or crisis; the situational theory of publics, which is concerned with the factors that influence various publics' information seeking and information uptake; the heuristic–systemic model, which deals with the extent to which people make judgments about risks on the basis of superficial cues contained in messages or on the basis of a more systematic analysis of the information provided; and the deliberative process model, which emphasizes involving stakeholders in fashioning risk communication messages that take into account divergent viewpoints, with the aim of furthering the understanding of risks and of moving toward agreement as to their acceptability. These same authors have also identified other models that are appropriate in different phases of a disaster or crisis.

Several themes have emerged from the decades-long record of risk communication research and practice. These themes underscore the importance of several factors, for example communicating uncertainty appropriately; framing risks in ways that make it more likely that audiences will understand them – which necessitates understanding the actual information needs of those audiences (as opposed to what communicators think the audiences need); paying heed to barriers to acting on the basis of risk communications; and including in messages all the information people need to have in order to take action.

If there are overarching themes in the risk communication literature, one is that trust is an essential component in all risk communication activities: trust that risk communicators are legitimate, credible, and disinterested; trust that the communication process is fair and is being undertaken in the public's best interest; and trust in the institutions that produce and disseminate risk information. Additionally, because publics are heterogeneous, groups will vary in the levels of trust they attach to different communication sources and institutions.

Another theme emphasizes the importance of evaluating risk communication strategies. As Baruch Fischhoff, one of the foremost authorities on risk communication, points out, "[i]t is depressing how often even rudimentary evaluation is missing. Amateurish, unscientific communications can be worse than nothing, by creating the impression that the problem has been addressed" (Fischhoff 2012: 25).

If communicating risk information is difficult during normal, non-disaster times, those difficulties are multiplied in the context of imminent threats. A substantial body of research documents factors that positively and negatively affect warning responses. The length of the warning period associated with different disaster agents is one such factor. Some hazards, such as hurricanes and riverine floods, allow for longer warning periods, while for others, such as tornadoes and hazardous chemical releases, the time available to warn the public is very short or even nonexistent, and this presents special challenges. Threats such as wildfires and chemical and nuclear hazards can be very dynamic, requiring rapid warnings and updates. Warning system failures can be deadly, as seen in the tragic wildfires that devastated the town of Lahaina on the Hawaiian island of Maui in 2023.

Those interested in research and practice on risk communication are also challenged to better understand how technological developments have altered risk communication activities. Particularly with the explosion of social media in recent years, older notions of linear source–message–channel–receiver communication have been supplanted by a recognition that information networks have become increasingly complex, in ways that researchers are only beginning to grasp. This trend, combined with the tendency for members of the public to obtain information of all types – including information on risks and warnings – from an increasingly heterogeneous, fragmented, and polarized information marketplace, raises challenges for researchers and risk communicators alike. Within the context of new technologies and social media, the drive to better understand communication processes related to hazards and disasters has given rise to a new field of study, crisis informatics, which bridges the fields of social, information, and computer science (Palen et al. 2007; Palen, Vieweg, Liu, and Hughes 2009; Vieweg et al. 2008; Palen and Hughes 2018).

The need for this type of research was highlighted during the Covid-19 pandemic, when official efforts to communicate risk faltered and misinformation, disinformation, and malicious information dissemination flourished in an atmosphere of mistrust of institutions and "elites," political polarization and violence, vaccine denial, and attempts to profit from public anxiety by offering crackpot and outright dangerous "remedies" for the virus. The Covid experience should lead to a wholesale reassessment of what it means to communicate risk in a "post-truth" society, and should also lead to more research on combatting mis- and disinformation.

Mental health aspects of disasters

The third major contribution of the psychological sciences is to improve our understanding of the psychosocial aspects and effects both of disasters and of the interventions designed to reduce their negative impacts. Selected findings on the psychological and mental health consequences of disasters on disaster survivors were discussed earlier in Chapter 5, so here the topic will be discussed only briefly.

Historically, sociologists and psychologists have differed in their views on those impacts, sociologists tending to argue that the negative psychological effects of disasters are relatively mild and transient and psychologists being significantly more concerned with the capacity of disasters to lead to serious and lasting psychological problems, such as (typically) post-traumatic stress disorder (PTSD). Research findings that have accrued over time have painted a more nuanced picture. In 2002, psychologist Fran Norris and her collaborators

(Norris, Friedman, Watson et al. 2002; Norris, Friedman, and Watson 2002) published a landmark meta-analysis of 160 empirical studies conducted between 1981 and 2001 that identified the conditions under which disasters are more likely to lead to adverse psychological outcomes. Such conditions range from PTSD, major depression, and anxiety disorders to elevated stress, health problems (somatic complaints, excessive drinking), problems in living that are caused by disasters, increased vulnerability to subsequent stressors, and problems specific to youth. In adults, these adverse outcomes were associated with experiencing more severe disasters, being female, being middle-aged, being a member of an ethnic minority group, experiencing additional stressors after disaster exposure, having had prior psychiatric problems, and having diminished psychosocial coping resources. In youths, the most serious psychological effects are associated with having experienced mass violence, for instance terrorism, rather than a natural or technological disaster, and coming from the developing world.

Since the publication of Norris and colleagues' 2002 review, major disasters have occurred that led to extensive research on their mental health consequences. This research includes a few longitudinal studies of different lengths. Chief among them were studies devoted to the terrorist attacks of September 11, 2001 and to Hurricane Katrina. Research on the mental health effects of 9–11 includes both nationwide surveys (Silver et al. 2002) and studies on the more severely affected populations. The establishment in July 2002 of the World Trade Center Health Registry, the most extensive study of its kind at the time, made it possible to track health and mental health outcomes for the persons most directly affected by the New York City attacks who volunteered to take part. The Registry contains data on more than 70,000 rescue and recovery workers, schoolchildren and school staff members, building occupants and residents of the hardest hit areas in Lower Manhattan, and individuals who happened to be in those areas at the time of the attacks. Most of the data collected focused on the physical impacts of exposure, but a portion of the research conducted dealt with mental health outcomes at different points in time (Brackbill et al. 2013).

Other research on highly exposed populations focused on the incidence of serious mental health problems such as PTSD (Galea et al. 2003; Boscarino et al. 2011; for a review of studies, see Neria, DiGrande, and Adams 2011). Findings are not entirely consistent across studies, but the evidence suggests that an event such as the 9–11 attacks in New York can have lasting negative psychological effects on those most directly affected, in this case particularly on responders involved in rescue operations, remains recovery, and cleanup activities at the site of the attacks (Centers for Disease Control and Prevention 2004; Stellman et al. 2008).

Hurricane Katrina is another disaster that has been studied extensively. In terms of negative mental health consequences, Katrina can be considered something of an outlier among US disasters on account of its catastrophic nature and the protracted length of the recovery period, because so many people lost their social support networks through displacement and relocation, and because many of the victims were already vulnerable owing to factors such as minority racial status and poverty.

One long-term study, the Resilience in Survivors of Katrina (RISK) project, has followed and continues to follow the experiences and the health and mental health status of more than 1,000 mostly African American young women for whom baseline data had been collected before Katrina. In this case, study results from 2010 showed a relatively high incidence of post-Katrina PTSD – around 30 percent – as compared with pre-disaster levels, which are associated with factors such as loss of housing, trauma experienced in connection with the hurricane, and the death of a family member or friend. This model study also took into account post-traumatic growth and potential genetic and neighborhood factors that could influence survivors' mental health (Waters 2016). Longer-term research with the RISK sample showed that, while symptoms declined over time, one in six individuals still reported post-traumatic stress symptoms twelve years later.

Similar patterns were found among residents of the Greater Kobe area in Japan sixteen years after the 1995 Great Hanshin Awaji (Kobe) earthquake of 1995: victims who had experienced death in their families and damage to their homes still report lower levels of subjective well-being and life satisfaction, negative affect, and physical health problems (Oishi et al. 2015). Such findings suggest that in many cases the psychological problems engendered by the occurrence of disasters are not easily overcome.

Urban planning

The field of urban planning is concerned with shaping the trajectory of urban forms through legislation, policies, and plans. In the context of hazards and disasters, urban planning makes the most significant contributions in the pre-disaster mitigation phase, by employing strategies designed to reduce the negative impacts of future disasters, and in the post-disaster recovery phase, by providing guidance on prudent strategies for redevelopment and reconstruction, with the goal of incorporating disaster risk reduction into those strategies. Urban planners advocate a variety of pre-disaster measures designed to mitigate disaster impacts, primarily through the promotion of risk-aware land use practices. These include directing new development away from hazardous areas; relocating populations, existing structures, and land uses to safer areas; advocating measures that maintain the health and functionality of natural protections against disasters, for example wetlands; and identifying non-hazard-related plans that also provide opportunities to employ land use policies in order to enhance safety (Godschalk 2003). Similarly, after disasters, the goal of urban planning is to guide recovery processes in ways that maximize safety in the face of hazards but do not sacrifice other important community values such as livability, access to transportation, and overall quality of life.

The employment of land use measures to manage hazards was a key emphasis of the founders of the disaster research – for example Gilbert White, who counted land use among the key adjustments to natural hazards. Examples exist of a number of successful programs for applying land use measures in this fashion. In the United States, for example, the cities of Boulder in Colorado and Tulsa in Oklahoma are well known for their efforts to reduce flood losses through the adoption of progressive land use measures. Under White's direct influence, Boulder restricted most development in its floodplain and began using the floodplain for other purposes, such as recreation. As we saw in Chapter 6, after a series of damaging and deadly floods, Tulsa adopted an ambitious risk reduction program that involved acquiring land in order to keep it from being developed, moving structures out of harm's way, and creating spaces within the urban environment that could serve as overflow reservoirs in the event of major flooding. To bolster such efforts, the National Flood Insurance Program (NFIP) offers communities incentives for flood risk reduction through its Community Rating System, which lowers flood insurance rates for the residents of communities that pursue recommended risk reduction policies. Examples also abound of coastal zone management policies that seek to protect people and property from hazards such as hurricane storm surge. With respect to earthquakes, a state law in California, the Alquist-Priolo Act, restricts the construction of multifamily structures near active fault zones, and other legislation has long required the incorporation of seismic safety elements into communities' general plans.

There are, however, significant barriers to the use of planning tools such as those discussed above to reduce disaster losses. First, despite the efforts of institutions such as the World Bank to highlight the importance of land use–focused measures as part of the effort to reduce future risks, such measures may be largely ignored in urban areas of poor countries, where residents and migrants seek to live in proximity to jobs and whatever services are available, without regard for the safety of those locations. Migrants gravitate to any areas that are available for settlement and, given the economic conditions under which they are forced to live, it is unlikely that they give much thought to whether those areas are exposed to hazards or not (Pelling 2003).

Second, even in developed societies such as the United States, training in urban planning generally neglects hazards and disasters, focusing instead on concepts such as smart growth, the new urbanism, and transit-oriented development. Few schools of urban planning emphasize the importance of integrating disaster risk reduction into urban planning activities, although the American Planning Association (APA) and its Hazards Planning Center are attempting to move education and practice in that direction. The gulf that exists between planners employed by local communities and community officials in disaster management roles only exacerbates this problem. Put simply, hazards are not a priority for urban planners, and disaster planning and urban planning are typically separate in most US communities. How, then, can we expect community planning to take into account disaster risk reduction objectives?

Third and perhaps most importantly, as I have discussed elsewhere (Tierney 1999; 2014) and earlier in Chapter 3, efforts to shape urban development in ways that take hazards into account typically incur opposition from real estate and development interests. Proponents of "growth" – which is socially constructed as beneficial to all community residents, although this is clearly not the case – expect to be able to build whatever, wherever, and whenever they want – and they have the political power to do so. In the face of these kinds of political constraints, urban planners who prioritize keeping their communities safe have their work cut out for them.

These challenges are evident in research on the implementation of the Disaster Mitigation Act of 2000. Known as DMA2K, this law required all local jurisdictions in the United States and its territories as well as all tribal governments to engage in mitigation planning, much of which revolves around assessing hazards and making decisions about how best to mitigate them. Studies suggest that mitigation plans developed by jurisdictions such as those located in coastal areas in the United States are generally of poor quality and do not necessarily contribute to hazard reduction activities (Kang, Peacock, and Husein 2010; Lyles, Berke, and Smith 2014). Perhaps those jurisdictions view DMA2K requirements as unfunded mandates – or perhaps their leaders are simply loath to do battle with powerful development interests.

Another, related set of issues concerns the extent to which plans designed to mitigate the impacts of disasters are consistent with the array of other plans that communities adopt. These issues have been a key concern for researchers at the Hazards Reduction and Recovery Center (HRRC) at Texas A&M University. For example, does a general community land use plan call for more development in a hazardous area, while a mitigation plan calls for less? Are plans for the construction of affordable housing or development near public transportation hubs coordinated with other plans, which address disaster risk? Or are plans and their implementation working at cross-purposes in ways that fail to reduce risk? On top of such concerns is the need to develop and implement plans that take into account a range of community needs, while also paying heed to both hazard mitigation and longer-term climate change adaptation. As a means of addressing some of these questions, and on the basis of research in multiple communities, the HRRC researchers developed the Plan Integration Resilience Scorecard, which can enable communities to better understand the degree to which various plans sync with one another and the points where they fail to do so. (For more information on this line of research, see Berke et al. 2019; 2021).

Concluding Observations

In this admittedly selective chapter I have introduced readers to perspectives from outside sociology that are foundational to an understanding of social–scientific disaster studies. There are fields I have not included here, such as public health, which provides insights into disaster-related mortality and morbidity and the epidemiology of disasters and pandemics. Nor have I emphasized historical research and how it contributes to the ways in which hazards and disasters have been conceived of and contended with over time. My objective has been to introduce readers who are perhaps new to the study of hazards and disasters to how sociological inquiry has been enriched by insights from outside the core of the discipline. This brief review has also set the stage for discussions in the next chapter: these discussions will focus on research trends that emphasize cross-disciplinary collaboration as a means of developing a more holistic understanding of hazard- and disaster-related challenges.

QUESTIONS AND EXERCISES

The most recent iteration of *Natural Hazard Mitigation Saves* (Multihazard Mitigation Council 2019) found that mitigation projects result in positive benefit–cost ratios. Describe the overall research strategy and methodology used in that study. What different disciplines came together to produce those results?

Hurricane Maria (Puerto Rico, 2017) is among the most devastating disasters in US history. What was the death toll in Maria in Puerto Rico? Is this death toll contested, and if so, why? What does newly published research say about the health and mental health consequences of Maria?

8

Confronting Disaster Research Challenges

Introduction

In a review of 225 published studies on the effects of disasters on mental health – a review conducted between 1981 and 2004 and involving more than 85,000 individuals who had experienced 132 different disaster events – Fran Norris (2006) found that the methods employed in those studies varied, but the most common type of design was cross-sectional and the studies themselves were conducted only after disasters had occurred (in other words, they did not incorporate baseline data), used convenience sampling, and worked with relatively small samples. Because research subjects tended not to be followed over long periods of time, little was learned about the longer-term effects of disasters. The small sample sizes used in mental health studies tended to rule out the possibility of sophisticated statistical analyses. Moreover, Norris noted, the methods used influenced the results that were obtained: studies employing pre- and post-disaster data showed smaller disaster effects than those that used only post-disaster methods, and smaller effects were also found in the studies that used larger sample sizes and convenience rather than random sampling – perhaps because subjects were chosen according to their accessibility. On top of that, although disasters have larger impacts on communities and societies in the global South, most studies were conducted in the global North.

I mention Norris's review not to highlight weaknesses in the research record, but rather because some of the shortcomings she identified are a result of the many constraints and challenges that accompany disaster research. For example, while for hazard- and disaster-related research during non-disaster periods funding is available from agencies such as the National Science Foundation (NSF), funding levels often increase only after major disaster events. However, those kinds of grants tend to favor relatively short-term studies, and also contribute to researchers' tendency to focus on large-scale disasters rather than on smaller and more common ones. Particularly for social scientists, research funding may not be substantial enough to support longer-term research, longitudinal and panel studies, or systematic efforts to achieve better response rates and better coverage of the populations of concern.

For reasons that will become evident in the discussions that follow, in disaster research any effort to increase research quality typically necessitates large budgets that many funding agencies may be unwilling to support except under special circumstances. That being the case, researchers sometimes have to choose between conducting research that is less than optimal methodologically and conducting no research at all.

Disaster Research Methods: How Distinctive Are They?

The data collection and analysis approaches used by sociologists and other social scientists who study disasters do not differ from those employed in social science research more generally. Disaster research methods include systematic observation, participant observation, interviewing, focus groups, collection and analysis of documentary and archival materials (including web-based studies), survey research, spatial social science methods, participatory research, evaluation research, and other approaches. Like other social scientists, disaster researchers use both qualitative and quantitative data collection and analytic strategies, although the types of qualitative and case study methods that have been used throughout the history of the field still predominate (Peek et al. 2020a).

What differs in many types of disaster studies, however, is the contexts and settings in which the research is conducted. Of course, this is not always the case. A considerable amount of research on hazards and disasters is carried out in non-disaster contexts; examples include research on risk perception, disaster mitigation and preparedness activities, disaster policy, and historical disasters. In such cases, research practices closely resemble those employed in other kinds of social–scientific studies. Challenges are much more likely to arise when researchers focus on actual disaster events and their consequences, largely because those studies have to be carried out in disturbed and turbulent environments. In the words of sociologist Robert Stallings,

> it is the context of research not the methods of research that makes disaster research unique ... Disaster researchers, therefore, need two types of training: first, they need training in research methods in general ... and second they need training in how, specifically, the circumstances surrounding disaster affect the implementation of these research methods. (Stallings 1997: 7)

Details that are typically taken for granted in research conducted in non-disaster times – for example, that a particular organization is in fact located at the address listed on its website, or that those who conduct telephone surveys will generally be able to reach working numbers – cannot be taken for granted in disaster situations. Disasters disrupt communities in ways that require extra effort and ingenuity on the part of those who wish to conduct disaster research.

This chapter is not intended to be a treatise on disaster research methods. There are many other publications that do a better job of providing detailed guidance on conducting research in disaster settings than is possible here (see Stallings 2002, 2007; Galea, Maxwell, and Norris 2008; Peek and Fothergill 2009; Henderson et al. 2009; Phillips 2014; Marlowe, Lou, Osman, and Zeba Alam 2015; Substance Abuse and Mental Health Services Administration 2016; Rivera 2022). Rather, in the sections that follow I first highlight practical, methodological, and ethical challenges disaster researchers face. I then go on to discuss important trends in the field that promise new advances.

Practical challenges

One obvious practical complication is that disasters arrive largely unannounced, although events like hurricanes generally allow for some warning. Studies conducted in non-disaster settings can be initiated and made to proceed on carefully planned schedules, developed in advance and largely predictable, but this is not the case for many studies of disasters. Disasters know no respect for teaching schedules, vacations, or holidays. Researchers wishing to carry out quick-response and even intermediate-term research must be able to confront and solve challenges associated with rapid or relatively rapid deployment in the field. Those whose research priorities require them to go into the field in the immediate aftermath of disasters must always be prepared.

Fortunately, there is a lot that can be done in advance to make post-disaster quick-response research proceed smoothly. Research protocols should be developed as much as possible ahead of time, and those who will be conducting the actual research should be trained in advance on what to expect, in terms of deployment and issues likely to be encountered in the field. Ideally, students who plan to do so should already have taken courses on the qualitative and quantitative methods they plan to employ and should have had training on methods specific to disaster research. Other important requirements, which are not specific to disaster research but become more pressing in those situations, include understanding travel policies and requirements for reimbursement and, where applicable, having a passport and obtaining the vaccinations required for travel to disaster-affected countries. Additionally, it is important that those who may be deployed to the field on short notice always keep their human subjects' certifications current.

Institutional review boards and human subjects' concerns

Disaster research is still a small field and many institutional review boards (IRBs) are unfamiliar with it and may have difficulty acting rapidly on requests for protocol approval. One strategy for dealing with such issues is to meet with human subjects officials when a proposal is submitted or before sending protocols for review, to explain the purpose of the research and typical disaster research strategies. A good deal of the work required for developing IRB review requests, such as conducting literature reviews on disaster research methods and writing descriptions of the risks and benefits of participating in disaster studies, is typically done at the research proposal stage.

Researchers should be aware that IRB officials and committee members may automatically consider anyone who is in a disaster area to be vulnerable to being harmed as a consequence of research involvement and thus may be overly conservative when reviewing the protocols. Issues related to the potential vulnerability of all research participants, including disaster survivors, are important and, in submitting protocols to IRBs, researchers will need to provide the best available information about the potential vulnerabilities of research participants and the risks and benefits of taking part in post-disaster studies.

Research participants' vulnerability is a concern in many types of social science research, not just disaster research. Levine (2004) notes that much has been written about the vulnerability of a wide range of populations, including those identified in US federal regulations as requiring extra protections – children, prisoners, pregnant women, fetuses, and newborns – but also poor people; individuals who are discriminated against, stigmatized, and marginalized; persons without political and economic power; members of minority racial and ethnic groups; people of low intelligence; and individuals who have been deprived of basic human and civil rights. However, she characterizes vulnerability in research as "an extraordinarily elastic concept, capable of being stretched to cover almost any person, group, or situation, and then of being snapped back to describe a narrow range of characteristics like age or incarceration" and warns that, with extensive stretching of the concept's meaning, "[i]f everyone is vulnerable, then the concept is so nebulous that it becomes almost meaningless" (2004: 398). There are inherent problems with assuming, in research settings, that entire groups of people are vulnerable simply because they have some trait in common, such as being African American or living in poverty. There is likely to be considerable intragroup variation in the risks faced by members of groups who are deemed vulnerable, and vulnerably can also vary over time (Browne and Peek 2014).

In my view there is no a priori reason for assuming that disaster survivors are so highly vulnerable that they require special protections beyond those that are provided to other research subjects (Newman and Kaloupek 2004; National Institute of Mental Health 2007; Substance Abuse and Mental Health Services Administration 2016). Of course, there are exceptions – for example, people who have been exposed to extreme trauma or have lost loved ones – and those should be treated as special cases. Similarly, some disaster survivors, such as refugees fleeing from wars and disasters and persons who are not in their country legally, may face special risks, and how those risks will be managed should be part of the research design and consent process. (For an interesting exchange on whether or not studying disasters requires a special code of conduct, see Gaillard and Peek 2019; Kendra and Wachtendorf 2020).

IRB applications require analyses of the risks and benefits of research participation, but here again the costs and benefits of participating in disaster research do not look all that different from those associated with research with other individuals who have undergone painful and disruptive experiences in their lives and have experienced various degrees of suffering – or with research subjects in general, for that matter. The small amount of research that exists on groups that have experienced trauma indicates that participation can cause distress to some of those who are asked to discuss their experiences. Interestingly, however, studies have also shown that a large majority of those who indicate that they felt some discomfort during the research process still do not regret participating. Instead, it appears that even those who find it in some ways disturbing to take part in research view their participation as having positive effects: for instance they can gain insight into their own experiences, improve their self-esteem, and feel that they have made a contribution to society (Levine 2004; Newman and Kaloupek 2004).

Collogan and colleagues advise that, in addressing the risks and benefits of research participation,

> [a]dministrators and IRB members who are charged with protecting the interests of human participants in research may be benefited in their considerations by having access to data on the low likelihood of significant risk of research post-disaster when conducted in appropriate settings with sensitivity to the needs of participants ... Evidence of the important benefits that disaster-focused research participants experience may also be useful to reviewers when weighing the risk–benefit ratio of participation. (Collogan et al. 2004: 369)

Again regarding institutional review, researchers should be aware that there may be other IRBs outside their own institutions that will need to give their approval before research can begin. In the United States, after the 1995 Oklahoma City bombing, the governor of Oklahoma designated the University of Oklahoma Health Sciences Center as the lead IRB for all projects related to research on that bombing, regardless of the institutions and investigators behind them. Although this occurs rarely, restrictions can also be placed on the ability to collect data after disasters. For example, on February 23, 2011 – the day after the most serious earthquake in the Christchurch, New Zealand earthquake sequence of 2010–2011 – the government of New Zealand instituted a moratorium on social science research that was in effect until May

1 of that year. This was done in an effort to reduce burdens on emergency responders and earthquake survivors that the government believed might result from researcher convergence. Another consideration is that certain kinds of research typically require additional privacy waivers, as is the case in other fields. Research with photographs or videotaping, where participants can be identified, is a case in point.

By their very nature, some disasters can be expected to generate controversy, intense scrutiny, and legal disputes. Under such circumstances, researchers may wish to obtain additional human subjects protection in the form of certificates of confidentiality. These certificates, which are issued by the US National Institutes of Health, are designed to protect research information from forced disclosure and breaches of privacy, such as court orders and subpoenas. I obtained a certificate of confidentiality for all the research conducted by the Disaster Research Center on the World Trade Center (WTC) terrorist attacks because I believed that there was a high potential for lawsuits and forced disclosure. (I was also approached by a lawyer from the city's legal department and told to stop contacting interviewees for our project, but that is another story.) One of the reasons why I wanted to obtain those additional protections was that I was aware of the many ways in which scholars who had conducted research on the Exxon Valdez oil spill were harassed by Exxon, and also of the corporation's efforts to force researchers to disclose data about their study participants (Picou 1996a; 1996b). A caution regarding certificates of confidentiality is that researchers' institutions must be willing to support them if subpoenas are issued. If forced disclosure is a possibility, it is prudent to consult in advance with the institution's legal representatives about strategies for research participant protection. (For additional discussion on IRB issues, including measures that can streamline the process in multi-institutional collaborations, see Peek et al. 2021.)

Other practical concerns

In social science research, researchers often offer payment or some other kind of incentive to study participants; and in disaster settings where survivors have suffered material losses this seems especially appropriate. Because researchers typically assure research subjects of confidentiality, they need to work out payment arrangements in advance with their institutions, if they are to fulfill that promise and protect confidentiality. Additionally, care must be taken to ensure that the gifts provided to participants are large enough to show appreciation for participation, but not so large as to place undue pressure on them to participate.

Researcher safety is another practical concern in many disaster settings. Widespread criminality is, typically, not a problem in the aftermath of disasters, particularly in the United States, but some countries and communities are more lawless than others, and it is always prudent to be aware of the potential for danger and to manage that risk.

Along these lines, cultural competence and sensitivity are required. To give just one example, researchers must be sensitive to norms on proper dress and demeanor in different societal settings, out of concern that missteps might trigger negative reactions from residents in disaster-stricken areas, or even from authorities. For example, although my fieldwork in Iran after the 2003 Bam earthquake was largely uneventful, I did experience a few uncomfortable moments in Bam when, in 120-degree Fahrenheit (48.8°C) heat, I could not stand to wear my long black covering. I was wearing instead a long-sleeved white tunic, long khaki pants, and a headscarf. That might have been acceptable garb in Tehran, but it wasn't in conservative Bam, as I found out. When the much-feared morality police headed for me in a public market, an engineer in our team who had grown up mainly in Iran and spoke the language quickly asked them to direct me to a place in the market where I could purchase an appropriate covering, and all was well. This incident also speaks to the value of working with researchers who are familiar with local cultural norms and practices.

Disaster settings present a variety of other safety challenges. Earthquakes are always followed by aftershocks that can do additional damage and even kill, and hazardous chemicals are invariably found in floodwaters. Drinking water can be contaminated as a consequence of disaster impacts. Debris-covered streets can be hazardous, especially when lighting is lacking as a result of a disaster – or never existed in the first place. Technological disasters may create unsafe conditions for researchers, just as they do for disaster survivors. For all these reasons, training for researchers should always address safety issues, and when necessary IRB protocols should discuss how the safety of researchers as well as that of research subjects will be addressed.

Being able to obtain access to places and people is another practical concern. Sometimes access to hard-hit areas is impossible for a period of time, as happens, for example, when major transportation routes are blocked or airports are shut down as a result of damage. Researchers need up-to-date information on the accessibility of disaster sites, but that information is often difficult to obtain. Simply navigating in disaster-stricken areas is difficult when landmarks and signage have been destroyed. Additionally, authorities typically restrict access to highly damaged areas, and may also block entry to emergency shelters and temporary housing sites. Researchers wishing to observe emergency response activities in the field or in emergency operation centers should expect to encounter varying degrees of resistance from the authorities. This is doubly true for terrorism-related events, where security is paramount.

There are a number of strategies that can be used when access to sites is being blocked: obtaining approval from the leadership of agencies that are in charge; presenting credentials such as researchers' photos and other identification, which identify the sponsoring funding agency and institution; and, equally if not more importantly, getting in touch with prior contacts in the affected area who can vouch for the legitimacy of the research. For example, the entrée and access that the Disaster Research Center field team was able to achieve after the 9–11 terrorist attacks in New York were predicated almost entirely on a relationship that had been developed with a high-ranking member of New York's Mayor's Office of Emergency Management before those events. Lead team members Tricia Wachtendorf and James Kendra spent most of the two months after the attacks making observations in the emergency operations center and other sites such as Ground Zero; sitting in on meetings that were held to determine the course of the response and early recovery; shadowing those who were coordinating emergency management activities; and collecting other kinds of perishable data – activities that would have been very difficult without an inside advocate.

Methodological challenges

In addition to practical problems, disaster researchers face methodological challenges that typically do not arise in other types of studies, or do so to a lesser degree. Displacement is one concern: community residents may no longer be in their homes, and agencies and organizations may also have been forced to operate from new locations. Those who are displaced are likely to differ in sociologically significant ways from those who are able to remain in or return rapidly to disaster-stricken areas; for example, they may be low-income residents who had been living in substandard or manufactured housing that sustained very severe damage. In the Katrina catastrophe, many New Orleans residents were displaced on a long-term or permanent basis because they were evacuated to places far from their homes and because the city of New Orleans demolished a lot of low-income housing not long after the hurricane, making it difficult for low-income residents to return.

In discussing efforts to conduct telephone surveys after Hurricane Katrina, Henderson et al. (2009) noted a number of challenges that were related in part to displacement. At a time when landlines were still common, a phone survey contacting landlines began six weeks after Katrina and therefore was more likely to reach early returnees. A cell phone survey began three months after the catastrophe, but probably missed potential respondents whose cell phone contracts expired – more likely among lower-income groups. Like other researchers who employ telephone surveys, these researchers were challenged by other factors, such as the sociodemographic differences between landline and cell phone–only individuals and households.

Research on businesses affected by disasters has been discussed earlier. Until recently, owing to resource constraints, business-related research tended to focus on those businesses that could be located and contacted months or years after a disaster. In other words, studies mainly focused on surviving businesses located in roughly the same geographic areas where they had been doing business before experiencing disaster. Businesses that had moved to distant locations or had ceased operating as a result of experiencing a disaster or for other reasons were left out of such studies, partly because of the difficulty of tracking them. Researchers have gone on to improve business tracking methods. In research on the impacts of Hurricane Katrina on small businesses in Mississippi, Holly Schrank, Maria Marshall, and their collaborators (Schrank et al. 2013; Marshall and Schrank 2014) developed elaborate and time-consuming strategies to locate businesses that had moved or had gone out of business in subsequent years.

Following disasters, efforts to interview or obtain records from agency and organizational representatives are often challenging. Organizations involved directly in responding to disasters are typically so overwhelmed with simply carrying out their disaster-related functions that they have little or no time for working with researchers. Agencies providing services to disaster victims may likewise feel overwhelmed, or may feel a need to withhold information from researchers on the assumption that their clients are already traumatized and overburdened and need to be protected.

Many types of research require layers of consent before data can be obtained from research subjects. Studies with school-age children are a case in point. Obtaining consent typically means getting permission from school systems, individual schools, parents, and the children themselves. Educational researchers are familiar with these kinds of hurdles, but research in disaster settings is even more fraught than research conducted during non-disaster times. Educational institutions may be overwhelmed as a result of disaster impacts and thus may be less inclined to participate in research. Schools and parents may worry about the negative effects of research on children whose lives have been disrupted. Owing to their own dislocation, parents may be difficult to find and, even when located, may be too overburdened to consider researchers' requests.

Barron Ausbrooks, Barrett, and Martinez-Cosio (2009) conducted a post–Hurricane Katrina study that involved surveys with displaced middle school and high school students, their parents and teachers, school principals, school social workers, and school district personnel. The many challenges they had to overcome included tracking the displaced students to their new homes, assuring ethical protections for children at risk, obtaining the requisite permissions from school districts and individual schools, and obtaining parents' permission and students' consent to participate in the study. Students had to be able to return signed parental permission forms to school – which some did not. Parents themselves were difficult to contact; the researchers noted that, as a result of Katrina, it was sometimes the case that "students were living with relatives while parents looked for work, took care of business back in Louisiana, or had been evacuated elsewhere. The transience of displaced disaster survivors places a distinctive twist on obtaining informed consent" (Barron Ausbrooks et al. 2009: 97). Additionally, student records are protected by federal law, and students cannot be required to participate in studies that touch upon topics such as their psychological well-being (which this study did) without their parents' and their own permission. None of the schools or school districts would give researchers access to the addresses of students who had been relocated as a result of Katrina, so these researchers had to develop alternative ways of locating students. Schools were generally reluctant to work with the research team because they already felt overburdened, and personnel such as school counselors felt the same way. Delays in obtaining necessary permissions and the participation of research subjects meant that the research could not proceed on its planned time schedule.

As noted earlier, funding agencies are typically more willing to provide research support in the aftermath of severe disasters. This means that most studies that attempt to assess the impacts of disasters on affected populations do so without the benefit of having baseline pre-disaster data that would make it possible to distinguish disaster-related effects from other factors that could have influenced the outcomes in question. As Galea and colleagues note with respect to mental health research in the disaster context,

> [h]aving to rely on post-only designs means that researchers have limited ability to determine the extent to which disasters caused the mental health consequences being documented after these events . . . absent an assessment of what the population of interest was like before the event, we are limited in our inference as to whether what we see after an event is truly a change or simply a reflection of pre-disaster circumstances. (Galea et al. 2008: S24)

These authors note that there are various strategies for compensating for the lack of baseline data, but those strategies have limitations themselves. For example, researchers can ask study participants to provide information on how they were faring before they experienced a disaster, but participants may have problems with recall or may have a tendency to retrospectively view pre-disaster conditions in light of their current post-disaster situations. Earlier chapters have provided examples of studies in which researchers were in the field prior to disasters, allowing for serendipitous pre- and post-disaster data collection.

Ethical challenges

Regarding ethical concerns, disaster researchers come across all the challenges related to informed consent, confidentiality, and protection of the interests of research participants that other sociological and social science researchers encounter; but they often confront additional ones, too. Because some of those who have been affected by disasters, be they community residents or emergency responders, have already experienced high levels of stress, special measures may be required to ensure their protection and, as noted earlier, IRBs are likely to require assurances in that regard. Such measures typically include assuring those involved in research that they can withdraw consent at any time, or those involved in interview studies that they can refuse to answer particular questions. Supplementary safeguards must be provided for those who could be disproportionately at risk. This category may include people who have lost family members or have been injured, children, frail elderly persons and nursing-home residents, and refugees from disasters and civil wars. Researchers must also be able to refer study participants to local resources such as crisis counselors when necessary. In some cases the participation of professionals qualified to assess the presence of serious negative reactions in research subjects may be warranted.

That said, it is important to consider the kinds of studies that could trigger elevated levels of distress, as well as the kinds of participants who could experience such stress. In many cases, the likelihood of stressful responses is remote or nonexistent. For example, research that consists of unobtrusively observing disaster operations is unlikely to place pressure on those who are observed. Because of population heterogeneity and variations in disaster experiences, large surveys with randomly selected households in a community that has experienced a disaster are unlikely to induce severe stress in the vast majority of participants. We can contrast them with hypothetical studies involving face-to-face interviews with first responders who searched for and recovered bodies after a disaster, or with survivors who lost children. The potential for creating additional stress for study participants exists on a continuum and, here again, there is no formula that can be applied easily to all types of studies and affected populations.

Scholars have also inquired whether those who have gone through disasters, particularly those who have experienced severe impacts, are capable of giving informed consent, in light of the fact that they may be under extreme stress. Like participants in studies of other kinds of trauma, disaster survivors fall somewhere on a continuum between having difficulty with giving informed consent and being fully capable of it; those who are truly unable to consent are a very small minority. Put another way, there appears to be nothing about experiencing a disaster that would make survivors uniquely unable to give conscious consent to take part in research (Rosenstein 2004; Collogan et al. 2004; National Institute of Mental Health 2007). Here again, however, researchers must take care to ensure that consent to participate in studies is indeed being given consciously and voluntarily.

A related ethical issue for researchers is the question of when and how – and even whether – to go into the field in the immediate aftermath of disaster. The logic that undergirds quick-response research is twofold: the data that researchers plan to collect are perishable; and, for reasons of validity, observing activities directly, as they occur in real time, is preferable to hearing about them or reading later accounts. This commitment to "experience-near" research has been part of the field since its inception, but there are also reasons to question whether other sorts of motives may underlie the efforts to get into the field quickly after disasters – motives that could be ethically questionable. The eagerness to collect data and publish them as soon as possible after disasters has been likened to a gold rush (Gomez and Hart 2013; Gaillard and Gomez 2015) in which researchers descend on disaster-stricken areas with little or no coordination and little or no familiarity with the distinctive cultural settings they are attempting to study. Critics suggest that some disaster scholars may be more interested in getting credit from their institutions and professions for publishing study results quickly than in doing high-quality research that has the potential to benefit its subjects. They also note that convergent researchers represent a draw on resources that could be used more productively in responding to disasters. As Gaillard and Gomez put it,

> one may wonder whether it is appropriate for outsiders less familiar with the affected place, who may lack prior cultural and language skills, to converge on places where people are struggling to rebuild their lives and livelihoods, and have other priorities than answering questions about the recent events. (Gaillard and Gomez 2015: 2)

These authors are referring in particular to culturally insensitive researchers who take advantage of populations in disaster areas, but it is important to recognize that these ethical dilemmas can be present in all types of post-disaster research, and indeed in research in general: researchers must not put their own professional interests before those of research participants. When researchers go into the field after disasters, they must do so for valid research-related reasons and their timing must reflect legitimate research concerns. The need to collect perishable data does provide a rationale for going into the field as soon as possible after a disaster event. Examples include gathering data on disaster-induced damage at particular locations before debris is cleared or structures are demolished; observing emergency response and sheltering operations while these are under way; collecting samples that indicate exposure to hazardous materials or toxins soon after disaster impact; and capturing data related to early recovery planning that cannot be obtained by other means. Here again, presence in the field at a particular time should be determined by the research questions at stake.

Obligations toward study participants

Ethical questions regarding what is owed to participants in research can be especially poignant in the case of disaster studies. The Belmont Report, which provides guidelines for all research with human subjects, emphasizes three critical ethical obligations: respect for persons, beneficence, and justice. Respect for persons refers to the obligation to acknowledge and support the decision-making autonomy of research participants and to protect those who may have diminished decision-making capacity. Individuals cannot make autonomous decisions without understanding what taking part in research will mean for them, and thus respect for the autonomy of research subjects necessarily entails the obligation to make clear the parameters of the research being undertaken, including the nature of subjects' participation and potential research risks and benefits. The principle of beneficence refers to the obligation to be concerned with the welfare of research subjects. Beneficence requires efforts to maximize potential benefits for research participants while avoiding doing harm. To fulfill this obligation effectively, researchers must be aware of the potential harms that study participants face and must make every effort to mitigate those risks. At the same time, while being concerned with the well-being of research subjects, researchers cannot overpromise with respect to possible direct benefits of participation. Justice in research requires researchers to treat all participants fairly. This means, for example, that the burdens of taking part in research must not fall disproportionately on particular individuals or groups.

At a more general level, researchers are ethically obligated not to use whatever power they may have to compel individuals or groups to participate in research, or to make non-participation difficult. This obligation is especially relevant when there are already large power differences between researchers and potential subjects, as happens, for example, when westerners attempt to carry out research in less developed countries. In such circumstances, there is a special obligation not to perpetuate colonialist and extractive practices – in this case, the extraction of knowledge.

Research carried out in disaster settings must also take into account other special circumstances created by those settings. Some disaster survivors may have lost everything and may be so overwhelmed with their own problems that they have no time for taking part in research. Others may believe that participating in a study will help them obtain some needed assistance. Still others may view participation as a form of therapy; this is a belief termed the "therapeutic misconception." There is also the possibility that the research itself disrupts the provision of emergency services (Kelman 2005), which would be ethically unacceptable. To block this possibility, researchers who go into the field immediately after disaster impact often opt for engaging at first only in the observation of response activities, as opposed to carrying out formal or even informal interviewing.

Particularly in the case of large-scale disasters, researchers from many disciplines – physical scientists, engineers, social scientists, medical researchers, and others, both domestic and international – often converge on disaster-stricken communities, which creates the potential for overburdening both the affected population and public officials. Physical scientists and engineers want to be taken on tours of the affected areas in order to collect data. Social scientists want access to members of the public, public officials, leaders of community institutions, and so on. People with responsibilities for dealing with disaster response and recovery are often forced to field multiple inquiries; and, similarly, victims may be approached by multiple research teams.

While most scientists and engineers rightly chafe at the notion that a "disaster research czar" should be put in charge of managing researcher convergence and while, as researchers, we resist measures aimed at exercising prior constraint over research, the potential for excessive burden creates a legitimate ethical concern in disaster settings. The best way to deal with the threat of unacceptable levels of burdensome research is for research teams to communicate and collaborate voluntarily – for example by sharing information on the topics they are studying and on the timing of their research activities, or by exploring ways to consolidate data collection and data sharing. Funding agencies have an important role to play in encouraging coordination but should not mandate it. A later section of this chapter focuses on such efforts.

Regarding other obligations, it is universally accepted that those who conduct research have an obligation to provide feedback on research findings to study participants. This does not mean distributing copies of articles from scholarly journals or jargon-filled technical reports. Rather it means making information available in ways that research subjects can access and understand. This can be done through printed material, a website, community briefings, engaging with the media through interviews or op-ed articles, or a combination of those approaches. Whatever method (or combination of methods) is selected, a paramount concern is to give back to those who have given their time to contributing to the success of disaster-related research projects and to provide information that could be useful to their lives and their communities.

The issue of compensating study participants financially or in some other way was discussed earlier in this chapter, but is worth revisiting through the lens of research ethics. Here again, there are no blanket rules or easy solutions. Limits are typically placed on providing compensation for public officials, but there could be conditions under which they would merit compensation – if, for example, they provide consultant services to a research project on their own time and are included as part of the research budget. Regarding members of the general public, provisions for compensation, when deemed appropriate, should be incorporated into budgets and justified in research proposals through reference to the literature that exists in the area. One simple rule is that compensation should be commensurate with what is being asked of research participants in terms of extensiveness of participation and potential inconvenience, as well as in terms of participants' resources and capabilities. Referring back to the principles of respect for persons, beneficence, and justice, compensation arrangements should enable participant agency, cause no harm, and potentially provide benefits to those who elect to take part in research activities.

Some types of research, such as participatory action research, require the active engagement of research participants during all phases of a project, from initial problem formulation to the production and dissemination of study results. Additionally, participatory methods have as one of their key aims the empowerment of communities that are engaged in research collaborations, so that they may exercise greater agency and press for change. Some critics have questioned whether disaster researchers who claim to be carrying out participatory action research are really following this guidance. These critics point out for example that, particularly in the context of developing countries, concepts such as participation and empowerment are often nothing more than buzzwords that funders expect to hear (Le De, Gaillard, and Friesen 2015). Researchers who wish to employ participatory action research strategies are ethically obliged to do so in good faith, keeping in mind that those strategies require not only collecting and analyzing data but also supporting communities in their social change efforts. Providing such support is, typically, a long-term endeavor.

Community consultation and engagement are also frequently recommended, even for studies that are not explicitly emancipatory in their aims. For example, the guidelines produced by the Working Group on Disaster Research and Ethics, which focus to a great extent on research conducted after disasters in less developed countries, recommend collaboration with the affected communities throughout the research process. The extent to which researchers consult and engage with community members and groups will vary according to study types and objectives. On the one hand, in large-scale surveys that employ modules that have been selected by investigators in advance, as is often the case with post-disaster mental health studies, apart from the actual data collection phase, engagement with members of the community may be minimal or entirely absent. On the other hand, for participant observation research, engagement is essential. In still other cases, such as hazard and disaster research involving citizen science, the main objective of the research is coproduction of knowledge, and engagement with participants is critical to the project's success.

Regardless of study design, to be ethical, consultation and engagement with disaster-affected communities must be authentic. Researchers cannot go into a community with preexisting ideas about exactly how a study should proceed and then pretend to be obtaining community input on the conduct of the study. They may not deceive community members into believing that they are actually having an influence on the research when they are not; nor can they say that they have consulted with a community when they have merely informed the community about their research plans.

Obligations toward those who assist with research

Another related ethical question centers on what "outside" disaster researchers owe to colleagues who reside in disaster zones. Here again, researchers are obligated not to overburden those who are in a position to assist them in their work. Among other forms of assistance, local researchers may provide background information on affected communities and populations, arrange meetings with contacts, and even provide housing. After Hurricane Katrina, for example, New Orleans– and Gulf-based researchers extended hospitality and provided assistance to many non-local researchers, and later some felt exploited by ungrateful colleagues. Those who provide valued assistance to disaster researchers should be included as collaborators and given appropriate credit in subsequent papers and publications. In particular, researchers who rely extensively on the expertise of junior scholars, such as graduate students from institutions in disaster-stricken areas, must take care to ensure that the contributions of these students are recognized appropriately.

Lead investigators have other obligations toward colleagues and collaborators, particularly those who have less seniority and experience, such as graduate students and early career researchers working under their direction. It is unethical to exploit junior colleagues; the obligation to avoid exploitation is explicitly laid out in ethical guidelines provided by the American Sociological Association. Beyond that, senior researchers working in disaster settings have an ethical obligation to attend to the welfare of those who are working for them. First and foremost, this means considering any and all issues that team members could encounter in the field and addressing those issues.

Conducting research with disaster survivors and other groups, such as first responders, and particularly research that uses participant observation and face-to-face interviewing methods, can be upsetting and draining even for the most experienced researcher. Empathy is a valued trait in fieldwork, but empathizing can be highly stressful, particularly when researchers spend long hours listening to disaster survivors recount their experiences of pain and loss and when there are physical hardships associated with the conduct of research. Individuals involved in post-disaster studies may find their accommodations and transportation arrangements less than ideal, which further adds to the stress they experience (Mukherji, Ganapati, and Rahill 2014). For these sorts of reasons, lead investigators must be aware of emotional reactions and problems that could arise among team members in the course of research and should consider practices such as regular debriefings during or after trips to the field. When the research requires long-term presence in disaster-affected areas, breaks from engagement should be incorporated into research plans.

I have provided general guidance here, but the practice of disaster research is anything but formulaic. Researchers should expect to encounter practical, ethical, and methodological dilemmas throughout the research process. As Browne and Peek (2014) put it in their influential article, this involves thinking on an ongoing basis that goes well beyond the IRB, to a consideration of what it means to be allowed into the lives of those who experience what may be a once-in-a-lifetime trauma.

Covid-19 and Disaster Research

The Covid-19 pandemic upended the plans of numerous researchers, including disaster researchers. Travel to remote field sites was largely suspended, participant observation research had to be postponed, and studies with methods like face-to-face interviewing had to be redesigned to employ online data collection methods or Zoom interviews. Such adjustments presented both practical and methodological challenges. Fortunately at the time of the pandemic guidance already existed, in the form of resources for conducting online surveys, using social media to facilitate research, and other strategies that researchers of all stripes would be required to adopt because of Covid (Hewson, Vogel, and Laurent 2016; Whitaker, Stevelink, and Fear 2017; Kozinets 2019; Carter et al. 2021; see also the crowdsourced guidance on conducting research during Covid in Lupton 2021).

It is too soon to assess how the modifications in research strategies necessitated by the pandemic have affected the quality of disaster research. Did distanced methods affect willingness to take part in research or the quality of the information provided? Did modified designs that adopted online data collection ignore persons who were not internet- or social media–savvy? Which groups were more likely to be disadvantaged in the use of such methods? When surveys are conducted online, which groups are likely to be disadvantaged? More generally, to what extent did modified research approaches approximate the gold standard for disaster research – and research more generally? If there was an upside to the disruption engendered by Covid it was that it challenged all researchers – including those who study disasters – to innovate and to carefully interrogate their methods.

Trends in the Study of Disasters

Social science disaster research has evolved in significant ways since its inception. Here I briefly touch upon a few of the most important recent developments: advances in big data and technology; the increased use of multidisciplinary teams in which sociologists take part; efforts to diversify the research workforce; and efforts to bring about greater research coordination and improve the practice of disaster research (for lengthier discussions of such topics, see Peek et al. 2020a).

First, researchers have been able to take advantage of access to ever larger datasets to analyze hazards, disasters, and their impacts in new ways. Over several decades, there have been major developments in areas such as remote sensing, geospatial analytic technologies, network analysis, and data fusion, and they often resulted in the development of products for applications such as catastrophic loss modeling for insurance industry and for emergency decision support. One example of the latter is the Prompt Assessment of Global Earthquakes for Response (PAGER) system (also mentioned in Chapter 7), developed by the US Geological Survey. It is not unusual nowadays to see systematic studies that merge data on multiple hazard exposures, social vulnerability, and built-environment vulnerability and that take into account both direct and cascading disaster impacts (see e.g. Drakes and Tate 2022). Advances in crisis informatics have made it possible to pore over mountains of data to track online processes such as convergence, rumoring, and the spread of misinformation (Calo et al. 2021). In short, disaster research has entered the era of big data.

Second, while a substantial proportion of sociological research on disasters remains discipline-based and funded by relatively small grants (if at all), sociologists are also increasingly taking part in multidisciplinary team-based research, in part owing to some funding agencies' preference for that kind of research, but also out of a recognition that such collaboration can be best suited for tackling complex research questions such as those surrounding hazards and disasters. In many cases, large amounts of funding are devoted to such work. One example among many is a project called Coastal Hazards, Equity, Economic Prosperity, and Resilience (CHEER), an NSF-sponsored research program that brings together engineers, physical scientists, and social scientists, including a sociologist who acts as one of the principal investigators. Another is the Center for Risk-Based Community Resilience Planning, funded by the US National Institute of Standards and Technology, in which sociologists work in collaboration with engineers, economists, and data scientists, among others. The disaster loss estimation studies and the mitigation benefit studies discussed in the previous chapter are also examples of cross-disciplinary collaboration.

Large-scale projects and centers involving investigators from multiple disciplines can supply welcome resources for sociologists who wish to study hazards and disasters. At the same time, there can be difficulties. One such problem centers on what I call the "handmaiden" research model, in which a sociologist (or some other social scientist) is more or less told by others – say, engineers or earth scientists – what that person's role will be in the overall project, or is given translational or end user–related tasks but had no input into the problem definition and research design at the outset. Or a sociologist may be put on a team for window dressing, to satisfy funder requirements, but has little say in influencing the direction of a study. Or a sociologist may be given a small share of the overall project or center budget, but that share is insufficient for exploring the topic in question in any depth, or for generating publishable results.

Working closely with investigators from other disciplines also requires considerable effort to become familiar with concepts, terms, and methods used in those disciplines – not to master them, of course, but to be able to communicate productively across disciplines and understand how contributions from different members of a large team project fit into the whole: woe betide the sociologist trying to study earthquakes who doesn't know the difference between the Richter magnitude and Modified Mercalli intensity scales! Often geospatial science provides the glue that makes integration possible. In other cases, that glue may be a team's focus on a particular at-risk or disaster-stricken community, where various aspects of vulnerability and resilience are explored.

Third, from the time of its inception and for many decades, the disaster research workforce was almost exclusively male and white. (Indeed, even the organizations that were focused on in early studies, such as fire and police departments and civil defense and emergency management agencies, were also gendered.) Women began to join the disaster research ranks in small numbers in the 1970s and now make up a substantial share of the workforce. But the field still lags behind significantly when it comes to opportunities available for researchers of color. For example, a 2018 survey of self-described social science disaster researchers worldwide found that 60 percent identify as white, while only about 5 percent identify as black or African American (Peek et al. 2020a).

Clearly this is a situation that calls for enhanced efforts toward diversity, equity, and inclusion (DEI) in the field, and some (admittedly small) steps have already been taken. For a short time, NSF sponsored a disaster research training program called Minority Scholars from Underrepresented Groups in Engineering and the Social Sciences (SURGE), which provided support and fieldwork opportunities for graduate students. For example, as part of their activities, students traveled to the US Virgin Islands to document the impacts of hurricanes Maria and Irma, which struck the islands in 2017. A few graduate students specializing in disasters have obtained support from the American Sociological Association's minority fellowship program. At the undergraduate level, some recipients of McNair scholarships for underrepresented groups take part in disaster studies – appropriately, since astronaut Ronald McNair, the second African American to go into space, was killed in the 1986 Challenger disaster. Both out of commitment to the values of the field and in response to DEI initiatives at their universities, sociological disaster researchers have stepped up their efforts to recruit talented students of color to work on their projects.

Founded in 2014, the William A. Anderson Fund, named after sociologist William (Bill) Anderson, a pioneering African American disaster researcher and longtime leader in the field (and also the founding director of the American Sociological Association Minority Fellowship Program), supports PhD students of color from sociology and other fields. The Fund's activities are diverse and designed to help fellows navigate their graduate programs and overcome obstacles they often face, both as students of color and as members of a relatively small research subfield. Workshops for fellows are held three times a year and focus on topics such as developing relationships with mentors, writing dissertation and grant proposals, preparing and submitting papers for publication, presenting at conferences, and job search strategies. Support is also provided for participation in meetings and conferences. A key Fund strategy is to develop a network of disaster researchers of color who can "lift as they climb" – that is, a network of more experienced fellows and alumni who will help those coming along in subsequent cohorts. To date, there are over one hundred current fellows and alumni, and many fellows have gone on to build successful careers in academia, at different levels of government, and in the private sector. Operating as it does as a nonprofit organization, the Fund faces ongoing fundraising challenges.

You will likely be impressed not by how much is being done to make the field more diverse, but rather by how little is being done to diversify the research workforce. You could rightly ask whether the diversity issue in the disaster research field is best addressed by short-term, low-dollar, and nonprofit-based initiatives, however beneficial such programs may be for the small number of scholars who are able to participate. You could also question how diversity-targeted efforts will fare in a political atmosphere in which DEI-focused programs of all kinds are under attack. Lawsuits have already been filed against programs that seek to provide financial opportunities for members of historically disadvantaged groups, and DEI programs at universities are under attack.

Fourth, significant efforts have been made to improve research coordination and data quality and comparability. Two key programs, Social Sciences Extreme Events Research (SSEER) and Coordinated Social Science, Engineering, and Extreme Events Research (CONVERGE), both of which are funded by NSF, are led by the Natural Hazards Center at the University of Colorado Boulder (see Peek et al. 2020b). SSEER seeks to identify and link social science disaster researchers in different parts of the world. The broader CONVERGE platform brings together SSEER researchers with researchers from other disciplines, such as geology and geotechnical and structural engineering. Importantly, in addition to its research coordinating role in disasters, CONVERGE offers online training modules on topics such as collecting and sharing perishable data, survey research and sampling, focus group research, cultural competence, institutional review boards and the ethics of disaster research, and reciprocity between researchers and the communities they study.

Programs like SSEER and CONVERGE seek to address issues that have plagued the disaster research field: the ad hoc nature of many disaster studies; the failure to employ standardized, consistent measures of key concepts; uncoordinated field operations; and a lack of data sharing. Both programs emphasize the importance of research ethics, and they also seek to increase the cohesiveness of the field itself, by making information on members of the research community more widely available.

Additionally, as its name suggests, CONVERGE seeks to promote convergence research – that is, research that goes well beyond single-discipline investigations to encompass multidisciplinary, interdisciplinary, and transdisciplinary research advances. In the disaster context, convergence is defined as

an approach to knowledge production and action that involves diverse teams working together in novel ways – transcending disciplinary and organizational boundaries – to address vexing social, economic, environmental, and technical challenges in an effort to reduce disaster losses and promote collective well-being. (Peek et al. 2020a: 2)

As discussed earlier, efforts toward bringing about convergence are challenging, especially for sociologists and other social scientists whose work requires them to engage with researchers from the physical sciences and engineering. And many sociologists may choose to stay in their own lane. At the same time, a convergence approach seems especially appropriate for problem-focused studies like those on hazards and disasters. As the late sociologist and disaster researcher Dennis Mileti often said, "nature never went to college," meaning that solutions to the big problems posed by disasters and climate change don't reside in any one neatly separated and defined discipline.

Concluding Comments

This chapter has looked briefly at the practical, methodological, and ethical aspects of carrying out research in disaster settings and has emphasized what makes those settings distinctive. We have also surveyed trends in the field. The intent has been to show that, while the general social science methods literature offers a great deal in the way of guidance, applying those methods to disaster settings often requires considerable ingenuity. I have used examples from my own research and lessons identified by other researchers to make this point. At the same time, I have also attempted to show that, as in all types of research, there are no hard and fast rules that can be automatically applied to the conduct of disaster research. Instead researchers are challenged to make numerous judgment calls in their work, and to do it on the basis of their knowledge, training, past experience, and common sense.

QUESTIONS AND EXERCISES

Go to the CONVERGE portion of the Natural Hazards Center website. Sign up for and complete one of its training modules. What did you learn from that training?

Gaillard and Peek (2019) and Kendra and Wachtendorf (2020) had a dialogue on whether disaster research requires a special code of conduct. What did each side argue? What do you personally think about these contrasting claims?

What factors stand in the way of conducting high-quality research on the short- and longer-term mental health impacts of disasters? What would be needed to overcome the limitations researchers face in this area?

9

What the Future Holds
Greater Risks and Impacts or Greater Coping Capacity?

Introduction: A Changing Landscape of Risk

Those who try to predict the future are often wrong. In 1995, responding to a prediction that people would soon be using the internet to buy books and newspapers, purchase airline tickets, and make restaurant reservations, astronomer Clifford Stoll argued in a *Newsweek* article that those ideas were far-fetched; "how come," he asked, if "cyberbusiness" was so useful, "my local mall does more business in an afternoon than the entire internet handles in a month?" Only twenty years ago, it was almost impossible to foresee a future that would include pervasive social media, smart phones, driverless cars, 3D printers, AI, and wearable devices. Trying to predict the future is risky. Even so, enough information exists to give us some idea about the landscape of future disasters. Such projections are not mere opinion or speculation; rather they are based on scientific knowledge and on an understanding of where environmental and societal trends are heading. Scientists and sociologists who study disasters and other types of crises have offered various views of the disasters to come. In this chapter I employ some of these insights, along with data, to think about what the future holds in the way of disasters. In addition to considering disasters that could occur in the future, we will also look at known hazards with catastrophic potential and at hazards associated with climate change. Finally, we will explore the extent to which policies and programs based on the idea of increasing disaster resilience can help with bringing about a safer future.

New Sources of Vulnerability

In a 1996 article, Henry Quarantelli pointed to a number of trends that he believed would influence twenty-first-century disasters. One of his key points was that, because of the forces of social change, future disasters are likely to be different from those of the past. This didn't mean that the hazards we are accustomed to would go away – only that new and different ones would appear. I summarize just a few of his projections here. He predicted, for example, disasters that were to result from failures in ever more intercon-nected cyber infrastructures and from accidents in biotechnology facilities. He also noted that the impacts of future disasters would spread far beyond the areas initially affected. Presciently in light of the 2011 catastrophe in Japan, he predicted that natural disaster agents could cause major accidents in nuclear and chemical facilities. Because of the rapid pace of urbanization, which included development and population growth in hazard-prone areas, increasing numbers of people and properties would be put at risk. Changes in the demographic composition of populations around the world would mean that vulnerable populations were to increase: in Japan, the problem would be an aging population; in less developed countries with younger demographic profiles, children and youths would be more at risk (Quarantelli 1996).

Later on, Quarantelli followed up with additional projections. Once again he expressed the idea that biotechnology is a significant hazard: "Sooner or later there will be the creation of, or the escape from control of, some altered organism that cannot be checked by presently known means ... we are not talking of an unreal movie like Jurassic Park, but of real possibilities" (Quarantelli 2001b: 234). A recent investigative journalistic account, *Pandora's Gamble* (Young 2023) – which, as the subtitle tells us, deals with lab leaks, accidents, and near misses in the laboratories that handle pathogens – bears out this concern.

Quarantelli also argued that nation-states are declining in importance with the rise of transnational corporations and international bodies and that globalization requires global hazard and disaster governance systems that have yet to emerge. At the same time, he questioned whether powerful entities such as global corporations would have the legitimacy in the eyes of the world, or even the interest, to manage future crises. Because of a lack of effective global-scale institutions, he argued, disasters that cross borders will be difficult to manage – a point I take up later in this section.

In *The Next Catastrophe*, sociologist Charles Perrow (2006) revealed why the potential for large-scale disasters is growing. As we have seen in Chapter 4, one of his main points is that the roots of disasters can be found in concen-trations, by which he means larger, denser populations living in high-risk geographic areas, as well as larger amounts of dangerous substances being used and stored near population centers. Additionally, for Perrow, the fact that economic power is increasingly concentrated in the hands of ever larger corporations means that decisions regarding safety and security are now made in corporate headquarters by people who are likely to be unfamiliar with conditions at local facilities. Like Quarantelli, Perrow pointed to vulner-abilities associated with our massively interconnected cyber infrastructure: it leaves open the possibility of cybercrime and malicious hacking, which can cause electric power grid failures and the hijacking of the control systems of chemical and nuclear facilities. Perrow recounted a number of past instances in which computer systems were hacked or taken over for nefarious purposes; but from what we know now such threats loom even larger, and the potential for cyber warfare is widely accepted.

One of Quarantelli's key points was that the disasters of the future, although perhaps not seen before, will not be entirely new but rather will have their roots in past and present societal conditions. It is not difficult to see how social change is contributing to risk buildup and sets the stage for disasters. Wildfires in the United States are a case in point. Development has increased at the wildland–urban interface (WUI) – that is, the area where the built environment and the natural environment intermingle. Development is also increasing in exurbia – places that are remote from both cities and suburbs. Population increases in such areas are in part a consequence of amenity migration, or population movement into areas valued for their beauty and recreational opportunities. With incomes rising for some, better-off segments of the population are able to own second (and even more) homes. Even if these are located in wildland areas, those homes are easier to access because of improved transportation systems. At the same time, advances in computer technology and the traumas of Covid-19 have made remote work more common, making it possible for residents of the WUI and exurbia to work from those locations (for details on WUI growth, see Radeloff et al. 2018). Institutional forces have also been important in increasing wildfire potential; suppressing fires, as opposed to letting forests burn naturally, as they have throughout history, has led to the buildup of fuels. More people living in wildland areas means more ignition sources in areas that are ripe for burning. Climate change is also responsible for the growing incidence and intensity of wildfires. One result: more people and structures than ever are exposed to wildfire hazards, and there is more potential for human-induced wildfire ignitions. Another result: for at least a decade, the US Department of Agriculture's Forest Service has spent more money annually fighting fires than it has spent on forest management (US Department of Agriculture 2015).

Similarly, increases in economic losses from hurricanes in the United States are the result of migration and increased development in at-risk coastal areas (Pielke et al. 2008). As seen in Houston when Hurricane Harvey struck in 2017, development in areas exposed to flood hazards, coupled with the expansion of impermeable surfaces and the destruction of ecosystems that provide flood protection, is setting the stage for the hurricane and flood disasters of the future. Here again, past conditions and trends have combined to elevate current and future risks.

Both Quarantelli and Perrow warned that technological developments can present new threats. One such threat that has recently emerged is induced seismicity. As hydraulic fracturing, or fracking, is being employed in oil production, the injection of wastewater from fracking into the earth is resulting in very large increases in the frequency of earthquakes. For example, owing to wastewater injection, the state of Oklahoma has seen a precipitous rise in earthquake activity since 2009 and is now the most seismically active state in the United States, surpassing even California (Hincks, Aspinall, Cooke, and Gernon 2018). Fracking also contributes to greenhouse gas emissions and thus to climate change.

Quarantelli also noted that future disasters will have an impact on multiple nation-states and regions.[1] Disasters that affect two or more societies – "transboundary (or transborder) social ruptures" – are becoming increasingly common. To give just a few examples, in Europe in 2000, a break in a dam holding toxic waste at a gold mine in Baia Mare, Romania sent large quantities of cyanide into the Somes River, then into the Tisa River, the second largest river in Hungary, and on into the Danube River, affecting Serbia and Bulgaria. The spill poisoned drinking water for millions of people and resulted in massive fish kills. In early 2003, an outbreak of severe acute respiratory syndrome (SARS) began in the Pearl River Delta region in China and ultimately spread to thirty-seven countries, with major impacts in places as far apart geographically as Hong Kong and Toronto, Canada. In 2004, the Indian Ocean earthquake and tsunami killed hundreds of thousands in fourteen countries in the Indian Ocean region. In the fall of 2017, Hurricane Irma cut a swathe through the Caribbean and the United States, affecting island nations and territories within the jurisdictions of the United States, the United Kingdom, France, and the Netherlands, along with the nations of Cuba, the Dominican Republic, Haiti, and the United States itself. Then Hurricane Maria proceeded to devastate some of those same places, the US territory of Puerto Rico, and other nations, such as Dominica and Turks and Caicos. In 2020 Covid-19, which originated in China, caused a pandemic of global proportions, killing over 7 million worldwide, including 1 million in the US.

Transboundary disasters have several attributes. They often begin with small accidents, failures, or outbreaks, but subsequently their effects spread more broadly, often in unexpected ways. Even existing pandemic plans never anticipated the illnesses, hospitalizations, and deaths that Covid-19 would cause on a global scale, or the massive disruption it would engender to virtually every aspect of life. Globalization in areas such as finance and industry means that financial crises have increasingly far-reaching effects. The 2008 crisis that caused the Great Recession began in the United States but spread rapidly worldwide, nearly collapsing the global financial system. Earlier in this century, earthquakes in Taiwan and floods in Thailand, and, later, the triple disaster in Japan in 2011 caused major disruptions in global supply chains, affecting trade in such products as semiconductors, hard drives, and auto parts. But even those losses were dwarfed by the massive disruptions to supply chains, travel, and virtually every aspect of social life that were caused by Covid-19.

Another characteristic of transboundary disasters is that, as they unfold, officials in the affected or potentially affected countries have difficulty getting a full picture of what is actually happening, in part because of the uncertainties associated with such crises, but also because officials in different countries may never have communicated with one another before in a crisis context. Additionally, there can be legal or political barriers to information sharing across borders, or nations may outright deny or cover up major transborder threats, as happened in the Soviet Union with the Chernobyl nuclear disaster in 1986 and in China with SARS in 2003 and again with Covid-19 in 2020.

These kinds of upheavals have the potential for creating legitimacy crises for the governments and institutions involved. We saw this, for example, with the SARS outbreak, when the credibility and crisis management capability of the Chinese government were so widely criticized that the leadership was forced to revamp the country's emergency management system (Lim 2021). The Japanese government's handling of the 2011 disasters, especially problems with its management of the Fukushima nuclear plant meltdowns, resulted in a significant loss of trust on the part of the public. Japan has long depended on nuclear power for its energy needs, but Fukushima also caused a public drop in confidence in the industry. In the United States, the Covid-19 pandemic led to unprecedented challenges to the credibility of the government and of agencies such as the Centers for Disease Control and Prevention, along with widespread opposition to official self-protective directives.

Disasters that affect multiple nations are of course not new. The Lisbon earthquake of 1755 was felt all over Europe and in northern Africa, and tsunamis created by the earthquake affected places as far away as England and Ireland. The earthquake had wide-ranging social, economic, and cultural impacts. For example, it struck a blow to Portugal's imperial ambitions and helped move European societies toward a less religious, more secular view of the origins of disasters.

However, what is new is that we are now beginning to understand the special challenges that societies face in our specific twenty-first-century social and economic context. With respect to transboundary disasters, this social and economic context has two key characteristics. First, we live in a globalized world that can amplify societal and infrastructural vulnerabilities. Second, globalization means that societies and economies are more interconnected and interdependent than ever before, and frequently in ways that are not well understood. For example complex, interconnected global systems of travel mean that viruses like SARS and Covid-19 could spread widely before the authorities in the affected societies were even aware of the phenomenon. At the same time, we lack transnational governance structures to manage the risks associated with transboundary disasters.

In a globalized world, corporations and other enterprises have to be extremely large in order to compete. Size is usually considered an advantage in terms of the ability to prepare for and respond to crises, but this is not always true because, as noted earlier, large global entities may lack an understanding of localized hazards and risks in the places where they do business. They may not care about those hazards and risks enough to take action, either. For example, having experienced deadly accidents in its US plants, British Petroleum professed to be improving its safety record, but the corporation actually cut off funds that would have made that possible – right up until the catastrophic 2010 Deepwater Horizon blowout and oil spill (Tierney 2014). Global integration can also mean that risky and even criminal practices spread more widely across borders, as happened in the run-up to the 2008 financial meltdown.

Governance mechanisms for managing transboundary risks and crises are nascent, weak, or entirely lacking. Hazards and disasters cross borders, but often the capacity to manage them does not. Global efforts like the United Nations International Strategy for Disaster Reduction are primarily nation-state–focused and are voluntary. As Cameron (2017) indicates, "[u]nlike armed conflict, natural disasters have no legally binding set of regulations to govern the actions of those involved in aid and recovery." Feldman and Fish (2015) also point out that transnational legal regimes for disaster management are poorly developed. Entities such as the International Federation of Red Cross and Red Crescent Societies and the United Nations Office for the Coordination of Humanitarian Assistance have developed nonbinding guidelines for aid provision, but that guidance mainly relates to donor countries that offer disaster assistance to less developed nations, as opposed to two or more national governments that collaborate to manage a transboundary crisis. Agreements that do exist tend to focus on responding to particular types of hazards. Examples include the Joint Contingency Plan, which provides for cooperation between the United States and Mexico in situations related to oil and hazardous materials spills along their shared border; Europe's Directive 2007/60/EC on the Assessment and Management of Flood Risk; and the Arctic Council's Agreement on Cooperation on Marine Oil Pollution, Preparedness, and Response in the Arctic (Tierney 2012; Feldman and Fish 2015).

John Hannigan refers to the parties that are involved one way or another in the management and politics of hazards and disasters within and across borders as a "global policy field" that consists of

> national states and local governments; regional organizations, interna-
> tional finance institutions (IFIs); United Nations disaster agencies and
> other international governmental organizations (IGOs); nongovernmental
> organizations (NGOs); multi-actor initiatives and partnerships; scientific,
> technical, and academic communities; private actors; and the mass media.
> (Hannigan 2012: 22)

Typically, there is only weak or sporadic coordination among such entities and, even within specific sectors such as the NGO one, there is often a lack of coordination.

The Evil We Know: Hazards with Catastrophic Potential

In an earlier publication (Tierney 2014), I called attention to some hazards that have the potential to cause major and even catastrophic disasters. Here I discuss some of them briefly. Speaking of earthquakes, the Great Tohoku earthquake and tsunami of 2011 caused massive death and destruction, but it was not the truly "big one" that Japan has been awaiting for decades. Scientists note that the Great Tokai earthquake – a predicted magnitude 8 event – is overdue and that the likelihood of such an event in the next twenty years approaches 90 percent. The magnitude 8 Tokai earthquake will strike not far from Tokyo, in the Nankai Trough, where the Philippine Sea Plate is sliding under the Eurasian Plate. When it occurs, this earthquake will cause a major tsunami and, like the 2011 mega disaster, the tsunami will threaten nuclear power plants in the region. Direct property damage from that event is conservatively estimated at $310 billion. This total does not take into account indirect losses that could result, for example, from the disruption of economic activities in the densely populated impact region. Following Perrow's reasoning, the deaths and massive damages waiting to be caused by the Great Tokai earthquake will be a consequence of concentrations – of people, economic activity, and built environment.[2]

A major earthquake in the New Madrid Seismic Zone (NMSZ) in the central United States, although much less likely than the Great Tokai earthquake, would also have devastating impacts. The earthquakes that occurred in the NMSZ in the winter of 1811–1812 were the largest seismic events ever to strike in the contiguous United States. Scenarios suggest that a 7.7 magnitude earthquake in the NMSZ could kill as many as 86,000, displace 7.2 million people, damage over half a million homes, and disrupt bridges, highways, and pipelines in an eight-state area, the most severe disruption occurring in Tennessee, Arkansas, and Missouri. A major earthquake in the NMSZ would be a truly catastrophic event.

Both the 2004 Indian Ocean tsunami and the 2011 Japan triple disaster were caused by subduction-related seismic events – that is, geologic conditions in which one tectonic plate slides beneath another – and the same will be true of the coming Great Tokai earthquake. Another area of concern in this respect is the Cascadia Subduction Zone (CSZ) in the Pacific Northwest. The CSZ is about 700 miles long, stretching from northern California to southern British Columbia in Canada. In the past thirty-odd years, researchers have been exploring the hazards that are associated with the CSZ and engaging in efforts to communicate those findings to the public. Since awareness of the magnitude of the threat associated with this seismic zone is relatively recent, buildings and infrastructure in the region were not designed to resist the kinds of forces that a large CSZ earthquake could generate. According to a scenario developed by the Cascadia Region Earthquake Workgroup (CREW) in 2013, the CSZ is capable of producing earthquakes in the 9.0 range, as well as tsunamis – all comparable to the events that occurred in Japan in 2011. The zone is close to the shore in many areas, so a tsunami could strike some communities as soon as fifteen minutes after the earthquake occurs. Those living, working, and traveling in tsunami inundation zones would have to evacuate immediately or lose their lives. A large CSZ earthquake would significantly damage ports, airports, highways, and bridges and do extensive damage to buildings, especially those constructed before current seismic codes (Cascadia Region Earthquake Workgroup 2013).

Climate Change–Related Threats

A multidimensional hazard

Climate change looms large in thought about the disasters of the future. It is already affecting societies around the world, and as it progresses its impacts will be even more profound. A recent report that did not even take into account the impacts of climate-driven disasters found that, on the basis of changes that are already "locked in" – meaning they would persist even if emissions were drastically cut today – climate change damages will total an estimated $38 trillion per year by 2050, causing average income losses worldwide of 19 percent, and those losses will be significantly higher in many parts of the global South. On the other hand, the measures required to respond to climate change would cost less than one sixth of that amount (Kotz, Levermann, and Weng 2024).

The Intergovernmental Panel on Climate Change (IPCC) is a United Nations–sponsored body that represents 195 UN member states charged with producing consensus reports on the state of scientific findings on climate change and its impacts. The IPCC does not conduct its own independent research; rather it develops state-of-the-art syntheses of existing empirical studies. The first IPCC report was published in 1990, and the most recent was issued in 2022.

The IPCC is divided into working groups that deal with different aspects of climate change; the most sociologically relevant IPCC findings come from Working Group II, which focuses on climate change impacts, adaptation, and vulnerability. While it is not possible to enumerate here all the issues discussed in the most recent Working Group II report, Box 9.1 lists just a few of the impacts the authors identified with a high degree of confidence. An

Box 9.1 Selected Findings from the 2022 IPCC Report on Climate Change Impacts, Adaptation, and Vulnerability

- Climate change has negatively affected health, mental health, and livelihoods worldwide and has also contributed to humanitarian crises.
- Global warming reaching 1.5°C (2.7°F) in the near term (that is, by 2040) will cause increases in multiple climate hazards and extreme events.
- Climate change risks are numerous, including biodiversity loss, declining water availability and food production, and increases in premature deaths.
- Climate change and its impacts, such as sea-level rise, flooding, and droughts, will lead to involuntarily migration.
- Climate change and associated impacts and risks are becoming more complex, with multiple hazards occurring simultaneously, creating compound risks and cascading effects.
- Climate extremes are causing economic and societal effects that cross regional and national boundaries.
- While climate change adaptation is well underway globally, such efforts are currently insufficient.

earlier special IPCC report on climate change and disasters (Field, Barros, Stocker, and Dahe 2012) had already concluded that climate change will affect the frequency, intensity, spatial extent, timing, and duration of weather and climate events while at the same time increasing vulnerability and damaging the coping and adaptive capacity among affected populations.

In the United States, the Global Change Research Act of 1990 created the US Global Change Research Program (USGCRP), which coordinates the climate change–related research activities of fifteen federal agencies, including the departments of Health and Human Services, Interior, Transportation, and Commerce, and agencies such as the Federal Emergency Management Agency (FEMA) and the Environmental Protection Agency. Among other activities, the USGCRP is charged with overseeing the development of national climate assessments, which are produced about every four years. The most recent assessment, called the Fifth Assessment or NCA5, was published in late 2023 (for an online version, see https://nca2023.globalchange.gov). NCA5 provides a comprehensive view on climate change trends and impacts at national and regional levels; gives numerous examples of programs designed to reduce greenhouse gas emissions and to adapt to climate change that are under way at federal, state, local, tribal, and territorial levels; explains what can be expected in the future under different strategies for reducing the effects of climate change; and outlines the social and economic benefits that can result from such strategies, such as the creation of jobs and new industries. The information in NCA5 is vast, so here I emphasize just a few key points.

As we have already seen, the report emphasizes that disasters are becoming increasingly frequent and costly. On average, the United States experiences a disaster that causes $1 billion or more in damages every three weeks. The report also discusses the increased frequency of compound events caused by a combination of climate change effects and extreme events, by concurrent disasters, and by events that have cascading effects. For example, climate change affects the health of forests, increasing wildfire risks; and, as the frequency and severity of wildfires intensifies, the particulate emissions from these fires spread, causing respiratory problems. Or consider the convergence of drought, extreme heat, and wildfires, as seen in recent years in the Pacific Northwest. Fires scour out landscapes, practically ensuring that subsequent rainfall events (which will be more intense in some areas) will cause flash flooding and mudslides. One report (Miller 2018) indicates that California will experience this type of "whiplash" cycle, in which drought and subsequent wildfires will be followed by years of heavy rainfall that cause flooding and debris flows – a cycle that will lead to escalating social impacts and losses. Climate change is contributing to ocean acidification, which in turn threatens marine ecosystems, and these are a source of food for millions and offer protection from extreme events. We have already seen, in Superstorm Sandy, in 2012, that rising sea levels caused by climate change engender higher storm surges, endangering cities like New York and Miami.

Another point of emphasis in the NCA5 report that is consistent with our discussions here is that the negative impacts of climate change are falling disproportionately on those who are already vulnerable. As we saw earlier, extreme heat disproportionately affects those who are elderly and socially isolated. Higher daytime and nighttime temperatures and heat waves will make life more difficult for poor residents and for those who are unhoused, in places like Phoenix and Las Vegas, as well as for people whose jobs require them to work outdoors, such as farm and construction workers. The demand for air conditioning will soar during heat waves, putting an excessive strain on power systems and on people's budgets. Asthma and other respiratory problems are prominent in inner-city neighborhoods, and climate change will worsen those conditions.

Climate change and coastal flooding

To focus on just one hazard, coastal flooding is exacerbated by climate change as sea levels rise. Hallegatte et al. (2013) conducted research to assess future economic losses to be incurred by 2050 from climate change–related coastal flooding in the 136 largest urban agglomerations worldwide. Their analyses show that by that year average annual losses from coastal flooding for those cities will rise to between $60 and $63 billion. They ranked urban areas in terms of the size of projected losses for 2050, taking into account anticipated social and economic trends, environmental changes such as subsidence and sea-level rise, and investments that cities have made in adaptation. The study also took into account annualized flood losses in relation to gross domestic product (GDP) in each of the 136 cities and urban agglomerations. Table 9.1 lists the ten cities with the highest projected economic losses from coastal flooding by 2050, along with changes in loss projection from a baseline year of 2005 and the share of GDP that future losses will represent.

As the table indicates, two cities in China's Pearl River Delta, Guangzhou and Shenzhen, are among the top ten in terms of projected flood losses; losses are expected to be highest in Guangzhou, which is also the city with the highest losses in proportion to its GDP. Three cities – Tianjin, Kolkata, and Miami – will see the largest increases vis-à-vis the losses measured in 2005. In some areas, such as New York–Newark, losses will be high but will constitute small percentages of their overall GDPs. Even so, the numbers are significant. Cities in less developed countries predominate on this list; and, with the exception of New Orleans and Miami, these are also the cities that will see the highest losses in proportion to their GDPs.

Table 9.1 Cities with the highest projected economic losses from coastal flooding–related hazards in 2050

Urban Agglomeration	Average Annualized (AA) Losses in US $million	Percent Increase over 2005 AA Losses	Losses as a Percentage of City GDP
Guangzhou, China	13,200	11%	1.46%
Mumbai, India	6,414	5%	0.49%
Kolkata, India	3,350	24%	0.26%
Guayaquil, Ecuador	3,189	13%	1.08%
Shenzhen, China	3,136	7%	0.40%
Miami, United States	2,549	21%	0.36%
Tianjin, China	2,276	26%	0.30%
New York–Newark, United States	2,056	5%	0.08%
Ho Chi Minh City, Vietnam	1,953	12%	0.83%
New Orleans, United States	1,864	18%	1.42%

Source: Compiled from data in Hallegatte, Green, Nicholls, and Corfee-Morlot 2013.

The Next Pandemic

This century has been marked by several outbreaks of infectious and zoonotic disease – SARS (2003), HIV/AIDS, Ebola, Middle East Respiratory Syndrome (MERS), H1N1 (swine flu), and Zika – and one global pandemic: SARS Covid-19. In an important review article, Baker et al. (2022) discuss technological, socio-demographic, and climate change–related factors that contribute to increased outbreak and pandemic vulnerability worldwide. A short list of these factors includes greatly increased air travel, urbanization and overcrowding in slum conditions, aging populations that can be immunocompromised, migration that can fuel the spread of viruses and bacteria, increasing worker contact with host species in agricultural industries, trade in animals that can be pathogen hosts, changing climate conditions that are conducive to the growth and spread of host species and disease vectors, and inequities in access to health care. The big picture is that, despite monumental accomplishments in eradicating or preventing the spread of many diseases, such as smallpox and polio, the threat of existing and emerging infectious diseases is very much with us.

Experts appear to have converged in their predictions about the next possible pandemic. That pandemic would be triggered by the spread of the H5N1 influenza virus, a type of bird flu that in the United States has already spread to mammals such as domestic cattle as well as to farm workers, and has been found in the nation's milk supply. Two issues are causes for concern. First, the virus could mutate in ways that would allow for easier spread to humans. And, second, even though existing vaccines could be calibrated to fight the virus, questions remain about whether the global healthcare system has the resources to deliver vaccines to at-risk populations in a timely manner (McKie 2024).

Scientists' views on the next pandemic also focus on a yet unknown virus labeled "disease X," a relative of Covid-19 (McKie 2024). This designation is a reflection on the extent to which the source, infectiousness, contagiousness, and lethal potential of existing and emerging pathogens are uncertain. In our lifetimes, the world may still see the emergence and spread of "disease X," or even of a known pathogen that mutates in ways that encourage its spread and make it more deadly.

In response to the Covid-19 pandemic and under the auspices of the World Health Organization, governments around the world have come together to forge an agreement on a new international pact that centers on pandemic prevention, preparedness, and response and proposes measures such as vaccine sharing, should the conditions for a pandemic materialize. At the time of this writing, negotiations are moving slowly and the progress of that initiative is a topic for ongoing research.

Can Resilience-Centered Approaches Reduce
Future Disaster Impacts?

In this volume I have explored how long-term global and societal trends contribute to the buildup of risk and set the stage for the occurrence of disasters when some force of nature or some technological failure serves as a trigger. In the present chapter we have so far taken a brief look at what the future holds, in order to see how social and environmental processes and anthropogenic threats such as climate change, cyber insecurity, and emerging infectious diseases are setting the stage for future disasters. In the face of looming threats like the ones discussed here, societies and communities have essentially two options: to continue with business as usual or to adopt measures that can dramatically reduce vulnerability and contain losses.

In light of what has been discussed in earlier chapters, business as usual will have predictable effects. Disaster-related losses in the form of death, injury, illness, and economic costs will continue to rise. Those effects will be borne disproportionately by the poorer countries of the world and by vulnerable groups in both developed and less developed countries. In countries at the periphery and semi-periphery of the world system, disasters will drive more people into poverty, prevent the poor from escaping it, and slow or reverse development efforts. Disaster events will interact with other social ills, for example wars and civil wars, to produce severe and complex humanitarian crises. As weather extremes become more common as a consequence of climate change, floods, droughts, and other perils will increase food insecurity and threaten livelihoods. Conflicts over resources will become more frequent. An already poorly functioning international disaster relief system will face mounting challenges.

In developed countries, the model of business as usual will become increasingly costly and disruptive. Many wealthy countries, or communities and regions in those countries, have adopted and implemented disaster risk reduction measures; but even with such measures in place losses will continue to rise, because historical practices of development have put more people and property in harm's way and because construction and population growth continue in hazardous areas. Similarly, greenhouse gas mitigation and climate adaptation programs have been adopted by many nations, communities, and sectors, but their implementation has likely come too late to slow the rate of global climate change and to head off its consequences.

Under a business-as-usual scenario, political and economic forces will continue to operate in ways that magnify the burgeoning risks. Climate change adaptation projects will proceed as planned, but retreat and relocation will increasingly be coping strategies of choice, as life in coastal areas and other disaster-prone zones becomes more and more untenable. Jurisdictions worldwide will face the challenge of extensively retrofitting, relocating, or abandoning critical infrastructure elements such as ports, highways, and power plants. Distinctive local and regional cultures threatened by disasters and climate change, such as those dependent on fishing and other subsistence activities, will weaken or disappear.

In the United States, the case of homeowner insurance offers a preview of trends to come. In Florida, a number of private insurance companies have left the market, and in many cases the rates offered by the companies that remain are unaffordable. The Florida Citizens Property Insurance Corporation, set up as an "insurer of last resort" for those who cannot afford to pay premiums offered by private companies, is now the state's largest insurer (First Street Foundation 2023). In recent years FEMA's National Flood Insurance Program (NFIP) has doubled its rates in high-risk parts of states like Florida and Louisiana.

Regarding wildfire hazards in California, of the twelve private insurance companies that have been operating and that are behind 85 percent of the policies, seven have stopped offering homeowners' insurance. In 2023, State Farm, the state's largest private insurer, stopped offering new policies owing to concern with burgeoning wildfire losses (Chabria and Smith 2023). Homeowners in areas of high wildfire risk face higher rates of policy non-renewals and significant increases in their premiums and are more and more turning to the state's Fair Access to Insurance Requirements (FAIR) program, another insurer of last resort (Liao al. 2022). At the same time there are concerns that California's FAIR plan may not be able to cover antici-pated future losses (Sumagaysay 2024). One report noted that "the system is becoming overwhelmed and officials are warning that it might be on the brink of insolvency" (Ramos 2024).

Property owners in many regions now struggle to decide what to do in the face of increasing insurance expenses. Some opt for going without insurance, as has happened in some high-risk areas with the NFIP. So do others whose mortgages are paid off, which removes some requirements regarding hazard insurance. Still others consider moving but face the prospect that high insurance rates would drive prospective buyers away. Because they add to the financial burdens of home ownership, high rates also contribute to the crisis of housing affordability.

There will of course be winners as well as losers in our business-as-usual scenario. Rebuilding after increasingly destructive disasters will provide jobs for developers and for individuals who work in the design and construction trades, and financial institutions in stricken communities will benefit from an influx of disaster assistance funds. Consulting companies that manage the disbursement of disaster assistance monies and private contractors who work in the disaster recovery space will thrive, as will professionals with expertise in areas such as land use planning, risk analysis, catastrophic risk modeling, and risk securitization. Coastal residents displaced by climate change and by repeated disasters will have to move somewhere, which may be beneficial for sectors of the economy that rely on property development and construction. Healthcare-related institutions should see their fortunes improve, as larger numbers of people experience the adverse effects of disasters and climate change – provided that those victims are adequately insured. Similarly, institutions and professions that offer psychological first aid and mental health and other forms of support will see the demand for their services increase in tandem with disaster-related losses and disruption. Climate-change adaptation and energy-transition activities will also be engines of job creation. That said, we may well ask what "winning" means in a world in which extreme heat and deadly and destructive disasters are routine.

A Resilient Future?

In the face of dire predictions regarding future impacts and losses, new programs are being advanced to address the twin perils of disasters and climate change. In earlier chapters we saw how government expenditures to reduce the impacts of climate change have increased as a consequence of recent legislation such as the Inflation Reduction Act of 2022, the largest investment in combatting climate change in US history. Programs such as FEMA's Community Disaster Resilience Zones, or Justice 40, promise to advance disaster- and climate-related environmental justice efforts. On the international scene, in 2023, at the United Nations Climate Change Conference of the Parties (Cop28), affluent countries pledged to set up a "damage and loss" program to compensate nations that are especially vulnerable to climate change for damages they had already incurred, on the logic that countries that contribute the most to greenhouse gas emissions and climate change ought to make amends and repay those that contributed far less, but bear the brunt of those impacts.

At first glance such programs seem promising, but there is cause for concern. Legislation can be repealed, and initiatives set up by executive order, like Justice40, can be reversed at the stroke of a pen. Disaster and climate change risk reduction efforts remain hostage to political and economic forces, and even temporary reversals or reductions in their momentum diminish the time available to avert more severe or even irreversible impacts. Since 2023, contributions to the loss and damage fund totaled around $700 million, but that is a mere pittance by comparison with losses that vulnerable developing countries are experiencing annually as a result of climate change (Lakhani 2023). Despite the multiplicity of risk reduction efforts that are under way worldwide at different levels of government, the current scenario is one of "too little, too late." Experts now conclude that there is no chance of limiting the warming to 1.5°C and achieving the target set for 2050, and that a 2-degree increase is likely in the not distant future.

As we saw in Chapter 6, the concept of resilience currently represents the holy grail of disaster risk reduction. Embraced in many parts of the developed world, in particular in the United States, and framed as a broad set of measures that address pre- and post-disaster protections and services, the disaster resilience construct promises an alternative to an increasingly dismal business-as-usual future. But can it achieve that objective? Given what we already know, there is reason for skepticism.

As I noted earlier and discussed elsewhere (Tierney 2015), at the individual and household levels, becoming more resilient is an attractive idea for those who are already capable of choosing among risk reduction options and exercising agency. These are well-off individuals and households with equity in their homes, adequate savings, insurance they can still afford to cover their losses, and an understanding of how to access the aid to which they are entitled when disaster does strike. Those lacking in such assets are at a disadvantage in terms of becoming disaster-resilient. How exactly can you be disaster-resilient if you are a single mother who already pays more than half her income to rent a unit in a poorly constructed and poorly maintained apartment complex? How resilient can a woman or a girl become if she is living in a male-dominated society governed by patriarchal norms? How resilient can you be if you are an elderly person on a fixed income who lives in a house with a paid-off mortgage and cannot afford to purchase hazard insurance – or chooses not to? We would do well to remember points made in Chapter 5 about the root causes of disaster vulnerability and their relationship with social inequality.

If resilience has been framed as the holy grail of disaster risk reduction, then in some views social capital is the holy grail of disaster resilience. Social capital, we are told, is a resource that is available to all those who wish to become resilient in the face of disasters, even – or perhaps especially – the poor. Yet social capital is unevenly distributed across the social order: those at the upper end of the class hierarchy possess not only high levels of bonding and bridging capital but also the all-important linking form, which connects them to those with political and economic power. Those on the disadvantaged side of the class divide rely on their bonding networks of social support for problem-solving on an everyday basis, but they typically lack the access to power that the linking ties represent – the very kinds of connections that matter most when disasters strike. We already have evidence that, after disasters, social capital works differently for the well-off, who can mobilize support from geographically distant sources, and for the poor, whose more localized networks may be frayed and unable to function well in the aftermath of disasters (Elliott, Haney, and Sams-Abiodun 2010). How will those who are disadvantaged recover if their ongoing support networks are damaged or destroyed by disaster, if post-disaster policies and programs do further damage to their networks of support, and if the aid that is available is insufficient to put them back on their feet?

Among the many criticisms that have been launched against the concept of resilience in recent years, perhaps the most compelling arguments center on its negative implications for political agency. Too often, discourses on resilience take for granted the assumption that individuals, families, communities, and other social actors have no choice but to adapt to a world in which hazards that are beyond their control – atmospheric, geologic, technological, and climate-related forces – wreak havoc. In this view, resilience requires adaptability and adjustment. Too often, discussions about ways of increasing resilience turn people's attention away from the need to reverse the social, political, and economic processes that combine to produce vulnerability and disasters. As Béné and colleagues observe with respect to the resilience of cities,

> what is missing in the present literature on urban resilience is the social justice and political dimensions of the concept and a clearer understanding of the advantages but also the dangers of adopting such a concept as a new policy narrative without specifically acknowledging the political economy dimension of urbanization. (Béné et al. 2018: 129)

An emphasis on resilience as currently framed in mainstream disaster discourse ignores the fact that people are political actors who can seize opportunities to create substantial social change in order to reduce their vulnerability to disasters and other stressors. Viewing potential victims as having no choice but to adapt to inevitable hazards in a resilient fashion obscures this point. Accepting the mainstream view of resilience means that we seek to improve our ability to respond to catastrophic oil spills and to adapt to climate change, rather than engaging in political activity that should reduce our reliance on fossil fuels while working toward an alternative-energy future. We look for social capital–based solutions to disaster preparedness rather than demanding, as political actors, that the poor not be housed in buildings that will kill them, should an earthquake or a hurricane occur.

With respect to climate change, under the resilience rubric, those who live in affluent societies expect the populations of low-income countries to become more resilient to climate-induced stressors and events. But, as Cannon and Müller-Mahn (2010: 633) state bluntly (and they are echoed in the aforementioned 2024 Kotz et al. study on climate change impacts on incomes worldwide), "[w]ith climate change, it is impossible to ignore the fact that the expected increase in poverty of hundreds of millions of people in developing countries is being caused by the behavior of the economies of richer countries." Or, as Friend and Moench (2015: 648) put it, what is needed is a "fundamental social transformation not just on supporting people who are already poor to cope with various shocks and crises, but addressing the factors determining why such people are poor in the first place and setting agendas of enhancing wellbeing and prosperity." However, rather than shouldering the burden of ameliorating projected increases in poverty and advancing transformative strategies, well-off nations carry on with business as usual while urging the poor and the powerless to become more resilient.

Resilience has a lot in common with the earlier concept of sustainable development, which promised a pathway to improving living conditions in less well-off societies. Like sustainable development, resilience has its origins in the global North and likely finds little resonance in the global South (Aguirre 2002; Tierney 2015). Here again, disaster resilience frameworks underemphasize the extent to which reducing disaster vulnerability necessitates reducing social inequality, empowering those who are vulnerable, and taking decisive action to diminish the burdens placed on poor nations and communities.

Even as discourses in the United States and other parts of the global North extoll the virtues of disaster resilience, neoliberal policies that roll back social provisions and benefit the 1 percent at the expense of others, who rank lower in the social class hierarchy, undermine the very support networks that make social resilience possible. If policymakers were genuinely committed to helping individuals, households, businesses, and communities become more resilient in the face of disasters, they would champion policies that promote a living wage, access to health care, high-quality education, community cohesion, safe housing for all, and community empowerment. The super-rich would allow themselves to be taxed fairly and would devote their funds to improving conditions in their own societies instead of spinning fantasies about life on the moon or Mars. Such measures would constitute the starting point for achieving durable, effective disaster resilience programs and outcomes. Studies like those discussed in this volume emphasize a basic but profound truth: those who cannot provide decent living conditions and food and clothing for their families cannot and will not commit time and resources to becoming disaster-resilient. Without a social and economic infrastructure to support it, disaster resilience is nothing more than a hollow promise.

My work in the field has led me to conclude that programs for managing hazards and disasters and promoting resilience are and always will be insufficient, unless they are part of a broader program intended to confront the political–economic forces that drive risk production in the first place. This will inevitably require transformative actions – not incremental ones – that challenge the hegemony of entities, institutions, and interests that benefit from putting our families, communities, and the planet at risk. Promising trends in this vein are lawsuits that identify the reduction of greenhouse gas emissions as a human right and that seek damages from the fossil fuel industry for its impact on global warming and subsequent losses, including those caused by extreme events. The numerous and diverse social movements that have emerged to press for greater equity in the face of climate change and disasters also hold the potential for transformative change under the right conditions.

Throughout this book I have emphasized the nexus between power and vulnerability: the power of local growth machines to act as boosters for development that ignores hazards; the power to relegate people of color to hazardous areas and sacrificial zones; the power of nation-states to promote activities that contribute to risk buildup; the power of international financial institutions to determine the fates of nations in the developing world; and the power that makes it possible for nations at the core of the world system to export hazards to dependent states at the periphery. Because the exercise of these kinds of power constitutes the social, political, and economic source of disaster risk, vulnerability, and victimization, it follows logically that reducing risk requires challenges to that hegemonic power – challenges that are organized, systematic, and persistent.

QUESTIONS AND EXERCISES

As noted here, climate experts concur that the world has essentially no chance of reaching the goal of no more than 1.5°C of warming above pre-industrial levels by 2050. Some believe that a 2.0 degree increase is likely. What would 2.0 degrees of warming look like? What are the implications of so much warming for future hazards?

In the United States, "managed retreat" is being promoted for some communities that are facing disaster- and climate-related risks. One such community is Isle de Jean Charles in Louisiana. Do some research on what has been going on to date in this community and its population.

This chapter briefly mentioned lawsuits that have been launched against polluters for damages that resulted from global warming and climate change. Focus on one such lawsuit and how it has been proceeding. What evidence is there to date regarding the success of such lawsuits?

Notes

Note to Chapter 1

1 This definition of hazard mitigation should not be confused with the way the term is used in climate change circles, where mitigation refers to efforts to limit greenhouse gas emissions and reduce global warming.

Note to Chapter 2

1 White and his collaborators later acknowledged this blind spot, noting that "[a]long with growth of interest in the concept of vulnerability has come a recognition of the role of broader, deeper and more powerful social forces which constrain choice and which cannot be countered with technical or social fixes" (White, Kates, and Burton 2001: 91).

Notes to Chapter 3

1 More information on the nondisclosure of hazards in Texas can be found in the 2016 *Houston Chronicle* series "Chemical Breakdown."
2 It should be noted, however, that "growth" doesn't always mean more construction. Capital accumulation can also take place when limits on growth, whether natural or legally enforced, cause housing prices to soar, as seen, for example, in the city of San Francisco.
3 At the time of that race riot, Tulsa was home to the wealthiest African American community in the United States and to what was then called "Black Wall Street."

Notes to Chapter 5

1 The term "Matthew effect" is based on the biblical gospel of Matthew, which states (13:12): "Whoever has will be given more … Whoever does not have, even what they have will be taken from them." Merton's original use of the concept referred to the fact that, in science, scientists who already have high status are given more credit for their discoveries than less eminent researchers, even if the latter made more

substantive contributions to discoveries. As a consequence, resources accrue to more famous senior scientists at the expense of equally creative and accomplished junior ones.

2 This number includes both the people who died during the heat wave (70,000) and subsequent deaths that were attributed to exposure to extreme heat (7,000). The study also includes deaths that occurred during periods of extreme heat in June, as well as during high-heat periods in August.

3 SoVI scores and publications that employ SoVI in vulnerability assessment can be found on the website of the University of South Carolina's Hazards and Resilience Research Institute (http://artsandsciences.sc.edu/geog/hvri/front-page).

Notes to Chapter 6

1 This literature refers to "families," but I prefer "households," which can include unrelated members, so I will use both terms interchangeably.

2 At the time when the Tangshan earthquake took place, China was much more of a centralized, Soviet-style state, with strong governmental control over most aspects of its social and economic life. It was poorer, more rural, and much less developed than it is today. Like the Soviet Union, China did not permit the dissemination of information about the disasters that took place within its borders. The outside world learned about the Tangshan catastrophe only gradually, over a period of years.

Note to Chapter 9

1 Recall that recent decades have seen growth in the number of nation-states. Former regions in the Soviet Union are now sixteen separate nation-states. Additionally, other entities have declared independence, breaking off into smaller national units; for example, the former Yugoslavia is now five separate countries, and the former Czechoslovakia is now two countries: the Czech Republic and Slovakia.

2 As of this writing, the Japanese government has issued notice of the heightened probability of a Nankai Trough event.

Bibliography

Abalansa, S., El Mahrad, B., Icely, J., and Newton, A. (2021) Electronic waste, an environmental problem exported to developing countries: The GOOD, the BAD and the ugly. *Sustainability* 13(9). doi: 10.3390/su13095302.

Adams, V. (2012) The other road to serfdom: Recovery by the market and the affect economy in New Orleans. *Public Culture* 24(1), 185–216.

Adams, V. (2013) *Markets of Sorrow, Labors of Faith: New Orleans in the Wake of Katrina*. Duke University Press: Durham, NC.

Adams, V., Van Hattum, T., and English, D. (2009) Chronic disaster syndrome: Displacement, disaster capitalism, and the eviction of the poor from New Orleans. *American Ethnologist* 36(4), 615–636.

Adams, V., Kaufman, S.R., Van Hattum, T., and Moody, S. (2011) Aging disaster: Mortality, vulnerability, and long-term recovery among Katrina survivors. *Medical Anthropology* 30(3), 247–270.

Adeola, F.O. and Picou, J.S. (2012) Race, social capital, and the health impacts of Katrina: Evidence from the Louisiana and Mississippi Gulf Coast. *Human Ecology Review* 19(1), 10–24.

Adeola, F.O. and Picou, J.S. (2014) Social capital and the mental health impacts of hurricane Katrina: Assessing long-term patterns of psychosocial distress. *International Journal of Mass Emergencies and Disasters* 32(1), 121–156.

Adger, W.N. (2000) Social and ecological resilience: Are they related? *Progress in Human Geography* 24, 347–364.

Adger, W.N. (2003) Social capital, collective action, and adaptation to climate change. *Economic Geography* 79(4), 387–404.

Aerts, J.C.J.H., Botzen, W.J.W., Emanuel, K., Lin, N., de Moel, H., and Michel-Kerjan, E.O. (2014) Evaluating flood resilience strategies for coastal megacities. *Science* 344(6183), 473–475.

Aguirre, B.E. (2002) Can sustainable development sustain us? *International Journal of Mass Emergencies and Disasters* 20, 111–125.

Aguirre, B.E., Wenger, D., and Vigo, G. (1998) A test of the emergent norm theory of collective behavior. *Sociological Forum* 13(2), 301–320.

Agyeman, J., Bullard, R.D., and Evans, B. (2003) *Just Sustainabilities: Development in an Unequal World*. Earthscan: London.

Aida, J., Kawachi, I., Subramanian, S.V., and Kondo, K. (2013) Disaster, social capital, and health. In I. Kawachi, S. Takao, and S.V. Subramanian, eds., *Global Perspectives on Social Capital and Health*. Springer: New York, 167–187.

Albala-Bertrand, J.M. (1993) *Political Economy of Large Natural Disasters*. Clarendon: Oxford.

Albala-Bertrand, J.M. (2006) The unlikeliness of an economic catastrophe: Localization and globalization. Working Paper 576, Queen Mary University of London, School of Economics and Finance, London.

Albright, E.A. and Crow, D.A. (2015) Learning processes, public and stakeholder engagement: Analyzing responses to Colorado's extreme flood events of 2013. *Urban Climate* 14, 79–93.

Albright, E.A. and Crow, D.A. (2016) Learning in the aftermath of extreme floods: Community damage and stakeholder perceptions of future risk. *Risk, Hazards & Crisis in Public Policy* 6(3), 308–328.

Aldrich, D.P. (2010) Fixing recovery: Social capital in post-crisis resilience. *Journal of Homeland Security*, http://works.bepress.com/daniel_aldrich/7.

Aldrich, D.P. (2011) The externalities of strong social capital: Post-tsunami recovery in Southeast India. *Journal of Civil Society* 7(1), 81–99.

Aldrich, D.P. (2012a) *Building Resilience: Social Capital in Post-Disaster Recovery*. University of Chicago Press: Chicago, IL.

Aldrich, D.P. (2012b) Social capital in post disaster recovery: Towards a resilient and compassionate East Asian community. In Y. Sawada and S. Oum, eds., *Economic and Welfare Impacts of Disasters in East Asia and Policy Responses*. ERIA: Jakarta, 157–178.

Aldrich, D.P. (2012c) Social, not physical, infrastructure: The critical role of civil society after the 1923 Tokyo earthquake. *Disasters* 36(3), 398–419.

Aldrich, D.P. (2019) *Black Wave: How Networks and Governance Shaped Japan's 3/11 Disasters*. University of Chicago Press: Chicago, IL.

Aldrich, D.P. and Crook, K. (2008) Strong civil society as a double-edged sword: Siting trailers in post-Katrina New Orleans. *Political Research Quarterly* 61(3), 379–389.

Aldrich, D.P. and Meyer, M.A. (2015) Social capital and community resilience. *American Behavioral Scientist* 59(2), 254–269.

Alesch, D.J., Arendt, L.A., and Petak, W.J. (2005) Seismic Safety in California Hospitals: Assessing an Attempt to Accelerate the Replacement or Seismic Retrofit of Older Hospital Facilities. Multidisciplinary Center for Earthquake Engineering Research, SUNY: Buffalo.

Alesch, D.J., Arendt, L.A., and Petak, W.J. (2012) *Natural Hazard Mitigation Policy Implementation, Organizational Choice, and Contextual Dynamics*. Springer: Dordrecht.

Alesch, D.J. and Holly, J.N. (1998) Small business failure, survival, and recovery: Lessons from the January 1994 Northridge Earthquake. In *Proceedings of the NEHRP Conference and Workshop on Research on the Northridge, California Earthquake of January 17, 1994*. Consortium of Universities for Research in Earthquake Engineering: Richmond, CA, 48–55.

Alesch, D.J., Holly, J.N., Mittler, E., and Nagy, R. (2001) *Organizations at Risk: What Happens When Small Businesses and Not-for-Profits Encounter Natural Disasters.* Public Entity Risk Institute: Fairfax, VA.

Alesch, D.J. and Petak, W.J. (1986) *The Politics and Economics of Earthquake Hazard Mitigation: Unreinforced Masonry Buildings in Southern California.* Institute of Behavioral Science, University of Colorado: Boulder.

Alexander, D.E. (2013) Resilience and disaster risk reduction: An etymological journey. *Natural Hazards and Earth System Sciences* 13(11), 2707–2716. doi: 10.5194/nhess-13-2707-2013.

Allen, B.L. (2007) Environmental justice, local knowledge, and after-disaster planning in New Orleans. *Technology in Society* 29, 153–159.

American Red Cross, National Immigration Law Center, and National Council of La Raza (2007) *Fact Sheet: Immigration Eligibility for Disaster Assistance,* http://www.nilc.org/wp-content/uploads/2015/11/disasterassist_immeligibility_2007-062.pdf.

American Society of Civil Engineers Hurricane Katrina External Review Panel (2007) *The New Orleans Hurricane Protection System: What Went Wrong and Why.* ASCE: Reston, VA.

Andersen, M.L. and Collins, P.H. (2016) *Race, Class, and Gender: An Anthology,* 9th edn. Cengage Learning: Boston, MA.

Anderson, G.B. and Bell, M.L. (2012) Lights out: Impact of the August 2003 power outage on mortality in New York, NY. *Epidemiology* 23, 189–193.

Anderson, W.A. (2005) Bringing children into focus on the social science disaster research agenda. *International Journal of Mass Emergencies and Disasters* 23, 159–175.

Anderson, W.A. (2014) The Great Alaska Earthquake and the dawn of US social science earthquake research. In *Proceedings of the 10th National Conference in Earthquake Engineering.* Earthquake Engineering Research Institute: Anchorage, AK, https://datacenterhub.org/resources/12948/download/10NCEE-001678.pdf.

Ansell, C., Boin, A., and Keller, A. (2010) Managing transboundary crises: Identifying the building blocks of an effective response system. *Journal of Contingencies and Crisis Management* 18(4), 195–207.

Applied Technology Council (2016) *Critical Assessment of Lifeline System Performance: Understanding Societal Needs in Disaster Recovery.* National Institute of Standards and Technology: Gaithersburg, MD.

Arbon, P., Steenkamp, M., Cornell, V., Cusack, L., and Gebbie, K. (2016) Measuring disaster resilience in communities and households: Pragmatic tools developed in Australia. *International Journal of Disaster Resilience in the Built Environment* 7, 201–215.

Arif, A., Robinson, J., Stanek, S., Fichet, E.S., Townsend, P., Worku, Z., and Starbird, K. (2017) A closer look at the self-correcting crowd: Examining corrections in online rumors. *Proceedings of the ACM 2017 Conference on*

Computer-Supported Cooperative Work and Social Computing (CSCW '17). ACM: Portland, OR, 155–168.

Arnold, C. (2014) Once upon a mine: The legacy of uranium on the Navajo nation. *Environmental Health Perspectives* 122, A44–A49.

Aronoff, M. and Gunter, V. (1992) Defining disaster: Local constructions for recovery in the aftermath of chemical contamination. *Social Problems* 39, 345–365.

Arup (2015) *City Resilience Index*. London, http://www.arup.com/projects/city-resilience-index.

Arvai, J. and Rivers, L., eds. (2014) *Risk Communication: Learning from the Past, Charting a Course for the Future*. Taylor & Francis: London.

Ash, K.D., Cutter, S.L., and Emrich, C.T. (2013) Acceptable losses? The relative impacts of natural hazards in the United States, 1980–2009. *International Journal of Disaster Risk Reduction* 5, 61–72.

Asia-Pacific Economic Cooperation (2015) *Annex A: APEC Disaster Risk Reduction Framework*. APEC, http://www.apec.org/Meeting-Papers/Annual-Ministerial-Meetings/2015/2015_amm/annexa.

Associated Press (2021) Puerto Rico cleanup by US military will take more than a decade. NBC News, March 26.

Auyero, J. and Swistun, D. (2008) The social production of toxic uncertainty. *American Sociological Review* 73, 357–379.

Bair, J., Anner, M., and Blasi, J. (2020) The political economy of private and public regulation in post-Rana plaza Bangladesh. *ILR Review* 73(4), 969–994.

Bajak, F. and Olson, L. (2018) Hurricane Harvey's toxic impact deeper than public told. Associated Press and Houston Chronicle, March 23.

Baker, R.E., Mahmud, A.S., Miller, I.F., Rajeev, M. et al. (2022) Infectious disease in an era of global change. *Nature Reviews Microbiology* 20: 193–205.

Bankoff, G. and Hilhorst, D., eds. (2022) *Why Vulnerability Still Matters: The Politics of Disaster Risk Creation*. Routledge: New York.

Bankoff, G., Frerks, G., and Hilhorst, D. (2004) *Mapping Vulnerability: Disasters, Development and People*. Earthscan: London.

Barr, D.A. (2014) *Health Disparities in the United States: Social Class, Race, Ethnicity, and Health*. Johns Hopkins University Press: Baltimore, MD.

Barrios, R.E. (2017) What does catastrophe reveal for whom? The anthropology of crises and disasters at the onset of the Anthropocene. *Annual Review of Anthropology* 46, 151–166.

Barron Ausbrooks, C.Y., Barrett, E.J., and Martinez-Cosio, M. (2009) Ethical issues in disaster research: Lessons from Hurricane Katrina. *Population Research and Policy Review* 28(1), 93–106.

Barrows, H.H. (1923) Geography as human ecology. *Annals of the Association of American Geographers* 13, 1–14.

Barry, J. (1997) *Rising Tide: The Great Mississippi Flood of 1927 and How It Changed America*. Simon & Schuster: New York.

Bartlett, S. (2008) The implications of climate change for children in lower-income countries. *Children, Youth, and Environments* 18(1), 71–98, http://www.jstor.org/stable/10.7721/chilyoutenvi.18.1.0071.

Bates, K.A. and Swan, R.S. (2010) *Through the Eye of Katrina: Social Justice in the United States.* Carolina Academic Press: Durham, NC.

Bauman, Z. (2017) *Wasted Lives: Modernity and Its Outcasts.* Polity: Cambridge.

Beamish, T.D. (2002a) *Silent Spill: The Organization of an Industrial Crisis.* MIT Press: Cambridge, MA.

Beamish, T.D. (2002b) Waiting for crisis: Regulatory inaction and ineptitude and the Guadalupe dunes oil spill. *Social Problems* 49, 150–177.

Bean, H. (2019) *Mobile Technology and the Transformation of Public Alert and Warning.* Praeger Security International: Santa Monica, CA.

Bean, H. and Grevstad, N. (2023) Wireless emergency alerts: Public understanding, trust, and preferences following the 2021 US nationwide test. *Journal of Contingencies and Crisis Management* 31, 273–288, https://doi.org/10.1111/1468-5973.12438.

Bean, H., Liu, B.F., Madden, S., Sutton, J., Wood, M.M., and Mileti, D.S. (2016) Disaster warnings in your pocket: How audiences interpret mobile alerts for an unfamiliar hazard. *Journal of Contingencies and Crisis Management* 24(3), 136–147.

Bean, H., Sutton, J., Liu, B.F., Madden, S., Wood, M.M., and Mileti, D.S. (2015) The study of mobile public warning messages: A research review and agenda. *Review of Communication* 15(1), 60–80. doi: 10.1080/15358593.2015.1014402.

Becvar, D.S. (2013) *Handbook of Family Resilience.* Springer: New York.

Belli, A. and Falkenberg, L. (2005) 24 nursing home evacuees die in bus fire. *Houston Chronicle*, September 24, http://www.chron.com/news/hurricanes/article/24-nursing-home-evacuees-die-in-bus-fire-1946742.php.

Béné, C., Mehta, L., McGranahan, G., Cannon, T., Gupte, J., and Tanner, T. (2018) Resilience as a policy narrative: Potentials and limits in the context of urban planning. *Climate and Development* 10(2), 116–133, http://dx.doi.org/10.1080/17565529.2017.1301868.

Benson, C. and Twigg, J. (2004) *Measuring Mitigation: Methodologies for Assessing Natural Hazard Risks and the Net Benefits of Mitigation: A Scoping Study.* ProVention Consortium and the International Federation of Red Cross and Red Crescent Societies: Geneva.

Berger, P.L. (1963) *Invitation to Sociology: A Humanistic Perspective.* Doubleday: New York.

Berger, P.L. and Luckmann, T. (1966) *The Social Construction of Reality: A Treatise in the Sociology of Knowledge.* Anchor Books: New York.

Berke, P.R., Kates, J., Malecha, M., Masterson, J. et al. (2021) Using a resilience scorecard to improve local planning for vulnerability to hazards and climate change: An application to two cities. *Cities* 119. doi: https://doi.org/10.1016/j.cities.2021.103408.

Berke, P.R., Matthew, L., Malecha, M.L., Yu, S., Lee, J., and Masterson, J.H. (2019) Plan integration for resilience scorecard: Evaluating networks of plans in six US coastal cities. *Journal of Environmental Planning and Management* 62(5), 901–920. doi: 10.1080/09640568.2018.1453354.

Berke, P., Newman, G., Lee, J., Combs, T., Kolosna, C., and Salvesen, D. (2015) Evaluation of networks of plans and vulnerability to hazards and climate change: A resilience scorecard. *Journal of the American Planning Association* 81(4), 287–302.

Berliner, P.F. (1994) *Thinking in Jazz: The Art of Improvisation.* University of Chicago Press: Chicago, IL.

Bevc, C.A. (2010) *Working on the Edge: Examining Covariates in Multi-Organizational Networks on September 11th Attacks on the World Trade Center.* Doctoral dissertation, University of Colorado, Boulder.

Bevc, C.A., Nicholls, K., and Picou, J.S. (2010) Community recovery from Hurricane Katrina: Storm experiences, property damage, and the human condition. In D.L. Brunsma, D. Overfelt, and J.S. Picou, eds., *The Sociology of Katrina: Perspectives on a Modern Catastrophe,* 2nd edn. Rowman & Littlefield: Lanham, MD, 135–156.

Birkland, T.A. (1997) *After Disaster: Agenda Setting, Public Policy, and Focusing Events.* Georgetown University Press: Washington, DC.

Birkland, T.A. (2007) *Lessons of Disaster: Policy Change after Catastrophic Events.* Georgetown University Press: Washington, DC.

Birkmann, J. (2006) Measuring vulnerability to promote disaster-resilient societies: Conceptual frameworks and definitions. In J. Birkmann, ed., *Measuring Vulnerability to Natural Hazards: Towards Disaster Resilient Societies.* United Nations University Press: Tokyo, 9–54.

Black, B.A., Pearl, J.K., Pearson, C.L., Pringle, P.T. et al. (2023) A multifault earthquake threat for the Seattle metropolitan region revealed by mass tree mortality. *Science Advances* 9(39), eadh4973.

Black, K. and Lobo, M. (2008) A conceptual review of family resilience factors. *Journal of Family Nursing* 14(1), 33–55.

Blaikie, P., Cannon, T., Davis, I. and Wisner, B. (1994) *At Risk: Natural Hazards, People's Vulnerability, and Disasters.* Routledge: London.

Blitzer, J. (2023) Jim Jordan's conspiratorial quest for power. *New Yorker,* October 21.

Blumenfeld, W.J. (2016) God and natural disasters: It's the gays' fault? *Huffington Post,* February 2, https://www.huffingtonpost.com/warren-j-blumenfeld/god -and-natural-disasters-its-the-gays-fault_b_2068817.html.

Blumer, H. (1939) Collective behavior. In R.E. Park, ed., *Principles of Sociology.* Barnes and Noble: New York, 219–280.

Blumer, H. (1969) *Symbolic Interactionism: Perspective and Method.* Prentice-Hall: Englewood Cliffs, NJ.

Board of Governors of the Federal Reserve System (2023) Economic well-being of US households in 2022. May, https://www.federalreserve.gov/publications /files/2022-report-economic-well-being-us-households-202305.pdf.

Bobb, J.F., Peng, R.D., Bell, M.L., and Dominici, F. (2014) Heat-related mortality and adaptation to heat in the United States. *Environmental Health Perspectives* 122(8), 811–816.

Boin, A. (2009) The new world of crises and crisis management: Implications for policy and research. *Review of Policy Research* 26(4), 367–377.

Boin, A., Busuioc, M., and Groenleer, M. (2013) Building European union capacity to manage transboundary crises: Network or lead-agency model? *Regulation & Governance* 8(4), 1–20.

Boin, A. and 't Hart, P. (2012) Aligning executive action in times of adversity: The politics of crisis co-ordination. In M. Lodge and K. Wegrich, eds., *Executive Politics in Times of Crisis*. Palgrave: Basingstoke, 179–196.

Bolin, B., Grineski, S., and Collins, T. (2005) The geography of despair: Environmental racism and the making of South Phoenix, Arizona, USA. *Human Ecology Review* 12(2), 156–168.

Bolin, B. and Kurtz, L.C. (2018) Race, class, ethnicity, and disaster vulnerability. In H. Rodríguez, W. Donner, and J.E. Trainor, eds., *Handbook of Disaster Research*, 2nd edn. Springer: Cham, Switzerland, 181–203.

Bolin, R.C. and Stanford, L. (1990) Shelter and housing issues in Santa Cruz county. In R.C. Bolin, ed., *The Loma Prieta Earthquake: Studies of Short-Term Impacts*. Institute of Behavioral Science, University of Colorado: Boulder.

Bolin, R.C. and Stanford, L. (1993) Emergency sheltering and housing of earthquake victims: The case of Santa Cruz county. In P.A. Bolton, ed., *The Loma Prieta, California, Earthquake of October 17, 1989: Public Responses*. US Government Printing Office: Washington, DC, B43–B50.

Bolin, R.C. and Stanford, L. (1998) *The Northridge Earthquake: Vulnerability and Disaster*. Routledge: London.

Bonanno, G.A., Brewin, C.R., Kaniasty, K., and LaGreca, A.M. (2010) Weighing the costs of disaster: Consequences, risks, and resilience in individuals, families, and communities. *Psychological Science in the Public Interest* 11, 1–49.

Bondi, L. (1990) Feminism, postmodernism, and geography: Space for Women? *Antipode* 22(2), 156–167.

Boscarino, J.A., Kirchner, H.L., Hoffman, S.N., Sartorius, J., and Adams, R.E. (2011) PTSD and alcohol use after the World Trade Center attacks: A longitudinal study. *Journal of Traumatic Stress* 24(5), 515–525.

Bostrom, A., Fischhoff, B., and Morgan, M.G. (1992) Characterizing mental models of hazardous processes: A methodology and an application to radon. *Journal of Social Issues* 48(4), 85–100.

Bosworth, S.L. and Kreps, G.A. (1986) Structure as process: Organization and role. *American Sociological Review* 51, 699–716.

Bourdieu, P. (1986) The forms of capital. In J.G. Richardson, ed., *Handbook of Theory and Research for the Sociology of Education*. Greenwood Press: New York, 241–258.

Bourke, L.K. (2021) Regulatory capture at the FAA. *Claremont Journal of Law and Public Policy*, November 12, https://www.5clpp.com/?p=4026.

Bourque, L.B., Mileti, D.S., Kano, M., and Wood, M.M. (2012) Who prepares for terrorism? *Environment and Behavior* 44(3), 374–409, http://dx.doi.org/10.1177/0013916510390318.

Bourque, L.B., Siegel, J.M., Kano, M., and Wood, M.M. (2006) Weathering the storm: The impact of hurricanes on physical and mental health. *The Annals of the American Academy of Political and Social Science* 604(1), 129–151.

Bourque, L.B., Siegel, J.M., Kano, M., and Wood, M.M. (2007) Morbidity and mortality associated with disasters. In H. Rodríguez, E.L. Quarantelli, and R.R. Dynes, eds., *Handbook of Disaster Research*. Springer: New York, 97–112.

Bours, D., McGinn, C., and Pringle, P. (2014a) *Guidance Note 1: Twelve Reasons Why Climate Change Adaptation M&E Is Challenging*. Sea Change, Phnom Penh, Cambodia & UKCIP: Oxford.

Bours, D., McGinn, C., and Pringle, P. (2014b) *Guidance Note 3: Theory of Change Approach to Climate Change Adaptation Programming*. Sea Change, Phnom Penh, Cambodia & UKCIP: Oxford.

Boyd, J., Epanchin-Niell, R., and Siikamaki, J. (2015) Conservation planning: A review of return on investment analysis. *Review of Environmental Economics and Policy* 9(1), 23–42.

Boykoff, M.T. and Boykoff, J.M. (2004) Balance as bias: Global warming and the US prestige press. *Global Environmental Change* 14, 125–136.

Brackbill, R.M., Stellman, S.D., Perlman, S.E., Walker, D.J., and Farfel, M.R. (2013) Mental health of those directly exposed to the World Trade Center disaster: Unmet mental health care need, mental health treatment service use, and quality of life. *Social Science & Medicine* 81, 110–114.

Bragg, R. (1999) Storm over South Florida building codes. *New York Times*, May 27.

Brody, S.D., Kang, J.E., and Bernhardt, S.P. (2010) Identifying factors influencing flood mitigation at the local level in Texas and Florida: The role of organizational capacity. *Natural Hazards* 52, 167–184, http://dx.doi.org/10.1007/s11069-009-9364-5.

Brody, S.D., Kang, J.E., Zahran, S., and Bernhardt, S.P. (2009) Evaluating local flood mitigation strategies in Texas and Florida. *Built Environment* 35(4), 492–515.

Brouillette, J.R. and Quarantelli, E.L. (1971) Types of patterned variation in bureaucratic adaptations to organizational stress. *Sociological Inquiry* 41, 39–46.

Brown, P. (1995) Race, class, and environmental health: A review and systemization of the literature. *Environmental Research* 69(1), 15–30.

Brown, P. (2007) *Toxic Exposures: Contested Illnesses and the Environmental Health Movement*. Columbia University Press: New York.

Browne, K.E. (2015) *Standing in Need: Culture, Comfort, and Coming Home after Katrina*. University of Texas Press: Austin, TX.

Browne, K.E. and Peek, L. (2014) Beyond the IRB: An ethical toolkit for long-term disaster research. *International Journal of Mass Emergencies and Disasters* 32(1), 82–120.

Bruder, J. (2017) *Nomadland: Surviving American in the Twenty-First Century*. Norton: New York.

Bruine de Bruin, W., Saw, H.-W., and Goldman, D.P. (2020) Political polarization in US residents' COVID-19 perceptions, policy preferences, and protective behaviors. *Journal of Risk and Uncertainty* 61(2), 177–194.

Brulle, R.J. and Pellow, D.N. (2006) Environmental justice: Human health and environmental inequalities. *Annual Review of Public Health* 27, 103–124, http://dx.doi.org/10.1146/annurev.publhealth.27.021405.102124.

Bruneau, M., Chang, S.E., Eguchi, R.T. et al. (2003) A framework to quantitatively assess and enhance the seismic resilience of communities. *Earthquake Spectra* 19, 733–752. doi: 10.1193/1.1623497.

Bryant, B. and Mohai, P. (1992) *Race and the Incidence of Environmental Hazards: A Time for Discourse*. Westview Press: Boulder, CO.

Bryant, M. and Sigurjonsson, T. O. (2022) Iceland's financial crisis 2008: Not a normal accident. *Journal of Governance and Regulation* 11(4) (special issue), 353–364.

Buchele, M. (2022) One year later, many question the "official" number of deaths linked to the Texas blackout. KUT News, February 15.

Bullard, R.D. (1990) *Dumping in Dixie: Race, Class, and Environmental Quality*. Westview Press: Boulder, CO.

Bullard, R.D. and Wright, B., eds. (2009) *Race, Place, and Environmental Justice after Hurricane Katrina*. Westview Press: Boulder, CO.

Bullard, R.D. and Wright, B. (2012) *The Wrong Complexion for Protection: How the Government Response to Disaster Endangers African American Communities*. NYU Press: New York.

Bullock, J.A., Haddow, G.D., Haddow, K.S. (2008) *Global Warming, Natural Hazards, and Emergency Management*. CRC Press: Boca Raton, FL.

Burby, R.J., ed. (1998) *Cooperating with Nature: Confronting Natural Hazards with Land-Use Planning for Sustainable Communities*. Joseph Henry Press: Washington, DC.

Burby, R.J. (2006) Hurricane Katrina and the paradoxes of government disaster policy: Bringing about wise governmental decisions for hazardous areas. *Annals of the American Academy of Political and Social Science* 604, 171–191.

Bureau of Labor Statistics (2013) Marriage and divorce: Patterns by gender, race, and educational attainment. *Monthly Labor Review*. doi: 10.21916/mlr.2013.32.

Burt, R. (1992) *Structural Holes: The Social Structure of Competition*. Harvard University Press: Cambridge, MA.

Burton, C. and Cutter, S.L. (2008) Levee failures and social vulnerability in the Sacramento-San Joaquin Delta area, California. *Natural Hazards Review* 9(3), 136–149. doi: 10.1061/(ASCE)1527–6988(2008)9:3(136).

Burton, C., Mitchell, J.T., and Cutter, S.L. (2011) Evaluating post-Katrina recovery in Mississippi using repeat photography. *Disasters* 35(3), 488–509.

Burton, I., Kates, R.W., and White, G.F. (1978) *The Environment as Hazard.* Oxford University Press: New York.

Bush, E.M. (2014) Homeless individuals and families are especially vulnerable during disasters and emergencies. *Michigan State University Extension,* July 7, http://msue.anr.msu.edu/news/homeless_individuals_and_families_are_especially_vulnerable_during_disaster.

Button, G. (2016) *Disaster Culture: Knowledge and Uncertainty in the Wake of Human and Environmental Catastrophe.* Routledge: New York.

Button, G. and Schuller, M., eds. (2016) *Contextualizing Disaster.* Berghan Books: New York.

Butts, C.T., Acton, R.M., and Marcum, C.S. (2012) Interorganizational collaboration in the Hurricane Katrina response. *Journal of Social Structure* 13, 1–17, http://www.cmu.edu/joss/content/articles/volume13/ButtsActonMarcum.pdf.

Butts, C.T., Petrescu-Prahova, M., and Cross, B.R. (2007) Responder communication networks in the World Trade Center disaster: Implications for modeling of communication within emergency settings. *Journal of Mathematical Sociology* 31(2), 121–147. doi: 10.1080/00222500601188056.

Cable, S., Shriver, T.E., and Mix, T.L. (2008) Risk society and contested illness: The case of nuclear weapons workers. *American Sociological Review* 73, 380–401.

Calo, R., Coward, C. Spiro, E.S., Starbird, K., and West, J.D. (2021) How do you solve a problem like misinformation? *Science Advances* 7(50). doi: 10.1126/sciadv.abn0481.

Cameron, E. (2017) Natural disasters and international law. Peace Palace Library, September 14, https://www.peacepalacelibrary.nl/2017/09/natural-disasters-and-international-law.

Campbell, N. (2016) *Trial by flood: Experiences of older adults in disaster.* Doctoral dissertation, Department of Sociology, University of Colorado, Boulder.

Campbell, N. M. (2019) Disaster recovery among older adults: Exploring the intersection of vulnerability and resilience. In F. Rivera, ed., *Emerging Voices in Natural Hazards Research.* Butterworth Heinemann: Cambridge, MA, 83–119.

Campisi, N. (2021) From inherent racial bias to incorrect data: The problems with current credit scoring models. *Forbes,* February 26.

Cannon, T. and Müller-Mahn, D. (2010) Vulnerability, resilience and development discourses in context of climate change. *Natural Hazards* 55, 621–635.

Cardona, O.D. (2010) *Indicators of Disaster Risk and Risk Management: Summary Report, Program for Latin America and the Caribbean.* Inter-American Development Bank: Washington, DC.

Cardona, O.D. (2011) Disaster risk and vulnerability: Concepts and measurement of human and environmental insecurity. In H.G. Brauch, U.O. Spring, C. Mesjasz et al., eds., *Coping with Global Environmental Change, Disasters and Security.* Springer-Verlag: Berlin, Germany, 107–121.

Cardona, O.D., Ordaz, M.G., Marulanda, M.C., Barbat, A.H., and Carreño, M.L. (2010) Earthquake risk from the financial protection perspective: A metric for fiscal vulnerability evaluation in the Americas. Paper presented at the 14th European Conference on Earthquake Engineering, Ohrid, Macedonia.

Cardona, O.D., Ordaz, M.G., Marulanda, M.C., Carreño, M.L., and Barbat, A.H. (2010) Disaster risk from a macroeconomic perspective: A metric for fiscal vulnerability evaluation. *Disasters* 34(4), 1064–1083.

Carpenter, S., Walker, B., Anderies, J.M., and Abel, N. (2001) From metaphor to measurement: Resilience of what to what? *Ecosystems* 4, 765–781.

Carr, L.J. (1932) Disaster and the sequence-pattern concept of social change. *American Journal of Sociology* 38(2), 207–218, http://www.jstor.org/stable /2766454.

Carter, S.M., Shi, P., Williams, J., Degeling, C., and Mooney-Somers, J. (2021) Conducting qualitative research online: Challenges and solutions. *Patient* 14(6), 711–718, https://doi: 10.1007/s40271-021-00528-w.

Cartlidge, E. (2014) Updated: Appeals court overturns manslaughter convictions of six earthquake scientists. *Science*, November 10, http://www.sciencemag.org /news/2014/11/updated-appeals-court-overturns-manslaughter-convictions-six -earthquake-scientists.

Cascadia Region Earthquake Workgroup (2013) *Cascadia Subduction Zone Earthquakes: A Magnitude 9.0 Earthquake Scenario*. CREW: Seattle, WA.

Center for Disaster Philanthropy (n.d.) LGBTQIA+ Communities and disasters, https://disasterphilanthropy.org/resources/lgbtqia-communities-and -disasters.

Centers for Disease Control and Prevention (2004) Mental health status of World Trade Center rescue and recovery workers and volunteers: New York City, July 2002–August 2004. *Center for Disease Control and Prevention Morbidity and Mortality Weekly Report* 53(35), 812–815.

Centre for Research on the Epidemiology of Disasters (CRED) (2016) *Poverty and Death: Disaster Mortality 1996–2015*. CRED, Institute of Health and Society, Université catholique de Louvain: Brussels.

Cerulo, K. (2008) *Never Saw It Coming: Cultural Challenges to Envisioning the Worst*. University of Chicago Press: Chicago, IL.

Chabria, A. and Smith, A.D. (2023) Time to panic? The home insurance market in California is collapsing because of climate change. *Los Angeles Times*, September 14.

Chakraborty, J., Collins, T.W., Montgomery, M.C., and Grineski, S.E. (2014) Social and spatial inequities in exposure to flood risk in Miami, Florida. *Natural Hazards Review* 15(3). doi: 10.1061/(ASCE)NH.1527–6996.0000140.

Chamlee-Wright, E.L. (2010) *The Cultural and Political Economy of Recovery: Social Learning in a Post-Disaster Environment*. Routledge: London.

Chamlee-Wright, E.L. and Storr, V.H. (2009) "There's no place like New

Orleans": Sense of place and community recovery in the ninth ward after Hurricane Katrina. *Journal of Urban Affairs* 31, 615–634.

Chamlee-Wright, E.L. and Storr, V.H., eds. (2010) *The Political Economy of Hurricane Katrina and Community Rebound.* Edward Elgar: Cheltenham.

Chamlee-Wright, E.L. and Storr, V.H. (2011) Social capital as collective narratives and post-disaster community recovery. *Sociological Review* 59(2), 266–282.

Chang, S.E. (2000) Disasters and transport systems: Loss, recovery, and competition at the port of Kobe after the 1995 earthquake. *Journal of Transport Geography* 8(1), 53–65.

Chang, S.E. (2010) Urban disaster recovery: A measurement framework with application to the 1995 Kobe Earthquake. *Disasters* 34(2), 303–327.

Chang, S.E. and Rose, A.Z. (2012) Towards a theory of economic recovery from disasters. *International Journal of Mass Emergencies and Disasters* 32(2), 171–181.

Chauhan, A. and Hughes, A.L. (2017) Providing online crisis information: An analysis of official sources during the 2014 Carlton Complex wildfire. In *Proceedings of the 25th International Conference on Human Factors in Computing Systems (CHI 2017).* ACM: New York, 399–408.

Chen, W., Cutter, S.L., Emrich, C.T., and Shi, P. (2013) Measuring social vulnerability to natural hazards in the Yangtze River Delta region, China. *International Journal of Disaster Risk Science* 4(4), 169–181.

Children's Health Fund and National Center for Disaster Preparedness (2010) *Legacy of Katrina: The Impact of a Flawed Recovery on Vulnerable Children of the Gulf Coast: A Five-Year Status Report: Significant Emotional Distress, Behavioral Problems and Instability Persist among Children Affected by the 2005 Disaster.* Columbia University: New York.

Chung, B., Jones, L., Campbell, L.X., Glover, H., Gelberg, L., and Chen, D.T. (2008) National recommendations for enhancing the conduct of ethical health research with human participants in post-disaster situations. *Ethnicity & Disease* 18, 378–383.

Clark, B. and Foster, J.B. (2009) Ecological imperialism and the global metabolic rift: Unequal exchange and the guano/nitrates trade. *International Journal of Comparative Sociology*, 50(3–4), 311–334, https://doi.org/10.1177/0020715209105144.

Clark, B. and Jorgenson, A.K. (2012) The treadmill of destruction and the environment impacts of militaries. *Sociology Compass* 6(7), 557–569.

Clarke, L. (1993) The disqualification heuristic: When do organizations misperceive risk? In W.R. Freudenburg and T.I.K. Youn, eds., *Research in Social Problems and Public Policy.* JAI Press: Greenwich, CT, vol. 5, 289–312.

Clarke, L. (2002) Panic: Myth or reality? *Contexts* 1, 21–26.

Clarke, L. (2006) *Worst Cases: Terror and Catastrophe in the Popular Imagination.* University of Chicago Press: Chicago, IL.

Clarke, L. (2008) Possibilistic thinking: A conceptual tool for thinking about extreme events. *Social Research: An International Quarterly* 75(3), 669–690.

Clouston, S.A. and Link, B.G. (2021) A retrospective on fundamental cause theory: State of the literature, and goals for the future. *Annual Review of Sociology* 47(1), 131–156.

Cobb, J.A. (2013) Flood of Lies: The St. Rita's Nursing Home Tragedy. Pelican: Gretna, LA.

Coleman, J.S. (1988) Social capital in the creation of human capital. *American Journal of Sociology* 94, S95–S120.

Collins, P.H. and Bilge, S. (2016) *Intersectionality*. Polity: Malden, MA.

Collins, T. (2010) Marginalization, facilitation, and the production of unequal risk: The 2006 Paso del Norte floods. *Antipode* 42, 258–288.

Collins, T. and Bolin, B. (2009) Situating hazard vulnerability: negotiating wildfire hazard in the US southwest. *Environmental Management* 44, 441–459.

Collogan, L.K., Tuma, F., Dolan-Sewell, R., Borja, S., and Fleischman, A.R. (2004) Ethical issues pertaining to research in the aftermath of disaster. *Journal of Traumatic Stress* 17(5), 363–372.

Comfort, L.K., Boin, A., and Demchak, C.C., eds. (2010) *Designing Resilience: Preparing for Extreme Events*. University of Pittsburgh Press: Pittsburgh, PA.

Commission on Racial Justice (1987) *Toxic Wastes and Race in the United States: A National Report on the Racial and Socio-Economic Characteristics on Communities with Hazardous Waste Sites*. United Church of Christ: New York.

Community and Regional Resilience Institute (2013) *Building Resilience in America's Communities: Observations and Implications of the CRS Pilots*. CARRI: Washington, DC.

Coppola, D.P. (2007) *Introduction to International Disaster Management*. Elsevier: Boston, MA.

Cosentino, G. (2020) *Social Media and the Post-Truth Order: The Global Dynamics of Misinformation*. Palgrave: Cham.

Courtney-Long, E.A., Carroll, D.D., Zhang, Q.C., Stevens, A.S., Griffin-Blake, S., Armour, B.S., and Campbell, V.A. (2015) Prevalence of disability and disability type among adults, United States, 2013. *Centers for Disease Control and Prevention: Morbidity and Mortality Weekly Report* 64(29), 777–808.

Crenshaw, K. (1991) Mapping the margins: Intersectionality, identity politics, and violence against women of color. *Stanford Law Review* 43(6), 1241–1299, http://www.jstor.org/stable/1229039.

Cummings, C.L., Berube, D.M., and Lavelle, M.E. (2013) Influences of individual-level characteristics on risk perceptions to various categories of environmental health and safety risks. *Journal of Risk Research* 16(10), 1277–1295. doi: 10.1080/13669877.2013.788544.

Cutter, S.L. (1996) Vulnerability to environmental hazards. *Progress in Human Geography* 20(4), 529–539.

Cutter, S.L., ed. (2001) *American Hazardscapes: The Regionalization of Hazards and Disasters*. Joseph Henry Press: Washington, DC.

Cutter, S.L. (2003) The vulnerability of science and the science of vulnerability. *Annals of the Association of American Geographers* 93(1), 1–12. doi: 10.1111/1467-8306.93101.

Cutter, S.L. (2016) The landscape of disaster resilience indications in the USA. *Natural Hazards* 80, 741–758.

Cutter, S.L. (2017) The forgotten casualties redux: Women, children, and disaster risk. *Global Environmental Change* 42, 117–121.

Cutter, S.L. (2024) The origin and diffusion of the Social Vulnerability Index (SoVI) *International Journal of Disaster Risk Reduction* 109, July, 104576.

Cutter, S.L., Ash, K.D., and Emrich, C.T. (2014) The geographies of community disaster resilience. *Global Environmental Change* 29, 65–77.

Cutter, S.L., Ash, K.D., and Emrich, C.T. (2016) Urban-rural differences in disaster resilience. *Annals of the American Association of Geographers* 106(6), 1236–1252. doi: 10.1080/24694452.2016.1194740.

Cutter, S.L., Barnes, L., Berry, C., Burton, C., Evans, E., Tate, E., and Webb, J. (2008) A place-based model for understanding community resilience to natural disasters. *Global Environmental Change* 18, 598–606. doi: 10.1016/j.gloenvcha.2008.07.013.

Cutter, S.L., Boruff, B.J., and Shirley, W.L. (2003) Social vulnerability to environmental hazards. *Social Science Quarterly* 84(2), 242–261.

Cutter, S.L., Burton, C., and Emrich, C.T. (2010) Disaster resilience indicators for benchmarking baseline conditions. *Journal of Homeland Security and Emergency Management* 7(1), 1–22.

Cutter, S.L., Emrich, C.T., Mitchell, J.T., Piegorsch, W.W., Smith, M.M., and Weber, L. (2016) *Hurricane Katrina and the Forgotten Coast of Mississippi*. Cambridge University Press: New York.

Cutter, S.L. and Huang, Q. (2022) The persistence of COVID-19 and inequities in the US experience. *Environment: Science and Policy for Sustainable Development* 64(5–6), 4–16.

Cutter, S.L., Schumann, R.L., and Emrich, C.T. (2014) Exposure, social vulnerability and recovery disparities in New Jersey after Hurricane Sandy. *Journal of Extreme Events* 1(1). doi: 10.1142/S234573761450002X.

Dahlhamer, J.M. and Tierney, K. (1998) Rebounding from disruptive events: Business recovery following the Northridge earthquake. *Sociological Spectrum* 18(2), 121–141.

Daly, M. and Silver, H. (2008) Social exclusion and social capital: A comparison and critique. *Theory and Society* 37(6), 537–566.

D'Andrea, M.A. and Reddy, G.K. (2018) The development of long-term adverse health effects in oil spill cleanup workers of the Deepwater Horizon offshore drilling rig disaster. *Frontiers in Public Health*, April 26.

Darrah, N. (2017) Florida nursing home deaths during Hurricane Irma ruled homicides. *Fox News*, November 22, http://www.foxnews.com/us/2017/11/22/florida-nursing-home-deaths-during-hurricane-irma-ruled-homicides.html.

Dash, N. and Peacock. W.G. (2003) Long-term recovery from Hurricane Andrew:

A comparison of two ethnically diverse communities. Paper presented at the annual meeting of the Southwestern Sociological Association, San Antonio.

Dastagir, A.E. (2017) What do men get that women don't? Here are a few things. *USA Today*, March 1.

Davis, E.A., Hansen, R., Kett, M., Mincin, J., and Twigg, J. (2013) Disability. In D.S.K. Thomas, B.D. Phillips, W.E. Lovekamp, and A. Fothergill, eds., *Social Vulnerability to Disasters*, 2nd edn. CRC Press: Boca Raton, FL, 199–234.

Davis, M. (1999) *Ecology of Fear: Los Angeles and the Imagination of Disaster*. Henry Holt: New York.

Davis, M. (2006) *Planet of Slums*. Verso: London.

De Loyola Hummell, B.M., Cutter, S.L., and Emrich, C.T. (2016) Social vulnerability to natural hazards in Brazil. *International Journal of Disaster Risk Science* 7, 111–122.

Denton, F., Wilbanks, T.J., Abeysinghe, A.C., Burton, I., Gao, Q., Lemos, M.C., Masui, T. et al. (2014) Climate-resilient pathways: Adaptation, mitigation, and sustainable development. In C.B. Field, V.R. Barros, D.J. Dokken, K.J. Mach, M.D. Mastrandrea, T.E. Bilir, M. Chatterjee et al., eds., *Climate Change 2014: Impacts, Adaptation, and Vulnerability, Part A*. Cambridge University Press: Cambridge, 1101–1131.

Department of Health and Human Services (2012) *Gaps Continue to Exist in Nursing Home Preparedness and Response During Disasters, 2007–2010*. Office of the Inspector General: Washington, DC.

Department for International Development (2011) *Defining Disaster Resilience: A DFID Approach Paper*. DFID: London.

Dhawan, R. and Jeske, K. (2006) How resilient is the modern economy to energy price shocks? *Economic Review (Federal Reserve Bank of Atlanta)*, January, https://www.researchgate.net/publication/5025718.

Dietz, T., Schwom, R.L., and Whitley, C.T. (2020) Climate change and society. *Annual Review of Sociology* 46, 135–158.

DiGangi, C. (2016) How many Americans have bad credit? *Credit*, February 12, http://blog.credit.com/2016/02/how-many-americans-have-bad-credit-136868.

Dilley, M., Chen, R.S., Deichmann, U., Lerner-Lam, A.L., Arnold, M., Agwe, J., Buys, P. et al. (2005) *Natural Disaster Hotspots: A Global Risk Analysis* [English]. World Bank: Washington, DC.

Dominey-Howes, D., Gorman-Murray, A., and McKinnon, S. (2014) Queering disasters: On the need to account for LGBTI experiences in natural disaster contexts. *Gender, Place & Culture* 21(7), 905–918. doi: 10.1080/0966369X.2013.802673.

Donovan, J., Dreyfuss, E., and Frieberg, B. (2022) *Meme Wars: The Untold Story of the Online Battles Upending Democracy in America*. Bloomsbury: New York.

Donovan, J., Friedberg, B., Lim, G., Leaver, N. et al. (2021) Mitigating medical disinformation: A whole-of-society approach to countering spam, scams, and hoaxes. Report. Shorenstein Center, Harvard University, Cambridge, MA.

Doocy, S., Gorokhovich, Y., Burnham, G., Balk, D., and Robinson, C. (2007) Tsunami mortality estimates and vulnerability mapping in Aceh, Indonesia. *Research and Practice* 97(S1), S146–S151.

Dormady, N., Roa-Henriquez, A., and Rose, A. (2019) Economic resilience of the firm: A production theory approach. *International Journal of Production Economics* 208, 446–460.

Downey, L. (2006a) Environmental inequality in metropolitan America in 2000. *Sociological Spectrum* 26(1), 21–41.

Downey, L. (2006b) Environmental racial inequality in Detroit. *Social Forces* 85(2), 771–796.

Downey, L. (2006c) Using geographic information systems to reconceptualize spatial relationships and ecological context. *American Journal of Sociology* 112(2), 567–612.

Downey, L. (2015) *Inequality, Democracy, and the Environment.* NYU Press: New York.

Downey, L., DuBois, S., Hawkins, B., and Walker, S. (2008) Environmental inequality in metropolitan America. *Organization & Environment* 21(3), 270–294.

Downey, L. and Hawkins, B. (2008) Race, income, and environmental inequality in the United States. *Sociological Perspectives* 51(4), 759–781.

Drabek, T.E. (1985) Managing the emergency response. *Public Administration Review* 45, 85–92.

Drabek, T.E. (1986) *Human System Responses to Disaster: An Inventory of Sociological Findings.* Springer-Verlag: New York.

Drabek, T.E. (1987) Emergent structures. In R.R. Dynes, B. DeMarchi, and C. Pelanda, eds., *Sociology of Disasters: Contribution of Sociology to Disaster Research.* Franco Angeli: Gorizia, 190–259.

Drabek, T.E. (1989) Disasters as non-routine social problems. *International Journal of Mass Emergencies and Disasters* 7, 253–264.

Drabek, T.E. (1996) *Sociology of Disaster: Instructor's Guide.* Federal Emergency Management Agency, Emergency Management Institute: Emmitsburg, MD.

Drabek, T.E. (2007) Social problems perspectives, disaster research, and emergency management: Intellectual contexts, theoretical extensions, and policy implications. Paper presented at the annual meeting of the American Sociological Association, New York.

Drabek, T.E. and Haas, J.E. (1969) Laboratory simulation of organizational stress. *American Sociological Review* 34, 223–238.

Drabek, T.E. and Hoetmer, G. (1991) *Emergency Management: Principle and Practice for Local Government.* International City and County Management Association: Washington, DC.

Drabek, T.E. and McEntire, D.A. (2003) Emergent phenomena and the sociology of disaster: Lessons, trends and opportunities from the research literature. *Disaster Prevention and Management: An International Journal* 12(2), 97–112. doi: 10.1108/09653560310474214.

Drabek, T.E., Tamminga, H.L., Kilijanek, T.S., and Adams, C.R. (1981) *Managing Multiorganizational Emergency Responses: Emergent Search and Rescue Networks in Natural Disaster and Remote Area Settings*. Natural Hazards Center, University of Colorado: Boulder.

Drakes, O. and Tate, E., (2022) Social vulnerability in a multi-hazard context: A systematic review. *Environmental Research Letters* 17(3), https://iopscience.iop.org/article/10.1088/1748-9326/ac5140/pdf.

Dunlap, R.E. and McCright, A.M. (2015) Challenging climate change: The denial countermovement. In R.E. Dunlap and R.J. Brulle, eds., *Climate Change and Society: Sociological Perspectives*. Oxford University Press: New York, 300–322.

Durham, C. and Miller, D.S. (2010) Native Americans, disasters, and the U.S. government: where responsibility lies. In J.D. Rivera, and D.S. Miller, eds., *How Ethnically Marginalized Americans Cope with Catastrophic Disasters: Studies in Suffering and Resilience*. Edwin Mellen Press: Lampeter, Wales, 17–49.

Dynes, R.R. (1970) *Organized Behavior in Disasters*. DC Health: Lexington, MA.

Dynes, R.R. (1988) Cross-cultural international research: Sociology and disaster. *International Journal of Mass Emergencies and Disasters* 6, 101–129.

Dynes, R.R. (1993) Disaster reduction: The importance of adequate assumptions about social organization. *Sociological Spectrum* 13, 175–192.

Dynes, R.R. (1994) Community emergency planning: False assumptions and inappropriate analogies. *International Journal of Mass Emergencies and Disasters* 12(2), 141–158.

Dynes, R.R. (2000) The dialogue between Voltaire and Rousseau on the Lisbon earthquake: The emergence of a social science view. *International Journal of Mass Emergencies and Disasters* 18(1), 97–115.

Dynes, R.R. (2006) Social capital: Dealing with community emergencies. *Homeland Security Affairs* 2(2), 1–26, http://hdl.handle.net/10945/25095.

Dynes, R.R., De Marchi, B., and Pelanda, C., eds. (1987) *Sociology of Disasters: Contribution of Sociology to Disaster Research*. Franco Angeli: Milan.

Eden, L. (2004) *Whole World on Fire: Organizations, Knowledge, and Nuclear Weapons Devastation*. Cornell University Press: Ithaca, NY.

Edgington, S. (2009) *Disaster Planning for People Experiencing Homelessness*. National Health Care for the Homeless Council: Nashville, TN.

Elliott, J.R., Haney, T.J., and Sams-Abiodun, P. (2010) Limits to social capital: Comparing network assistance in two New Orleans neighborhoods devastated by Hurricane Katrina. *Sociological Quarterly* 51, 624–648.

Elliott, J.R. and Howell, J. (2017) Beyond disasters: A longitudinal analysis of natural hazards' unequal impacts on residential instability. *Social Forces* 95(3), 1181–1207. doi: 10.1093/sf/sow086.

Elliott, J.R. and Pais, J. (2006) Race, class, and Hurricane Katrina: Social differences in human responses to disaster. *Social Science Research* 35(2), 295–321.

Elliott, J.R. and Sullivan, L. (2015) How the Red Cross raised half a billion dollars for Haiti and built six homes. *ProPublica*, https://www.propublica.org/article/how-the-red-cross-raised-half-a-billion-dollars-for-haiti-and-built-6-homes.

Ellsworth, W.L., Llenos, A.L., McGarr, A.F., Michael, A.J., Rubenstein, J.L., Mueller, C.S., Petersen, M.D. et al. (2015) Increasing seismicity in the US midcontinent: Implications for earthquake hazard. *Leading Edge* 34(6), 618–626. doi: 10.1190/tle34060618.1.

Emrich, C.T. and Cutter, S.L. (2011) Social vulnerability to climate-sensitive hazards in the southern United States. *Weather, Climate, and Society* 3, 193–208.

Enarson, E. and Chakrabarti, P.G.D., eds. (2009) *Women, Gender and Disaster: Global Issues and Initiatives*. SAGE: Thousand Oaks, CA.

Enarson, E., Fothergill, A., and Peek, L. (2018) Gender and disaster: Foundations and new directions for research and practice. In H. Rodríguez, W. Donner, W., and J.E. Trainor, eds., *Handbook of Disaster Research*, 2nd edn. Springer: Cham, Switzerland, 205–223.

Enarson, E. and Morrow, B.H. (1997) A gendered perspective: The voices of women. In W.G. Peacock, B.H. Morrow, and H. Gladwin, eds., *Hurricane Andrew: Ethnicity, Gender and the Sociology of Disasters*. Routledge: London, 115–140.

Enarson, E. and Morrow, B.H., eds. (1998) *The Gendered Terrain of Disaster: Through Women's Eyes*. Praeger: Westport, CT.

Enarson, E. and Pease, B., eds. (2016) *Men, Masculinities, and Disaster*. Routledge: New York.

Engle, N.L. (2011) Adaptive capacity and its assessment. *Global Environmental Change* 21(2), 647–656.

Erikson, K.T. (1976) *Everything in Its Path*. Simon & Schuster: New York.

Erikson, K.T. (1995) *A New Species of Trouble*. Norton: New York.

Erikson, K. and Peek, L. (2022) *The Continuing Storm: Learning from Katrina*. University of Texas Press: Austin.

Eyerman, R. (2015) *Is This America? Katrina as Cultural Trauma*. University of Texas Press: Austin.

Faas, A.J. (2023) *In the Shadow of Tungurahua: Disaster Politics in Highland Ecuador*. Rutgers University Press: New Brunswick, NJ.

Faas, A.J. and Barrios, R. (2015) Applied anthropology of risks, hazards, and disasters. *Human Organization* 74(4), 287–296.

Fairlie, R.W. and Robb, A.M. (2010) *Disparities in Capital Access between Minority and Non-Minority-Owned Businesses: The Troubling Reality of Capital Limitations Faced by MBEs*. US Department of Commerce, Minority Business Development Agency: Washington, DC.

Farazmand, A., ed. (2014) *Crisis and Emergency Management*, 2nd edn. CRC Press: Boca Raton, FL.

Fatemi, F., Ardalan, A., Aguirre, B., Mansouri, N., and Mohammadfam, I. (2017) Social vulnerability indicators in disasters: Findings from a systematic review. *International Journal of Disaster Risk Science* 22, 219–227. doi: 10.1016/j.ijdrr.2016.09.006.

Feather, J. (2014) Why older adults face more danger in natural disasters. Huffington Post, February 17, https://www.huffingtonpost.com/entry/why-older-adults-face-mor_b_4461648.html.

Federal Emergency Management Agency (2017) Draft Interagency Concept for Community Resilience Indicators and National-Level Measures. FEMA, Mitigation Framework Leadership Group, US Department of Homeland Security: Washington, DC.

Feldman, E.A. and Fish, C. (2015) Natural disasters, nuclear disasters, and global governance. Paper 1552, University of Pennsylvania, Philadelphia, 1–54, http://scholarship.law.upenn.edu/faculty_scholarship/1552.

Field, C.B., Barros, V., Stocker, T.F., and Dahe, Q., eds. (2012) Managing the Risks of Extreme Events and Disasters to Advance Climate Change Adaptation: Special Report of the Intergovernmental Panel on Climate Change. Cambridge University Press: Cambridge.

Finch, C., Emrich, C.T., and Cutter, S.L. (2010) Disaster disparities and differential recovery in New Orleans. Population and Environment 31(4), 179–202, http://www.jstor.org/stable/40587588.

Fink, S. (2013) Five Days at Memorial: Life and Death in a Storm-Ravaged Hospital. Crown: New York.

Finucane, M.L., Slovic, P., Mertz, C.K., Flynn, J., and Satterfield, T.A. (2000) Gender, race, and perceived risk: The "white male" effect. Health, Risk & Society 2(2), 159–172. doi: 10.1080/713670162.

First Street Foundation (2023) The 9th National Risk Assessment. First Street Foundation: New York.

Fischhoff, B. (2005) A hero in every aisle seat. New York Times, August 7, http://www.nytimes.com/2005/08/07/opinion/a-hero-in-every-aisle-seat.html.

Fischhoff, B. (2012) Risk perception and communication. In B. Fischhoff, ed., Risk Analysis and Human Behavior. Earthscan: London, 3–32.

Fitzhugh, S.M., Gibson, C.B., Spiro, E.S., and Butts, C.T. (2016) Spatio-temporal filtering techniques for the detection of disaster-related communication. Social Science Research 59, 137–154. doi: 10.1016/j.ssresearch.2016.04.023.

Flora, C.B. and Flora, J. (2008) Rural Communities: Legacy and Change, 3rd edn. Westview Press: San Francisco, CA.

Flynn, J., Slovic, P., and Mertz, C.K. (1994) Gender, race, and the perception of environmental health risk. Risk Analysis 14, 1101–1108.

Folke, C., Carpenter, S., Elmqvist, T., Gunderson, L., Holling, C.S., and Walker, B. (2002) Resilience and sustainable development: Building adaptive capacity in a world of transformations. Ambio 31(5), 437–440.

Fordham, M. (1998) Making women visible in disasters: Problematising the private domain. Disasters 22, 126–143.

Fordham, M., Lovekamp, W.E., Thomas, D.S.K., and Phillips, B.D. (2013) Understanding social vulnerability. In D.S.K. Thomas, B.D. Phillips, W.E. Lovekamp, and A. Fothergill, eds., Social Vulnerability to Disasters, 2nd edn. CRC Press: Boca Raton, FL, 1–29.

Fortun, K. and Frickel, S. (2013) Making a case for disaster science and technology studies. An STS Forum on the East Japan Disaster. Online forum, https://fukushimaforum.wordpress.com/online-forum-2/online-forum /making-a-case-for-disaster-science-and-technology-studies.

Foster, J.B. and Holleman, H. (2014) The theory of unequal ecological exchange: A Marx–Odum dialectic. *Journal of Peasant Studies* 41(2), 199–233.

Fothergill, A. (1996) Gender, risk, and disaster. *International Journal of Mass Emergencies and Disasters* 14(1), 33–56.

Fothergill, A. (1998) The neglect of gender in disaster work: An overview of the literature. In E. Enarson and B.H. Morrow, eds., *The Gendered Terrain of Disaster: Through Women's Eyes*. Praeger: Westport, CT, 11–25.

Fothergill, A., Maestas, E.G., and Darlington, J.D. (1999) Race, ethnicity and disasters in the United States: A review of the literature. *Disasters* 23(2), 156–173.

Fothergill, A. and Peek, L. (2004) Poverty and disasters in the United States: A review of recent sociological findings. *Natural Hazards* 32, 89–110.

Fothergill, A. and Peek, L. (2013) Permanent temporariness: Displaced children in Louisiana. In L. Weber and L. Peek, eds., *Displaced: Life in the Katrina Diaspora*. University of Texas Press: Austin, 119–43.

Fothergill, A. and Peek, L. (2015) *Children of Katrina*. University of Texas Press: Austin.

Foucault, M. (1965) *Madness and Civilization*. Pantheon: New York.

Fraga, R. (2012) The Greening of Oz: Sustainable Architecture in the Wake of a Tornado. Wasteland Press: Shelbyville, KY.

Frank, A.G. (1966) *The Development of Underdevelopment*. Monthly Review Press: New York.

Frank, A.G. (1969) Capitalism and Underdevelopment in Latin America: Historical Studies of Chile and Brasil. Modern Reader Paperbacks: New York.

Frank, A.G. (1979) *Dependent Accumulation and Underdevelopment*. Monthly Review Press: New York.

Frank, T. (2020) LGBTQ people are at higher risk in disasters. E&E News, December 23.

Freudenburg, W.R. (1997) Contamination, corrosion and the social order: An overview. *Current Sociology* 45(3), 19–39.

Freudenburg, W.R., Gramling, R., Laska, S., and Erikson, K.T. (2009) *Catastrophe in the Making: The Engineering of Katrina and the Disasters of Tomorrow*. Island Press: Washington, DC.

Frickel, S. and Vincent, M.B. (2007) Hurricane Katrina, contamination, and the unintended organization of ignorance. *Technology in Society* 29(2), 181–188.

Friedman, L. (2017) Scientists fear Trump will dismiss blunt climate report. *New York Times*, August 7.

Friend, R. and Moench, M. (2015) Rights to urban climate resilience: Moving beyond poverty and vulnerability. *WIREs Climate Change* 6(6), 643–651.

Fritz, C.E. (1961) Disasters. In R.K. Merton and R.A. Nisbet, eds., *Contemporary Social Problems*. Harcourt: New York, 651–694.

Fussell, E. (2015) The long-term recovery of New Orleans' population after Hurricane Katrina. *American Behavioral Scientist* 59(10), 1231–1245.

Fussell, E., Sastry, N., and Van Landingham, M. (2010) Race, socioeconomic status, and return migration to New Orleans after Hurricane Katrina. *Population and Environment* 31, 20–42.

Gaddis, E.B., Miles, B., Morse, S., and Lewis, D. (2007) Full-cost accounting of coastal disasters in the United States: Implications for planning and preparedness. *Ecological Economics* 63(2 & 3), 307–318.

Gaillard, J.C. and Gomez, C. (2015) Post-disaster research: Is there gold worth the rush? *Jàmbá: Journal of Disaster Risk Studies* 7(1), a120. doi: 10.4102/jamba.v7i1.120.

Gaillard, J.C. and Peek, L. (2019) Comment: Disaster-zone research needs a code of conduct. *Nature* 575(7783): 440–442.

Gaillard, J.C., Gorman-Murray, A., and Fordham, M. (2017) Sexual and gender minorities in disaster. *Gender, Place & Culture* 24(1), 18–26. doi: 10.1080/0966369X.2016.1263438.

Gaillard, J.C., Sanz, K., Balgos, B.C., Dalisay, S.N.M., Gorman-Murray, A., Smith, F., and Toelupe, V. (2017) Beyond men and women: A critical perspective on gender and disaster. *Disasters* 41(3), 429–447.

Galea, S., Maxwell, A.R., and Norris, F. (2008) Sampling and design challenges in studying the mental health consequences of disasters. *International Journal of Methods in Psychiatric Research* 17(S2), 21–28.

Galea, S., Vlahov, D., Resnick, H., Ahern, J., Susser, E., Gold, J. Bucuvalas, M., and Kilpatrick, D. (2003) Trends of probable post-traumatic stress disorder in New York City after the September 11 terrorist attacks. *American Journal of Epidemiology* 158(6), 514–524. doi: 10.1093/aje/kwg187.

Gallopín, G.C. (2006) Linkages between vulnerability, resilience, and adaptive capacity. *Global Environmental Change* 16, 293–303.

Garcia-Acosta, V. (ed.) (2020) *The Anthropology of Disasters in Latin America: State of the Art*. Routledge: New York.

Gauchat, G. (2012) Politicization of science in the public sphere: A study of public trust in the United States, 1974 to 2010. *American Sociological Review* 77(2), 167–187.

Ghuman, S.J., Brackbill, R.M., Stellman, S.D., Farfel, M.R., and Cone, J.E. (2014) Unmet mental health care need 10–11 years after the 9/11 terrorist attacks, 2011–2012 results from the World Trade Center Health Registry. *BMC Public Health* 14(491). doi: 10.1186/1471-2458-14-491.

Gilbert, D.L. (2018) *The American Class Structure in an Age of Growing Inequality*, 10th edn. SAGE: Thousand Oaks, CA.

Gilbert, S.W., Burtry, D.T., Helgeson, J.F., and Chapman, R.E. (2015) *Community Resilience Economic Decision Guide for Buildings and Infrastructure Systems*. NIST

Special Publication 1197, National Institute of Standards and Technology, US Department of Commerce.

Gill, D.A. and Picou, J.S. (1998) Technological disaster and chronic community stress. *Society & Natural Resources* 11(8), 795–815.

Gill, D.A., Picou, J.S., and Ritchie, L.A. (2012) The 2010 BP oil spill and 1989 Exxon Valdez oil spill: A comparison of initial social impacts. *American Behavioral Scientist* 56(1), 3–23.

Gin, J.L., Eisner, R.K., Der-Martirosian, C., Kranke, D., and Dobalian, A. (2017) Preparedness is a marathon, not a sprint: A tiered maturity model for assessing preparedness in homeless residential organizations in Los Angeles. *Natural Hazards Review* 19(1). doi: 10.1061/(asce)nh.1527–6996.0000276

Gin, J.L., Kranke, D., Saia, R., and Dobalian, A. (2016) Disaster preparedness in homeless residential organizations in Los Angeles county: Identifying needs, assessing gaps. *Natural Hazards Review* 17(1), 1–8. doi: 10.1061/(ASCE)NH.1527–6996.0000208.

Giroux, H. (2007) Violence, Katrina, and the biopolitics of disposability. *Theory, Culture, and Society* 24(7–8): 305–309.

Glade, S., Niles, S., Roudbari, S., Pezzulo, P.C. et al. (2022) Disaster resilience and sustainability of incarceration infrastructure: A review of the literature. *International Journal of Disaster Risk Reduction* 80, article 103190.

Glade, S., Schmitz, C., Barron, B., Dashti, S., et al. (2023) Hazards and incarceration facilities: Evaluating facility level exposure to floods, extreme heat, and landslides in Colorado. *Natural Hazards Review* 25(1). doi: 10.1061/NHREFO.NHENG-1556.

Glassman, J. (2010) Critical geography II: Articulating race and radical politics. *Progress in Human Geography* 34(4), 506–512.

GOAL (2015) *Toolkit for Measuring Community Disaster Resilience: Guidance Manual.* GOAL, https://www.goalglobal.org/images/GOAL_Toolkit_Disaster_Resilience_Guidance_Manual_May_2015.compressed.pdf.

Godschalk, D.R. (2003) Urban hazard mitigation: Creating resilient cities. *Natural Hazards Review* 4(3), 136–143.

Goldberg, D. (2002) *The Racial State.* Blackwell: Oxford.

Golding, G. (2023) Texas electrical grid remains vulnerable to extreme weather events. Federal Reserve Bank of Dallas, January 17.

Goldman, E. and Galea, S. (2014) Mental health consequences of disasters. *Annual Review of Public Health* 35, 169–183.

Gomez, C. and Hart, D.E. (2013) Disaster gold rushes, sophisms and academic neocolonialism: Comments on "earthquake disasters and resilience in the global North." *Geographical Journal* 179(3), 272–277.

Gosling, M. and Hiles, A. (2010) Business continuity statistics: Where myth meets fact. Continuity Central, http://www.continuitycentral.com/feature0660.html.

Gotham, K.F. (2012) Disaster, Inc.: Privatization and post-Katrina rebuilding in New Orleans. *Perspectives on Politics* 10(3), 633–646.

Gotham, K.F. (2014) Racialization and rescaling: Post-Katrina rebuilding and the Louisiana Road Home program. *International Journal of Urban and Regional Research* 38(3), 773–790.

Gottesdeiner, L. and Graham, D. (2021) Haiti quake revives anger over aid response to disasters. Reuters, August 16.

Gould, K.A., Pellow, D.N., and Schnaiberg, A. (2004) Interrogating the treadmill of production: Everything you wanted to know about the treadmill but were afraid to ask. *Organization & Environment* 17(3), 296–316.

Gould, K.A., Pellow, D.N., and Schnaiberg, A. (2016) *Treadmill of Production: Injustice and Unsustainability in the Global Economy.* Routledge: New York.

Government Accountability Office (2015a) *Hurricane Sandy: An Investment Strategy Could Help the Federal Government Enhance National Resilience for Future Disaster.* GAO: Washington, DC.

Government Accountability Office (2015b) *An Investment Strategy Could Help the Federal Government Enhance National Resilience for Future Disasters.* GAO: Washington, DC.

Grant K., Goldizen F.C., Sly P.D., Brune M.N., Neira M., et al. (2013) Health consequences of exposure to e-waste: A systematic review. *Lancet Global Health* 1(6), e350–61. doi: 10.1016/S2214-109X(13)70101-3.

Gray, I. (2021). The treadmill of protection: How public finance constrains climate adaptation. *Anthropocene Review*, 8(2), 196–218, https://doi.org/10.1177/20530196211015326.

Grineski, S.E., Collins, T.W., Chakraborty, J., and Montgomery, M. (2015) Hazardous air pollutants and flooding: A comparative interurban study of environmental injustice. *GeoJournal* 80(1), 145–158.

Grineski, S.E., Collins, T.W., Romo Aguilar, L., and Aldouri, R. (2010) No safe place: Environmental hazards and injustice along Mexico's northern border. *Social Forces* 88, 2241–2266.

Gronlund, C.J., Zanobetti, A., Schwartz, J.D., Wellenius, G.A., and O'Neill, M.S. (2014) Heat, heat waves, and hospital admissions among the elderly in the United States, 1992–2006. *Environmental Health Perspectives* 122(11), 1187–1192.

Guha-Sapir, D. and Hoyois, P. (2015) *Estimating populations affected by disasters: A review of methodological issues and research gaps.* Centre for Research on the Epidemiology of Disasters, Institute of Health and Society, Université catholique de Louvain: Brussels.

Guillard-Gonçalves, C., Cutter, S.L., Emrich, C.T., and Zêzere, J.L. (2015) Application of social vulnerability index (SoVI) and delineation of natural risk zones in Greater Lisbon, Portugal. *Journal of Risk Research* 18(5), 651–674, http://dx.doi.org/10.1080/13669877.2014.910689.

Gunter, V.J., Aronoff, M., and Joel, S. (1999) Toxic contamination and communities: Using an ecological–symbolic perspective to theorize response contingencies. *Sociological Quarterly* 40(4), 623–640.

Gupta, A. and Ferguson, J. (1997) *Culture, Power, Place: Explorations in Critical Anthropology*. Duke University Press: Durham, NC.

Haas, J.E., Kates, R.W., and Bowden, M.J., eds. (1977) *Reconstruction Following Disaster*. MIT Press: Cambridge, MA.

Haddow, G.D., Bullock, J.A., and Coppola, D.P. (2016) *Introduction to Emergency Management*, 6th edn. Elsevier: Oxford.

Hall, C.M., Malinen, S., Vosslamber, R., and Wordsworth, R., eds. (2016) *Business and Post-Disaster Management: Business, Organisational, and Consumer Resilience and the Christchurch Earthquakes*. Routledge: New York.

Hallegatte, S., Green, C., Nicholls, R.J., and Corfee-Morlot, J. (2013) Future flood losses in major coastal cities. *Nature Climate Change* 3, 802–806.

Hamza, M. and Zetter, R. (1998) Structural adjustment, urban systems and disaster vulnerability in developing countries. *Cities* 15(4), 291–299.

Haney, T.J., Elliott, J.R., and Fussell, E. (2010) Families and hurricane response: Risk, roles, resources, race and religion. In D. Brunsma, D. Overfelt, and J.S. Picou, eds., *The Sociology of Katrina: Perspectives on a Modern Catastrophe*, 2nd edn. Rowman & Littlefield, Lanham, MD, 77–102.

Hannigan, J. (2012) *Disasters without Borders*. Polity: Cambridge.

Harlan, S.L., Brazel, A.J., Prashad, L., Stefanov, W.L., and Larsen, L. (2006) Neighborhood microclimates and vulnerability to heat stress. *Social Science & Medicine* 63, 2847–2863.

Harlan, S.L., Declet-Barreto, J.H., Stefanov, W.L., and Petitti, D.B. (2013) Neighborhood effects on heat deaths: Social and environmental predictors of vulnerability in Maricopa County, Arizona. *Environmental Health Perspectives* 121(2), 197–204.

Harrald, J.R. (2006) Agility and disciple: Critical success factors in disaster response. *Annals of the American Academy of Political and Social Science* 604, 256–272.

Harvey, D. (1973) *Social Justice and the City*. University of Georgia Press: Athens, GA.

Harvey, D. (1993) *Justice, Nature, and the Geography of Difference*. Blackwell: Oxford.

Harvey, D. (2001) *Spaces of Capital: Toward a Critical Geography*. Routledge: New York.

Hawkins, R.L. and Maurer, K. (2010) Bonding, bridging and linking: How social capital operated in New Orleans following Hurricane Katrina. *British Journal of Social Work* 40, 1777–1793.

Hawley, K., Moench, M., and Sabbag, L. (2012) *Understanding the Economics of Flood Risk Reduction: A Preliminary Analysis*. Institute for Social and Environmental Transition-International: Boulder, CO.

He, W., Goodkind, D., and Kowal, P. (2016) *An Aging World: 2015* (International Population Reports). US Department of Commerce, US Census Bureau: Washington, DC, https://www.census.gov/content/dam/Census/library/publications/2016/demo/p95-16-1.pdf.

Healy, A. and Malhotra, N. (2009) Myopic voters and natural disaster policy. *American Political Science Review* 103(3), 387–406, http://dx.doi.org/10.1017/S0003055409990104.

Heid, A.R., Pruchno, R., Cartwright, F.P., and Wilson-Genderson, M. (2017) Exposure to Hurricane Sandy, neighborhood collective efficacy, and post-traumatic stress symptoms in older adults. *Aging & Mental Health* 21(7), 742–750. doi: 10.1080/13607863.2016.1154016.

Hellden, D., Anderson, C., Nelson, M., Ebi, K., Friberg, P., and Alfven, T. (2021) Climate change and child health: A scoping review and an expanded conceptual framework. *Lancet Planetary Health* 5e: 164–175.

Helliwell, J.F. and Putnam, R.D. (1995) Economic growth and social capital in Italy. *Eastern Economic Journal* 21(3), 295–307.

Henderson, T.L., Sirois, M., Chen, A.C.-C., Airriess, C., Swanson, D.A., and Banks, D. (2009) After a disaster: Lessons in survey methodology from Hurricane Katrina. *Popular Research and Policy Review* 28(1), 67–92.

Henry, C.S., Morris, A.S., and Harrist, A.W. (2015) Family resilience: Moving into the third wave. *Family Relations* 64, 22–43.

Hewitt, K. (1983a) The idea of calamity in a technocratic age. In K. Hewitt, ed., *Interpretations of Calamity: From the viewpoint of human ecology*. Allen & Unwin: Boston, MA, 3–32.

Hewitt, K. (1983b) *Interpretations of Calamity: From the Viewpoint of Human Ecology*. Allen & Unwin: Boston, MA.

Hewitt, K. and Burton, I. (1971) *The Hazardousness of a Place: A Regional Ecology of Damaging Events*. University of Toronto Press: Toronto.

Hewson, C., Vogel, C., and Laurent, D. (2016) *Internet Research Methods*, 2nd edn. SAGE: Thousand Oaks, CA.

Highfield, W. and Brody, S.D. (2013) Evaluating the effectiveness of local mitigation activities in reducing flood losses. *Natural Hazards Review* 14(4), 229–236.

Hilgartner, S. and Bosk, C.L. (1988) The rise and fall of social problems: A public arenas model. *American Journal of Sociology* 94, 53–78.

Hincks, T., Aspinall, W., Cooke, R., and Gernon, T. (2018) Oklahoma's induced seismicity strongly linked to wastewater injection depth. *Science* 359(6381), 1251–1255. doi: 10.1126/science.aap7911.

Hinkel, J., Dorninger, C., Wieland, H., and Suwandi, I. (2022) Imperialist appropriation in the world economy: Drain from the global South through unequal exchange, 1990–2015. *Global Environmental Change* 73, article 102467.

Hinshaw, R.E. (2006) *Living with Nature's Extremes: The Life of Gilbert Fowler White*. Johnson Books: Boulder, CO.

Hiroi, O., Mikami, S., and Miyata, K. (1985) A study of mass media reporting in emergencies. *International Journal of Mass Emergencies and Disasters* 3, 21–49.

Hisham, T., Patherage, C., and Fernando, T. (2021) Measuring community disaster resilience at local levels: An adaptable resilience framework. *International Journal of Disaster Risk Reduction* 62, article 102358.

Hochrainer, S. (2009) Assessing the macroeconomic impacts of natural disasters: Are there any? Policy Research Working Paper 4968, World Bank, Global Facility for Disaster Reduction and Recovery, Washington, DC.

Hoffman, S.M. (1998) Eve and Adam among the embers: Gender patterns after the Oakland Berkeley firestorm. In E. Enarson and B.H. Morrow, eds., *The Gendered Terrain of Disaster: Through Women's Eyes*. Praeger: Westport, CT, 55–61.

Hoffman, S.M. and Oliver-Smith, A., eds. (2002) *Catastrophe and Culture: The Anthropology of Disaster*. School for Advanced Research Press: Santa Fe, NM.

Holland, K. (2015) 45 million Americans are living without a credit score. CNBC, http://www.cnbc.com/2015/05/05/credit-invisible-26-million-have-no -credit-score.html.

Holling, C.S. (1973) Resilience and stability of ecological systems. *Annual Review of Ecology and Systematics* 4, 1–23, http://www.jstor.org/stable/2096802.

Hooks, G. (1994) Regional processes in the hegemonic nation: Political, economic, and military influences on the use of geographic space. *American Sociological Review* 59(5), 746–772, http://www.jstor.org/stable/2096446.

Hooks, G. and Smith, C.L. (2004) The treadmill of destruction: National sacrifice areas and Native Americans. *American Sociological Review* 69(4), 558–575, http://www.jstor.org/stable/3593065.

Hooks, G. and Smith, C.L. (2005) Treadmills of production and destruction: Threats to environment posed by militarism. *Organization & Environment* 18(1), 19–37.

Horney, J., Dwyer, C., Aminto, M., Berke, O., and Smith, G. (2017) Developing indicators to measure post-disaster community recovery in the United States. *Disasters* 41(1), 124–149.

HoSang, D., LaBennett, O., and Pulido, L., eds. (2012) *Racial Formation in the 21st Century*. University of California Press: Berkeley, CA.

Hoynes, H., Miller, D.L., and Schaller, J. (2012) Who suffers during recessions? *Journal of Economic Perspectives* 26, 27–48.

Hughes, A. and Chauhan, A. (2015) Online media as a means to affect public trust in emergency responders. In L. Palen, M. Buscher, T. Comes, and A. Hughes, eds., *Proceedings of the ISCRAM 2015 Conference, May 24–27, Kristiansand, Norway*. ISCRAM: Kristiansand, 171–181.

Hughes, A., Palen, L., Sutton, J., Liu, S.B., and Vieweg, A. (2008) "Site-seeing" in disaster: An examination of on-line social convergence. In F. Friedrich and B. Van De Walle, eds., *Proceedings of the 5th International ISCRAM Conference*. Academic Press: Washington, DC, http://www.amandaleehughes.com /OnlineConvergenceISCRAM08.pdf.

Hughes, A., St. Denis, L., Palen, L., and Anderson, K.M. (2014) Online public communications by police and fire services during the 2012 Hurricane

Sandy. In *Proceedings of the SIGCHI 2014 Conference on Human Factors in Computing Systems*. ACM: New York, 1505–1514.

Human Rights Campaign (2012) *Working with the Lesbian, Gay, Bisexual and Transgender Community: A Cultural Guide for Emergency Responders and Volunteers*. HRC: Washington, DC.

Hunt, M., Tansey, C.M., Anderson, J., Boulanger, R.F., Eckenwiler, L., Pringle, J., and Schwartz, L. (2016) The challenge of timely, responsive and rigorous ethics review of disaster research: Views of research ethics committee members. *PLoS ONE* 11(6), 1–15.

Hurlbert, J.S., Haines, V.A., and Beggs, J.J. (2000) Core networks and tie activation: What kinds of routine networks allocate resources in nonroutine situations? *American Sociological Review* 65, 598–618.

Igan, D. and Lambert, D. (2019) Bank lobbying: Regulatory capture and beyond. International Monetary Fund working paper, WP/19/171.

Institute on Statelessness and Inclusion (2014) *The World's Stateless*. ISI: Eindhoven, Netherlands.

Interagency Performance Evaluation Task Force (2008) *Performance Evaluation of the New Orleans and Southeast Louisiana Hurricane Protection System: Final Report of the Interagency Performance Evaluation Task Force*. US Army Corps of Engineers: Washington, DC.

Intergovernmental Panel on Climate Change (2022) Impacts, adaptation and vulnerability: Report of WGII. IPCC Sixth Assessment Report, https://www.ipcc.ch/report/ar6/wg2.

Internal Displacement Monitoring Center (2017) *Recovery Postponed: The Long-Term Plight of People Displaced by the 2011 Great East Japan Earthquake, Tsunami and Nuclear Radiation Disaster*. Internal Displacement Monitoring Center: Geneva.

International Gay and Lesbian Human Rights Commission (n.d.) *The Impact of the Earthquake, and Relief and Recovery Programs on Haitian LGBT People*. IGLHRC: New York.

Isadore, C. (2024) A terrifying 10-minute flight adds to years of Boeing's quality control problems. CNN, January 8.

Islam, M.S., Kamal, A.M., Kabir, A. et al. (2021) COVID-19 vaccine rumors and conspiracy theories: The need for cognitive inoculation against misinformation to improve vaccine adherence. *PLoS One*. 16(5), article e0251605.

Jacob, M. (2010) Ethnography, memory, and culture: Healing the soul wound of technological disaster. In J.D. Rivera and D.S. Miller, eds., *How Ethnically Marginalized Americans Cope with Catastrophic Disasters: Studies in Suffering and Resilience*. Edwin Mellen Press: Lampeter, Wales, 37–49.

Jaeger, C.C., Renn, O., Rosa, E.A., and Webler, T. (2001) *Risk, Uncertainty, and Rational Action*. Earthscan: London.

Janoske, M., Liu, B.F., and Sheppard, B. (2012) *Understanding Risk Communication Best Practices: A Guide for Emergency Managers and Communicators*. National

Consortium for the Study of Terrorism and Responses to Terrorism, University of Maryland, College Park, MD.

Janssen, M.A. and Ostrom, E. (2006) Resilience, vulnerability, and adaptation: A cross-cutting theme of the international human dimensions programme on global environmental change. *Global Environmental Change* 16, 237–239.

Jensen, J. (2011) *Preparedness: A Principled Approach to Return on Investment.* International Association of Emergency Managers: Falls Church, VA.

Jensen, J. and Thompson, S. (2016) The incident command system: A literature review. *Disasters* 40, 158–182.

Jha, A.K., Miner, T.W., and Stanton-Geddes, Z., eds. (2013) *Building Urban Resilience: Principles, Tools, and Practice.* World Bank: Washington, DC.

Johnson, C. (2004) *The Sorrows of Empire: Militarism, Secrecy, and the End of the Republic.* Metropolitan Books: New York.

Johnson, L.A. and Olshansky, R.B. (2016) *After Great Disasters: An In-Depth Analysis of How Six Countries Managed Community Recovery.* Lincoln Institute of Land Policy: Cambridge, MA, 1–72.

Johnson, N.R. (1987) Panic at "the Who concert stampede": An empirical assessment. *Social Problems* 34, 362–373.

Johnson, N.R. (1988) Fire in a crowded theater: A descriptive analysis of the emergence of panic. *International Journal of Mass Emergencies and Disasters* 6, 7–26.

Johnson, N.R., Feinberg, W.E., and Johnston, D.M. (1994) Microstructure and panic: The impact of social bonds on individual action in collective flight from the Beverly Hills Supper Club fire. In R.R. Dynes and K. Tierney, eds., *Disasters, Collective Behavior, and Social Organization.* University of Delaware Press: Newark, 168–189.

Johnston, B. (2007) Half-lives, half-truths, and other radioactive legacies of the Cold War. In B. Johnson, ed., *Half-Lives and Half-Truths: Confronting the Radioactive Legacies of the Cold War.* SAR Press: Santa Fe, NM, 1–24.

Jorgenson, A.K. (2006) Unequal ecological exchange and environmental degradation: A theoretical proposition and cross-national study of deforestation, 1990–2000. *Rural Sociology* 71(4), 685–712.

Jorgenson, A.K., Clark, B., Thombs, R.P., Kentor, J. et al. (2023) Guns versus climate: How militarization amplifies the effects of economic growth on carbon emissions. *American Sociological Review* 88(3), 418–453.

Kahn, M.E. (2005) The death toll from natural disasters: The role of income, geography, and institutions. *Review of Economics and Statistics* 87(2), 271–284.

Kahneman, D. (2011) *Thinking, Fast and Slow.* Farrar, Straus & Giroux: New York.

Kahneman, D., Slovic, P., and Tversky, A. (1982) *Judgements under Uncertainty: Heuristics and Biases.* Cambridge University Press: Cambridge.

Kahneman, D. and Tversky, A. (1972) Subjective probability: A judgement of representativeness. *Cognitive Psychology* 3, 430–454.

Kahneman, D. and Tversky, A. (1979) Prospect theory: An analysis of decision under risk. *Econometrica* 47, 263–291.

Kang, J.E., Peacock, W.G., and Husein, R. (2010) An assessment of coast zone hazard mitigation plans in Texas. *Journal of Disaster Research* 5(5), 526–534.

Kapucu, N. and Garayev, V. (2016) Structure and network performance: Horizontal and vertical networks in emergency management. *Administration & Society* 48(8), 931–961.

Kapucu, N., Hawkins, C.V., and Rivera, F.I. (2013) *Disaster Resiliency: Interdisciplinary Perspectives*. Routledge: New York.

Karoly, L.A. (2008) Valuing Benefits in Benefit–Cost Studies of Social Programs. RAND: Santa Monica, CA.

Kates, R.W. (2011) *Gilbert F. White, 1911–2006: A Biographical Memoir*. National Academy of Sciences: Washington, DC.

Katz, J.M. (2013) *The Big Truck That Went by: How the World Came to Save Haiti and Left Behind a Disaster*. St. Martin's Press: New York.

Keating, A., Campbell, K., Mechler, R., Michel-Kerjan, E., Mochizuki, J., Kunreuther, H., Bayer, J. et al. (2014) *Operationalizing Resilience against Natural Disaster Risk: Opportunities, Barriers, and a Way Forward*. Zurich Flood Resilience Alliance: Zurich.

Keating, J.P., Loftus, E.F., and Manber, M. (1983) Emergency evacuations during fires: Psychological considerations. In R.F. Kidd and M.J. Saks, eds., *Advances in Applied Social Psychology*. Lawrence Erlbaum Associates: Hillsdale, NJ, 83–99.

Keller, C., Bostrom, A., Kuttschreuter, M., Savadori, L., Spence, A., and White, M. (2012) Bringing appraisal theory to environmental risk perception: A review of conceptual approaches of the past 40 years and suggestions for future research. *Journal of Risk Research* 15(3), 237–256. doi: 10.1080/13669877.2011.634523.

Keller, R.C. (2015) *Fatal Isolation: The Devastating Paris Heatwave of 2003*. Chicago, IL: University of Chicago Press.

Kelman, I. (2005) Operational ethics for disaster research. *International Journal of Mass Emergencies and Disasters* 23(3), 141–158.

Kempner, J., Merz, J.F., and Bosk, C.L. (2011) Forbidden knowledge: Public controversy and the production of nonknowledge. *Sociological Forum* 26(3), 475–500.

Kendra, J.M., Clay, L.A., and Gill, K.B. (2018) Resilience and disasters. In H. Rodríguez, W. Donner, and J.E. Trainor, eds., *Handbook of Disaster Research*, 2nd edn. Springer: Cham, Switzerland, 87–107.

Kendra, J.M. and Wachtendorf, T. (2003) Elements of community resilience in the World Trade Center attack. *Disasters* 27(1), 37–53.

Kendra, J.M. and Wachtendorf, T. (2006) The waterborne evacuation of lower Manhattan on September 11: A case of distributed sensemaking. Preliminary paper no. 355, Disaster Research Center, University of Delaware, Newark, DE.

Kendra, J.M. and Wachtendorf, T. (2016) *American Dunkirk: The Waterborne Evacuation of Manhattan on 9/11*. Temple University Press: Philadelphia, PA.

Kendra, J. and Wachtendorf, T. (2020) Disaster-zone research: No need for a customized code of conduct. *Nature* 578 (7795). doi: 10.1038/d41586-020-00459-w.

Kessler, R.C., Galea, S., Gruber, M.J., Sampson, N.A., Ursano, R.J., and Wessely, S. (2008) Trends in mental illness and suicidality after Hurricane Katrina. *Molecular Psychiatry* 13(4), 374–384.

Kilpatrick, D.G. (2004) The ethics of disaster research: A special section. *Journal of Traumatic Stress* 17(5), 361–362.

Kingdon, J. (1995) *Agendas, Alternatives, and Public Policies*. Addison-Wesley: Boston, MA.

Kingdon, J. (2011) *Agendas, Alternatives, and Public Policies: Update Edition, with an Epilogue on Health Care*. Pearson Education: New York.

Kiyota, E., Tanaka, Y., Arnold, M., and Aldrich, D.P. (2015) Elders leading the way to resilience. *SSRN Electronic Journal*. doi: 10.2139/ssrn.2575382.

Klein, N. (2007) *The Shock Doctrine: The Rise of Disaster Capitalism*. Henry Holt: New York.

Klein, R.J.T., Nicholls, R.J., and Thomalla, F. (2003) Resilience to natural hazards: How useful is this concept? *Global Environmental Change Part B: Environmental Hazards* 5(1 & 2), 35–45.

Kleindorfer, P., Kunreuther, H., and Ou-Yang, C. (2012) Single-year and multi-year insurance policies in a competitive market. *Journal of Risk and Uncertainty* 45, 51–78.

Klinenberg, E. (2002) *Heat Wave: A Social Autopsy of Disaster in Chicago*. University of Chicago Press: Chicago, IL.

Klinenberg, E., Araos, M., and Koslov, L. (2020) Sociology and the climate crisis. *Annual Review of Sociology* 46, 649–669.

Knoke, D. (1990) *Political Networks: The Structural Perspective*. Cambridge University Press: Cambridge.

Knowles, S.G. (2011) *The Disaster Experts: Mastering Risk in Modern America*. University of Pennsylvania Press: Philadelphia.

Knox, R. (2016) A $1 pill that could save thousands of lives: Research suggests cheap way to avoid U.N.-caused cholera. WBUR CommonHealth, http://www.wbur.org/commonhealth/2016/02/05/antibiotic-pill-cholera-united-nations.

Kok, M.T.J., Narain, V., Wonink, S., and Jager, J. (2006) Human vulnerability to environmental change: An approach for UNEP's global environmental outlook (GEO). In J. Birkmann, ed., *Measuring Vulnerability to Natural Hazards: Towards Disaster Resilient Societies*. United Nations University Press: Tokyo, 128–147.

Koks, E.E., Carrera, L., Jonkeren, O., Aerts, J.C.J.H., Husby, T.G., Thissen, M., Standardi, G. et al. (2016) Regional disaster impact analysis: Comparing input–output and computable general equilibrium models. *Natural Hazards and Earth System Sciences*, 16, 1911–1924.

Kopp, R.J., Krupnick, A.J., and Toman, M.A. (1997) Cost–benefit analysis and regulatory reform: An assessment of the science and art. RFF Discussion Paper 97–19, Resources for the Future, Washington, DC.

Korten, T. (2015) In Florida, officials ban term "climate change." *Miami Herald*, March 8.

Kotkin, J. and Cox, W. (2017) Rising rents are stressing out tenants and heightening America's housing crisis. *Forbes*, October 19.

Kotz, M., Levermann, A., and Weng, L. (2024) The economic commitment of climate change. *Nature Climate Change* 628, 551–557.

Kousky, C. (2014) Informing climate adaptation: A review of the economic costs of natural disasters. *Energy Economics* 46, 576–592.

Kowalska-Duplaga, K. and Duplaga, M. (2023) The association of conspiracy beliefs and the uptake of COVID-19 vaccination: A cross-sectional study. *BMC Public Health* 23(1). doi: 10.1186/s12889-023-15603-0.

Kozinets, R.V. (2019) *Netography: The Essential Guide to Qualitative Social Media Research*. SAGE: Thousand Oaks, CA.

Kraus, L. (2017) *2016 Disability Statistics Annual Report*. Institute of Disability, University of New Hampshire: Durham, NH.

Kreps, G.A. (1984) Sociological inquiry and disaster research. *Annual Review of Sociology* 10, 309–330.

Kreps, G.A. (1985) Disaster and the social order. *Sociological Theory* 3(1), 49–64, http://www.jstor.org/stable/202173.

Kreps, G.A., ed. (1989) *Social Structure and Disaster*. University of Delaware Press: Newark.

Kreps, G.A. and Bosworth, S.L. (1993) Disaster, organizing, and role enactment: A structural approach. *American Journal of Sociology* 99, 428–463.

Kreps, G.A., Bosworth, S.L., Mooner, J.A., Russell, S.T., and Myers, K.A. (1994) *Organizing, Role Enactment, and Disaster: A Structural Theory*. University of Delaware Press: Newark.

Kreps, G.A. and Drabek, T.E. (1996) Disasters are nonroutine social problems. *International Journal of Mass Emergencies and Disasters* 14, 129–153.

Kroll-Smith, S., Baxter, V., and Jenkins, P. (2015) *Left to Chance: Hurricane Katrina and the Story of Two New Orleans Neighborhoods*. University of Texas Press: Austin.

Kuligowski, E.D. (2011) *Terror Defeated: Occupant Sensemaking, Decision-Making and Protective Action in the 2001 World Trade Center Disaster*. Doctoral dissertation, Department of Sociology, University of Colorado: Boulder.

Kuligowski, E.D., Waugh, A., Sutton, J., and Cova, T.J. (2023) Ember alerts: Assessing wireless emergency alert (WEA) messages using the warning response model. University at Albany, SUNY.

Kull, D., Mechler, R., and Hochrainer-Stigler, S. (2013) Probabilistic cost–benefit analysis of disaster risk management in a development context. *Disaster* 37(3), 374–400.

Kunreuther, H.C., Pauly, M.V., and McMorrow, S. (2013) *Insurance and Behavioral Economics: Improving Decisions in the Most Misunderstood Industry*. Cambridge University Press: New York.

Kunreuther, H.C. and Rose, A.Z., eds. (2004a) *The Economics of Natural Hazards*, vol. 1. Edward Elgar: Cheltenham.

Kunreuther, H.C. and Rose, A.Z., eds. (2004b) *The Economics of Natural Hazards*, vol. 2. Edward Elgar: Cheltenham.

Kunreuther, H.C. and Roth, R.J., Sr., eds. (1998) *Paying the Price: The Status and Role of Insurance Against Natural Disasters in the United States*. Joseph Henry Press: Washington, DC.

Kunreuther, H.C. and Slovic, P. (1986) Decision making in hazard and resource management. In R.W. Kates and I. Burton, eds., *Geography, Resources, and Environment*, vol. 2: *Themes from the Work of Gilbert F. White*. University of Chicago Press: Chicago, IL, 153–187.

Kurokawa, K. (2012) *The Official Report of the Fukushima Nuclear Accident Independent Investigation Committee*. National Diet of Japan: Tokyo.

Kurtz, H. (2009) Acknowledging the racial state: An agenda for environmental justice research. *Antipode* 41(4), 684–704.

Laditka, S.B., Laditka, J.N., Xirasagar, S., Cornman, C.B., Davis, C.B., and Richter, J.V.E. (2008) Providing shelter to nursing home evacuees in disasters: Lessons from Hurricane Katrina. *American Journal of Public Health* 98(7), 1288–1293.

Lakhani, N. (2023) $700m pledged to loss and damage fund at Cop28 covers less than 0.2% needed. *Guardian*, December 6.

Lasswell, H.D. (1948) The structure and function of communication in society. In L. Bryson, ed., *Communication of Ideas*. Harper: New York, 37–51.

Le De, L., Gaillard, J.C., and Friesen, W. (2015) Academics doing participatory disaster research: How participatory is it? *Environmental Hazards* 14(1), 1–15. doi: 10.1080/17477891.2014.957636.

Leap, B., Stalp, M.C., and Kelly, K. (2022) Raging against the "neoliberal hellscape": Anger, pride, and ambivalence in civil society responses to the COVID-19 pandemic in the USA. *Antipode* 54(4), 1166–1187.

Lee, A.V., Vargo, J., and Seville, E. (2013) Developing a tool to measure and compare organizations resilience. *Natural Hazards Review* 14, 29–41. doi: 10.1061/(ASCE)NH.1527–6996.0000075.

Lerner, J.S. and Keltner, D. (2001) Fear, anger, and risk. *Journal of Personality and Social Psychology* 81(1), 146–159. doi: 10.1037//0022–3514.81.1.146.

Levine, C. (2004) The concept of vulnerability in disaster research. *Journal of Traumatic Stress* 17(5), 395–402.

Liao, Y., Walls, M.A., Wibbenmeyer, M., and Pesek, S. (2022) Insurance availability and affordability under increasing wildfire risk in California. November. Resources for the Future, Issue Brief 22-09.

Lim, W.K. (2021) *Designing Emergency Management: China's Post-SARS Experience, 2003–2012*. Routledge: New York.

Lin, N. (1999) Building a network theory of social capital. *Connections* 22(1), 28–51.

Lin, R., Xia, R., and Smith, D. (2014) UC releases list of 1,500 buildings: Big step for LA quake safety. *Los Angeles Times*, January 25, http://articles.latimes.com /2014/jan/25/local/la-me-ln-concrete-buildings-list-20140125.

Lin, S., Fletcher, B.A., Luo, M., Chinery, R., and Hwang, S. (2011) Health impact in New York City during the Northeast blackout of 2003. *Public Health Reports* 126(3), 384–393.

Lind, B.E., Tirado, M., Butts, C.T., and Petrescu-Prahova, M. (2008) Brokerage roles in disaster response: Organisational mediation in the wake of Hurricane Katrina. *International Journal of Emergency Management* 5(1 & 2), 75–99.

Lind, D. (2017) Fear of deportation could keep Texans from evacuating for Harvey – and Trump is making it worse. *Vox*, August 25, http://www.vox .com/policy-and-politics/2017/8/25/16205040/hurricane-harvey-checkpoints -immigration-border.

Lindell, M.K., Alesch, D., Bolton, P.A., Greene, M.R., Larson, L.A. et al. (1997) Adoption and implementation of hazard adjustments. *International Journal of Mass Emergencies and Disasters* 15 (special issue), 327–453.

Lindell, M.K., Arlikatti, S., and Prater, C.S. (2009) Why people do what they do to protect against earthquake risk: Perceptions of hazard adjustment attributes. *Risk Analysis* 29, 1072–1088.

Lindell, M.K. and Perry, R.W. (1992) *Behavioral Foundations of Community Emergency Management*. Hemisphere Publishing Corporation: Washington, DC.

Lindell, M.K. and Perry, R.W. (2000) Household adjustment to earthquake hazard: A review of research. *Environment and Behavior* 32, 590–630.

Lindell, M.K. and Perry, R.W. (2004) *Communicating Environmental Risk in Multiethnic Communities*. SAGE: Thousand Oaks, CA.

Lindell, M.K. and Perry, R.W. (2012) The protective action decision model: theoretical modifications and additional evidence. *Risk Analysis* 32(4), 616–632.

Liu, S.B. and Palen, L. (2010) The new cartographers: Crisis map mashups and the emergence of neogeographic practice. *Cartography and Geographic Information Science* 37(1), 69–90.

Liu, S.B., Palen, L., Sutton, J., Hughes, A.L., and Vieweg, S. (2008) In search of the bigger picture: The emergent role of on-line photo sharing in times of disaster. In F. Friedrich and B. Van De Walle, eds., *Proceedings of the 5th International ISCRAM Conference*. Academic Press: Washington, DC, https:// works.bepress.com/vieweg/11.

Logan, J. and Molotch, H. (1987) *Urban Fortunes: The Political Economy of Place*. University of California Press: Berkeley.

Ludwig, S. (2015) Credit scores in American perpetuate racial injustice. Here's how. *Guardian*, October 13. www.theguardian.com/commentisfree/2015/oct /13/your-credit-score-is-racist-heres-why.

Luhby, T. (2023) White Americans have far more wealth than Black Americans: Here's how big the gap is. CNN, October 31.

Lundgren, R. and McMakin, A. (2009) *Risk Communication: A Handbook for Communicating Environmental, Safety, and Health Risks*, 4th edn. John Wiley & Sons, Inc.: Hoboken, NJ.

Lupton, D. (Ed.) 2021. Doing fieldwork in a pandemic. Crowdsourced document, revised version, https://antle.iat.sfu.ca/wp-content/uploads/Doing-Fieldwork-in-a-pandemic-Resources.pdf.

Lyles, L.W., Berke, P., and Smith, G. (2014a) A comparison of local hazard mitigation plan quality in six states, USA. *Landscape and Urban Planning* 122, 89–99.

Lyles, L.W., Berke, P., and Smith, G. (2014b) Do planners matter? Examining factors driving incorporation of land use approaches into hazard mitigation plans. *Journal of Environmental Planning and Management* 57(5), 792–811.

Macauley, M.K. (2006) The value of information: Measuring the contribution of space-derived earth science date to resource management. *Space Policy* 22, 274–282.

Magesh, S., John, D., Li, W.T., Li, Y. et al. (2022) Disparities in COVID-19 by race, ethnicity, and socioeconomic status: A systematic review and meta-analysis. *JAMA Network Open* 4 (11), article e2134147.

Malo, S. (2022) Air Force sued over plan to recommence burning of waste munitions on Guam. Reuters, January 26.

Maricopa County (2024) 2023 Heat-related deaths report. Department of Public Health, Phoenix, Arizona.

Marlon, J., Howe, P., Mildenberger, M., and Leiserowitz, A. (2016) *Yale Climate Opinion Maps, US 2016*. Yale Program on Climate Communication, Yale University: New Haven, CT.

Marlowe, J.M., Lou, L., Osman, M., and Zeba Alam, Z. (2015) Conducting post-disaster research with refugee background peer researchers and their communities. *Qualitative Social Work* 14(3), 383–398.

Marshall, M.I., Niehm, L.S., Sydnor, S.B., and Schrank, H.L. (2015) Predicting small business demise after a natural disaster: An analysis of pre-existing conditions. *Natural Hazards* 79, 331–354.

Marshall, M.I. and Schrank, H.L. (2014) Small business disaster recovery: A research framework. *Natural Hazards* 72(2), 597–616.

Marshall, S. and McCormick, K. (2015) *Returns on Resilience: The Business Case.* Urban Land Institute: Washington, DC.

Massey, D.S. and Denton, N.A. (1998) *American Apartheid: Segregation and the Making of the Underclass.* Harvard University Press: Cambridge, MA.

Masten, A.S. and Monn, A.R. (2015) Child and family resilience: A call for integrated science, practice, and professional training. *Family Relations* 64, 5–21. doi: 10.1111/fare.12103.

Masterson, J.H., Peacock, W.G., Van Zandt, S.S., Grover, H., Schwarz, L.F., and Cooper Jr., J.T. (2014) *Planning for Community Resilience: A Handbook for Reducing Vulnerability to Disasters.* Island Press: Washington, DC.

Matejowsky, T. (2015) Merchant resiliency and climate hazard vulnerability in the urban Philippines: Anthropological perspectives on 2011 typhoons Nesat and Nalgae. In D.C. Wood, ed., *Climate Change, Culture, and Economics: Anthropological Investigations* (Research in Economic Anthropology 35). Emerald Group Publishing Limited: Bingley, UK, 239–262.

Mathur, D. (2022) *Available to Be Poisoned: Toxicity as a Form of Life*. Lexington Books: Lanham, MD.

Matthewman, S. (2015) *Disasters, Risks and Revelation*. Palgrave Macmillan: New York.

May, P.J. (1991) Reconsidering policy design: Policies and publics. *Journal of Public Policy* 11(2), 187–206.

May, P.J. (1992) Policy learning and failure. *Journal of Public Policy* 12(4), 331–354, http://www.jstor.org/stable/4007550.

May, P.J. (1999) Fostering policy learning: A challenge for public administration. *International Review of Public Administration* 4(1), 21–31. doi: 10.1080/12294659.1999.10804920.

May, P.J. and Feeley, T.J. (2000) Regulatory backwaters: Earthquake risk reduction in the Western United States. *State & Local Government Review* 32(1), 20–33, http://www.jstor.org/stable/4355248.

May, P.J., Jochim, A.E., and Sapotichne, J. (2011) Constructing homeland security: An anemic policy regime. *The Policy Studies Journal* 39(2), 285–307.

Mayer, B., Running, K., and Bergstrand, K. (2015) Compensation and community corrosion: Perceived inequalities, social comparisons, and competition following the Deepwater Horizon oil spill. *Sociological Forum* 30(2), 369–390.

Mayhorn, C.B. (2005) Cognitive aging and the processing of hazard information and disaster warnings. *Natural Hazards Review* 6(4), 165–170.

Mayunga, J.S. (2009) *Measuring the Measure: A Multidimensional Scale Model to Measure Community Disaster Resilience in the US Gulf Coast Region*. Doctoral dissertation, Urban and Regional Sciences, Texas A&M University, College Station.

McCoy, B. and Dash, N. (2013) Class. In D.S.K. Thomas, B.D. Phillips, W.E. Lovekamp, and A. Fothergill, eds., *Social Vulnerability to Disasters*, 2nd edn. CRC Press: Boca Raton, FL, 83–112.

McDonald, K.E., Keys, C.B., and Balcazar, F.E. (2007) Disability, race/ethnicity and gender: Themes of cultural oppression, acts of individual resistance. *American Journal of Community Psychology* 39, 145–161.

McEntire, D.A. (2007) *Disciplines, Disasters, and Emergency Management*. Charles C. Thomas: Springfield, IL.

McEntire, D.M. (2022) *Disaster Response and Recovery: Strategies and Tactics for Resilience*. John Wiley & Sons: Hoboken, NJ.

McGoey, L. (2019) *The Unknowers: How Strategic Ignorance Rules the World*. Zed Books Ltd: London.

McKie, R. (2024) The next pandemic likely to be caused by flu virus, scientists warn. *Guardian*, April 12.

McNamara, D.E., Rubinstein, J.L., Myers, E., Smoczyk, G., Benz, H.M., Williams, R.A., Hayes, G. et al. (2015) Efforts to monitor and characterize the recent increasing seismicity in central Oklahoma. *Leading Edge* 34(6), 628–639. doi: 10.1190/tle34060628.1.

McPhee, J. (1989) *The Control of Nature*. Farrar, Straus & Giroux: New York.

Meerkatt, H., Kolo, P., and Renson, Q. (2015) *UNICEF/WFP Return on Investment for Emergency Preparedness Study*. Boston Consulting Group, UNICEF, and the World Food Programme, https://www.unicef.org/publications/files/UNICEF _WFP_Return_on_Investment_for_Emergency_Preparedness_Study.pdf

Melamed, J. (2015) Racial capitalism. *Critical Ethnic Studies* 1(1), 76–85, http://www. jstor.org/stable/10.5749/jcritethnstud.1.1.0076.

Mendonça, D. and Wallace, W.A. (2007) A cognitive model of improvisation in emergency management. *IEEE Transactions on Systems, Man and Cybernetics, Part A: Systems and Humans* 38(4), 547–561.

Mendonça, D., Webb, G., Butts, C. and Brooks, J. (2014) Cognitive correlates of improvised behaviour in disaster response: The cases of the Murrah Building and the World Trade Center. *Journal of Contingencies and Crisis Management* 22(4), 185–195.

Meo, M., Ziebro, B., and Patton, A. (2004) Tulsa turnaround: From disaster to sustainability. *Natural Hazards Review* 5, 1–9.

Merton, R.K. (1957) The role-set: Problems in sociological theory. *British Journal of Sociology* 8(2), 106–120.

Merton, R.K. (1968) The Matthew effect in science. *Science* 159(3810), 56–63.

Meyer, M.A. (2018) Social capital in disaster research. In H. Rodríguez, W. Donner, and J.E. Trainor, eds., *Handbook of Disaster Research*, 2nd edn. Springer: Cham, Switzerland, 263–286.

Michel-Kerjan, E., Hochrainer-Stigler, S., Kunreuther, H., Linnerooth-Bayer, J., Mechler, R., Muir-Wood, R., Ranger, N. et al. (2013) Catastrophe risk models from evaluating disaster risk reduction investments in developing countries. *Risk Analysis* 33(6), 984–999.

Miles, S.B. and Chang, S.E. (2003) *Urban Disaster Recovery: A Framework and Simulation Model*. Multidisciplinary Center for Earthquake Engineering Research, University at Buffalo: Buffalo, NY.

Miles, S.B. and Chang, S.E. (2006) Modeling community recovery from earthquakes. *Earthquake Spectra* 22(2), 439–458.

Miles, S.B. and Chang, S.E. (2011) ResilUS: A community disaster resilience model. *Cartography and GIS* 38, 36–51.

Mileti, D.S. (1975) *Natural Hazards Warning Systems in the United States*. Institute of Behavioral Science, University of Colorado: Boulder.

Mileti, D.S. (1999) *Disasters by Design: A Reassessment of Natural Hazards in the United States*. Joseph Henry Press: Washington, DC.

Mileti, D.S. and Darlington, J.D. (1997) The role of searching in shaping reactions to earthquake risk information. *Social Problems* 44, 89–103.

Mileti, D.S., Drabek, T.E., and Haas, J.E. (1975) *Human Systems in Extreme Environments*. Institute of Behavioral Science, Program on Environment and Behavior, University of Colorado: Boulder.

Mileti, D.S. and Fitzpatrick, C. (1993) *The Great Earthquake Experiment: Risk Communication and Public Action*. Westview Press: Boulder, CO.

Mileti, D.S., Fitzpatrick, C., and Farhar, B.C. (1990) *Risk Communication and Public Response to the Parkfield Earthquake Prediction Experiment*. Hazards Assessment Laboratory and Department of Sociology, Colorado State University: Fort Collins.

Mileti, D.S. and O'Brien, P. (1992) Warnings during disaster: Normalizing communicated risk. *Social Problems* 39, 40–57.

Mileti, D.S. and Peek, L. (2000) The social psychology of public response to warnings of a nuclear power plant accident. *Journal of Hazardous Materials* 75, 181–194.

Mileti, D.S. and Sorensen, J.H. (1987) Natural hazards and precautionary behavior. In N.D Weinstein, ed., *Taking Care: Understanding and Encouraging Self-Protective Behavior*. Cambridge University Press: Cambridge, 189–207.

Mileti, D.S. and Sorensen, J.H. (1990) *Communication of Emergency Public Warnings*. Oak Ridge National Laboratory: Oak Ridge, TN.

Miller, B. (2018) Climate change could leave Californians with "weather whiplash." CNN, http://www.cnn.com/2018/04/23/us/climate-change -california-whiplash-wxc/index.html.

Miller, D.S. and Rivera, J.D. (2011) Tragedy has brought us together: Responding to new and emerging regional catastrophes. In D.S. Miller and J.D. Rivera, eds., *Comparative Emergency Management: Examining Global and Regional Responses Disasters*. CRC Press: Boca Raton, FL, xxix–xliii.

Mitchell, B.C. and Chakraborty, J. (2015) Landscapes of thermal inequity: Disproportionate exposure to urban heat in the three largest US cities. *Environmental Research Letters* 10(11), http://iopscience.iop.org/article/10.1088 /1748–9326/10/11/115005/meta.

Moench, M., Tyler, S., and Lage, J., eds. (2011) *Catalyzing Urban Climate Resilience: Applying Resilience Concepts to Planning Practice in the ACCCRN Program*. Institute for Social and Environmental Transition-International: Boulder, CO.

Mohai, P., Pellow, D., and Roberts, J.T. (2009) Environmental Justice. *Annual Review of Environment and Resources* 34, 405–430. doi: 10.1146/ annurev-environ-082508-094348.

Molotch, H. (1976) The city as a growth machine: Toward a political economy of place. *American Journal of Sociology* 82(2), 309–332, http://www.jstor.org/stable /2777096.

Monroe, I. (2016) Hurricane Katrina's struggling black gay community. Huffington Post, September 2, https://www.huffingtonpost.com/irene -monroe/hurricane-katrinas-strugg_b_8074408.html.

Monroe, R. (2022) Why Texas's power grid still hasn't been fixed. *New Yorker*, February 9.

Monte, L.M. (2021) Household pulse survey shows many don't trust COVID vaccine, worry about side effects. US Census Bureau, Washington, DC.

Montgomery, M.C. and Chakraborty, J. (2015) Assessing the environmental justice consequences of flood risk: A case study in Miami, Florida. *Environmental Research Letters* 10, 1–11.

Moore, S., Daniel, M., Linnan, L., Campbell, M., Benedict, S., and Meier, A. (2004) After Hurricane Floyd passed: Investigating the social determinants of disaster preparedness and recovery. *Family & Community Health* 27(3), 204–217.

Morgan, M.G., Fischhoff, B., Bostrom, A., and Atman, C.J. (2002) *Risk Communication: A Mental Models Approach*. Cambridge University Press: Cambridge.

Moss, P. and Falconer Al-Hindi, K., eds. (2008) *Feminisms in Geography: Rethinking Space, Place, and Knowledges*. Rowman & Littlefield: Lanham, MD.

Mueller, J. and Stewart, M.G. (2011a) Balancing the risks, benefits, and costs of homeland security. *Homeland Security Affairs* 7, 1–27.

Mueller, J. and Stewart, M.G. (2011b) *Terror, Security, and Money: Balancing the Risks, Benefits, and Costs of Homeland Security*. Oxford University Press: New York.

Mueller, J. and Stewart, M.G. (2012) The terrorism delusion: America's overwrought response to September 11. *International Security* 37, 81–110.

Muir-Wood, R. (2017) Billions in liabilities: Man-made earthquakes at Europe's biggest gas field. RMS, http://www.rms.com/blog/2017/01/26/billions-in-liabilities-man-made-earthquakes-at-europes-biggest-gas-field.

Mukherji, A., Ganapati, N.E., and Rahill, G. (2014) Expecting the unexpected: Field research in post-disaster settings. *Natural Hazards* 73(2), 805–828.

Multihazard Mitigation Council (2004) *Natural Hazard Mitigation Saves*. National Institute of Building Sciences: Washington, DC.

Multihazard Mitigation Council (2005) *Natural Hazard Mitigation Saves: An Independent Study to Assess the Future Savings from Mitigation Activities*, vol. 2: Study Documentation. National Institute of Building Sciences: Washington, DC.

Multihazard Mitigation Council (2019) *Natural Hazard Mitigation Saves: 2019 Report*. National Institute of Building Sciences: Washington, DC.

Muramatsu, N. and Akiyama, H. (2011) Japan: Super-aging society preparing for the future. *Gerontologist* 51(4), 425–432. doi: 10.1093/geront/gnr067.

Murphy, B.L. (2007) Locating social capital in resilient community-level emergency management. *Natural Hazards* 41, 297–315.

Nakagawa, Y. and Shaw, R. (2004) Social capital: A missing link to disaster recovery. *International Journal of Mass Emergencies and Disasters* 22(1), 5–34.

Nakahara, S. and Ichikawa, M. (2013) Mortality in the 2011 tsunami in Japan. *Journal of Epidemiology* 23(1), 70–73.

National Academies (2018) *Emergency Alert and Warning Systems: Current Knowledge and Future Research Directions*. National Academies Press: Washington, DC.

National Center for Disaster Preparedness (2010) *Impact on Children and Families of the Deepwater Horizon Oil Spill: Preliminary Findings of the Coaster Population Impact Study.* Columbia University: New York.

National Center for Disaster Preparedness (2013) *Children's Health and Disasters: Children's Health after the Oil Spill: A Four-State Study Findings from the Gulf Coast Population Impact Project.* Columbia University: New York.

National Center for Disaster Preparedness (2015) *The Hurricane Sandy Person Report: Disaster Exposure, Health Impacts, Economic Burden, and Social Well-*Being (The Sandy Child and Family Health Briefing Report Series). Columbia University: New York.

National Center on Family Homelessness (2014) *America's Youngest Outcasts: A Report Card on Child Homelessness.* American Institutes for Research: Waltham, MA.

National Coalition for the Homeless (2017) *Substance Abuse and Homelessness.* National Coalition for the Homeless: Washington, DC.

National Council on Disability (2006) *The Impact of Hurricanes Katrina and Rita on People with Disabilities: A Look Back and Remaining Challenges.* National Council on Disability: Washington, DC.

National Institute of Mental Health (2007) Ethical issues to consider in developing, evaluating, and conducting research post-disaster. National Institutes of Health: Bethesda, MD, http://www.nimh.nih.gov/funding/grant-writing-and-application-process/ethical-issues-to-consider-in-developing-evaluating-and-conducting-research-post-disaster.shtml.

National Institute of Standards and Technology (2015a) *Community Resilience Planning Guide for Buildings and Infrastructure Systems,* vol. 1 (NIST Special Publication 1190). NIST: US Department of Commerce.

National Institutes of Standards and Technology (2015b) *Community Resilience Planning Guide for Buildings and Infrastructure Systems,* vol. 2 (NIST Special Publication 1190). NIST: US Department of Commerce.

National Institute of Standards and Technology (2016) *Critical Assessment of Lifeline System Performance: Understanding Societal Needs in Disaster Recovery.* NIST: US Department of Commerce.

National Preparedness Leadership Initiative (n.d.) *Investing in Resilience, Investing in the Whole Community.* National Preparedness Leadership Initiative, Harvard Kennedy School, Harvard School of Public Health: Cambridge, MA.

National Research Council (1989) *Improving Risk Communication.* National Academies Press: Washington DC.

National Research Council (1996) *Understanding Risk: Informing Decisions in a Democratic Society.* National Academies Press: Washington, DC.

National Research Council (2006) *Facing Hazards and Disasters: Understanding Human Dimensions.* National Academies Press: Washington, DC.

National Research Council (2011) *Building Community Disaster Resilience through Public–Private Collaboration.* National Academies Press: Washington, DC.

National Research Council (2012) *Disaster Resilience: A National Imperative.*

Committee on Increasing National Resilience to Hazards and Disasters, Committee on Science, Engineering and Public Policy. National Academies Press: Washington, DC.

National Research Council (2013a) *Geotargeted Alerts and Warnings: Report of a Workshop on Current Knowledge and Research Gaps*. National Academies Press: Washington, DC.

National Research Council (2013b) *Public Response to Alerts and Warnings Using Social Media: Report of a Workshop on Current Knowledge and Research*. National Academies Press: Washington, DC.

NBC News (2008) Illegal immigrants opted to stay during Gustav. NBC News, September 2, http://www.nbcnews.com/id/26513677/ns/us_news-life/t/illegal-immigrants-opted-stay-during-gustav/#.WwhQhYoh2Uk.

NBC News (2017) Majority of northern California fire victims were senior citizens. NBC News, October 21, https://www.nbcbayarea.com/news/local/North-Bay-Fires-Victims-451678753.html.

Neal, D.M. and Phillips, B.D. (1990) Female-dominated local social movement organizations in disaster-threat situations. In G. West, G. and R.L. Blumberg, eds., *Women and Social Protest*. Oxford University Press: New York, 243–255.

Neria, Y., DiGrande, L., and Adams, B.G. (2011) Posttraumatic stress disorder following the September 11, 2001, terrorist attacks: A review of the literature among highly exposed populations. *American Psychologist* 66(6), 429–446.

Newman, E. and Kaloupek, D.G. (2004) The risks and benefits of participating in trauma-focused research studies. *Journal of Traumatic Stress* 17(5), 383–394.

Newsome, B.O. and Jarmon, J.A. (2016) *A Practical Introduction to Homeland Security and Emergency Management: From Home to Abroad*. CQ Press: Thousand Oaks, CA.

New York Times (2022) The ransom. *New York Times*, May 22.

New York Times Editorial Board (2013) Hurricane Sandy and New York's poor. *New York Times*, December 23.

Ngo, E.B. (2001) When disasters and age collide: Reviewing vulnerability of the elderly. *Natural Hazards Review* 2(2), 80–89.

Nigg, J.M., Riad, J.K., Wachtendorf, T., Tweedy, A., and Reshaur, L. (1998) Disaster resistant communities initiative: Evaluation of the pilot phase. Final Project Report #40, University of Delaware Disaster Research Center, Newark, DE.

Norgaard, K.M. (2006) "People want to protect themselves a little bit": Emotions, denial, and social movement nonparticipation. *Sociological Inquiry* 76(3), 372–396.

Norgaard, K.M. (2011) *Living in Denial: Climate Change, Emotions, and Everyday Life*. MIT Press: Cambridge, MA.

Norris, F.H. (2006) Disaster research methods: Past progress and future directions. *Journal of Traumatic Stress* 19(2), 173–184.

Norris, F.H., Friedman, M.J., and Watson, P.J. (2002) 60,000 disaster victims speak, part ii: Summary and implications of the disaster mental health research. *Psychiatry: Interpersonal and Biological Processes* 65(3), 240–260. doi: 10.1521/psyc.65.3.240.20169.

Norris, F.H., Friedman, M.J., Watson, P.J., Byrne, C.M., Diaz, E., and Kaniasty, K. (2002) 60,000 disaster victims speak, part i: An empirical review of the empirical literature, 1981–2001. *Psychiatry: Interpersonal and Biological Processes* 65(3), 207–239. doi: 10.1521/psyc.65.3.207.20173.

Norris, F.H., Galea, S., Friedman, M.J., and Watson, J., eds. (2006) *Methods for Disaster Mental Health Research*. Guilford Press: New York.

Norris, F.H., Stevens, S.P., Pfefferbaum, B., Wyche, K.F., and Pfefferbaum, R.L. (2008) Community resilience as a metaphor, theory, set of capacities, and strategy for disaster resilience. *American Journal of Community Psychology* 41, 127–150. doi: 10.1007/s10464–007–9156–6.

O'Brien, P. and Mileti, D.S. (1992) Citizen participation in emergency response following the Loma Prieta earthquake. *International Journal of Mass Emergencies and Disasters* 10, 71–89.

Office of Management and Budget (1992) *Circular No. A-94, Revised*. OMB: Washington, DC.

Oishi, S., Kimura, R., Hayashi, H., Tatsuki, S. et al. (2015) Psychological adaptation to the Great Hanshin-Awaji earthquake of 1995: 16 years later victims still report lower levels of subjective well-being. *Journal of Research in Personality* 55, 84–90.

Okuyama, Y. (2007) Economic modeling for disaster impact analysis: Past, present, and future. *Economic Systems Research* 19(2), 115–124.

Oliver, M. and Shapiro, T.M. (1995) *Black Wealth/White Wealth: A New Perspective on Racial Inequality*. Routledge: New York.

Oliver-Smith, A. (1996) Anthropological research on hazards and disasters. *Annual Review of Anthropology* 25, 303–328, http://www.jstor.org/stable/2155829.

Oliver-Smith, A. (2010) Haiti and the historical construction of disasters. *NACLA Report on the Americas* 43(4), 32–36. doi: 10.1080/10714839.2010.11725505.

Oliver-Smith, A. (2015a) Hazards and disaster research in contemporary anthropology. In J.D. Wright, ed., *International Encyclopedia of the Social and Behavioral Sciences*, 2nd edn. Elsevier: Amsterdam, 546–553.

Oliver-Smith, A. (2015b) Disaster risk reduction and climate change adaptation: The view from applied anthropology. *Human Organization* 72(4), 275–282.

Oliver-Smith, A. and Hoffman, S.M. (1999) *The Angry Earth*. University of Florida: Routledge: New York.

Olshansky, R.B. and Johnson, L.A. (2010) *Clear as Mud: Planning for the Rebuilding of New Orleans*. Routledge: New York.

Omi, M. and Winant, H. (1994) *Racial Formation in the United States: From the 1960s to the 1990s*, 2nd edn. Routledge: New York.

Orengo-Aguayo, R., Stewart, R.W., and de Arrellano, M.A. (2019) Disaster exposure and mental health among Puerto Rican youths after Hurricane Maria. *JAMA Network Open* 2(4). doi: 10.1001/jamanetworkopen.2019.2619.

Oreskes, N. and Conway, E.M. (2010) *Merchants of Doubt: How a Handful of Scientists Obscured the Truth on Issues from Tobacco Smoke to Climate Change.* Bloomsbury: New York.

Oreskes, N. and Conway. E.M. (2023) *The Big Myth: How American Business Taught Us to Loathe Government and Love the Free Market.* Bloomsbury: New York.

Organisation for Economic Co-Operation and Development (2013) *OECD Skills Outlook 2013: First Results from the Survey of Adult Skills.* OECD Publishing. doi: 10.1787/9789264204256-en.

Otani, J. (2010) *Older People in Natural Disasters: The Great Hanshin Earthquake of 1995.* Kyoto University Press/Trans Pacific Press: Kyoto/Victoria, Australia.

Palen, L., Anderson, J., Bica, M., Castillos, C., Crowley, J. et al. (2020) Crisis Informatics: Human-Centered Research on Tech & Crises: A Guided Bibliography Developed by Crisis Informatics Researchers. HAL, hal-02781763.

Palen, L. and Hughes, A. (2018) Social media in disaster communication. In H. Rodríguez, W. Donner, and J.E. Trainor, eds., *Handbook of Disaster Research*, 2nd edn. Springer: Cham, Switzerland, 497–518.

Palen, L. and Liu, S.B. (2007) Citizen communications in crisis: Anticipating a future of ICT-supported public participation. *Proceedings of the CHI Conference: Emergency Action.* ACM: New York, 727–736.

Palen, L., Vieweg, S., Liu, S.B., and Hughes, A. (2009) Crisis in a networked world: Features of computer-mediated communication in the April 16, 2007 Virginia Tech event. *Social Science Computing Review* 27, 467–480.

Palen, L., Vieweg, S., Sutton, J., Liu, S.B., and Hughes, A. (2007) Crisis informatics: Studying crisis in a networked world. Paper presented at the Third International Conference on E-Social Science, October 7–9, Ann Arbor, Michigan, http://citeseerx.ist.psu.edu/viewdoc/download?doi=10.1.1.113.5750&rep=rep1&type=pdf.

Pardee, J.W. (2012) Living through displacement: Housing insecurity among low-income evacuees. In L. Weber and L. Peek, eds., *Displaced: Life in the Katrina Diaspora.* University of Texas Press: Austin, 63–78.

Park, J., Cho, J. and Rose, A. (2011) Modeling a major source of economic resilience to disasters: recapturing lost production. *Natural Hazards* 58(1), 163–182.

Park, R.E. (1936) Human ecology. *American Journal of Sociology* 42, 1–15.

Parrott, W.G. (2017) Role of emotions in risk perception. In G. Emilien, R. Weitkunat, and F. Lüdicke, eds., *Consumer Perception of Product Risks and Benefits.* Springer: Cham, Switzerland, 221–232.

Paton, D. and Johnston, D., eds. (2006) *Disaster Resilience: An Integrated Approach.* Charles C. Thomas: Springfield, IL.

Patrick, K. (2017) Income security, National snapshot: Poverty among women and families, 2016. National Women's Law Center, https://nwlc.org/wp-content/uploads/2017/09/Poverty-Snapshot-Factsheet-2017.pdf.

Patt, A.G., Tadross, M., Nussbaumer, P., Asante, K., Metzger, M., Rafael, J., Goujon, A. et al. (2010) Estimating least-developed countries' vulnerability to climate-related extreme events over the next 50 years. *Proceedings of National Academy of Sciences* 107(4), 1333–1337. doi: 10.1073/pnas.0910253107.

Patt, A.G., Schroter, D., Klein, R.J.T., and de la Vega-Leinert, A.C., eds. (2010) *Assessing Vulnerability to Global Environmental Change*. Earthscan: London.

Patterson, O., Weil, F., and Patel, K. (2010) The role of community in disaster response: Conceptual models. *Population Research and Policy Review* 29(2), 127–141.

Patton, A., ed. (1994) *From Rooftop to River: Tulsa's Approach to Floodplain and Stormwater Management*. Department of Public Works: Tulsa, OK.

Peacock, W.G. (2003) Hurricane mitigation status and factors influencing mitigation status among Florida's single-family homeowners. *Natural Hazards Review* 4(3), 149–158.

Peacock, W.G. and Girard, C. (1997) Ethnic and racial inequalities in disaster damage and insurance settlements. In W.G. Peacock, B.H. Morrow, and H. Gladwin, eds., *Hurricane Andrew: Ethnicity, Gender and Sociology of Disasters*. Routledge: London, 171–190.

Peacock, W.G., Morrow, B.H., and Gladwin, H. (1997) *Hurricane Andrew: Ethnicity, Gender and the Sociology of Disasters*. Routledge: London.

Peake, L. and Sheppard, E. (2014) The emergence of radical/critical geography within North America. *ACME: An International E-Journal for Critical Geographies* 13(2), 305–327.

Peck, J. (2010) *Constructions of Neoliberal Reason*. Oxford University Press: Oxford.

Peck, J. and Tickell, A. (2002) Neoliberalizing space. *Antipode* 34(3), 380–404.

Peek, L. (2008) Children and disasters: Understanding vulnerability, developing capacities, and promoting resilience: An introduction. *Children, Youth, and Environments* 18(1), 1–29, http://www.jstor.org/stable/10.7721/chilyoutenvi.18.1.0001.

Peek, L. (2010) Age. In B.D. Phillips, D.S.K. Thomas, A. Fothergill, and L. Blinn-Pike, eds., *Social Vulnerability to Disasters*. CRC Press: Boca Raton, FL, 155–185.

Peek, L. (2012) They call it "Katrina fatigue": displaced families and discrimination in Colorado. In L. Weber and L. Peek, eds., *Displaced: Life in the Katrina Diaspora*. University of Texas Press: Austin, 31–46.

Peek, L. (2013) Age. In D.S.K. Thomas, B.D. Phillips, W.E. Lovekamp, and A. Fothergill, eds., *Social Vulnerability to Disasters*, 2nd edn. CRC Press: Boca Raton, FL, 167–198.

Peek, L. (2022) A new system for disaster research. *American Scientist* 110(4), 226–231.

Peek, L., Abramson, D.M., Cox, R.S., Fothergill, A., and Tobin, J. (2018) Children and disasters. In H. Rodriguez, W. Donner, and J.E. Trainor, eds., *Handbook of Disaster Research*. Springer: Cham, Switzerland, 241–262.

Peek, L., Champeau, H., Austin, J., Mathews, M., and Wu, H. (2020a) What methods do social scientists use to study disasters? An analysis of the Social

Science Extreme Events Research Network. *American Behavioral Scientist* 64(8), 1066–1094.

Peek, L. and Fothergill, A. (2009) Using focus groups: Lessons from studying daycare centers, 9/11, and Hurricane Katrina. *Qualitative Research* 9(1), 31–59.

Peek, L., Tobin, J., Adams, R.M., Wu, H., and Mathews, M.C. (2020b) A framework for convergence research in the hazards and disaster field: The natural hazards engineering research infrastructure CONVERGE facility. *Frontiers in Built Environment* 6, July 6.

Peek, L., Tobin, J., van de Lindt, J., and Andrews, A. (2021) Getting interdisciplinary teams into the field: Institutional review board pre-approval and multi-institution authorization agreements for rapid response disaster research. *Risk Analysis: An International Journal* 41(7), 1204–1212.

Pelling, M. (2003) *The Vulnerability of Cities: Natural Disasters and Social Resilience.* Routledge: New York.

Pelling, M. (2011) *Adaptation to Climate Change: From Resilience to Transformation.* Routledge: New York.

Pellow, D. (2000) Environmental inequality formation: Toward a theory of environmental justice. *American Behavioral Scientist* 43(4), 581–601.

Pellow, D. (2007) *Resisting Global Toxics: Transnational Movements for Environmental Justice.* MIT Press: Cambridge, MA.

Perrings, C. (1998) Resilience in the dynamics of economy-environment systems. *Environment and Resource Economics* 113(3–4), 503–520.

Perrings, C. (2006) Resilience and sustainable development. *Environmental and Development Economics* 11, 417–427. doi: 10.1017/S1355770X06003020.

Perrow, C. (1984) *Normal Accidents: Living with High-Risk Technologies.* Basic Books: New York.

Perrow, C. (2006) *The Next Catastrophe: Reducing our Vulnerabilities to Natural, Industrial, and Terrorist Disasters.* Princeton University Press: Princeton, NJ.

Perrow, C. (2011) Fukushima and the inevitability of accidents. *Bulletin of the Atomic Scientists* 67 (6), 44–52.

Perry, R.W. and Hirose, H. (1983) *Volcano Management in the United States and Japan.* JAI Press, Greenwich, CT.

Perry, R.W. and Lindell, M.K. (1991) The effects of ethnicity on evacuation. *International Journal of Mass Emergencies and Disasters* 9, 47–68.

Perry, R.W. and Lindell, M.K. (2007) *Emergency Planning.* John Wiley & Sons, Inc.: Hoboken, NJ.

Petrescu-Prahova, M. and Butts, C.T. (2005) Emergent coordination in the World Trade Center disaster. Paper No. 36, Institute for Mathematical Behavioral Sciences, University of California, Irvine, http://citeseerx.ist.psu.edu/viewdoc/summary?doi=10.1.1.59.8310.

Pfeffer, F.T., Danziger, S., and Schoeni, R.F. (2013) Wealth disparities before and after the Great Recession. *Annals of the American Academy of Political and Social Science* 650(1), 98–123.

Pfefferbaum, B., Reissman, D.B., Pfefferbaum, R.L., Klomp, R.W., and Gurwitch, R.H. (2007) Building resilience to mass trauma events. In L.S. Doll, S.E. Bonzo, J.A. Mercy, D.A. Sleet, and E.N. Haas, eds., *Handbook of Injury and Violence Prevention.* Springer: New York, 347–358.

Pfefferbaum, R.L., Pfefferbaum, B., and Van Horn, R.L. (2011) *Communities Advancing Resilience Toolkit (CART): The Cart Integrated System.* Terrorism and Disaster Center at the University of Oklahoma Health Sciences Center: Oklahoma City.

Pfefferbaum, R.L., Pfefferbaum, B., Van Horn, R.L., Klomp, R.W., Norris, F.H., and Reissman, D.B. (2013) The communities advancing resilience toolkit (CART): An intervention to build community resilience to disasters. *Journal of Public Health Management & Practice* 19(3), 250–258.

Pfefferbaum, R.L., Pfefferbaum, B., Zhao, Y.D., Van Horn, R.L., McCarter, G.S., and Leonard, M.B. (2016) Assessing community resilience: A CART survey application in an impoverished urban community. *Disaster Health* 3(2), 45–56.

Phelan, J.C., Link, B.G., and Tehranifar, P. (2015) Fundamental causes of health inequalities: Theory, evidence, and policy implications. *Journal of Health and Social Behavior* 51, 528–540.

Phillips, B.D. (1993) Cultural diversity in disasters: Sheltering, housing, and long term recovery. *International Journal of Mass Emergencies and Disasters* 11, 99–110.

Phillips, B.D. (1998) Sheltering and housing of low-income and minority groups in Santa Cruz county after the Loma Prieta earthquake. In J.M. Nigg, ed., *The Loma Prieta, California, Earthquake of October 17, 1989: Recovery, Mitigation, and Reconstitution* (US Geological Survey Professional Paper 1553-D), US Government Printing Office: Washington, DC, 17–28.

Phillips, B.D. (2009) *Disaster Recovery.* CRC Press: Boca Raton, FL.

Phillips, B.D. (2014) Qualitative disaster research. In P. Leavy, ed., *The Oxford Handbook of Qualitative Research.* Oxford University Press: Oxford. doi: 10.1093/oxfordhb/9780199811755.013.010.

Phillips, B.D. and Jenkins, P. (2013) Violence. In D.S.K. Thomas, B.D. Phillips, W.E. Lovekamp, and A. Fothergill, eds., *Social Vulnerability to Disasters*, 2nd edn. CRC Press: Boca Raton, FL, 311–340.

Phillips, B.D., Thomas, D.S.K., Fothergill, A. and Blinn-Pike, L., eds. (2010) *Social Vulnerability to Disasters.* CRC Press: Boca Raton, FL.

Philo, C. (2005) The geographies that wound. *Population, Space and Place* 11, 441–454.

Picou, J.S. (1996a) Compelled disclosure of scholarly research: Some comments on "high stakes litigation." *Law & Contemporary Problems* 59(3), 149–157.

Picou, J.S. (1996b) Sociology and compelled disclosure: Protecting respondent confidentiality. *Sociological Spectrum* 16(3), 209–237.

Picou, J.S. (1996c) Toxins in the environment, damage to the community:

Sociology and the toxic tort. In P. Jenkins and S. Kroll-Smith, eds., *Witnessing for Sociology: Sociologists in Court*. Greenwood Press: Westport, CT, 210–223.

Picou, J.S., Marshall, B.K., and Gill, D.A. (2004) Disaster, litigation, and the corrosive community. *Social Forces* 82(4), 1493–1522. doi: 10.1353/sof.2004.0091.

Pielke, R.A. (1999) Who decides? Forecasts and responsibility in the 1997 Red River flood. *Applied Behavior Science Review* 7(2), 83–101.

Pielke, R.A., Gratz, J., Landsea, C.W., Collins, D., Saunders, M.A., and Musulin, R. (2008) Normalized hurricane damage in the United States: 1900–2005. *Natural Hazards Review* 9(1), 29–42.

Pielke, R.A. and Landsea, C.W. (1998) Normalized hurricane damages in the United States: 1925–1995. *Weather and Forecasting* 13(3), 621–631.

Pincha, C. (2008) *Indian Ocean Tsunami through the Gender Lens: Insights from Tamil Nadu, India*. Earthworm Books: Mumbai.

Plodinec, J.M. (2009) *Definitions of Resilience: An Analysis*. Community and Regional Resilience Institute, Oak Ridge National Laboratory: Oak Ridge, TN.

Pollard, M.S. and Davis, L.M. (2022) Decline in trust in the Centers for Disease Control and Prevention during the COVID-19 pandemic. *Rand Health Quarterly* 9(3), article 23. PMID35837520.

Polsky, C., Neff, R., and Yarnal, B. (2007) Building global change vulnerability assessments: The vulnerability scoping diagram. *Global Environmental Change* 17, 472–485.

Population Reference Bureau (2015) *2015 World Population Data Sheet*. PRB: Washington, DC.

Portes, A. (1998) Social capital: Its origins and applications in modern sociology. *Annual Review of Sociology* 24, 1–24. doi: 10.1146/annurev.soc.24.1.1.

Poursanidis, D. and Chrysoulakis, N. (2017) Remote sensing, natural hazards and the contribution of ESA Sentinels missions. *Remote Sensing Applications: Society and Environment* 6, 25–38. doi: 10.1016/j.rsase.2017.02.001.

Price, G.N. (2013) Hurricane Katrina as an experiment in housing mobility and neighborhood effects: Were the relocated poor black evacuees better-off? *Review of Black Political Economy* 40, 121–143.

Prince, S.H. (1920) *Catastrophe and Social Change: Based upon a Sociological Study of the Halifax Disaster*. Columbia University Press: New York.

Proctor, B.D., Semega, J.L., and Kollar, M.A. (2016) *Income and Poverty in the United States: 2015: Current Population Reports*. United States Census Bureau: Washington, DC.

Proctor, R.N. and Schiebinger, L., eds. (2008) *Agnotology: The Making and Unmaking of Ignorance*. Stanford University Press: Palo Alto, CA.

Pulido, L. (2000) Rethinking environmental racism: White privilege and urban development in southern California. *Annals of the Association of American Geographers* 90(1), 12–40.

Pulido, L. (2016) Flint, environmental racism, and racial capitalism. *Capitalism Nature Socialism* 27(3), 1–16. doi: 10.1080/10455752.2016.1213013.

Pulido, L. (2017) Geographies of race and ethnicity II: Environmental racism, racial capitalism and state-sanctioned violence. *Progress in Human Geography* 41(4), 1–10. doi: 10.1177/0309132516646495.

Purdum, J.C. (2019) Hazardous or vulnerable? Prisoners and emergency planning in the US. In F.I. Rivera, ed., *Emerging Voices in Natural Hazards Research*. Butterworth Heinemann: Oxford, 179–209.

Purdum, J.C. and Meyer, M. (2020) Prison labor through the life cycle of disasters. *Risk, Hazards, and Crises in Public Policy* 11(3), 296–319.

Purdum., J.C., Dominick, A., and Dixon, B. (2022) Extreme temperatures and COVID-19 in Texas prisons. Report 22-01R. Hazards Reduction and Recovery Center, College Station, Texas. doi: 10.13140/RG.2.2.25080.11522.

Putnam, R.D. (1995) Bowling alone: America's declining social capital. *Journal of Democracy* 6(1), 65–78.

Putnam, R.D. (2000) *Bowling Alone: The Collapse and Revival of American Community*. Simon & Schuster: New York.

Putnam, R.D. (2001) Social capital: Measurement and consequences. *Isuma: Canadian Journal of Policy Research* 2, 41–51.

Quarantelli, E.L. (1954) The nature and conditions of panic. *American Journal of Sociology* 60, 267–275.

Quarantelli, E.L. (1974) Weaknesses in disaster planning. *Proceedings of the Human Factors and Ergonomics Society Annual Meeting* 18(3), 321–322.

Quarantelli, E.L. (1977) Panic behavior: Some empirical observations. In D.J. Conway, ed., *Human Response to Tall Buildings*. Dowden, Hutchinson, and Ross, Inc.: Stroudsburg, PA, 336–350.

Quarantelli, E.L. (1987) Disaster studies: An analysis of the social historical factors affecting the development of research in the area. *International Journal of Mass Emergencies and Disasters* 5, 285–310.

Quarantelli, E.L. (1988) The NORC research on the Arkansas tornado: A fountainhead study. *International Journal of Mass Emergencies and Disasters* 6, 283–310.

Quarantelli, E.L. (1995) Emergent behaviors and groups in the crisis time of disasters. Preliminary Paper #226, Disaster Research Center, University of Delaware, Newark.

Quarantelli, E.L. (1996) The future is not the past repeated: Projecting disasters of the 21st century from present trends. Preliminary Paper #229, Disaster Research Center, University of Delaware, Newark.

Quarantelli, E.L. (1998) *What Is a Disaster? Perspectives on the Question*. Routledge: London.

Quarantelli, E.L. (2001a) Another selective look at future social crises: Some aspects of which we can already see in the present. *Journal of Contingencies and Crisis Management* 9(4), 233–237.

Quarantelli, E.L. (2001b) Sociology of panic. In N.J. Smelser and P.B. Baltes, eds. *International Encyclopedia of the Social and Behavioral Sciences*. Pergamon Press: Oxford, 11020–11023.

Quarantelli, E.L. and Dynes, R.R. (1970) Property norms and looting: Their patterns in community crises. *Phylon* 31, 168–182.

Quarantelli, E.L. and Dynes, R.R. (1972) When disaster strikes (it isn't much like what you've heard and read about). *Psychology Today* 5, 66–70.

Quarantelli, E.L., Lagadec, P., and Boin, R.A. (2007) A heuristic approach to future disasters and crisis: New, old, and in-between types. In H. Rodríguez, E.L. Quarantelli, and R.R. Dynes, eds., *Handbook of Disaster Research*. Springer: New York, 16–41.

Quarantelli, E.L., Taylor, V.A., and Tierney, K. (1977) Delivery of emergency medical services in disasters. Preliminary Paper #46, Disaster Research Center, University of Delaware, Newark.

Quarantelli, E.L., Wenger, D., Mikami, S., and Hiroi, O. (1993) The reporting of news in disaster: A comparative study of Japanese and American communities. Historical and Comparative Series #8. Disaster Research Center, University of Delaware, Newark.

Radeloff, V.C., Helmers, D.P., Kramer, H.A., Mockrin, M.H., Alexandre, P.M., Bar-Massada, A., Butsic, V. et al. (2018) Rapid growth of the US wildland–urban interface raises wildfire risk. *Proceedings of the National Academy of Sciences USA* 115(13), 3314–3319.

Raker, E.J. (2022) Climate-related disasters and children's health: Evidence from Hurricane Harvey. *Socius* 8, https://doi.org/10.1177/23780231221135971.

Ramos, J. (2024) California FAIR plan warns major disaster could wipe out insurer of last resort. CBS News, March 25.

Rayner, S. (2012) Uncomfortable knowledge: The social construction of ignorance in science and environmental policy discourses. *Economy and Society* 41(1), 107–125. doi: 10.1080/03085147.2011.637335.

Red Cross (2012) *Understanding Community Resilience and Program Factors That Strengthen Them: A Comprehensive Study of Red Cross Red Crescent Societies Tsunami Operation*. International Federation of Red Cross and Red Crescent Societies: Geneva, http://www.ifrc.org/PageFiles/96984/Final_Synthesis_Characteristics _Lessons_Tsunami.pdf.

Reid, J. (2013) Interrogating the neoliberal biopolitics of the sustainable development-resilience nexus. *International Political Sociology* 7, 353–367.

Reininger, B.M., Rahbar, M.H., Lee, M. et al. (2013) Social capital and disaster preparedness among low income Mexican Americans in a disaster prone area. *Social Science & Medicine* 83, 50–60.

Renschler, C.S., Frazier, A.E., Arendt, L.A., Cimellaro, G.P., Reinhorn, A.M. and Bruneau, M. (2010) Developing the "peoples" resilience framework for defining and measuring disaster resilience at the community scale. *Proceedings of the 9th US National and 10th Canadian Conference on Earthquake Engineering, July 25–29, Toronto*. Earthquake Engineering Research Institute: Oakland, CA, 1152–1161.

Resilience Measurement Evidence and Learning Community of Practice

(2016) *Analysis of Resilience Measurement Frameworks and Approaches*. Overseas Development Institute: London.

Richards, E.G. (2015) Finding fault: Induced earthquake liability and regulation. *Field Report: Columbia Journal of Environmental Law*, April 1, https://www.cailaw .org/media/files/IEL/Publications/2015/earthquakes-shakeup-vol9no3.pdf.

Risk to Resilience Study Team (2009) *Catalyzing Climate and Disaster Resilience: Processes for Identifying Tangible and Economically Robust Strategies*. Risk to Resilience Study: Kathmandu, Nepal.

Ritchie, L.A. (2004) *Voices of Cordova: Social Capital in the Wake of the Exxon Valdez Oil Spill*. Doctoral dissertation, Mississippi State University, Department of Sociology, Anthropology, and Social Work, Starkville.

Ritchie, L.A. (2012) Individual stress, collective trauma, and social capital in the wake of the Exxon Valdez oil spill. *Sociological Inquiry* 82(2), 187–211.

Ritchie, L.A. and Gill, D.A. (2007) Social capital theory as an integrating theoretical framework in technological disaster research. *Sociological Spectrum* 27(1), 103–129. doi: 10.1080/02732170601001037.

Ritchie, L.A. and Gill, D.A. (2011). The role of community capitals in disaster recovery. Paper presented at the PERI Symposium "Community Recovery from Disaster," http://www.riskinstitute.org/peri/content/view/1118/5.

Ritchie, L.A., Gill, D.A., and Farnham, C. (2013) Recreancy revisited: Beliefs about institutional failure following the Exxon Valdez oil spill. *Society and Natural Resources: An International Journal* 26, 655–671. doi: 10.1080/08941920.2012.690066.

Ritchie, L.A., Gill, D.A., and Hamilton, K. (2022) Winter storm Uri: Resource loss and psychosocial outcomes of critical infrastructure failure in Texas. *Journal of Critical Infrastructure Policy* 3(1), 83–103.

Ritchie, L.A., Gill, D.A., and Long, M.A. (2018) Mitigating litigating: An examination of psychosocial impacts of compensation processes associated with the 2010 BP Deepwater Horizon Oil Spill. *Risk Analysis*. doi: 10.1111/risa.12969.

Ritchie, L.A. and Tierney, K. (2011) Temporary housing planning and early implementation in the 12 January 2010 Haiti earthquake. *Earthquake Spectra* 27(S1), S487–S507.

Ritchie, L.A., Tierney, K., and Gilbert, B. (2010) Disaster preparedness among community-based organizations in the city and county of San Francisco: Serving the most vulnerable. In D. Miller and D.J. Rivera, eds., *Community Disaster Recovery and Resiliency: Exploring Global Opportunities and Challenges*. CRC Press: Boca Raton, FL, 251–280.

Rivera, F.I. (2019) *Emerging Voices in Natural Hazards Research*. Butterworth-Heinemann: Cambridge, MA.

Rivera, J.D., ed. (2022) *Disaster and Emergency Management Methods: Social Science Approaches in Application*. Routledge: New York.

Robbins, P. (2012) *Political Ecology*. Routledge: New York.

Roberts, K.H. (1989) New challenges in organizational research: High-reliability organizations. *Industrial Crisis Quarterly* 3, 111–125.

Roberts, K.H. (1990) Some characteristics of high reliability organizations. *Organization Science* 2, 160–176.

Roberts, K.H. (1993) Cultural characteristics of reliability enhancing organizations. *Journal of Managerial Issues* 5(2), 165–181.

Roberts, K.H. and Bea, R.G. (2001) Must accidents happen? Lessons from high reliability organizations. *Academy of Management Perspectives* 15, 70–78.

Roberts, P.S. (2016) *Disasters and the American State: How Politicians, Bureaucrats, and the Public Prepare for the Unexpected*. Cambridge University Press: New York.

Roberts, P.S., Ward, R., and Wamsley, G. (2012) The evolving federal role in emergency management: Policies and processes. In C.B. Rubin, ed., *Emergency Management: The American Experience, 1900–2010*, 2nd edn. CRC Press: Boca Raton, FL, 247–276.

Roberts, P.S., Ward, R., and Wamsley, G. (2014) The evolution of emergency management in America: From a troubling past to an uncertain future. In A. Farazmand, ed., *Crisis and Emergency Management: Theory and Practice*, 2nd edn. CRC Press: Boca Raton, FL, 167–187.

Robine, J.A. (2017) When climate change encounters the revolution in adult longevity. *Aging Clinical and Experimental Research* 29(6), 1073–1074.

Robine, J.M., Cheung, S.L., Le Roy, S., Van Oyen, H., and Herrmann, F.R. (2007) *Report on Excess Mortality in Europe during Summer 2003* (2003 Heat Wave Project). Inserm: Paris.

Rodin, J. (2014) *The Resilience Dividend: Being Strong in a World Where Things Go Wrong*. Rockefeller Foundation: New York.

Rose, A.Z. (1995) Input–output economics and computable general equilibrium models. *Structural Change and Economic Dynamics* 6(3), 295–304.

Rose, A.Z. (2007) Economic resilience to natural and man-made disasters: Multidisciplinary origins and contextual dimensions. *Environmental Hazards* 7(4), 383–398.

Rose, A.Z. (2009) *Economic Resilience to Disasters*. Community and Regional Resilience Institute, Oak Ridge National Laboratory: Oak Ridge, TN.

Rose, A.Z. and Krausmann, E. (2013) An economic framework for the development of a resilience index for business recovery. *International Journal of Disaster Risk Reduction* 5, 73–83. doi: 10.1016/j.ijdrr.2013.08.003.

Rose, A.Z. and Liao, S. (2005) Modeling regional economic resilience to disasters: A computable general equilibrium analysis of water service disruptions. *Journal of Regional Science* 45(1), 75–112.

Rose, A.Z., Oladosu, G., Lee, B., and Asay, G.B. (2009) The economic impacts of the September 11 terrorist attacks: A computable general equilibrium analysis. *Peace Economics, Peace Science and Public Policy* 15(2), https://doi.org/10.2202/1554-8597.1161.

Rose, G. (1993) *Feminism and Geography: The Limits of Geographical Knowledge*. Polity: Cambridge.

Rose-Redwood, R.S. (2006) Governmentality, geography, and the geo-coded world. *Progress in Human Geography* 30(4), 469–486.

Rosenstein, D.L. (2004) Decision-making capacity and disaster research. *Journal of Traumatic Stress* 17(5), 373–381.

Ross, A.D. (2014) *Local Disaster Resilience: Administrative and Political Perspectives*. Routledge: New York.

Rossi, P.J., Wright, J.D., and Weber-Burdin, E. (1982) *Natural Hazards and Public Choice: The State and Local Politics of Hazard Mitigation*. Academic Press: Cambridge.

Rubin, C.B. (2012) An introduction to 110 years of disaster response and emergency management. In C.B. Rubin, ed., *Emergency Management: The American Experience, 1900–2010*, 2nd edn. CRC Press: Boca Raton, FL, 1–12.

Rudel, T.K., Timmons, R.J., and Carmin, J. (2011) Political economy of the environment. *Annual Review of Sociology* 37, 221–238. doi: 10.1146/annurev.soc.012809.102639.

Rugh, J.S., Albright, L., and Massey, D.S. (2015) Race, space, and cumulative disadvantage: A case study of the subprime lending collapse. *Social Problems* 62(2), 186–218.

Rutter, M. (1987) Psychosocial resilience and protective mechanisms. *American Journal of Orthpsychiatry* 57(3), 316–331. doi: 10.1111/j.1939–0025.1987.tb03541.x.

Sagan, S. D. (1993) *The Limits of Safety: Organizations, Accidents, and Nuclear Weapons*. Princeton, NJ: Princeton University Press.

Salcedo, A., Lazo, L., and Powell, L. (2023) Miles-long trains are blocking first responders when every minute counts. *Washington Post*, May 25.

Saltman, K.J. (2024) *The Disaster of Resilience: Education, Digital Privatization, and Profiteering*. Bloomsbury: London.

Samuelson, W. and Zeckhauser, R.J. (1988) Status quo bias in decision making. *Journal of Risk and Uncertainty* 1, 7–59.

Sandman, P.M. (2012) *Responding to Community Outrage: Strategies for Effective Risk Communication*. American Industrial Hygiene Association, http://www.psandman.com/media/RespondingtoCommunityOutrage.pdf.

Santos-Hernández, J. and Morrow, B.H. (2013) Language and literacy. In B. Phillips, D.S.K. Thomas, A. Fothergill, and L. Blinn-Pike, eds., *Social Vulnerability to Disasters*, 2nd edn. CRC Press: Boca Raton, FL.

Sarnoff, N. (2017) Apartment rents rising in Harvey's wake. *Houston Chronicle*, October 5.

Sassen, S. (2012) *Cities in the World Economy*, 4th edn. Pine Forge Press: Thousand Oaks, CA.

Sassen, S. (2014) *Expulsions: Brutality and Complexity in the Global Economy*. Harvard University Press: Cambridge, MA.

Sassen, S. (2015) At the systemic edge. *Cultural Dynamics* 27(1), 173–181.

Scanlon, J. (1997) Human behaviour in disaster: The relevance of gender. *Australian Journal of Emergency Management* 11, 2–7.

Schipper, E.L.F. and Langston, L. (2015) A comparative overview of resilience measurement frameworks. Working Paper 422, Overseas Development Institute, London.

Schnaiberg, A. (1980) *The Environment: From Surplus to Scarcity*. Oxford University Press: New York.

Schnaiberg, A. and Gould, K.A. (1994) *Environment and Society: The Enduring Conflict*. St. Martin's Press: New York.

Schrank, H.L., Marshall, M.I., Hall-Phillips, A., Wiatt, R.F., and Jones, N.E. (2013) Small-business demise and recovery after Katrina: Rate of survival and demise. *Natural Hazards* 65, 2353–2374.

Schroeder, A., Wamsley, G.L., and Ward, R. (2001) The evolution of emergency management in America: From a painful past to a promising but uncertain future. In A. Farazmand, ed., *Handbook of Crisis and Emergency Management*. CRC Press: Boca Raton, FL, 357–418.

Schulman, P.R. (1993) The negotiated order of organizational reliability. *Administration and Society* 25, 353–372.

Schweinberger, M., Petrescu-Prahova, M., and Vu, D.Q. (2014) Disaster response on September 11, 2001 through the lens of statistical network analysis. *Social Networks* 37, 42–55.

Semple, K. (2016) When the kitchen is also a bedroom: Overcrowding worsens in New York. *New York Times*, February 29.

Sharifi, A. (2016) A critical review of selected tools for assessing community resilience. *Ecological Indicators* 69, 629–647. doi: 10.1016/j.ecolind.2016.05.023.

Sheffi, Y. (2005) *The Resilient Enterprise: Overcoming Vulnerability for Competitive Advantage*. MIT Press: Cambridge, MA.

Sheffi, Y. (2017) *The Power of Resilience: How the Best Companies Manage the Unexpected*. MIT Press: Cambridge, MA.

Sherwin, B. (2019) After the storm: The importance of acknowledging environmental justice in sustainable development and disaster preparedness. *Duke Environmental Law & Policy Journal* 29, 273–300.

Silver, R.C., Holman, E.A., McIntosh, D.N., Poulin, N., and Gil-Rivas, V. (2002) Nationwide longitudinal study of psychological responses to September 11. *Journal of the American Medical Association* 288(10), 1235–1244.

Shaw, R. and Sharma, A. (2011) *Climate and Disaster Resilience in Cities*. Emerald Group: Bingley, UK.

Slovic, P. (1999) Trust, emotion, sex, politics, and science: Surveying the risk-assessment battlefield. *Risk Analysis* 19(4), 689–701.

Slovic, P. (2010) *The Feeling of Risk: New Perspectives on Risk Perception*. Earthscan: London.

Slovic, P., Finucane, M.L., Peters, E., and MacGregor, D.G. (2004) Risk as analysis and risk as feelings: Some thoughts about affect, reason, risk, and rationality. *Risk Analysis* 24(2), 311–322.

Slovic, P., Finucane, M.L., Peters, E., and MacGregor, D.G. (2007) The affect heuristic. *European Journal of Operational Research* 177, 1333–1352.

Slovic, P., Fischhoff, B., and Lichtenstein, S. (1978) Judged frequency of lethal events. *Journal of Experimental Psychology: Human Learning and Memory* 4(6), 551.

Slovic, P., Fischhoff, B., and Lichtenstein, S. (1979) Rating the risks. *Environment* 21(3), 14–39.

Slovic, P., Fischhoff, B., and Lichtenstein, S. (1981) Facts and fears: Societal perception of risk. In K.B. Monroe, ed., *NA: Advances in Consumer Research*, vol. 8. Association for Consumer Research: Ann Arbor, MI, 497–502.

Smelser, N.J. (1962) *Theory of Collective Behavior*. Free Press: New York.

Smith, G. and Wenger, D. (2007) Sustainable disaster recovery: Operationalizing an existing agenda. In H. Rodríguez, E.L. Quarantelli, and R.R. Dynes, eds., *Handbook of Disaster Research*. Springer: New York, 234–257.

Soden, R. and Palen, L. (2014) From crowdsourced mapping to community mapping: The post-earthquake work of OpenStreetMap Haiti. In C. Rossitto, L. Ciofi, D. Martin, and B. Conein, eds. *COOP 2014: Proceedings of the 11th International Conference on the Design of Cooperative Systems, 27–30 May 2014, Nice (France)*, 311–326.

Soja, E.W. (1989) *Postmodern Geographies: The Reassertion of Space in Critical Social Theory*. Verso: New York.

Soja, E.W. (2000) *Postmetropolis: Critical Studies of Cities and Regions*. Blackwell: Malden, MA.

Soja, E.W. (2009) The city and spatial justice. Paper prepared for presentation at the Spatial Justice Conference, Nanterre, Paris, France, March 12–14.

Solari, C.D. and Mare, R.D. (2012) Housing crowding effects on children's wellbeing. *Social Science Research* 41(2), 464–476.

Solnit, R. (2009) *A Paradise Built in Hell: The Extraordinary Communities That Arise in Disaster*. Viking: New York.

Somers, M.R. (2008) *Genealogies of Citizenship: Markets, Statelessness, and the Right to Have Rights*. Cambridge University Press: Cambridge.

Somers, S. (2009) Measuring resilience potential: An adaptive strategy for organizational crisis planning. *Journal of Contingencies and Crisis Management* 17(1), 12–23.

Sosa Pascual, O., Wiscovich, J., Train, A.B., Hernandez, A.R., and Moriarty, D. (2023) More people are dying in Puerto Rico as its health-care system crumbles. *Washington Post*, November 28.

Spiro, E.S., Acton, R.M., and Butts, C.T. (2013) Extended structures of mediation: Re-examining brokerage in dynamic networks. *Social Networks* 35, 130–143. doi: 10.1016/j.socnet.2013.02.001.

Staeheli, L.A., Kofman, E., and Peake, L.J., eds. (2004) *Mapping Women, Making Politics: Feminist Perspectives on Political Geography*. Routledge: New York.

Stallings, R.A. (1995) *Promoting Risk: Constructing the Earthquake Threat*. Aldine de Gruyter: Hawthorne, NY.

Stallings, R.A. (1997) Methods of disaster research: Unique or not? *International Journal of Mass Emergencies and Disasters* 15(1), 7–19.

Stallings, R.A., ed. (2002) *Methods of Disaster Research*. International Research Committee on Disasters: Newark, DE.

Stallings, R.A. (2007) Methodological issues. In H. Rodríguez, E.L. Quarantelli, and R.R. Dynes, eds., *Handbook of Disaster Research*. Springer: New York, 55–82.

Stallings, R.A. and Quarantelli, E.L. (1985) Emergent citizen groups and emergency management. *Public Administration Review* 45, 93–100.

Starbird, K., Spiro, E.S., Edwards, I., Zhou, K., Maddock, J., and Narasimhan, S. (2016) Could this be true? I think so! Expressed uncertainty in online rumoring. In *Proceedings of the 2016 CHI Conference on Human Factors in Computing Systems*. ACM: New York, 360–371.

Stehling-Ariza, T., Park, Y.S., Sury, J.J., and Abramson, D. (2012) Measuring the impact of Hurricane Katrina on access to a personal healthcare provider: The use of the National Survey of Children's Health for an external comparison group. *Maternal and Child Health Journal* 16(S1), S170–S177.

Stellman, J.M., Smith, R.P., Katz, C.L, Sharma, V., Charney, D.S., Herbert, R., Moline, J. et al. (2008) Enduring mental health morbidity and social function impairment in World Trade Center rescue, recovery, and cleanup workers: The psychological dimension of an environmental health disaster. *Environmental Health Perspectives* 116(9), 1248–1253.

Stephenson, A., Vargo, J., and Seville, E. (2010) Measuring and comparing organisational resilience in Auckland. *Australian Journal of Emergency Management* 25(2), 27–32.

Stevenson, J.R., Vargo, J., Ivory, V., Bowie, C., and Wilkinson, S. (2015) *Resilience Benchmarking and Monitoring Review*. Ministry of Business, Innovation, and Employment: Wellington, NZ.

Stocking, S. and Holstein, L. (2009) Manufacturing doubt: Journalists' roles and the construction of ignorance in a scientific controversy. *Public Understanding of Science* 18, 23–42.

Stough, L.M. and Kelman, I. (2018) People with disabilities and disasters. In H. Rodríguez, W. Donner, and J.E. Trainor, eds., *Handbook of Disaster Research*, 2nd edn. Springer: Cham, Switzerland, 225–242.

Stryckman, B., Grace, T.L., Schwarz, P., and Marcozzi, D. (2015) An economic analysis and approach for health care preparedness in a substate region. *Disaster Medicine and Public Health Preparedness* 9(4), 344–348. doi: 10.1017/dmp.2015.37.

Subcommittee on Disaster Reduction (2005) *Grand Challenges for Disaster Reduction*. Office of Science and Technology Policy: Washington, DC.

Substance Abuse and Mental Health Services Administration (2016) *Disaster Technical Assistance Center Supplemental Research Bulletin: Challenges and Considerations in Disaster Research*, www.samhsa.gov/sites/default/files/dtac / supplemental-research-bulletin-jan-2016.pdf.

Sumagasy, L. (2024) 350,000 Californians are now on the FAIR plan, the last resort for fire insurance: Now what? CalMatters, January 23.

Sun, L., Deng, Y., and Qi, W. (2018) Two impact pathways from religious belief to public disaster response: Findings from a literature review. *International Journal of Disaster Risk Reduction* 27, 588–595.

Sun, S. (2023) National snapshot: Poverty among women and families. National Women's Health Center, Washington, DC, https://nwlc.org/wp-content /uploads/2023/02/2023_nwlc_PovertySnapshot-converted.pdf.

Superu (2015) Family resilience. *In Focus*, August, 14, https://thehub.sia.govt.nz /resources/in-focus-family-resilience.

Susman, P., O'Keefe, P., and Wisner, B. (1983) Global disasters: A radical interpretation. In K. Hewitt, ed., *Interpretations of Calamity: From the Viewpoint of Human Ecology*. Allen & Unwin: Boston, MA, 263–283.

Sutcliffe, K.M. and Vogus, T.J. (2003) Organizing for resilience. In K. Cameron, J.E. Cutton, and R.E. Quinn, eds., *Positive Organizational Scholarship*. Berrett-Koehler Publishers: San Francisco, CA, 94–110.

Sutton, J. (2010) Twittering Tennessee: Distributed networks and collaboration following a technological disaster. In *Proceedings of the 7th International ISCRAM Conference*. Information Systems for Crisis Response and Management: Brussels, http://citeseerx.ist.psu.edu/viewdoc/download?doi=10.1.1.701.9623& rep=rep1&type=pdf.

Sutton, J. (2012) When online is off: Public communications following the February 2011 Christchurch, NZ earthquake. In L. Rothkrants, J. Ristvej, and Z. Franco, eds., *Proceedings of the 9th International ISCRAM Conference, April, Vancouver, Canada*, http://www.iscram.org/legacy/ISCRAM2012/proceedings /ISCRAM2012_proceedings.pdf

Sutton, J., Gibson, C.B., Phillips, N.E., Spiro, E.S., League, C., Johnson, B., Fitzhugh, S.M. et al. (2015) A cross-hazard analysis of terse message retransmission on Twitter. *Proceedings of the National Academy of Sciences* 112(48), 14793–14798. doi: 10.1073/pnas.1508916112.

Sutton, J., Gibson, C.B., Spiro, E.S., League, C., Fitzhugh, S.M., and Butts, C.T. (2015) What it takes to get passed on: Message content, style, and structure as predictors of retransmission in the Boston marathon bombing response. *PLoS ONE* 10(8), 1–19. doi: 10.1371/journal.pone.0134452.

Sutton, J., League, C., Sellnow, T. and Sellnow, D. (2015) Emergency public health messaging in a disaster event: Content and style factors for terse messages. *Health Communication* 30(2), 135–143.

Sutton, J., Palen, L., and Shklovski, I. (2008) Back-channels on the front-lines: Emerging use of social media in the 2007 Southern California wildfires. In F. Friedrich and B. Van De Walle, eds., *Proceedings of the 5th International ISCRAM Conference*. Academic Press: Washington, DC, 624–631, http://cmci.colorado .edu/~palen/Papers/iscram08/BackchannelsISCRAM08.pdf.

Sutton, J., Spiro, E.S., Butts, C.T., Fitzhugh, S.M., Johnson, B.A., and Greczek, M.

(2013) Tweeting the spill: Online informal communications, social networks, and conversational microstructures during the Deepwater Horizon oilspill. *International Journal of Information Systems for Crisis Response and Management* 5(1), 58–76.

Sutton, J., Spiro, E.S., Greczek, M., Johnson, B., Fitzhugh, S.M., and Butts, C.T. (2012) Connected communications: Network structures of official communications in disaster. In L. Rothkranz, J. Ristvej, and Z. Franco, eds., *Proceedings of the 9th International ISCRAM Conference, April, Vancouver, Canada*. ISCRAM: Vancouver, 1–10.

Sutton, J., Spiro, E.S., Johnson, B.A., Fitzhugh, S.M., Gibson, C.B., and Butts, C.T. (2014a) Terse message amplification in the Boston bombing response. In S.R. Hiltz, M.S. Pfaff, L. Plotnick, and P.C. Shih, eds., *Proceedings of the 11th International Conference on Information Systems for Crisis Response and Management, May 24*. Pennsylvania State University: University Park, 612–621.

Sutton, J., Spiro, E.S., Johnson, B.A., Fitzhugh, S.M., Gibson, C.B., and Butts, C.T. (2014b) Warning tweets: Serial transmission of warning messages during a disaster event. *Information, Communication, and Society* 17(6), 765–787.

Sutton, J. and Woods, C. (2016) Tsunami warning message interpretation and sense making: focus group insights. *Weather, Climate, and Society* 8, 389–398.

Swain, J. and French, S. (2008) *Disability on Equal Terms*. SAGE: Thousand Oaks, CA.

Swidler, A. (1986) Culture in action: Symbols and strategies. *American Sociological Review* 51(2), 273–286, http://www.jstor.org/stable/2095521.

Swiss Reinsurance (2014) *Mind the Risk: A Global Ranking of Cities under Threat from Natural Disasters*. Swiss Re: Zurich.

Sydnor, S., Niehm, L., Lee, Y., Marshall, M.I., and Schrank, H.L. (2017) Analysis of post-disaster damage and disruptive impacts on the operating status of small businesses after Hurricane Katrina. *Natural Hazards* 85(3), 1637–1663.

Sylves, R. (2015) *Disaster Policy and Politics*, 2nd edn. CQ Press: Thousand Oaks, CA.

Szasz, A. and Meuser, M. (1997) Environmental inequalities: Literature review and proposals for new directions in research and theory. *Current Sociology* 45(3), 99–120.

Sze, J. (2006) *Toxic Soup Redux: Why Environmental Racism and Environmental Justice Matter after Katrina*. Understanding Katrina: Social Science Research Council, http://understandingkatrina.ssrc.org/Sze.

Szentes, T. (1971) *The Political Economy of Underdevelopment*. Budapest: Akadémiai Kiadó.

Tang, Z., Brody, S.D., Quinn, C., and Chang, L. (2010) Moving from agenda to action: Evaluating local climate change action plans. *Journal of Environmental Planning and Management* 53(1), 41–62.

Tanne, J.H. (2021) Covid 19: US government committee hears how social media spreads misinformation. *British Medical Journal* 375. doi: 10.1136/bmj.n2834.

Tanner, T. and Rentschler, J. (2015) *Unlocking the "Triple Dividend" of Resilience: Why Investing in Disaster Risk Management Pays Off*. Overseas Development Institute/ World Bank: London/Washington, DC.

Tapia, A.H., Lalone, N., and Kim, H. (2014) Run amok: Group crowd participation in identifying the bomb and bomber from the Boston Marathon bombing. In S.R. Hiltz, M.S. Pfaff, L. Plotnick, and P.C. Shih, eds., *Proceedings of the 11th International ISCRAM Conference, May 24*. Pennsylvania State University: University Park, 265–274.

Tatsuki, S. (2013) Old age, disability, and the Tohoku-Oki earthquake. *Earthquake Spectra* 29, S403–S432.

Taylor, V.A. (1977) Good news about disasters. *Psychology Today*, October, 93–96.

Taylor, V.A., Ross, G.A., and Quarantelli, E.L. (1977) *Delivery of Mental Health Services in Disasters: The Xenia Tornado and Some Implications*. Disaster Research Center, University of Delaware: Newark.

Tchouakeu, M.N., Maitland, C., Tapia, A., and Kvasny, L. (2013) Humanitarian inter-organizational collaboration network: Investigating the impact of network structure and information and communication technology on organisation performance. *International Journal of Services Technology and Management* 19(1, 2, 3), 19–43.

Thaler, R. (2015) *Misbehaving: The Making of Behavioral Economics*. Norton: New York.

Thaler, R. and Sunstein, C. (2008) *Nudge: Improving Decisions about Health, Wealth, and Happiness*. Penguin Books: London.

Third National Climate Assessment (2014) *Climate Change Impacts in the United States*. US National Climate Assessment, US Global Change Research Program: Washington, DC.

Thomas, D.S.K., Phillips, B.D., Lovekamp, W.E., and Fothergill, A., eds. (2013) *Social Vulnerability to Disasters*, 2nd edn. CRC Press: Boca Raton, FL.

Thomas, W.I. and Thomas, D.S. (1928) *The Child in America: Behavior Problems and Programs*. Knopf: New York.

Tierney, K. (1994) Property damage and violence: A collective behavior analysis. In M. Baldassare, ed., *The Los Angeles Riots: Lessons for the Urban Future*. Westview Press: Boulder, CO, 149–173.

Tierney, K.J. (1999) Toward a critical sociology of risk. *Sociological Forum* 14, 215–242.

Tierney, K. (2007) From the margins to the mainstream? Disaster research at the crossroads. *Annual Review of Sociology* 33, 503–525.

Tierney, K. (2008) Hurricane Katrina: Catastrophic impacts and alarming lessons. In J.M. Quigley and A. Rosenthal, eds., *Risking House and Home: Disasters, Cities, Public Policy*. Institute of Governmental Studies Press: Berkeley, CA, 119–136.

Tierney, K. (2009) *Disaster Response: Research Findings and Their Implications for Resilience Measures* (CARRI Research Report 6). Natural Hazards Center, University of Colorado: Boulder.

Tierney, K. (2012) Critical disjunctures: Disaster research, social inequality, gender, and Hurricane Katrina. In E. David and E. Enarson, eds., *The Women of Katrina: How Gender, Race, and Class Matter in an American Disaster.* Vanderbilt University Press: Nashville, TN, 245–258.

Tierney, K. (2014) *The Social Roots of Risk: Producing Disasters, Promoting Resilience.* Stanford University Press: Palo Alto, CA.

Tierney, K. (2015) Resilience and the neoliberal project: Discourses, critiques, practices – and Katrina. *American Behavioral Scientist* 59(10), 1327–1342. doi: 10.1177/0002764215591187.

Tierney, K. (2018) Disaster as social problem and social construct. In A. Treviño, ed., *The Cambridge Handbook of Social Problems.* Cambridge University Press: Cambridge, 79–94.

Tierney, K. and Bruneau, M. (2007) Conceptualizing and measuring resilience: A key to disaster loss reduction. *TR News* 250, 14–17.

Tierney, K., Lindell, M.K., and Perry, R.W. (2001) *Facing the Unexpected: Disaster Preparedness and Response in the United States.* Joseph Henry Press: Washington, DC.

Tierney, K. and Oliver-Smith, A. (2012) Social dimensions of disaster recovery. *International Journal of Mass Emergencies and Disasters* 30, 122–146.

Tierney, K., Petak, W.J., and Hahn, H. (1988) *Disabled Persons and Earthquake Hazards.* Institute of Behavioral Science, Natural Hazards Center, University of Colorado: Boulder.

Tierney, K. and Taylor, V.A. (1977) EMS delivery in mass emergencies: Preliminary research findings. *Mass Emergencies* 2, 151–157.

Tobin, K. and Freeman, P. (2004) Emergency preparedness: A manual for homeless service providers. Center for Social Policy Publications 6. University of Massachusetts: Boston, MA, http://scholarworks.umb.edu/csp_pubs/30.

Tobin-Gurley, J. and Enarson, E. (2013) Gender. In D.S.K. Thomas, B.D. Philips, W.E. Lovekamp, and A. Fothergill, eds., *Social Vulnerability to Disasters*, 2nd edn. CRC Press: Boca Raton, FL, 139–165.

Toholske, C., Lynch, V.D., Spriggs, R., Ahn, Y. et al. (2024) Hazardous heat exposure among incarcerated people in the United States. *Nature Sustainability* 7, 394–398.

Topol, S.A. (2023) The America that Americans forget. *New York Times*, July 7.

Turner, R.H. and Killian, L.M. (1987) *Collective Behavior.* Prentice Hall: Englewood Cliffs, NJ.

Tversky, A. and Kahneman, D. (1973) Availability: A heuristic for judging frequency and probability. *Cognitive Psychology* 5(2), 207–232.

Tversky, A. and Kahneman, D. (1974) Judgement under uncertainty: Heuristics and biases. *Science* 185(4157), 1124–1131.

Tversky, A. and Kahneman, D. (1981) The framing of decisions and the psychology of choice. *Science* 211(4481), 453–458.

United Nations International Strategy for Disaster Reduction (2007) Hyogo

Framework for Action 2005–2015: Building the resilience of nations and communities to disasters. UNISDR, https://www.unisdr.org/2005/wcdr /intergover/official-doc/L-docs/Hyogo-framework-for-action-english.pdf.

United Nations International Strategy for Disaster Reduction (2017) Terminology, https://www.unisdr.org/we/inform/terminology#letter-v.

Urban Institute (2017) Nine charts about wealth inequality in America (updated), http://apps.urban.org/features/wealth-inequality-charts.

US Army Corps of Engineers (2015) *Memorandum for Planning Community of Practice* (Economic Guidance Memorandum 16–01). Federal Interest Rates for Corps of Engineers Projects for Fiscal Year 2016, Department of the Army, US Army Corps of Engineers: Washington, DC.

USA Facts (2023) How has wealth distribution in the US changed over time? November 13, https://usafacts.org/articles/how-has-wealth-distribution-in-the -us-changed-over-time.

USA for UNHCR (2023) Rohingya refugee crisis explained, August 23, https:// www.unrefugees.org/news/rohingya-refugee-crisis-explained.

US Census Bureau (2016) *Income and Earnings Summary Measures by Selected Characteristics: 2015*. Department of Commerce, Census Bureau: Washington, DC.

US Census Bureau (2017) *Income and Earnings Summary Measures by Selected Characteristics: 2016*. Department of Commerce, Census Bureau: Washington, DC.

US Department of Commerce (2010) *Disparities in Capital Access between Minority and Non-Minority-Owned Businesses: The Troubling Reality of Capital Limitations Faced by MBEs*. US Department of Commerce, Minority Business Development Agency: Washington, DC.

US Department of Education (2009) *Issue Brief: English Literacy of Foreign-Born Adults in the United States: 2003*. US Department of Education: Jessup, MD.

US Department of Health and Human Services (2023) *Meeting the Needs of Lesbian, Gay, Bisexual, Transgender, and Intersex (LGBTQI+) Individuals During Disasters and Emergencies*. HHS Administration for Strategic Preparedness and Response.

US Department of Health and Human Services (n.d.) *Disaster Response for Homeless Individuals and Families: A Trauma-Informed Approach*. Office of the Assistant Secretary for Preparedness and Response, https://www.phe.gov /Preparedness/planning/abc/Documents/homeless-trauma-informed.pdf.

US Department of Homeland Security (2013) *National Response Framework*. Homeland Security: Washington, DC.

US Department of Interior (2011) *Report Regarding the Causes of the April 20, 2010 Macondo Well Blowout*, https://www.bsee.gov/sites/bsee.gov/files/reports/safety /dwhfinal.pdf.

US Department of Labor (2010) *Report of Investigation: Fatal Underground Mine Explosion, April 5, 2010*. Mine Safety and Health Administration, US Department of Labor.

US Department of Labor (2023) *Persons with a Disability: Labor Force Characteristics – 2023*. Bureau of Labor Statistics, Washington, DC.

US Department of Transportation (2004) *Effects of Catastrophic Events on Transportation System Management and Operations: August 2003 Northeast Blackout New York City*. Report no. DOT_VNTSC-FHWA-04–04. John A. Volpe National Transportation Systems Center: Cambridge, MA.

US General Accounting Office (1983) *Siting of Hazardous Waste Landfills and Their Correlation with Racial and Economic Status of Surrounding Communities*. US Printing Office: Washington, DC.

US Global Change Research Program (2016) *The Impacts of Climate Change on Human Health in the United States*. US Global Change Research Program: Washington, DC.

US Global Change Research Program (2023) *The Fifth National Climate Assessment*, https://nca2023.globalchange.gov.

US House of Representatives (2020) *The Design, Development, and Certification of the Boeing 737 Max*. House Committee on Transportation and Infrastructure.

Uscher-Pines, L., Chandra, A., Acosta, J., and Kellerman, A. (2012) Citizen preparedness for disasters: Are current assumptions valid? *Concepts in Disaster Medicine* 6(2), 170–173.

Van der Elst, N.J., Page, M.T., Weiser, D.A., Goebel, T.H.W., and Hosseini, S.M. (2016) Induced earthquake magnitudes are as large as (statistically) expected. *Journal of Geophysical Research: Solid Earth* 121, 4575–4590.

Van Willigen, J. (2002). *Applied Anthropology: An Introduction*. Greenwood: Santa Barbara, CA.

Van Willigen, M., Edwards, T., Edwards, B., and Hessee, S. (2002) Riding out the storm: Experiences of the physically disabled during Hurricanes Bonnie, Dennis, and Floyd. *Natural Hazards Review* 3, 98–106.

Vaughan, D. (1996) *The Challenger Launch Decision: Risky Technology, Culture, and Deviance at NASA*. University of Chicago Press: Chicago, IL

Vaughan, D. (2021) *Dead Reckoning: Air Traffic Control, System Effects, and Risk*. University of Chicago Press: Chicago, IL.

Vickery, J. (2017) *Every day is a disaster: Homelessness and the 2013 Colorado floods*. Doctoral dissertation, University of Colorado, Department of Sociology, Boulder.

Vieweg, S., Hughes, A., Starbird, K., and Palen, L. (2010) A comparison of microblogging behavior in two natural hazard events: What Twitter may contribute to situational awareness. *Proceedings of the ACM 2010 Conference on Human Factors in Computing Systems, Atlanta, GA*. ACM: New York, 1079–1088.

Vieweg, S., Palen, L., Liu, S.B., Hughes, A., and Sutton, J. (2008) Collective intelligence in disaster: Examination of the phenomenon in the aftermath of the 2007 Virginia Tech shooting. In F. Friedrich and B. Van De Walle, eds., *Proceedings of the 5th International ISCRAM Conference*. Academic Press: Washington, DC, 44–54.

Vigdor, J.L. (2007) The Katrina effect: Was there a bright side to the evacuation of greater New Orleans? Working Paper 13022, National Bureau of Economic Research, Cambridge, MA.

Vogel, J.M. and the Family Systems Collaborative Group (2017) *Family Resilience and Traumatic Stress: A Guide for Mental Health Providers*. National Center for Child Traumatic Stress: Los Angeles, CA, https://www.nctsn.org/sites/default/files/resources//family_resilience_and_traumatic_stress_providers.pdf

Vogel, J.M. and Pfefferbaum, P. (2016) Family resilience after disasters and terrorism. In R. Pat-Horenczyk, D. Brom, and J.M. Vogel, eds., *Helping Children Cope with Trauma: Individual, Family and Community Perspectives*. Routledge: New York, 81–100.

Wachtendorf, T. (2004) *Improvising 9/11: Organizational improvisation in the World Trade Center disaster*. Doctoral dissertation, University of Delaware, Department of Sociology, Newark.

Wachtendorf, T. (2009) Trans-system social ruptures: Exploring issues of vulnerability and resiliency. *Review of Policy Research* 26, 379–393.

Wachtendorf, T. and Kendra, J.M. (2006) Improvising disaster in the city of jazz: Organizational response to Hurricane Katrina. Social Science Research Council, http://http://understandingkatrina.ssrc.org/Wachtendorf_Kendra.

Walaski, P.F. (2011) *Risk and Crisis Communications: Methods and Messages*. John Wiley & Sons, Inc.: Hoboken, NJ.

Walker, G. and Burningham, K. (2011) Flood risk, vulnerability and environmental justice: Evidence and evaluation of inequality in a UK context. *Critical Social Policy* 31(2), 216–240.

Walker, T.D. (2015) Enlightened absolutism and the Lisbon earthquake: Asserting state dominance over religious sites and the church in Eighteenth-century Portugal. *Eighteenth-Century Studies* 48(3), 307–328.

Wallace, J., Goldsmith-Pinkham, P., and Schwartz, J.L. (2023) Excess death rates for Republican and Democratic registered voters in Florida and Ohio during the COVID-19 pandemic. *JAMA Internal Medicine* 183 (9), 916–923.

Walsh, F. (2016) *Strengthening Family Resilience*, 3rd edn. Guilford Press: New York.

Warmbrodt, Z. and Meyer, T. (2017) How Washington lobbyists fought flood insurance reform. *Politico*, September 2.

Warner, W.L. (1949) *Social Class in America: A Manual of Procedure for the Measurement of Social Status*. Science Research Associates: Chicago, IL.

Waters, M.C. 2016. Life after Hurricane Katrina: The resilience in survivors of Katrina (RISK) project. *Sociological Forum* 31, 750–769.

Webb, G.R., Tierney, K., and Dahlhamer, J.M. (2000) Businesses and disasters: Empirical patterns and unanswered questions. *Natural Hazards Review* 1(2), 83–90.

Webb, G.R., Tierney, K., and Dahlhamer, J.M. (2002) Predicting long-term business recovery from disaster: A comparison of the Loma Prieta Earthquake to Hurricane Andrew. *Environmental Hazards* 4(2) 45–58. doi: 10.3763/ehaz.2002.0405.

Weber, L. and Peek, L., eds. (2012) *Displaced: Life in the Katrina Diaspora*. University of Texas Press: Austin.

Weick, K.E. (1993) The collapse of sensemaking in organizations: The Mann Gulch disaster. *Administrative Science Quarterly* 38, 628–652.

Weick, K.E. (1998) Improvisation as a mindset for organizational analysis. *Organization Science* 9(5), 543–555.

Weick, K.E. and Roberts, K.H. (1993) Collective mind in organizations: Heedful interrelating on flight decks. *Administrative Science Quarterly* 38, 357–381.

Weick, K. and Sutcliffe, K.M. (2007) *Managing the Unexpected: Resilient Performance in the Age of Uncertainty*, 2nd edn. Jossey-Bass: San Francisco, CA.

Weick, K.E., Sutcliffe, K.M., and Obstfeld, D. (1999) Organizing for high reliability: Processes of collective mindfulness. In R. Sutton and B. Staw, eds., *Research in Organizational Behavior*. Jai Press: Greenwich, CT, 81–123.

Weick, K.E., Sutcliffe, K.M., and Obstfeld, D. (2005) Organizing and the process of sensemaking. *Organization Science* 16(4), 409–421.

Weinstein, N.D. (1980) Unrealistic optimism about future life events. *Journal of Personality and Social Psychology* 39, 806–820.

Weinstein, N.D. (1989) Optimistic biases about personal risks. *Science* 246, 1232–1233.

Weissbecker, I., Sephton, S.E., Martin, M.B., and Simpson, D.M. (2008) Psychological and physiological correlates of stress in children exposed to disaster: Current research and recommendations of intervention. *Children, Youth and Environments* 18(1), 30–70, http://www.jstor.org/stable/10.7721/chilyoutenvi.18.1.0030.

Wenger, D.E. (1987) Collective behavior and disaster research. In R.R. Dynes, B. DeMarchi, and C. Pelanda, eds., *Sociology of Disasters: Contributions of Sociology to Disaster Research*. Franco Angeli: Milan, 213–237.

Wenger, D.E., Dykes, J.D., Sebok, T.D., and Neff, J.L. (1975) It's a matter of myths: An empirical examination of individual insight into disaster response. *Mass Emergencies* 1, 33–46.

Wenger, D.E. and James, T.F. (1994) The convergence of volunteers in a consensus crisis: The case of the 1985 Mexico City earthquake. In R.R. Dynes and K. Tierney, eds., *Disasters, Collective Behavior, and Social Organization*. University of Delaware Press: Newark, 229–243.

Western, B. (2006) *Punishment and Inequality in America*. Russell Sage Foundation: New York.

Western, B. and Pettit, B. (2010) Incarceration and social inequality. *Daedalus* 139, 8–19.

Wherry, F.F. and Chakrabarti, P. (2022) Accounting for credit. *Annual Review of Sociology* 48, 131–147.

Whitaker, C., Stevelink, S., and Fear, N. (2017) The use of Facebook in recruiting participants for health research purposes. *Journal of Medical Internet Research* 19(8), article e290. doi: 10.2196/jmir.7071.

White, C.M. (2011) *Social Media, Crisis Communications, and Emergency Management: Leveraging Web 2.0 Technologies*. CRC Press: Boca Raton, FL.

White, G.F. (1945) Human adjustment to floods. Research Paper 29, Department of Geography, University of Chicago, IL.

White, G.F., ed. (1974) *Natural Hazards: Local, National, Global*. Oxford University Press: New York.

White, G.F. and Haas, J.E. (1975) *Assessment of Research on Natural Hazards*. MIT Press: Cambridge, MA.

White, G.F., Kates, R.W., and Burton, I. (2001) Knowing better and losing even more: The use of knowledge in hazards management. *Environmental Hazards* 3, 81–92.

White House (2023) *National Climate Resilience Framework 2023*. White House, Washington, DC.

Wilhelmi, O.V. and Hayden, M.H. (2010) Connecting people and place: A new framework for reducing urban vulnerability to extreme heat. *Environmental Research Letters* 5(1), http://iopscience.iop.org/article/10.1088/1748-9326/5/1/014021/meta.

Williams, D.R., Mohammed, S.A., Leavell, J., and Collins, C. (2010) Race, socioeconomic status and health: Complexities, ongoing challenges and research opportunities. *Annals of the New York Academy of Sciences* 1186, 69–101.

Williams, D.R., Priest, N., and Anderson, N. (2016) Understanding associations between race, socioeconomic status and health: Patterns and prospects. *Health Psychology* 35(4), 407–411.

Williams, J. (2011) A sustainable return on investment. In S. Coyle, *Sustainable and Resilient Communities: A Comprehensive Actions Plan for Towns, Cities, and Regions*. John Wiley & Sons: Hoboken, NJ.

Williams, S. (2008) Rethinking the nature of disaster: From failed instruments of learning to a post-social understanding. *Social Forces* 87(2), 1115–1138.

Winderl, T. (2014) *Disaster Resilience Measurements: Stocktaking of Ongoing Efforts in Developing Systems for Measuring Resilience*. United Nations Development Program: New York, https://www.preventionweb.net/files/37916_disasterresiliencemeasurementsundpt.pdf.

Wisner, B. (1998) Marginality and disaster vulnerability: Why the homeless of Tokyo don't "count" in disaster preparations. *Applied Geography* 18(1), 25–33.

Wisner, B., Blaikie, P., Cannon, T., and Davis, I. (2004) *At Risk: Natural Hazards, People's Vulnerability, and Disasters*, 2nd edn. Routledge: London.

Wisner, B. and Walker, P. (2005) *The Making and Unmaking of Whiteness*. Duke University Press: Durham, NC.

Woo, B. and Jun, H.-J. (2020) Globalization and slums: How do economic, political, and social globalization affect slum prevalence? *Habitat International* 98, 102–152.

Wood, M.M. and Bourque, L.B. (2018) Morbidity and mortality associated with disaster. In H. Rodríguez, W. Donner, and J.E. Trainor, eds., *Handbook of Disaster Research*, 2nd edn. Springer: Cham, Switzerland, 357–383.

Wood, M.M., Mileti, D.S., Bean, H., Liu, B.F., Sutton, J., and Madden, S. (2018) Milling and public warnings. *Environment and Behavior* 50(5), 535–566.

World Bank Group (2013) *Building Resilience: Integrating Climate and Disaster Resilience into Development: The World Bank Group Experience. Global Facility for Disaster Risk Reduction*. World Bank: Washington, DC.

World Bank Group (2017) *Unbreakable: Building the Resilience of the Poor in the Face of Natural Disasters*. World Bank: Washington, DC.

World Economic Forum (2023) *The Global Gender Gap Report, 2023*. World Economic Forum, June 20, https://www3.weforum.org/docs/WEF_GGGR _2023.pdf.

Wozniak, K., Davidson, G., and Ankersen, T. (2012) *Florida's Coastal Hazards Law: Property Owner Perceptions of the Physical and Regulatory Environment with Conclusions and Recommendations*. Florida Sea Grant, National Oceanic and Atmospheric Administration, University of Florida: Gainesville.

Young, A. (2023) *Pandora's Gamble: Lab Leaks, Pandemics, and a World at Risk*. Hachette Book Group: New York.

Young, A.L. (2017) Displaced by the storm: Texas evacuees without options. *Texas Monthly*, October 6, https://www.texasmonthly.com/articles/displaced -by-the-storm-texas-evacuees-without-options.

Zahran, S., Peek, L., and Brody, S.D. (2008) Youth mortality by forces of nature. *Children, Youth and Environments* 18(1), 371–388, http://www.jstor.org/stable/10 .7721/chilyoutenvi.18.1.0371.

Zaval, L. and Cornwell, J.M. (2016) Cognitive biases, non-rational judgements, and public perceptions of climate change. In M.C. Nisbet, M. Schafer, E. Markowitz, S. Ho, S. O'Neill, and J. Thaker, eds., *The Oxford Encyclopedia of Climate Change Communication*. Oxford University Press: Oxford. doi: 10.1093/ acrefore/9780190228620.013.304.

Zavestoski, S. and the Contested Illness Research Group (2012) *Contested Illnesses: Citizens, Science, and Health Social Movements*. University of California Press: Oakland.

Zeng, L., Starbird, K., and Spiro, E.S. (2016) Rumors at the speed of light? Modeling the rate of rumor transmission during crisis. In *The 49th Hawaii International Conference on System Sciences*. Institute of Electrical and Electronics Engineers (IEEE): Piscataway, NJ, 1969–1978. doi: 10.1109/HICSS.2016.248.

Zhang, Y., Zhang, C., Drake, W., and Olshansky, R. (2014) Planning and recovery following the great 1976 Tangshan earthquake. *Journal of Planning History* 14(3), 224–243. doi: 10.1177/1538513214549435.

Zhang, Y., Drake, W., Xiao, Y., Olshansky, R., Johnson, L., and Song, Y. (2016) Disaster recovery planning after two catastrophes: the 1976 Tangshan earthquake and the 2008 Wenchuan earthquake. *International Journal of Mass Emergencies and Disasters* 34(2), 174–203.

Zottarelli, L.K. (2008) Post-Hurricane Katrina employment recovery: The interaction of race and place. *Social Science Quarterly* 89(3), 592–607.

Index

second assessment project, 23–24
Secure Livelihoods Research Consortium (SLRC), 157
self-protective measures, 8
Sendai Framework for Action, 148
Sendai Framework for Disaster Risk Reduction 2015–2030, 131
sensitivity, 199
September 11 attacks (2001), 26, 28, 61, 63, 75, 161, 183, 198
Serbia, affected by toxic waste, 218
service delivery systems, 15
severe acute respiratory syndrome (SARS), 2–3, 218–219, 226
sexual minorities in disasters, 100, 116–117
ShakeOut (earthquake), 181
Shapiro, Thomas, 92
Sharifi, A., 145
Shaw, R., 139
Shaw, Rajib, 139
sheltering, shelters, 56, 67, 95, 100, 106, 114–115, 117, 120, 123, 168, 199, 204
Shenzhen, China, 50, 225
Sheppard, B., 185
Shirley, W.L., 80
Sichuan earthquake (2008), 50
Silver, H., 144
situational theory of publics, 185–186
Slovic, P., 179
slums, 46, 48
Smith, F., 117
Smith, G., 166
social behavior in disasters, 3
social capital, 10, 137–141
  and disaster recovery, 167–169
  downside of, 142–145
  forms, 138
  influence of scholarship on, 139
social change, 217
social class, 87–91
social constructionism, 32–34
  and Covid-19, 34–35
  social construction of ignorance, 36–38
The Social Construction of Reality (Berger and Luckmann), 33
social embeddedness, 137–138

social inequality, 230, 232
social production of disaster risk and vulnerability, 41
social resilience, 136, 147
The Social Roots of Risk (Tierney), 9
social science disaster research, 25, 31, 209–210
Social Science Research Council (SSRC), 29
Social Sciences Extreme Events Research (SSEER), 25–26, 212–213
social systems, 130
social vulnerability, 83–85, 210
  gender and, 92–96
  race and ethnicity and, 91–92
  social class and, 87–91
Social Vulnerability Index (SoVI), 126, 127, 146
societal resilience, 131
"socio-political ecology," 24
sociology, 8–10, 31, 176
  fundamental cause theory, 89
  social science disaster research, 31
  study of emergent response networks, 28
  Thomas theorem, 35
  vulnerability 38–39
sociopolitical model of disability, 110
Soja, E., 182
Solnit, R., 139
Somers, M.R., 150
Sorensen, John, 66
source–message–channel–receiver–effect–feedback model, 66
space and disaster, 24–25
Spatial Hazard Event and Loss Database for the United States (SHELDUS), 127
spatial social science, 181–182, 194
Sri Lanka, 29, 157
Stallings, R., 194
Stalp, M., 173
Standing in the Need: Culture, Comfort, and Coming Home after Katrina (Browne), 177
Starbird, Kate, 65
state's role in vulnerability production, 98–100
stateless persons and vulnerability, 119–120